Taking Sides: Clashing Views
in Family and Personal
Relationships, 11/e

Don Dyson

http://create.mheducation.com

ISBN-10: 1260181545   ISBN-13: 9781260181548

Contents

Detailed Table of Contents

UNIT 1: What Makes a Family?

Issue: Are Traditional Families Better Than Nontraditional Families?
YES: Allan C. Carlson and Paul T. Mero, from "The Natural Family: A Manifesto," Howard Center (2006)
NO: Mark Good, from "Nontraditional Families and Childhood Progress through School," Original essay written for this volume (2012)

Allan Carlson is President of the Howard Center for Family, Religion & Society and Distinguished Fellow in Family Policy Studies at the Family Research Council in Washington, D.C. Paul Mero is President of the Sutherland Institute and a Trustee of the ALS Foundation. Carlson and Mero argue that America needs to return to a traditional family headed by a man and woman. Mark Good is a Professor of Counselor Education at West Chester University and the President of Opn-Wyd, a diversity and communication company. Good argues that diversity in traditional and nontraditional families is healthy. In fact, he argues that it can be damaging to hold up the traditional family as the ideal familial structure.

Issue: Are Teenagers Too Young to Become Parents?
YES: The National Campaign to Prevent Teen and Unplanned Pregnancy, from "One in Three: The Case for Wanted and Welcomed Pregnancy," The National Campaign to Prevent Teen and Unplanned Pregnancy (2007)
NO: Simon Duncan, Claire Alexander, and Rosalind Edwards, from "What's the Problem with Teenage Parents?" Tuffnell Press (2010)

The National Campaign to Prevent Teen and Unplanned Pregnancy is dedicated to reducing teenage pregnancy. Their research argues that teens face significant consequences if they have unplanned pregnancy. Simon Duncan, Claire Alexander, and Rosalind Edwards have written a chapter in a book about teen pregnancy and parenting. This chapter, which takes a global perspective by looking at another Western society, England, argues that teenage pregnancy and parenting is not a problem.

Issue: Is Polyamory a Good Alternative for Relationships and Families?
YES: Elisabeth Sheff, from "What You Can Learn from Polyamory," *Greater Good* (2017)
NO: Alan J. Hawkins, Betsy VanDenBerghe, and Lynae Barlow, from "The New Math of 'Consensual Nonmonogamy',"
National Review (2017)

Elisabeth Sheff, PhD, CASA, CSE is an educational consultant and expert witness serving sexual and gender minorities. She is the author of *The Polyamorists Next Door* and *When Someone You Love Is Polyamorous*, as well as numerous academic and legal articles about polyamory, gender, families, and sexual minorities. Sheff presents evidence that the basic tenets of polyamory are not only healthy, but can teach monogamists skills for healthier relationships. Alan J. Hawkins is a professor and Lynae Barlow an undergraduate student in the Brigham Young University School of Family Life. Betsy VanDenBerghe is a writer based in Salt Lake City. Hawkins and VanDenBerghe are the authors of the National Marriage Project report "Facilitating Forever." Hawkins, Barlow, and VanDenBerghe argue that power dynamics, individual suffering, and preservation of family norms are all key reasons why polyamory is untenable.

<u>**Issue: Should Same-sex Adoption Be Legal?**</u>
YES: Elizabeth A. Harris, from "Same-Sex Parents Still Face Legal Complications," *The New York Times* (2017)
NO: Jules Gomes, from "Is Gay Adoption Wrong? The Children Say Yes," *Anglican Ink* (2017)

Elizabeth Harris has been a culture reporter at *The New York Times* since 2009. In her tenure at the times, she has written from a variety of positions on issues from real estate to education foreign affairs. Harris argues that although same-sex adoption is legal in most cases, there are state-by-state laws that challenge potential parents and a shifting legal landscape that can result in a parent being a legal stranger to their own child simply by driving across a state line. Jules Gomes writes for The Anglican Ink, a publication of Anglican Television Ministries in Milford, Connecticut. Gomes reports on a study conducted in the United Kingdom by Robert Oscar Lopez and Brittany Klein titled: Jepthah's Children: the innocent casualties of same sex adoption. In his article, Gomes argues that bearing children is not a right, but a responsibility and a gift. He states that gay or lesbian adults should sacrifice their homosexuality and raise a child in a home with both a husband and wife (for the good of the child) or sacrifice their desire to have children.

<u>**Issue: Does Having a Transgender Parent Hurt Children?**</u>
YES: Brynn Tannehill, from "Here's What It's REALLY Like Having A Transgender Parent," *TheHuffingtonPost.com, Inc.* (2016)
NO: Caitlin White, from "A Void Wider Than Gender: Here's What My Life Has Been Like Since My Father Came Out as Trans," *Vice* (2015)

Brynn Tannehill graduated from the Naval Academy with a BS in computer science in 1997. She earned her Naval Aviator wings in 1999 and served as a campaign analyst while deployed overseas. In 2008, Brynn earned a MS in Operations Research from the Air Force Institute of Technology and transferred from active duty to the Naval Reserves. In 2008, Brynn began working as a senior defense research scientist in private industry. She left the drilling reserves and began transition in 2010. Since then she has written for *OutServe magazine*, The New Civil Rights Movement, and Queer Mental Health as a blogger and featured columnist. Brynn presents the first-person narrative of her 8th-grade daughter about what it is like to have a transgender parent. Caitlin White is a writer in Brooklyn, New York, and a regular contributor to *Brooklyn Magazine*. Caitlin writes poignantly about the challenges she experienced when her parent came out to her as transgender. While an advocate of trans people, she writes about the difficulties faced by a child whose parent changes their gender identity.

UNIT 2: Contemporary Issues in Relationships

<u>**Issue: Is Cybersex "Cheating"?**</u>
YES: Susan A. Milstein, from "Virtual Liaisons: Cybersex Is Cheating," Original essay written for this volume (2009)
NO: Crystal Bedley, from "Virtual Reality: Cybersex Is Not Cheating," Original essay written for this volume (2009)

Susan Milstein is a Certified Health Education Specialist and a Certified Sexuality Educator. She is an Associate Professor in the Department of Health Enhancement at Montgomery College in Maryland, as well as the Lead Consultant for Milstein Health Consulting. Milstein contends that while it is difficult to create a universal definition of cheating, the majority of people feel that cybersex outside of a primary relationship is cheating. Crystal Bedley argues that the anonymous nature of cybersex means that it is not cheating.

<u>**Issue: Is the Hookup Culture on College Campuses Bad for Heterosexual Girls?**</u>
YES: Amy Julia Becker, from "Hookup Culture Is Good for Women, and Other Feminist Myths," *Christianity Today* (2012)
NO: Timaree Schmit, from "Hookup Culture Can Help Build Stronger Relationships," Original essay written for this volume (2014)

Amy Julia Becker argues that hookup culture demeans women. From a Christian perspective, she argues that sex leads to greater life fulfillment when removed from the hookup culture. Timaree Schmit argues that hookup culture is nothing new and that it can be healthy for people to have different sexual experiences.

Donald Dyson is an associate professor of human sexuality education at Widener University and has served in leadership capacities at Widener University's Center for Human Sexuality studies. Dyson argues that there are essential qualities of a healthy relationship and that an open relationship can be successful. Stanley Kurtz, a writer and senior fellow at the Ethics and Public Policy Center, argues that allowing same-sex marriage will create a slippery slope, eventually leading to plural marriages. Kurtz contends that such marriages prove destructive to the institution of marriage itself.

UNIT 3: Contemporary Issues in Parenting

Calvin P. Johnson, Esq., is the attorney for the parents, Colleen and Anthony Hauser. Johnson argues that the government forcing medical care for the Hauser child violates his religious liberty and is abusive to this child. John R. Rodenberg is the District Court judge in this case. Rodenberg argues that all parties are acting out of convictions for the best interest of the child. He also argues that the state has a compelling interest to act against Hauser's religious views for medical care since the child is only thirteen years old.

Wayne Grinwis has been a Sexual Health Educator for Planned Parenthood for 15 years. He is also Adjunct Professor in the Department of Health at West Chester University. Grinwis credits Andrea Daniels for help with this article. Grinwis argues that pornography is all right for adults, but for teenagers, it can create unrealistic expectations about sex, provide a negative and inaccurate sexuality education, and increase sexual violence against women. Justin Sitron is an Assistant Professor of Education at Widener University. Sitron argues that pornography has no negative impact on teenagers and, in fact, has potential benefits. Sitron contends that Internet pornography can be helpful in providing teens an opportunity to see real bodies, a chance to learn about sex from seeing rather than doing, and an open door for communication with parents.

Lisa E. Soronen, Nicole Vitale, and Karen A. Haase are writing on legal issues for the National School Boards Association. This article encourages administrators to hand over cell phone sexting cases to the appropriate law enforcement agencies. Julie Hilden is a graduate of Harvard College and Yale Law School. A former clerk for Supreme Court Justice Stephen Breyer, she has more recently appeared on *Good Morning America*, Court TV, CNN, and NPR. Hilden argues that harsh penalties are extreme and unjust.

<u>**Issue: Is Traditional Masculinity Harmful to Boys and Men?**</u>
YES: Brianna Attard, from "Toxic Masculinity: How Our Current System of Gender is Harmful to People," *The Sydney Feminists* (2017)
NO: Paul Nathanson, from "A Requiem for Manhood," *Australian Institute of Male Health and Studies* (2018)

Brianna Attard is a researcher and writer at The Sydney Feminists, Inc. She wrote her first article for TSF on toxic masculinity. Brianna enjoys volunteering and working for organizations that operate within a feminist framework. She outlines Toxic Masculinity and its impact on women, men, and interpersonal interactions. Paul Nathanson has a BA (art history), a BTh (Christian theology), an MLS (library service), an MA (religious studies), and a PhD (religious studies). Of particular interest to him is the surprisingly blurry relation between religion and secularity: how religion underlies seemingly secular phenomena such as popular movies and political ideologies. Nathanson argues, through the use of cinematic examples, that there is a need among men for creating identity through masculinity.

<u>**Issue: Should Parents Allow Puberty Blocking Hormones for Their Transgender Children?**</u>
YES: Jacqueline Ruttimann, from "Blocking Puberty In Transgender Youth," *Endocrine News* (2013)
NO: Michelle Cretella, from "I'm a Pediatrician: Here's What I Did When a Little Boy Patient Said He Was a Girl," *The Daily Signal* (2017)

Jacqueline Ruttimann is a freelance writer living in Chevy Chase, Maryland. She argues that pubertal blockers allow transgender youth to carefully consider transition and decreases the need for cross-sex hormones later in life, which results in fewer health risks for the individual. Michelle Cretella, MD, is the president of the American College of Pediatricians, a national organization of pediatricians and other health-care professionals dedicated to the health and well-being of children. She argues that no one is born transgender, and that "gender confused" children should be supported in their biological sex through puberty.

UNIT 4: Families and Systems

<u>**Issue: Should Illegal Immigrant Families Be Able to Send Their Children to Public Schools?**</u>
YES: William Brennan, from Majority Opinion, *Plyler v. Doe*, U.S. Supreme Court (1982)
NO: Warren Burger, from Dissenting Opinion, *Plyler v. Doe*, U.S. Supreme Court (1982)

William Brennan is regarded as one of the greatest intellectual leaders of the twentieth-century -Supreme Court. He was regarded for writing extraordinarily forward-thinking opinions, especially regarding civil rights and civil liberties. This case proves no exception, as he captures an issue that seems even more pertinent today than when the Supreme Court addressed it. Brennan believes that children who are in the country and undocumented have a constitutional right to a public education. Warren Burger was the Chief Justice of the Supreme Court during a time in which it was slowly moving in a more conservative direction. He was an instrumental voice in many cases before the Supreme Court that had a more conservative outcome. Burger believes that undocumented immigrant children have no constitutional right to an education.

<u>**Issue: Should Teachers in Schools Have Firearms?**</u>
YES: Michael W. Goldberg, from "I'm a School Psychologist — And I Think Teachers Should Be Armed," *Forward* (2018)
NO: Eugene Scott, from "A Big Question in the Debate About Arming Teachers: What About Racial Bias?" *Washington Post* (2018)

Michael W. Goldberg is a School Psychologist. He earned his Masters in Psychology at SUNY New Paltz, and was born in Brooklyn in 1963, where he was raised by his Orthodox Jewish grandparents. He argues that arming specially trained teachers will decrease the likelihood of school shootings as well as decrease subsequent trauma for students. Eugene Scott writes about identity politics for The Fix. He was previously a breaking news reporter at CNN Politics. Scott argues that in schools, where racial bias among teachers has been well documented, arming teachers will likely result in the unwarranted deaths of students of color.

Issue: Should Cyber-Bullies Be Prosecuted?
YES: Brianna Flavin, from "Is Cyberbullying Illegal? When Comments Turn Criminal," Rasmussen College Blog (2017)
NO: J. Graffeo, from "People v Marquan M." *New York State Law Reporting Bureau* (2014)

Brianna Flavin is a freelance writer, content marketer, adjunct professor, and poet. She argues that cyberbullying is culturally pervasive and should be criminalized to prevent tragedies such as teen suicide and school shootings. The opposing view is presented by the verdict of the New York Court of Appeals in a case that argued that the cyberbullying law enacted was considered a violation of the defendant's First Amendment free speech.

Issue: Should Parents of School Shooters Be Held Responsible for Their Children's Actions?
YES: Alia E. Dastagir, from "After a School Shooting, are Parents to Blame?" *USA Today* (2018)
NO: John Cassidy, from "America's Failure To Protect Its Children From School Shootings Is A National Disgrace," *The New Yorker* (2018)

Alia E. Dastagir is a reporter covering cultural issues, including gender, race, and sexuality. She argues studies consistently show that teen violence is mitigated by consistent, nurturing adult influence and that those adults need to take their responsibility seriously. John Cassidy has been a staff writer at *The New Yorker* since 1995. In 2012, he began writing a daily column about politics and economics on newyorker.com. Cassidy argues that the federal government, in its unwillingness to stand up to gun lobbyists, is responsible for the ongoing epidemic of school shootings.

Issue: Is the Criminal Justice System Unfair to Black Families?
YES: Samantha Daley, from "The Criminal Justice System Is Failing Black Families," *Rewire.News* (2014)
NO: Kay S. Hymowitz, from "Did Mass Incarceration Destroy the Black Family? No, and Here's Why," *City Journal* (2015)

Samantha Daley is a reproductive justice activist and a supervisor at a homeless shelter for youth and a writer in Echoing Ida, a project of Forward Together. She argues that the criminal justice system's biased treatment toward black families creates a system that passes down racial disadvantage from generation to generation. Kay S. Hymowitz is the William E. Simon Fellow at the Manhattan Institute and a contributing editor of *City Journal*. She writes extensively on childhood, family issues, poverty, and cultural change in America. She argues that issues within Black families are an under-considered part of the mass incarceration problem.

Preface

Human beings are social animals. We have a fundamental need to connect with others, and it is often that need that drives our behavior throughout life. We see it in the complete dependence of an infant, in the socialization of a child, in the desire to fit in of adolescence, in the bonding of early adulthood, in the generativity of midlife, in the reflection of older adulthood, and in the legacies we long to leave in our ending years. Lives are characterized by the types and the qualities of the relationships we forge.

Most folks' first experience with relationships is in the context of families. For many, this is the first place that we learn to navigate and to understand interpersonal relationships. It is in the places that we are raised that we learn about the world, about human interactions, and about the myriad processes of relating to others. The modeling that we see provides us our first lessons about right and wrong, and becomes a foundational script for how we view the world. Those scripts, for better or for worse, influence our futures in ways that we may never fully understand.

As we progress through life, we learn the complexities of relationships. We encounter the joys that they bring. We suffer the hurt that comes from unexpected sources. Our hearts soar and break. We are both held up in the light and betrayed by the darkness in those that we encounter. Each moment of laughter and each drop of tears weave together to form intersections that affect how we understand others and ourselves.

Our journeys through life and relationships do not occur outside of the realities of the social environments in which we grow. The social systems in which we move mold our thinking. The expectations of a gendered world shape our understanding of our core selves, forcing us into boxes that have varying degrees of fit for each of us. The anti-black reality of cultures around the globe paints our villains in darker tones and our heroes in white, building both conscious and unconscious bias into our psyches. The systems of economic oppression teach us to value the wealthy, to suspect the poor, and to tie ourselves to a system that perpetuates service in the pursuit of riches or survival.

Our families, for better and worse; our interactions, that help and harm; our social locations, that privilege and oppress; all of these things create a complex tapestry from which we build the values and beliefs that guide our actions through life. It is within the context of these that we attempt to build connection and relationship with others. And at times it is hard.

Into this complex and difficult space, I offer this volume of *Taking Sides: Clashing Views in Family and Personal Relationships*. It is not designed to answer the great questions of our time. It is not designed to make your decisions for you. It is certainly not designed to give you ammunition in your fight against values and beliefs that differ from yours.

This volume is designed to offer different perspectives on issues that affect families and relationships. It is provided as a resource bank that provides access to thoughts, ideas, and beliefs that may be quite different than your own. It is put together in a way that helps to thoughtfully illuminate issues while avoiding the rhetoric and bullying that often occurs in electronic spaces. It is put out into a world in which views are becoming more polarized and newsfeeds more cultivated.

One of the most powerful and positive feelings that we can experience as people is being understood. We do not have to agree with each other about all things. That is an impossible goal to achieve. What we can do is try to understand one another. We can try to see the complex histories of joy and hurt that inform very different perspectives on issues about which we care deeply. We can attempt to see the social inequities and the pain they cause to those who sit outside of the privilege that they also bestow. We can look beyond the rhetoric to see the people. We can seek to understand one another and perhaps, in that understanding, to improve the relationships that we so desperately need in order to survive.

A Note to Instructors

Great educators know well that learning, for their students, does not happen until they can take an experience, analyze it, generalize from that analysis, and apply their learning in meaningful ways within their own lives. Without this complete process, education remains the conveyance of discreet facts from our mouths to our students' ears to their notes to our test without passing through the minds of anyone in the system. It is my sincere hope that your use of this resource will be one that goes beyond debate. The questions for thought and the common ground sections attempt to help students to build skills in perspective taking and emotional intelligence. It is my sincere hope that you build upon these things with additional activities that support complex understandings of the different perspectives found herein.

Dedication

This book is dedicated to Mollie Dyson, my indomitable mother, who taught me through her compassionate example that understanding others offers more to the world than judging them. "It's not mean if it's true, it's just true. What is kind or mean comes from what you do with that truth."

Editor of This Volume

DON DYSON, PHD, is an Associate Professor at Widener University's Center for Human Sexuality Studies. Dr. Dyson received his Masters in Social Service from Bryn Mawr Graduate School of Social Work and Social Research and his Doctorate in Philosophy from the University of Pennsylvania in Educational Leadership/Human Sexuality.

Introduction

This edition of *Taking Sides: Family and Personal Relationships* is being released at a time when the temperature of social debate seems to be reaching unprecedented heat. Political parties are more polarized than ever. Anger and hatred are emboldened by the anonymity of social media. Accusations fly as fast as memes can carry them. New feeds are cultivated to inflame rather than to inform. It can feel overwhelming and hopeless.

In a nation that is built on the equality of all people, learning how to engage in thoughtful dialogue is one of the most important skills that each of us can develop. Indeed, it is our only hope.

In this volume, you will find a series of issues that create tension and discord between people. Some of the issues are those with which you might be familiar. Some you may not have thought about yet. Some of the perspectives that you read will resonate with your own worldview, and others will make you uncomfortable and even angry. That's the whole point of this work. In every case, though, the people who have written what you read have given a good deal of thought to their perspective, and they have agreed to offer those works in this book.

Your task, as the reader, is to work hard to try to hear the perspective of those with whom you disagree. You do not have to be convinced. You do not have to change your own thinking. What I am asking you to do as the editor of the work is to try to understand. There is a great deal of power in understanding others. I want you to able to access that power.

To do this, I offer the brilliant framework of Courageous Conversations (Singleton & Linton, 2006). In 2006, Glenn E. Singleton and Curtis Linton published their work, *Courageous Conversations About Race: A field guide for achieving equity in schools*. While that work was specific to discussions of race, perhaps one of the most difficult conversations for folks to have, the framework that they offer can be incredibly helpful in developing understanding between people who may not share perspectives on controversial issues. Specifically, I'd like you to consider their Four Agreements and their Compass of Response.

The Four Agreements of Courageous Conversation begin with the agreement to stay engaged. When we are confronted with opinions and beliefs that differ from ours, our natural reaction is often to disengage. We want to move away from our discomfort and retreat into what is familiar and safe. That leads us back to our already strongly held beliefs and doesn't allow us to listen and try to understand. Staying engaged means that we work to hold our discomfort at bay while we try to understand a perspective other than our own. It is hard, but it is worth it.

The second agreement is to speak your truth. This means that we work to be honest with our thoughts and feelings, even if they are not what we think others want to hear, and owning that they are our beliefs and not necessarily the "right" or "only" perspective. In this instance, it involves taking the risk to hold an unpopular opinion, or even to voice the reality that we can understand some of the points that the "other side" is making, even if we don't agree with them.

The third agreement laid out by Singleton and Linton is to experience discomfort. This acknowledges that discomfort is inevitable whenever we are talking about sensitive issues. Courageous Conversations acknowledge that discomfort as a place where dialogue and learning can take place. If we are never uncomfortable, we never have a need to learn and grow.

The final agreement in the model is to expect and accept nonclosure. This asks that we allow the process of dialogue to happen and that we do not rush to quick conclusions. If we are truly going to learn to talk thoughtfully about difficult things, we need to accept that the end of the conversation might not give us the feeling of closure that we want. The purpose of the dialogue is not to convince the other or to win an argument. Instead, it is to keep the conversation going and be open to new perspectives.

With those four agreements in place, Singleton and Linton (2006) identify a four-point compass from which people respond to sensitive issues. Those four points are Emotional, Moral, Intellectual, and Social.

Emotional responses are the feelings that people have in response to an issue. Moral responses include a person's beliefs about a topic. Those beliefs can be evaluative (that something is good or bad) or values-based (how or if something *should* be done). Intellectual responses are the thoughts that one has about an issue. They are often broad or connected to scientific fact or observation. Social responses are how someone might react to an issue in a social setting. This may include their "professional" or "formal" response that they would give in front of a group of people.

With the four agreements in place, the questions at the end of each unit ask you to consider the compass responses that you identify in the readings. Can you identify the emotional, moral, intellectual, and social responses that the authors include in their work? Can you identify your own emotional, moral, intellectual, and social responses to the issue overall? Taking the time to identify those reactions can help us to better understand where our own perspectives come from. Listening to where the reactions of others come from can help us to better understand those who hold different views than our own. Taking the time to talk about them can help us to find common ground and to build a more thoughtful response.

That is the goal of this volume. If we can have thoughtful and compassionate dialogue about our differences, it is my firm belief that we can find a way through them that builds a more connected world for all of us.

Reference

Singleton, G.E. & Linton, C. (2006). *Courageous Conversations about Race: A Field Guide for Achieving Equity in Schools*. Corwin: Thousand Oaks, CA.

Unit 1

UNIT

What Makes a Family?

*F*amilies are considered by most people to be the bedrock of any given culture. It is in our families that we learn how to talk, how to walk, how to think, and how to grow. Yet there is not always agreement about what makes a family. Is it blood? If so, what about adoptive parents? Is it parenting? Then what about those raised by aunts and uncles, or those raised in foster care systems? Is it love? If so, then is that enough? This unit explores some of the controversies that arise when people try to define family and to decide what types of families are best for themselves and for others.

Selected, Edited, and with Issue Framing Material by:
Don Dyson, *Widener University*

ISSUE

Are Traditional Families Better Than Nontraditional Families?

YES: Allan C. Carlson and Paul T. Mero, from "The Natural Family: A Manifesto," Howard Center (2006)

NO: Mark Good, from "Nontraditional Families and Childhood Progress through School," Original essay written for this volume (2012)

Learning Outcomes

After reading this issue, you will be able to:

- Identify the major arguments made for and against the traditional family.
- Compare and contrast the competing arguments made for and against the traditional family in this issue.
- Evaluate the implications of changing family structure on children and the larger American society.

ISSUE SUMMARY

YES: Allan Carlson is President of the Howard Center for Family, Religion & Society and Distinguished Fellow in Family Policy Studies at the Family Research Council in Washington, D.C. Paul Mero is President of the Sutherland Institute and a Trustee of the ALS Foundation. Carlson and Mero argue that America needs to return to a traditional family headed by a man and woman.

NO: Mark Good is a Professor of Counselor Education at West Chester University and the President of Opn-Wyd, a diversity and communication company. Good argues that diversity in traditional and nontraditional families is healthy. In fact, he argues that it can be damaging to hold up the traditional family as the ideal familial structure.

Throughout most of American history, the concept of marriage and parenthood has seen a mild fluctuation. Ages for marriage may have changed a bit. Much has remained steady and intact, but over the past decades, we also have seen a fairly profound change in the nature of family.

Greater access to birth control, which was guaranteed to all married couples by the Supreme Court during the late 1960s, gave couples greater power over the timing of and frequency of child rearing. While women still face discrimination in terms of employment and wages, today's woman has more opportunities in the workplace than in generations past. Indeed, there was a time in American history when marriage was virtually the only way that women could secure their economic future. Today, women face different challenges than men, but millions manage to provide to support single mothers and their children. During times of economic distress, the discrepancy in wages can result in increased job security for women. For example, while there certainly is discrimination based on wages, in 2010, more women were employed than men.

Economic opportunities for women are by no means the only issue reconstructing our definition of families. For example, same-sex marriage, something not recognized in any of the 50 states just one decade ago, is legal in six states and Washington, D.C., and is likely to spread to additional states over the coming years. Today, the number of adults who have never married remains much higher than it had been for generations past. This trend is not absent of having children, as there is also a rise in single parents raising children in the United States.

What do these changes mean? These days, are adult generations living in diverse family structures at the expense of and to the detriment of children? Or have we reached a more democratic, egalitarian family structure that comes closer to embracing our nation's true diversity? The answer divides a wide array of Americans.

Each political party has a different view of the value of traditional versus nontraditional families. The 2008 Republican National Platform states the following:

Preserving Traditional Marriage

Because our children's future is best preserved within the traditional understanding of marriage, we call for a constitutional amendment that fully protects marriage as a union of a man and a woman. . . .

Republicans recognize the importance of having in the home a father and a mother who are married. The two-parent family still provides the best environment of stability, discipline, responsibility, and character. Children in homes without fathers are more likely to commit a crime, drop out of school, become violent, become teen parents, use illegal drugs, become mired in poverty, or have emotional or behavioral problems. We support the courageous efforts of single-parent families to provide a stable home for their children. . . .

As the family is our basic unit of society, we oppose initiatives to erode parental rights.

On which side of this debate would one find the Republican Party? If we look back to the Political Ideology continuum at the start of the chapter, where would the aforementioned views fall along the continuum? While supporting the traditional family, there is an acknowledgment of the "courage" of single parents. Why is this, when they cite a two-parent family as the ideal?

What about examining the Republican position through a Lakoffian Nation as Family framework, also cited in the Introduction. Does this represent Strict Father Morality? Nurturant Parent Morality? What does the language itself tell you about the larger worldview of the Republican Party as stated in this section of their platform?

The Democratic National Committee released its own platform that mentions families without using the word *traditional:*

Children and Families

If we are to renew America, we must do a better job of investing in the next generation of Americans. For parents, the first and most sacred responsibility is to support our children: setting an example of excellence, turning off the TV, and helping with the homework. But we must also support parents as they strive to raise their children in a new era. We must make it easier for working parents to spend time with their families when they need to. . . We also must recognize that caring for family members and managing a household is real and valuable work.

Fatherhood

Too many fathers are missing—missing from too many lives and too many homes. Children who grow up without a father are five times more likely to live in poverty and are more likely to commit crime, drop out of school, abuse drugs, and end up in prison. We need more fathers to realize that responsibility does not end at conception. We need them to understand that what makes a man is not the ability to have a child—it's the courage to raise one.

On which side of this debate would one find the Democratic Party? If we look back to the Political Ideology continuum at the start of the chapter, where would the aforementioned views fall along the continuum? While supporting the family, there is a listing of the qualities of good parents rather than a focus on the structure of the family. Why do Democrats avoid citing the structure of the ideal American family?

What about examining the Democratic position through a Lakoffian Nation as Family framework. Does this represent Strict Father Morality? Nurturant Parent Morality? What does the language itself tell you about the larger worldview of the Democratic Party, as stated in this section of their platform?

This issue contains two articles about whether the traditional family is the ideal family structure. *The Natural Family: A Manifesto* contains excerpts in this book intended to help the reader understand the case for the traditional (i.e., natural) family. The counterpoint by Professor Good argues that family diversity is itself a valuable goal in a pluralistic society.

YES

Allan C. Carlson and Paul T. Mero

The Natural Family: A Manifesto

What is the natural family? The answer comes to the woman and the man who take the risk of turning their love into promises of lifelong devotion.

In doing so, they will discover the story of the family, at once an ideal vision and a universal reality. In our time, they will also sense crisis, for malignant forces tear at the common source of freedom, order, virtue, and children. To set things right, they will need to look for clear principles, open goals, and a firm course of action. They also will need to reject false charges and weak compromise. Still, through these acts they shall come to know true liberty, a rekindled hearth, and a real homecoming, for themselves and for all humankind.

The Story of the Family

A young man and a young woman draw toward each other. They yearn to be as one. When they see the other, broad smiles appear. They sense the possibility of joy. Alone, they feel partial, incomplete. When together, they feel whole. The people among whom they live bless this bond in the celebration of marriage. The man and the woman exchange public vows with each other, and also with their kindred and neighbors, and the two become one flesh.

Over time, their joy and passion will be tested by the twists and surprises of life. They will cry together, sometimes in happiness, sometimes in sorrow. They will face sickness; they may know poverty; they could face dislocation or natural disaster; they might be torn apart by war. In times of despair or loss, they will find strength in each other. Facing death, they will feel the warm spiritual balm that heals the pain of physical separation. The conjugal bond built on fidelity, mutual duty, and respect allows both of them to emerge into their full potential; they become as their Creator intended, a being complete.

This marriage creates a new family, a home, the first and fundamental unit of human society. Here, husband and wife build a small economy. They share the work of provisioning, drawing on each one's interests, strengths, and skills. They craft a home which becomes a special place on earth. In centuries past, the small farm or the artisan's shop was the usual expression of this union between the sexual and the economic. Today, the urban townhouse, apartment, or suburban home are more common. Still, the small home economy remains the vital center of daily existence.

The wife and husband also build their home as a spiritual place. They learn that family and faith are, in fact, two sides of the same coin. The vital home rests on reverence, worship, and prayer.

From this same natural union flows new human life. Children are the first end, or purpose, of marriage. The couple watch with wonder as their first baby grows within the mother. Joy and awe drive away doubt and fear as they find their love transformed into a living child. Parts of their own beings have gone into the child's making, forming a new and unique person. The new father takes on the protection of the new mother in her time of vulnerability and dependence. A happiness follows the trial of childbirth as the new mother nurses her baby and as the father caresses his first born. Receiving a child through adoption sparks similar feelings. From such amazing moments, these parents are the child's first teachers; their home, the child's first, most vital school. They pass to the child the skills of living and introduce the satisfactions of talking, reading, reasoning, and exploring the world.

Inspired by love, the couple opens its union to additional children, filling their home, and filling the earth. These parents will know the delight of watching brothers and sisters grow together. They will watch with a mix of pride and worry as their children take their first steps, attempt their first chores, take on their first responsibilities. Among the children, there will be bruised knees, quarrels over toys, lost sport contests, tears, and laughter. As the children grow, they enter by steps a broader world. In all this, though, their parents stand as guides and guardians, and the home serves as a shelter and the focus of their common life.

Indeed, the natural family opens its home to other kin. The love and care which flow from parents to young children are mirrored in the care and love that adult children give to their aging parents. The truly rich family draws on the strengths of three or more generations. This family cares for its own. Each generation sees itself as a link in an unbroken chain, through which the family extends from and into the centuries.

A Time of Crisis

And yet, the natural family—*part of the created order, imprinted on our natures, the source of bountiful joy, the fountain of new life, the bulwark of ordered liberty*—stands reviled and threatened in the early 21st century. Foes have mounted attacks on all aspects of the natural family, from the bond of marriage to the birth of children to the true democracy of free homes. Ever more families show weaknesses and disorders. We see growing numbers of young adults rejecting the fullness and joy of marriage, choosing instead cheap substitutes or standing alone, where they are easy prey for the total state. Too many children are born outside of wedlock, ending as wards of that same state. Too few children are born inside married-couple homes, portending depopulation.

What has caused this alienation of humankind from its true nature and real home? Two basic assaults on the natural family have occurred, with their roots reaching back several hundred years: in brief, the challenge of industrialism and the assault of new, family-denying ideas.

On the one hand, the triumph of industrialism brought a "great disruption" or a "great transformation" in human affairs. The creation of wealth accelerated under the regime of industry. Yet this real gain rested on tearing productivity away from the hearth, on a disruption of the natural ecology of family life. The primal bond of home and work appeared to dissolve into air. Family-made goods and tasks became commodities, things to be bought and sold. Centralized factories, offices, and warehouses took over the tasks of the family workshop, garden, kitchen, and storeroom. Husbands, wives, and even children were enticed out of homes and organized in factories according to the principle of efficiency. Impersonal machines undermined the natural complementarity of the sexes in productive tasks. Children were left to fend for themselves, with the perception that their families no longer guided their futures; rather, the children now looked to faceless employers.

Politicians also embraced the industrial ideal and its claims to efficiency. New laws denied children a family-centered education and put them in mass state schools. Fertility tumbled, for "it . . . has yet to be [shown] . . . that any society can sustain stable high fertility beyond two generations of mass schooling." The state also invaded the home, seizing the protection of childhood from parents through the reform school movement and later schemes to "prevent child abuse." Family households, formerly function-rich beehives of useful, productive work and mutual support, tended to become merely functionless, overnight places of rest for persons whose active lives and loyalties lay elsewhere.

More critically, new ideas emerged over the same years that rejected the natural family. Some political thinkers held that the individual, standing alone, was the true cell of society; that family bonds—including those between husband and wife and between mother and child—showed merely the power of one selfish person over another. Other theorists argued that the isolated self, the lone actor in "the state of nature," was actually oppressed by institutions such as family and church. In this view, the central state was twisted into a supposed agent of liberation. It alone could free the enslaved individual from "the chains of tradition." From these premises emerged a terrible cloud of ideologies that shared a common target: the natural family. These idea systems included socialism, feminism, communism, sexual hedonism, racial nationalism, and secular liberalism.

By the 1990's, their campaign was global. Cynically, they used the International Year of the Family, 1994, to launch a series of United Nations conferences designed to tear down the natural family in the developing nations, as well. Cairo, Beijing, Istanbul, and Copenhagen were the arenas where they tried to impose this "post-family" order.

In our time, the partisans of a "post-family" world are still the ones on the offensive. For example, our pro-family movement has failed to restore legal protection to marriage by rolling back the "no-fault" revolution. Instead, by 2005, we are in a desperate fight simply to keep the vital institution of marriage from being fitted to homosexuals. And our two movements have failed to slow the war of governments on human fertility, despite the new likelihood of a catastrophic depopulation of the developed *and* developing nations through the global "empty cradle."

A Vision

And so, we advance here a new vision and a fresh statement of principles and goals appropriate for the 21st century and the third millennium.

We see a world restored in line with the intent of its Creator. We envision a culture—found both locally and universally—that upholds the marriage of a woman to a man, and a man to a woman, as the central aspiration for the young. This culture affirms marriage as the best path to health, security, fulfillment, and joy. It casts the home built on marriage as the source of true political sovereignty, the fountain of democracy. It also holds the household framed by marriage to be the primal economic unit, a place marked by rich activity, material abundance, and broad self-reliance. This culture treasures private property in family hands as the rampart of independence and liberty. It celebrates the marital sexual union as the unique source of new human life. We see these homes as open to a full quiver of children, the source of family continuity and social growth. We envision young women growing into wives, homemakers, and mothers; and we see young men growing into husbands, homebuilders, and fathers.

We see true happiness as the product of persons enmeshed in vital bonds with spouses, children, parents, and kin. We look to a landscape of family homes, lawns, and gardens busy with useful tasks and ringing with the laughter of many children. We envision parents as the first educators of their children. We see homes that also embrace extended family members who need special care due to age or infirmity. We view neighborhoods, villages, and townships as the second locus of political sovereignty. We envision a freedom of commerce that respects and serves family integrity. And we look to nation-states that hold the protection of the natural family to be their first responsibility.

Our Principles

To advance this vision, we advocates for the natural family assert clear principles to guide our work in the new century and millennium.

- We affirm that the natural family, not the individual, is the fundamental unit of society.
- We affirm the natural family to be the union of a man and a woman through marriage for the purposes of sharing love and joy, propagating children, providing their moral education, building a vital home economy, offering security in times of trouble, and binding the generations.
- We affirm that the natural family is a fixed aspect of the created order, one ingrained in human nature. Distinct family systems may grow weaker or stronger. However, the natural family cannot change into some new shape; nor can it be redefined by eager social engineers.
- We affirm that the natural family is the ideal, optimal, true family system. While we acknowledge varied living situations caused by circumstance or dysfunction, all other "family forms" are incomplete or are fabrications of the state.

- We affirm the marital union to be the authentic sexual bond, the only one open to the natural and responsible creation of new life.
- We affirm the sanctity of human life from conception to natural death; each newly conceived person holds rights to live, to grow, to be born, and to share a home with its natural parents bound by marriage.
- We affirm that the natural family is prior to the state and that legitimate governments exist to shelter and encourage the natural family.
- We affirm that the world is abundant in resources. The breakdown of the natural family and moral and political failure, not human "overpopulation," account for poverty, starvation, and environmental decay.
- We affirm that human depopulation is the true demographic danger facing the earth in this new century. Our societies need more people, not fewer.
- We affirm that women and men are equal in dignity and innate human rights, but different in function. Even if sometimes thwarted by events beyond the individual's control (or sometimes given up for a religious vocation), the calling of each boy is to become husband and father; the calling of each girl is to become wife and mother. Everything that a man does is mediated by his aptness for fatherhood. Everything that a woman does is mediated by her aptness for motherhood. Culture, law, and policy should take these differences into account.
- We affirm that the complementarity of the sexes is a source of strength. Men and women exhibit profound biological and psychological differences. When united in marriage, though, the whole becomes greater than the sum of the parts.
- We affirm that economic determinism is false. Ideas and religious faith can prevail over material forces. Even one as powerful as industrialization can be tamed by the exercise of human will.
- We affirm the "family wage" ideal of "equal pay for equal family responsibility." Compensation for work and taxation should reinforce natural family bonds.
- We affirm the necessary role of private property in land, dwelling, and productive capital as the foundation of familial independence and the guarantor of democracy. In a just and good society, all families will hold real property.
- And we affirm that lasting solutions to human problems rise out of families and small communities. They cannot be imposed by bureaucratic and judicial fiat. Nor can they be coerced by outside force.

Our Platform

From these principles, we draw out a simple, concrete platform for the new century and millennium. To the world, we say:

- We will build a new culture of marriage, where others would define marriage out of existence.
- We will welcome and celebrate more babies and larger families, where others would continue a war on human fertility.
- We will find ways to bring mothers, fathers, and children back home, where others would further divide parents from their children.
- And we will create true home economies, where others would subject families to the full control of big government and vast corporations.

To do these things, we must offer positive encouragements, and we must also correct the policy errors of the past. Specifically:

To Build a New Culture of Marriage . . .

- We will craft schooling that gives positive images of chastity, marriage, fidelity, motherhood, fatherhood, husbandry, and housewifery. We will end the corruption of children through state "sex education" programs.
- We will build legal and constitutional protections around marriage as the union of a man and a woman. We will end the war of the sexual hedonists on marriage.
- We will transform social insurance, welfare, and housing programs to reinforce marriage, especially the marriage of young adults. We will end state incentives to live outside of marriage.
- We will place the weight of the law on the side of spouses seeking to defend their marriages. We will end state preferences for easy divorce by repealing "no-fault" statutes.
- We will recognize marriage as a true and full economic partnership. We will end "marriage penalties" in taxation.
- We will allow private insurers to recognize the health advantages of marriage and family living, according to sound business principles. We will end legal discrimination against the married and child-rich.
- We will empower the legal and cultural guardians of marriage and public morality. We will end the coarsening of our culture.

To Welcome More Babies Within Marriage . . .

- We will praise churches and other groups that provide healthy and fertile models of family life to the young. We will end state programs that indoctrinate children, youth, and adults into the contraceptive mentality.
- We will restore respect for life. We will end the culture of abortion and the mass slaughter of the innocents.
- We will create private and public campaigns to reduce maternal and infant mortality and to improve family health. We will end government campaigns of population control.
- We will build special protections for families, motherhood, and childhood. We will end the terrible assault on these basic human rights.
- We will celebrate husbands and wives who hold open their sexual lives to new children. We will end the manipulation and abuse of new human life in the laboratories.
- We will craft generous tax deductions, exemptions, and credits that are tied to marriage and the number of children. We will end the oppressive taxation of family income, labor, property, and wealth.
- We will create credits against payroll taxes that reward the birth of children and that build true family patrimonies. We will end existing social insurance incentives toward childlessness.
- We will offer tax benefits to businesses that provide "natal gifts" and "child allowances" to their employees. We will end legal incentives that encourage business corporations to ignore families.

To Bring Mothers, and Fathers, Home . . .

- We will ensure that stay-at-home parents enjoy at least the same state benefits offered to day-care users. We will end all discriminations against stay-at-home parents.
- We will encourage new strategies and technologies that would allow home-based employment to blossom and prosper. We will end policies that unfairly favor large, centralized businesses and institutions.
- We will favor small property that reintegrates home and work. We will end taxes, financial incentives, subsidies, and zoning laws that discourage small farms and family-held businesses.

To Create a True Home Economy . . .

- We will allow men and women to live in harmony with their true natures. We will end the aggressive state promotion of androgyny.
- We will encourage employers to pay a "family wage" to heads of households. We will end laws that prohibit employers from recognizing and rewarding family responsibility.

- We will craft laws that protect home schools and other family-centered schools from state interference. We will give real control of state schools to small communities so that their focus might turn toward home and family. And we will create measures (such as educational tax credits) that recognize the exercise of parental responsibility. We will end discriminatory taxes and policies that favor mass state education of the young.
- We will hold up the primacy of parental rights and hold public officials accountable for abuses of their power. We will end abuse of the "child-abuse" laws.
- We will encourage self-sufficiency through broad property ownership, home enterprise, home gardens, and home workshops. We will end the culture of dependency found in the welfare state.
- We will celebrate homes that are centers of useful work. We will end state incentives for home building that assume, and so create, families without functions.

The Usual Charges

We know that certain charges will be leveled against us. Some will say that we want to turn back the clock, to restore a mythical American suburban world of the 1950's. Others will charge that we seek to subvert the rights of women or that we want to impose white, Western, Christian values on a pluralistic world. Still others will argue that we ignore science or reinforce patriarchal violence. Some will say that we block inevitable social evolution or threaten a sustainable world with too many children.

So, in anticipation, let us be clear:

We Look Forward with Hope, While Learning from the Past

It is true that we look with affection to earlier familial eras such as "1950's America." Indeed, for the first time in one hundred years, five things happened simultaneously in America (and in Australia and parts of Western Europe, as well) during this time: the marriage rate climbed; the divorce rate fell; marital fertility soared; the equality of households increased; and measures of child well-being and adult happiness rose. These were the social achievements of "the greatest generation." We look with delight on this record and aspire to recreate such results.

However, we also know that this specific development was a one-generation wonder. It did not last. Some children of the "baby boom" rebelled. Too often, this rebellion was foolish and destructive. Still, we find weaknesses in the family model of "1950's America." We see that it was largely confined to the white majority. Black families actually showed mounting stress in these years: a retreat from marriage; more out-of-wedlock births. Also, this new suburban model—featuring long commutes for fathers and tract homes without the central places such as parks and nearby shops where mothers and youth might have found healthy community bonds—proved incomplete. Finally, we see the "companionship marriage" ideal of this time, which embraced psychological tasks to the exclusion of material and religious functions, as fragile. We can, and we will, do better.

We Believe Wholeheartedly in Women's Rights

Above all, we believe in rights that recognize women's unique gifts of pregnancy, birthing, and breastfeeding. The goal of androgyny, the effort to eliminate real differences between women and men, does every bit as much violence to human nature and human rights as the old efforts by the communists to create "Soviet Man" and by the nazis to create "Aryan Man." We reject social engineering, attempts to corrupt girls and boys, to confuse women and men about their true identities. At the same time, nothing in our platform would prevent women from seeking and attaining as much education as they want. Nothing in our platform would prevent women from entering jobs and professions to which they aspire. We do object, however, to restrictions on the liberty of employers to recognize family relations and obligations and so reward indirectly those parents staying at home to care for their children. And we object to current attacks on the Universal Declaration of Human Rights, a document which proclaims fundamental rights to family autonomy, to a family wage for fathers, and to the special protection of mothers.

We Believe That the Natural Family Is Universal, an Attribute of All Humankind

We confess to holding Christian values regarding the family: the sanctity of marriage; the desire by the Creator that we be fruitful and multiply; Jesus' miracle at the wedding feast; His admonitions against adultery and divorce. And yet, we find similar views in the other great world faiths. Moreover, we even find recognition of the natural family in the marriage rituals of animists. Because it is imprinted on our natures as human beings, we know that the natural family can be grasped by all persons who open their minds to the evidence of their senses and their hearts to the promptings of their best instincts. Also, in the early 21st century, there is little that is "Western" about our views. The voices of the "post family" idea are actually today's would-be "Westernizers." They are the ones who largely rule in the child-poor, aging, dying lands of "the European West." It is they who seek to poison the rest of the world with a grim, wizened culture of death. Our best friends are actually to be found in the developing world, in the Third World, in the Middle East, Africa, South Asia, South America. Our staunchest allies tend not to be white, but rather people of color. Others seek a sterile, universal darkness. We seek to liberate the whole world—including dying Europa—for light and life, for children.

We Celebrate the Findings of Empirical Science

Science, honestly done and honestly reported, is the friend of the natural family. The record is clear from decades of work in sociology, psychology, anthropology, sociobiology, medicine, and social history: children do best when they are born into and raised by their two natural parents. Under *any* other setting—including one-parent, step-parent, homosexual, cohabiting, or communal households—children predictably do worse. Married, natural-parent homes bring health, learning, and success to the offspring reared therein. Science shows that these same homes give life, wealth, and joy to wives and husbands, as well. Disease, depression, and early death come to those who reject family life. This result should not really cause surprise. Science, after all, is the study of the natural order. And while the Creator forgives, nature never does.

We Seek to Reduce Domestic Violence

All families fall short of perfection and a few families fail. We, too, worry about domestic violence. We know that people can make bad choices, that they can fall prey to selfishness and their darker instincts. We also know that persons can live in places or times where they have few models of solid homes, few examples of good marriages. All the same, we also insist that the natural family is not the source of these human failures. The research here is clear. Women are safest physically when married and living with their husbands. Children are best sheltered from sexual, physical, and emotional abuse when they live with their married natural parents. In short, the natural family is the *answer* to abuse. We also know that all husbands and wives, all mothers and fathers, need to be nurtured toward and encouraged in their proper roles. These are the first tasks of all worthy social institutions.

We Believe That While Distinct Family Systems Change, the Design of the Natural Family Never Does

Regarding the natural family, we deny any such thing as social evolution. The changes we see are either decay away from or renewal toward the one true family model. From our very origin as a unique creature on earth, we humans have been defined by the long-term bonding of a woman and a man, by their free sharing of resources, by a complementary division of labor, and by a focus on the procreation, protection, and rearing of children in stable homes. History is replete with examples of distinct family systems that have grown strong and built great civilizations, only to fall to atomism, vice, and decay. Even in our Western Civilization, we can identify periods of family decline and disorder, followed by successful movements of renewal. It is true that the last forty years have been a time of great confusion and decay. We now sense a new summons to social rebirth.

We Seek a Sustainable Human Future

With sadness, we acknowledge that the new Malthusian impulse has succeeded in its war against children all too well. Fertility is tumbling around the globe. A majority of nations have already fallen into "the aging trap" of depopulation. As matters now stand, the predictable future is one of catastrophic population decline, economic contraction, and human tragedy. Our agenda actually represents the earth's best hope for a sustainable future.

Looking Forward

That large task requires new ways of thinking and acting. Our vision of the hearth looks forward, not to the past, for hope and purpose. We see the vital home reborn through startling new movements such as home schooling. We marvel at fresh inventions that portend novel bonds between home and work. We are inspired by a convergence of religious truth with the evidence of science around the vital role of the natural family. We see the prospect of a great civil alliance of religious orthodoxies, within nations and around the globe; not to compromise on doctrines held dear, but to defend our family systems from the common foe. With wonder, we find a shared happiness with people once distrusted or feared. We enjoy new friendships rooted in family ideals that cross ancient divides. We see the opportunity for an abundant world order built on the natural family.

We issue a special call to the young, those born over the last three to four decades. You are the children of a troubled age, a time of moral and social disorder. You were conceived into a culture of self-indulgence, of abortion, a culture embracing death. More than all generations before, you have known the divorce of parents. You have lived too often in places without fathers. You have been taught to deny your destinies as young women and young men. You have been forced to read books that mock marriage, motherhood, and fatherhood. Persons who should have protected you—teachers, judges, public officials—often left you as prey to moral and sexual predators. Many of you are in fact the victims of a kind of cultural rape: seduced into early sexual acts, then pushed into sterility.

And yet, you are also the ones with the power to make the world anew. Where some members of *our* generation helped to corrupt the world, you will be the builders. You have seen the darkness. The light now summons you. It is your time to lead, with the natural family as your standard and beacon. Banish the lies told to you. Claim your natural freedom to create true and fruitful marriages. Learn from the social renewal prompted by "the greatest generation" and call on them for special support. You have the chance to shape a world that welcomes and celebrates children. You have the ability to craft a true homecoming. Your generation holds the destiny of humankind in its hands. The hopes of all good and decent people lie with you.

The Call

A new spirit spreads in the world, the essence of the natural family. We call on all people of goodwill, whose hearts are open to the promptings of this spirit, to join in a great campaign. The time is close when the persecution of the natural family, when the war against children, when the assault on human nature shall end.

The enemies of the natural family grow worried. A triumph that, not so many years ago, they thought complete is no longer sure. Their fury grows. So do their attempts, ever more desperate, at coercion. Yet their mistakes also mount in number. They misread human nature. They misread the times.

We all are called to be the actors, the moral soldiers, in this drive to realize the life ordained for us by our Creator. Our foes are dying, of their own choice; we have a world to gain. Natural families of all races, nations, and creeds, let us unite.

"TO THE WORLD, WE SAY:
- We will build a new culture of marriage, where others would define marriage out of existence.
- We will welcome and celebrate more babies and larger families, where others would continue a war on human fertility.
- We will find ways to bring mothers, fathers, and children back home, where others would further divide parents from their children.
- And we will create true home economies, where others would subject families to the full control of big government and vast corporations."

ALLAN C. CARLSON is President of the Howard Center for Family, Religion & Society and Distinguished Fellow in Family Policy Studies at the Family Research Council in Washington, D.C.

PAUL T. MERO is President of the Sutherland Institute and a Trustee of the ALS Foundation. Carlson and Mero argue that American needs to return to a traditional family and is headed by a man and woman.

Mark Good

 **NO**

Nontraditional Families and Childhood Progress through School

What types of outcomes can be expected for children raised by same-sex couples, relative to children in other types of families? The answer is vitally important both for public policy relating to same-sex marriage and adoption (Eskridge 2002; Koppelman 2002), and for theories of how family structure matters. Supporters and opponents of same-sex marriage rights agree that the legal issue of same-sex marriage rights should revolve around the question of childhood outcomes for children raised by same-sex couples (Alvaré 2005; Patterson 2002). In this paper, I examine progress through school, i.e., normal progress versus grade retention, for children of same-sex couples compared to children of other family types, using data from the 2000 U.S. census.

The debate over same-sex unions and their children draws from and informs a more general literature concerning family structure's effect on children. The literature on family structure has generally focused on structural variations within heterosexual parented families, contrasting heterosexual married couples, heterosexual remarried couples, and (presumably heterosexual) single mothers (Cherlin 1992; McLanahan and Sandefur 1994). Even though same-sex couples are a small minority of all couples (1% of all couples in census 2000 were same-sex couples), the inclusion of same-sex couples can provide researchers with more leverage over the key question of how family structure matters in general.

Studies of family structure and children's outcomes nearly universally find at least a modest advantage for children raised by their married biological parents. The question which has bedeviled researchers, and which remains essentially unresolved, is *why* (Cherlin 1999). Some results have indicated that socioeconomic status explains most or all of the advantage of children raised by married couples (Biblarz and Raftery 1999; Gennetian 2005; Ginther and Pollak 2004), while other scholars find that family structure has an enduring effect on children net of all other factors (McLanahan and Sandefur 1994; Zill 1996). Married couples tend to be the most prosperous type of family unit, and this economic prosperity undoubtedly has certain advantages for children (but also see Mayer 1997).

Literature Review

Same-Sex Parenting

The modern reality of same-sex couples raising children long postdates the classical psychological theories of child development (for example, Freud [1905] 1975). Recent research on childhood socialization to gender roles has emphasized peer groups and genetics as much as direct parental influence (Harris 1998; Maccoby 1990). In-depth studies of the psychosocial development of children raised by lesbians or by same-sex couples has found that these children are normal and well adjusted (Chan, Raboy and Patterson 1998b; Flaks et al. 1995; Golombok et al. 2003), though as I discuss below, there are also critics of the small-N literature on same-sex couples and their children.

Same-sex couples become parents in three main ways. First, through one partner's (generally prior) heterosexual relationship; second, through adoption; third, through donor insemination or surrogate parenting (Stacey 2006). Same-sex couples cannot become parents through misuse or failure of birth control, the way heterosexual couples can. Parenthood is more difficult to achieve for same-sex couples than for heterosexual couples, which implies a stronger selection effect for same-sex parents. If gays and lesbians have to work harder to become parents, it could be the case that the gays and lesbians who do become parents are on average more dedicated to the hard work of parenting than their heterosexual peers, and this could be beneficial for their children.

In Judith Stacey's (2006 p. 39) discussion of gay adoption, she describes the gay men of Los Angeles as having to search through the state's ". . . overstocked warehouse of 'hard to place' children, the majority of whom . . . have been removed from families judged negligent, abusive, or incompetent. Most of the state's stockpiled children . . . are children of color, and disproportionately boys with 'special needs.'" If it is the case that same-sex couples who adopt mainly have access to 'special needs' children, the special needs of these children could exert a downward bias on the average outcomes for children of same-sex couples. Fortunately, the census distinguishes between the head of household's "own children," adopted children, stepchildren, and foster children.

Nearly all children of gay and lesbian parents attend schools and live in neighborhoods whose other children come overwhelmingly from families with heterosexual parents. In other words, children of same-sex couples share a common peer and school environment with children of heterosexual couples. To the extent that peer environment is a primary socializing environment for children (Harris 1998; Maccoby 1990; for a survey, see Rutter 2002), whatever differences sexual orientation of parents makes within the home may well be mediated and diffused by the common peer and school environments that children share regardless of the gender or sexual orientation of their parents.

How the Census Complements the Existing Literature

Our research lists 45 empirical studies of outcomes of children of same-sex couples, comprising all of the journal articles listed in Fiona Tasker's (2005) comprehensive survey which examined childhood outcomes, plus several more recent studies listed by Wald (2006), and all four studies listed by Meezan and Rauch (2005) as the highest quality studies in this field, and all the more recent studies which cite the earlier ones. None of the studies cited in our research find statistically significant disadvantages for children raised by gay and lesbian parents compared to other children.

The uniform finding of no significant disadvantage for children raised by gay or lesbian parents has been convincing to some scholars (Ball and Pea 1998; Meezan and Rauch 2005; Stacey and Biblarz 2001; Wald 2006), though others remain unconvinced (Lerner and Nagai 2001; Nock 2001; Wardle 1997). Several points are worth commenting upon. First, as the critics have noted, convenience sampling dominated this literature in the past (Nock 2001). More recent scholarship has answered this criticism by using nationally representative probability samples derived from the National Longitudinal Study of Adolescent Health (Add Health, see Wainright and Patterson 2006, 2008; Wainright et al. 2004), as well as studies constructed from a hybrid of probability sampling and convenience sampling (Golombok et al. 2003; Perry et al. 2004).

A second critique of the literature, that the sample sizes of the studies are too small to allow for statistically powerful tests, continues to be relevant. The mean number of children of gay or lesbian parents in these studies

is 39, and the median is 37, and both numbers would be slightly lower if studies without comparison groups were excluded. The nationally representative studies in the series found only 44 children who were raised by lesbian couples in the Add Health survey. Golombok et al (2003) found only 18 lesbian mothers out of 14,000 mothers in the Avon Longitudinal Study of Parents and Children, which is why they supplemented this sample with snowball sampling and their own convenience sample. The universally small sample sizes of the studies in the existing literature has left room for several critiques, including the critique that small sample studies would not have the statistical power to identify the effects of homosexual parents on childhood outcomes, even if such effects did exist (Lerner and Nagai 2001; Nock 2001). A third potential weakness of this literature is the narrowness of family structures under study (Tasker 2005). Of the 45 studies listed, only seven examined the children of gay fathers, and only two of these seven studies had a more traditional family control group built into the study.

Among the convenience sample studies, several of the most important have been based on samples of women who became parents through assisted reproductive technology (ART-Brewaeys et al. 1997; Chan et al. 1998b; Flaks et al. 1995). Because individuals who become parents through assisted means can be identified through the reproductive clinic and are therefore easier to recruit than the general population of same-sex couple parents, the literature on same-sex couple parenting has tended to feature studies of the kind of women who can afford ART: white upper middle class women. Nationally representative data tends to paint a different picture: in the U.S. census, same-sex couple parents tend to be more working class and are much more likely to be racially nonwhite compared to heterosexual married couples.

The debate over same-sex marriage and gay and lesbian adoption rights revolves around many competing sets of assumptions with political, religious, and ideological axes which cannot be resolved or even fully addressed in this paper. To the extent the debate is an empirical debate, that is to the extent that disagreement remains over the meaning of the empirical literature on the development of children of same-sex couples, this paper offers a new perspective.

To supplement the existing small-scale studies, I offer a large sample study of children from the U.S. Census, including 3,502 children of same-sex couples who had been living with both parents for at least five years (2,030 children living with lesbian mothers and 1,472 children living with gay fathers, see our research), and more than 700,000 children in grades 1–8 from other family types. This sample size more than satisfies Nock's (2001) criteria of 800 as the minimum number of gay and lesbian couples required for statistically useful study.

The U.S. census has several major disadvantages: normal progress through school is the only available children's outcome, and even this outcome is measured with less precision than one would hope for. Although the census data have several important limitations for the research questions considered here, the strengths of the census data (large sample, national representativity, and a full array of family structures) address important lacunae in the literature, and as such, this study offers a potentially useful new perspective on how family structure matters to children. Although the census data are far from ideal for the subject under study here, better data are nowhere on the horizon.

Grade Retention

Grade retention (the opposite of normal progress through school) has been increasing in U.S. schools since President Bill Clinton proposed ending social promotion in schools in his State of the Union address in 1998 (Alexander, Entwisle and Dauber 2003:viii; Hauser 2001). Grade retention is an important childhood outcome because retention in the primary grades is a strong indicator of a lack of childhood readiness for school, and we know that effective parenting is a crucial ingredient in school readiness (Brooks-Gunn and Markman 2005). Brooks-Gunn and Markman argue that the lower school readiness of racial minority children is due, in part, to parenting practices which differ from the authoritative parenting style favored in middle class white homes (Baumrind 1966; Lareau 2003).

Guo, Brooks-Gunn, and Harris (1996) studied grade retention among urban black children and found that some indicators of parental stress such as unemployment and welfare use were associated with increased grade retention for children; in other words, they found childhood grade retention to be a useful measure of difficulties the students were experiencing at home. Guo, Brooks-Gunn, and Harris (1996:218) identify three potential sources of grade retention: "weak cognitive ability, behavioral problems, and lack of engagement in school." Of these three causes of childhood grade retention, the second two might be partly associated with the quality of the home environment. Students with learning disabilities or physical disabilities which affect learning are also at risk of grade retention, and this type of grade retention would not be indicative of parenting deficits.

Grade retention is closely associated with more serious problems later in life. Students who are held back at least once are at much higher risk for eventually dropping out of high school (Alexander, Entwisle, and Horsey 1997; Guo et al. 1996; Moller et al. 2006; Roderick 1994; Rumberger 1987; Tillman, Guo, and Harris 2006). Failure to graduate from high school is associated with low earnings, high unemployment, low self-esteem, and high mortality rates (Guo et al. 1996; McLanahan 1985; Tillman et al. 2006). Even when grade retention takes place in the early grades, the "crystallization" of behaviors and academic abilities implies that difficulties a child experiences when he or she is 7 or 8 carry forward (more so for girls than for boys) into adolescence and young adulthood (Kowalesi-Jones and Duncan 1999).

There are several theoretical reasons for supposing that children of same-sex couples might have lower school readiness (and therefore higher rates of grade retention) than own children of heterosexual married couples, net of race, parental income, and parental education. First, the legal privileges of marriage are numerous and have direct consequences for the well being of children (Eskridge 1996; Pawelski et al. 2006). Second, evolutionary theory suggests that parents invest more in their own biological children (Wilson 2002; but see also Hamilton, Cheng, and Powell 2007), and same-sex couples (absent a prior sex change) cannot both be the biological parents of any one child. Third, the large majority of children of same-sex couples from the 2000 census were children from prior heterosexual relationships (only 11% were stepchildren, adopted children, or foster children of the head of household), meaning that most of the children being raised by same-sex couples at the time of the 2000 census had previously lived through divorce or parental breakup, which research has shown to be traumatic for some children (Amato and Cheadle 2005; Chase-Lansdale, Cherlin, and Kiernan 1995; McLanahan and Sandefur 1994; Wallerstein and Kelly 1980; Wallerstein, Lewis, and Blakeslee 2000).

The Benefits of Legal Marriage

Legal marriage confers a host of protections and advantages both to the couples who marry and to their children. Married couples generally share joint legal custody of their coresident children. In a system of employer-based health care insurance, either spouse in a married couple can usually provide health insurance for both spouses and all their children. Marriage is a long-term contract which allows and encourages parents to make long-term investments in their children (Waite and Gallagher 2000). Divorce rights, which are a corollary to marriage rights, provide guarantees for child support and visitation that are intended to minimize the damage of a breakup to a couple's children. Given the many practical, legal, economic, and social advantages of marriage as a childrearing family structure, it should come as no surprise that children of long-term married couples have the best outcomes (McLanahan and Sandefur 1994). The various benefits of marriage extend far beyond income, so one would generally expect children in married couples to have advantages even after SES is accounted for in regressions.

The moral claim for same-sex marriage rests in part on the many practical and psychological benefits of marriage, benefits which conservative family scholars have made the most careful and enthusiastic case for (Waite and Gallagher 2000; Wilson 2002). The benefits of marriage, combined with the exclusion of gays and lesbians (and their children) from those benefits, together form one cornerstone of the case for same-sex marriage (Eskridge 1996).

Relevant Comparison Sets for Same-Sex Couples

Along with the standard comparison to heterosexual married couples, heterosexual cohabiting couples are a second logical comparison group for same-sex cohabiting couples. Both heterosexual cohabiters and same-sex cohabiters are two-parent families living without the rights and benefits of marriage. Certainly, there are differences: heterosexual cohabiting couples can marry if they want to, whereas in the United States at the time of the 2000 census, same-sex couples could not marry. The comparison between children of same-sex cohabiting couples and children of heterosexual cohabiting couples allows for a more specific test of the effect of same-sex parenthood on children, while holding constant legal rights and the number of parents.

A third relevant comparison for children of same-sex couples are the children living in group quarters, since these are the children presumably available for adoption, and because same-sex couples are more likely than heterosexual couples to participate in the adoption market. Some of the difference between children in group quarters and children living with parents and guardians must be due to selection effects—the most troubled children available for adoption may not be adopted and may do poorly in school as a result of emotional or physical disabilities. On the other hand, if gay and lesbian adoptive parents are choosing from the middle or the bottom of the adoptive pool (Stacey 2006), rather than from the population of the most desirable potential adoptees, then the selection effect will be less important. In either case, the census, as a cross-sectional survey, is poorly suited to the analysis of selection effects. Nonetheless, census 2000 does provide strong controls for individual student disabilities, and any comparison between children living with families and children living in group quarters will be made after individual disabilities have been controlled for.

First-Order Predictors of Childhood Grade Retention

Because denominator school populations cover four years (grades 1–4, grades 5–8), but the students who can be identified as over age for their grade come only from the last grade of each four-year span (grades 4 and 8)5, the implied grade retention rate is four times higher than the observed grade retention rate. Our research shows both the observed grade retention rate and the implied grade retention rate, for primary school students using weighted data from the 2000 census.

Our research suggests that childhood grade retention is correlated with family type. Children of heterosexual married couples had the lowest implied rate of grade retention, 6.8%. Children of lesbian mothers and gay fathers had grade retention rates of 9.5% and 9.7%, respectively. Children of heterosexual cohabiting parents had a grade retention rate of 11.7%, while children of single parents had grade retention rates between 11.1% and 12.6%.

The differences in childhood grade retention between all types of non-group-quarters households were dwarfed by the high grade retention rates of children living in group quarters. According to our research, children living in group homes, many of them awaiting adoption or foster parents, had an implied grade retention rate of 34.4%. Children who were incarcerated had a grade retention rate of 78.0%. Later in the paper, I show that the enormous difference in grade retention between children raised in families and children living in group quarters remains even after individual level student disabilities are accounted for.

One way to gauge the advantage of living with families is to note that adopted children (10.6% grade retention) who spent the five years prior to the census living with their adoptive parents, and foster children (20.6% grade retention) with five years of residential stability performed considerably better than children who spent the same 5 years living at a single-group-quarters address (34.4% grade retention for non-inmates). The performance hierarchy which favors own children, and then (in declining order of school performance) adopted children, then foster children, then children in group quarters confirms the long standing research finding that children do best when living with parents who make a long term commitment to the children's development (Bartholet 1999). Selection bias (wherein the children with the most severe disabilities or children who have suffered the worst abuse are the least likely to be adopted) must also play a role, which unfortunately cannot be quantified with these data.

The rest of our research shows implied grade retention along several other dimensions. Asian children had the lowest rates of grade retention, while black children had the highest. Girls were less likely to be held back in the primary grades than boys were. Suburban schools had lower rates of grade retention than city schools, which in turn were lower than rural schools. Household socioeconomic status (SES) was a crucial predictor of childhood school performance. In households with income less than $25,000, 12.6% of the primary school students were left back, compared to only 5.3% for children in households with incomes over $100,000. Householder's education had an even stronger effect on children's progress through school: parents who had less than a high school degree had primary school children who were retained 14.3% of the time, whereas householders with college degrees had children who were retained only 4.4% of the time.

Our research shows that the strongest factor in making normal progress through elementary school is living with a family rather than living in group quarters. For children living in a family, whether the family is headed by a heterosexual married couple or by some less traditional parenting arrangement, the second most important factor in childhood progress through school appears to be parental educational attainment.

Socioeconomic Status by Family Type

Our research shows that gays and lesbians had a higher-than-average educational attainment of 13.6 years (i.e., 1.6 years of college) compared to 13.4 years for heterosexual married heads of household. Across family types, gay couples had the highest median household income at $61,000 per household. It should also be noted that men have higher earnings than women, and gay male couples are the only household type that relied on the earnings of two men. The second Nontraditional Families and Childhood Grade Retention P. 17 four family types are all single-parent (i.e., single-income) families, so their household incomes were roughly half as high as the household incomes of the first four family types.

Despite the fact that the cost of becoming parents may be higher for gays and lesbians than for heterosexual couples, our research shows that gay and lesbian couples who did have children had substantially lower income and educational attainment than gay and lesbian couples in general. While gay and lesbian cohabiters had relatively high household incomes, gay and lesbian parents had lower SES than heterosexual married parents ($50 thousand per household for gay parents compared to $58 thousand for heterosexual married parents). Excluding marital status recodes, the income and educational level of gay and lesbian parents was even lower. Among gay and lesbian couples, those with lower incomes are more likely to be raising children.

Not only were heterosexual married parents economically advantaged, the heterosexual married couples were also racially advantaged. Only 22.9% of children of heterosexual married couple were black or Hispanic, whereas 41.6% of children of gay men were black or Hispanic, and this percentage rose to 53.7% when dual marital status recodes were excluded. The children of lesbians were similarly likely (37.1%) to be black or Hispanic. Never-married mothers were the most likely parenting family type to have black or Hispanic children. The racial breakdown of parents was similar to the racial breakdown of children described in our research. Among heterosexual married heads of household, 22.2% were black or Hispanic, while 40.4% of gay fathers were black or Hispanic, and 36.1% of lesbian mothers were black or Hispanic (not shown in our research).

Among all family types, children of lesbian mothers were the most likely (more than 12%) to be adopted children, stepchildren, or foster children. Because economic disadvantage, minority racial status, and experience with the adoption or foster care system are all challenges for children, a careful analysis of the school performance of children of gay and lesbian parents must take these disadvantages into account.

Comparisons with Children of Unmarried Heterosexual Couples

Our research revisits the regressions from our research (with the same models, covariates, and summary statistics), comparing children raised by same-sex couples to children raised by heterosexual cohabiting couples. Our research shows that children raised by same-sex couples are more likely to make normal progress through school compared to children raised by heterosexual cohabiting couples, but the difference is statistically significant only in Model 1, before parental SES has been accounted for. If children living with dual marital status recoded couples are excluded, the signs are reversed (meaning children raised by heterosexual cohabiting couples do better), but none of the coefficients are statistically significant. These results suggest that (for the outcome of normal progress through school) children raised by same-sex cohabiting couple parents are no different, and perhaps slightly advantaged, compared to children being raised by heterosexual cohabiting couples. The similarity in school performance between children of same-sex couples and children of heterosexual cohabiting couples fails to support the gender essentialist theories of parenting, which argue that child development depends on having parental role models from both gender groups (Alvaré 2005; Popenoe 1996; Wardle 1997).

Comparisons with Children in Group Quarters

Our research represents a different variation on the type of analysis from. In our research, the sample of children includes children in group quarters, and these children are the comparison category for the analysis. Because neither household income nor parental education can be associated with children in group quarters, these variables are dropped from the analysis. The sample of children in our research includes own children, adopted children, stepchildren, group quarters children, and foster children. Since the children in group-quarters have no head of household to have a relationship with, it seemed appropriate to use the broadest definition of "children" for children who were living with families. Furthermore, the adopted and foster children probably include some children who formerly lived in group quarters.

Our research confirms the robustness of a previous finding from our research, that children who live with parents regardless of family type are much more likely to make normal progress through school than children living in group quarters. Even after student disabilities (more common among group-quarters children than among children living with families) are taken into account, the difference remained between children raised by families and children living in group quarters. Children living at least five years with same-sex couples and children living at least five years with unmarried heterosexual cohabiting couples had odds of making good progress through school that were twice as high as non-inmate children who had spent the previous five years in group-quarters. Using coefficients from Model 2 of our research, which controls for children's race and disabilities, children raised by same-sex couples had odds of making good progress through school that were 2.43 times higher than children living in group quarters (e.886 = 2.43). Children raised by heterosexual cohabiting couples were similarly advantaged compared to children in group quarters (e.810 = 2.25, coefficients from Model 2). The advantage of children raised by same-sex couples over children living in group quarters remains positive and statistically significant across all four models even after marital status recoded couples are excluded.

Discussion

Children raised by same-sex couples are one of the most difficult populations in the United States to study systematically because of their small numbers and their geographic dispersion. The census data are far from ideal, and better data would, of course, be welcome. However, until such time as better nationally representative data are available, the U.S. census is the only nationally representative dataset with a large enough sample of children raised by same-sex couples to allow for statistically powerful comparisons with children of other family types.

To the extent that normal progress through primary school is a useful and valid measure of child development, the results confirm that children of same-sex couples appear to have no inherent developmental disadvantage. Heterosexual married couples are the most economically prosperous, the most likely to be white, and the most legally advantaged type of parents; their children have the lowest rates of grade retention. Parental SES accounts for more than half of the relatively small gap in grade retention between children of heterosexual married couples and children of same-sex couples. When one controls for parental SES and characteristics of the students, children of same-sex couples cannot be distinguished with statistical certainty from children of heterosexual married couples.

Children of all non–group quarters family types, including households headed by same-sex couples, are dramatically more likely to make normal progress through school than students living in group quarters. Any policy that would deny gay and lesbian parents the right to adopt or foster children would force some children to remain in group quarters. A longer stay in group quarters would seem to be contrary to the best interest of the children. In recent years, scholars have arrived at a consensus that moving children out of group homes and into adoptive families should be the goal of public policy. Families, even suboptimal families, are better equipped than the state to raise children (Bartholet 1999; Goldstein, Freud, and Solnit 1979).

Historical restrictions against interracial adoption in the United States represent one relevant historical precedent for the current debate over the adoption rights of same-sex couples. Randall Kennedy (2003) argues that even though restrictions against interracial adoption have been proposed as a way of protecting children, such restrictions have victimized children by taking them away from loving homes or by forcing children to remain in group quarters for too long. Policies which limit the kinds of families that can adopt or foster children ignore the enormous advantages of personal attention that families have (even single parents and other nontraditional family types) over the state in raising children well.

The prior literature has found no evidence that children raised by same-sex couples suffer any important disadvantages (Chan et al. 1998b; Patterson 1995; Stacey and Biblarz 2001; Wald 2006). Yet this same literature has been heavily criticized on the methodological grounds that universally small sample sizes prevent the studies from having the statistical power to identify differences that might actually exist (Alvaré 2005; Lerner and Nagai 2001; Nock 2001). The analysis in this paper, using large-sample, nationally representative data for the first time, shows that children raised by same-sex couples have no fundamental deficits in making normal progress through school. The core finding here offers a measure of validation for the prior, and much debated, small-sample studies.

MARK GOOD is a Professor of Counselor Education at West Chester University and the President of Opn-Wyd, a diversity and communication company. Good argues that diversity in traditional and nontraditional is healthy. In fact, he argues that it can be damaging to hold the traditional family as the ideal familial structure.

EXPLORING THE ISSUE

Are Traditional Families Better Than Nontraditional Families?

Critical Thinking and Reflection

1. Can you identify the emotional, moral, intellectual, and social components in Carson and Mero's argument?
2. Can you identify the emotional, moral, intellectual, and social components in Good's argument?
3. Can you identify your own emotional, moral, intellectual, and social responses to this issue?
4. What are some similarities and differences between your responses and the authors'?

Is There Common Ground?

While we can debate the value of the traditional versus the nontraditional family, changing family structure is difficult to alter significantly. However, there are other qualities that need to be provided to ensure that children are afforded as many opportunities as possible. Let's identify those opportunities and advantages. What are some of the ways in which both traditional and nontraditional families can provide such opportunities?

Family structure will not remain static. Perhaps nontraditional families will be on the increase. Perhaps they will be on the decrease. What sort of projections would you make about changing family structure in the future?

How should a pluralistic democracy approach such changes in family structure?

Additional Resources

American Family Association:

www.afa.net

Focus on the Family:

www.focusonthefamily.com/

Human Rights Campaign:

www.hrc.org

Lambda Legal:

www.lambdalegal.org/

Internet References . . .

American Family Association

www.afa.net

Camp Mountain Meadow

www.queercamps.org/camps/mountainmeadow

Focus on the Family

www.focusonthefamily.com

Human Rights Campaign

www.hrc.org

Selected, Edited, and with Issue Framing Material by:
Don Dyson, *Widener University*

ISSUE

Are Teenagers Too Young to Become Parents?

YES: The National Campaign to Prevent Teen and Unplanned Pregnancy, from "One in Three: The Case for Wanted and Welcomed Pregnancy," National Campaign to Prevent Teen and Unplanned Pregnancy (May 2007)

NO: Simon Duncan, Claire Alexander, and Rosalind Edwards, from "What's the Problem with Teenage Parents?" Tuffnell Press (2010)

Learning Outcomes
After reading this issue, you will be able to: • Identify critical research about the state of and consequences of teenage parenting.   • Compare and contrast the major research cited and analysis used in examining teenage parenthood.   • Evaluate the impact of teen parenthood on teens themselves as well as on the larger American society.

ISSUE SUMMARY

YES: The National Campaign to Prevent Teen and Unplanned Pregnancy is dedicated to reducing teenage pregnancy. Their research argues that teens face significant consequences if they have unplanned pregnancy.

NO: Simon Duncan, Claire Alexander, and Rosalind Edwards have written a chapter in a book about teen pregnancy and parenting. This chapter, which takes a global perspective by looking at another Western society, England, argues that teenage pregnancy and parenting is not a problem.

Most people agree that it is important to reduce teenage pregnancy and parenthood. Teens involved in a pregnancy often did not plan that pregnancy. Indeed, about half of all pregnancies in the United States are unplanned—about 3 million each year.

Since the Clinton administration, there has been ongoing debate about the federal government's role in funding programs to reduce teen pregnancy: whether the best way to keep teenagers from having children is to teach them about contraception and abstinence, or only teach them about abstinence so that they fear the consequences of having sex. Although there is debate about whether abstinence-only or comprehensive sexuality education is the best approach, the goals tend to be the same: keep teenagers from pregnancy and parenthood.

In the United States, 30 percent of girls will become pregnant at least once by the age of 20. Many will terminate

their pregnancies while others will decide to become parents. Sometimes fathers remain involved; often teen mothers are left as single parents, perhaps with support from their parent(s), guardian(s), and/or caretaker(s).

This issue will focus on adult views of teenage parenthood. However, it is important to take some time to read the perspective of teenage parents themselves. On Pregnancystories.net, teens have posted some of the following stories about their young pregnancy and parenthood:

> **15 and pregnant**—well im 15 and two weeks pregnant. I told my boyfriend at the time and he was happy but as soon as his parents found out they said he was too young to be a dad. . . . Im looking forward to having my baby and iv got all the support i need. To all the girls who am pregnant and dont have a man . . . dont let him get you down cuz they aint worth it.
>
> Abi

my perfect accident—hey everyone my name is johanna, i am 18 years old and i have a 5 month old baby. when i was about 4 months off my 17th birthday me and one of my close guy friends started doing a friends with benefits sort of thing, at first it was great but then we let our emotions become involved and i fell in love with him. we decided to end it and he got a girlfriend pretty much straight away which hurt me. soon after i found out that i was pregnant and i told him, but he didnt believe me i had to confirm it with the doctor before anything happened. he was far from happy with it and started saying that it was all my fault i was a whore and a bitch, eventually his girlfriend broke up with him because of it. he still to this day hates me but i dont care i now have a beautiful 5 month old baby boy dominic jason, who is my world! my mum is so over the moon with everything and im happy to be a single mum, i now realize he did me a favor, i couldve never been with him after that or exposed dominic to that!

johanna

single mommy—Hi my name is Alex, I am 19 and i have a 1 year old daughter. it all started when I was 17 i got pregnant to my boyfriend of 2 years johnny, i was shocked and scared at first but eventually told him and everyone, we decided to keep the baby and be young parents, but as my pregnancy went on johnny started to push away, and eventually when I was 26 weeks he got a football scholarship to college, we talked about it and he wasnt ready to become a father, so he left for college a week later, i was devastated but i had my daughter to think of, i have birth to Lilliana Jayde 4 weeks after i turned 18, i am now 19 and lilliana is 13 and a half months old, we are very happy she is my world, i regularly send johnny pictures we keep in touch he still wants to know that lilliana is okay but she has never met him. But im happy i have a wonderful job, and im renting a nice 3 bedroom house, i have great friends and family.

What do you think about these narratives of teens who are currently or will soon be parents? Their perspective seems fairly positive. Do you think that their experience will meet their expectations? Are they providing a realistic view or an overly rosy view? In your view, are their expectations rational? Are they in denial? Can you see a difference in the support network that some teens have versus others? What impact will that have?

Although there are a great deal of publications about keeping teens from having sex, there is a lack of consensus on this issue—as seen from these teen voices. This Yes selection contains an research from the National Campaign to Prevent Teen and Unplanned Pregnancy, a mainstream American publication, stating that teens are too young to have children.

The opposing viewpoint comes from Europe, and it does so for a number of reasons. First, Europe is not having the same debate about *whether* teens should have sex at all, a topic which has proven highly controversial in the United States (e.g., see the U.S. debate about abstinence-only education versus comprehensive sexuality education). Second, England and much of Western Europe have a more extensive social safety net program than is typically found in the United States. Third, in examining family and personal relationships, it is sometimes valuable to take a global perspective. What does that culture have in common with ours? What is different? What is it about their perspective or approach that you find compelling? What is it about their perspective or approach that you find wrong or even damaging?

We also know that teens in the United States have a much higher rate of pregnancy than they do in England and Western Europe. Research tells us that there is not a significant difference in teenage sexual behavior between the countries. So what causes this difference? Is it an institutional issue of privilege and resources? In the United States, we have a higher proportion of poor citizens per capita than in Western Europe. Or is it a question of education? In the United States, children often receive little if any sexuality education, and many only learn about abstinence. In Western Europe, it is not regarded as controversial to teach children about contraception if they are at an age at which they may become sexually active.

Regardless of the difference in pregnancy rates, this issue provides readers with the opportunity to take a closer look at different views on whether this is a problem.

YES

**The National Campaign to Prevent
Teen and Unplanned Pregnancy**

One in Three: The Case for Wanted and Welcomed Pregnancy

Defining the Problem

The nation has made extraordinary progress in preventing early pregnancy and childbearing. The teen pregnancy rate declined 36 percent between 1991 and 2002 (the most recent data available) and the teen birth rate has declined by one-third. In fact, few social problems have improved as dramatically as has this one.

When the National Campaign to Prevent Teen Pregnancy began in 1996, we challenged the nation to reduce the teen pregnancy rate in the United States by one-third over a 10-year period. Ten years later, demographic projections suggest that the nation may well have achieved this goal. Even so, it is still the case that one-third of teen girls become pregnant before they are 20, and the rate of teen pregnancy in the United States remains far higher than in other comparable countries. Mindful of the continuing problem, in 2006 we challenged the nation to reduce the rate of teen pregnancy by *another* one-third over the next 10 years.

But when the progress among teens is looked at within the context of pregnancy and childbearing in America more generally, it is increasingly apparent that although teens are moving in the right direction, their older brothers and sisters, friends, relatives, and neighbors are not.

A new analysis of existing data by the National Campaign indicates that about one in three pregnancies in America are unwanted. In this analysis, unwanted pregnancies include (1) pregnancies that end in abortion (about 1.3 million), (2) births resulting from pregnancies that women *themselves* say they did not want at the time of conception or *ever* in the future (about 567,000); and (3) a smaller number of miscarriages that were also of unwanted pregnancies (179,000). In other words, just over 2 million of the 6.4 million pregnancies in America in 2001 (the most recent data available) were unwanted.

Moreover, between 1994 and 2001, the *rate* of unwanted pregnancy in the United States increased slightly (4 percent) from 31.9 to 33.2 unwanted pregnancies per 1,000 women aged 15–44. In fact, the rate of unwanted pregnancy increased among women in every age group with the exception of teens.

An unwanted pregnancy is not to be confused with a pregnancy that may have come at an inconvenient or awkward time; in fact, some women will say, for example, that their third child was a pleasant surprise, and sometimes pregnancy comes a bit sooner than a couple might wish. The children born months later from these mistimed pregnancies are often welcomed into stable and nurturing families.

But some pregnancies are more than unexpected or mistimed; they are greeted by women with anguish—sometimes even alarm—especially when they occur at a time in a woman's life when she is not prepared to raise a child—or, in many instances, *another* child. She may not have adequate personal or financial supports in place or have other serious problems or challenges. It is these pregnancies that are of particular concern, as detailed later in this monograph.

Of the 2 million unwanted pregnancies estimated to have occurred in 2001:

- More than half (54 percent) occurred to women in their twenties (1,092,000 pregnancies): about one third (32 percent) were to women aged 20–24 (651,000 pregnancies); more than one in five (22 percent) were to women aged 25–30 (441,000 pregnancies).
- About three in ten (28 percent) were to women aged 30–44 (577,000 pregnancies).
- About two in ten (18 percent) occurred to teens aged 15–19 (366,000 pregnancies).
- In addition, almost three fourths (72 percent) of unwanted pregnancies are to unmarried women (1,475,000 pregnancies), and just over a quarter (28 percent) of unwanted pregnancies occur to married women (565,000 pregnancies).

What the National Campaign Plans to Do

In response to these important statistics, the National Campaign to Prevent Teen Pregnancy is expanding its mission. We will continue to work on preventing teen pregnancy. And we will now *also* focus on reducing the high level of unwanted pregnancy in the United States among young adults in their twenties where the majority of such pregnancies occur. This expansion is made possible by the William and Flora Hewlett Foundation, which has made a ten-year commitment to preventing unwanted pregnancy and reducing the need for abortion in America.

In opening this new front, the National Campaign will use the experience and knowledge we have gained in our work with teens to encourage young adults to bring more intentionality and planning to their pregnancies. We will continue in a common sense, bipartisan, and research-based fashion using many of the same strategies that have contributed to the nation's progress in reducing teen pregnancy over the past 10 years. In this new work with young adults, we will encourage personal responsibility among women and men and responsible public policies as well. We will:

- work with opinion leaders, policymakers, and program leaders at the national and state levels;
- support public information and education about a wide range of topics;
- encourage careful, consistent use of family planning by all who are sexually active and not seeking pregnancy;
- encourage responsible, healthy relationships among young adults (which can include refraining from sexual activity in some circumstances) to help them achieve their future family and career goals;
- engage the entertainment media, faith communities, parents, and others;
- emphasize the role of men in pregnancy prevention and planning; and
- support practical, evidence-based polices that advance our mission.

Helping Americans reduce their high levels of unwanted pregnancy is a complex challenge, of course, and it will require intense attention and ongoing action from many sectors. Although the National Campaign has many ideas about what to do, there is much we need to learn about underlying causes and possible remedies. Accordingly, over the next several months, the National Campaign will be continuing to learn from a wide variety of experts, policymakers, those on the front lines, and young adults themselves about unwanted pregnancy and what might be done to improve the situation. This outreach has already begun and will be intensifying in the upcoming months.

Taking strong steps to increase the proportion of pregnancies that are fully wanted and welcomed is long overdue. It is worth repeating: one in three pregnancies—over *2 million* each year—are unwanted. We think the country can do far better.

Why Preventing Unwanted Pregnancy Matters

Reducing unwanted pregnancy will bring significant benefits to women, men, children, families, and society in general.

Increasing the proportion of pregnancies that are wanted and welcomed will help ensure healthier pregnancies, healthier babies, and enhanced child development.

New guidelines about preconception care from the Centers for Disease Control and Prevention underscore how planning for pregnancy and being at optimal health before pregnancy can help to dramatically improve a woman's chance of having a healthy pregnancy and baby. Unfortunately, women who experience an unwanted pregnancy often do not have the opportunity to engage in such preconception care.

Even when taking into account the existing social and economic factors, women experiencing an unwanted pregnancy are less likely to obtain prenatal care and their babies are at increased risk of both low birthweight and of being born prematurely, both of which increase the risk of many serious problems including infant mortality. These mothers are also less likely to breastfeed their infants.

Children born from unwanted pregnancies also face a range of developmental risks as well. For example, these children report poorer physical and mental health compared to those children born as the result of an intended pregnancy. They also have relationships with their mothers that are less close during childhood (and possibly into adulthood) when compared to peers who were born as the result of an intended pregnancy.

A new analysis from Child Trends indicates that, after controlling for numerous background factors, children two years old who were born as the result of an unwanted pregnancy have significantly lower cognitive test scores when compared to children born as the result of an intended pregnancy. These cognitive test scores include direct assessment of such skills as listening, vocabulary, exploring, problem solving, memory, and communication, as well as a child's overall mental ability relative to other children in his or her age group.

Increasing the proportion of pregnancies that are wanted and welcomed will help reduce both out-of-wedlock births and child poverty.

Over two decades of social science research makes clear that children fare better when their parents are older, have completed at least high school, are in stable and committed relationships—marriage, in particular—and are ready to take on the complex challenges of being parents. But many children born as the result of unwanted pregnancies are not welcomed into such families.

The majority of children from an unwanted pregnancy are born to women who are either single or cohabiting. This is important because children who are raised in single-parent families face a number of challenges. For example, when compared to similar children who grow up with two parents, children in one-parent families are twice as likely to drop out of high school, 2.5 times as likely to become teen mothers, 1.4 times as likely to be both out of school and out of work, and five times more likely to be poor. Even after adjusting for a variety of relevant social and economic differences, children in single-parent homes have lower grade-point averages, lower college aspirations, and poorer school attendance records. As adults, they also have higher rates of divorce.

Moreover, an analysis of data from 1970 to 1996 by National Campaign President Isabel Sawhill shows that virtually all of the increase in child poverty over that period was related to the growth of single-parent families. In the 1970s, some of this increase was the result of rising divorce rates, but since the early 1980s, virtually all of the increase has been driven by the increased numbers of never-married mothers.

All such data suggest that reducing unwanted pregnancy will increase the proportion of children born into circumstances that better support their growth and development. For example, the National Campaign estimates that preventing unwanted pregnancy has the potential to reduce non-marital childbearing by 26 percent.

Increasing the proportion of pregnancies that are wanted and welcomed will reduce the need for abortion.

Although there are many deeply felt and strongly held beliefs nationwide about the proper place of abortion in American life, virtually all of us see value in lessening the need for abortion and would prefer that fewer women have to confront an unwanted pregnancy in the first place. Through primary prevention—that is helping couples avoid unwanted pregnancy—the 1.3 million abortions in America each year can be dramatically decreased.

Increasing the proportion of pregnancies that are wanted and welcomed will help reduce disparities.

Disparities in unwanted pregnancy are on the rise. A woman below the poverty line is now nearly four times as likely as a woman at or above 200 percent of poverty to have an unintended pregnancy—a complex measure that includes *both* unwanted and mistimed pregnancy. Reflecting this trend, the abortion rate for low-income women increased 22 percent between 1994 and 2000. Still, 40 percent of all unintended pregnancies are to women at or above 200 percent of poverty.

Increasing the proportion of pregnancies that are wanted and welcomed will help women and men better plan their future.

That an unwanted pregnancy can derail the future plans of individuals is self-evident. For example, an unexpected, unwanted pregnancy can interrupt a young person's education and diminish future job prospects—a scenario that is becoming ever more serious with the increasing demand for a well-educated workforce. Reducing the high level of unwanted pregnancy in this country will unquestionably help many teens and adults achieve economic security and more stable relationships, which benefits not only them but also their children and society.

What the American Public Knows and Believes

Public opinion surveys conducted on behalf of the National Campaign by two widely respected communications firms, the Glover Park Group and Public Strategies Inc., make clear that there is broad and deep public support for the goal of reducing the number of unwanted pregnancies. In fact, over two-thirds (69 percent) of the

American public believes it is important to reduce the number of unwanted pregnancies in the United States.

The public also supports several ways to encourage more young adults to increase the proportion of pregnancies that are fully wanted and welcomed by both partners:

- 87 percent support strengthening a culture of *personal responsibility* regarding sex, getting pregnant, and bringing children into the world, as well as strengthening the norm of always practicing family planning when a couple is not ready to have a child.
- 82 percent support *responsible policies* that will increase the use of contraception, particularly by those who cannot afford it and by those at greatest risk for having an unwanted pregnancy.
- 90 percent of the public support the idea of providing *more education* to teens, parents, and young adults in their 20s and 30s that encourages them to take sex, pregnancy, and family formation seriously; stresses personal responsibility and respectful relationships; and includes extensive information about contraception.

In this same survey, the most commonly cited reason for reducing unwanted pregnancy was to improve the quality of life for children:

- 24 percent of adults say that the single most important reason for reducing teen and unwanted pregnancy is because children who grow up wanted have a better future.
- 20 percent say it is because more children are likely to grow up living with both a father and a mother.

More generally, the vast majority of Americans believe that young people should complete their education, have the means to raise a child, and be married before becoming pregnant:

- 88 percent of the American public believes that children generally do better when they are raised in two-parent, married families.
- 97 percent believe it is important to have the means to take care of a child without outside assistance before becoming a parent.
- 96 percent believe that finishing one's education before becoming a parent is important.
- 90 percent believe that being married before becoming pregnant is important.

Despite these widely shared sentiments, the *magnitude* of the unwanted pregnancy problem in the United

States—and which groups are most at risk—are not well understood. In particular, very few Americans realize that teens are only a small part of the problem. For example:

- Even though less than 20 percent of all abortions are to teens, 4 out of 5 Americans think that the percentage is higher (often much higher).
- 77 percent of Americans assume that teens have the highest number of unplanned pregnancies; in fact, young adults do.
- Only 15 percent of the public knows that unmarried teens are *more likely* than unmarried women in their 20s to have used an effective method of contraception the last time they had sex.

Teens Still Matter a Lot

This monograph makes the case that adults, not just teenagers, are having difficulty in overall pregnancy planning. Even so, there are two primary reasons why the nation should continue to focus on teen pregnancy given all its serious consequences.

Despite a one-third decline in teen pregnancy and birth rates since the early 1990s, the teen pregnancy rate in the United States is *still* the highest among comparable countries. One in three teens becomes pregnant at least once by age 20. For some subgroups, the news is even more sobering. For example, 51 percent of Latina teens become pregnant by the time they leave their teen years. There is also some evidence to suggest that the progress the nation has made in preventing teen pregnancy and childbearing has begun to slow or, in some cases, to reverse—all of which suggests that the nation's efforts going forward will need to be more intense and creative.

A crisp focus on preventing teen pregnancy and childbearing is also important because the knowledge, attitudes, and behavioral patterns that develop in adolescence strongly affect behavior in the years that follow. In other words, the teen years are a critical place to start to prevent unwanted pregnancy among women of all ages. In our work with teenagers, the National Campaign will continue to encourage teens to delay sexual activity—their best choice—and to practice family planning if they are sexually active.

A Final Note

Unwanted pregnancy among young adults is a complex problem, and getting people to change their behavior is a difficult proposition at best. Even so, we believe this nation can do far better and are optimistic about the chances for success. When the National Campaign began a decade ago, there was a sense that teen pregnancy was an intractable problem and the organization's goal of reducing the teen pregnancy rate by one-third was greeted with great skepticism. Ten years later, the situation has improved dramatically. This progress suggests that *adults* can do a better job, too, and that a higher proportion of all pregnancies can be wanted and welcomed.

If the National Campaign's efforts and those of others lead to less unwanted pregnancy, more young adults will be deliberate, serious, and intentional about pregnancy, childbearing, and family formation. In so doing, more children will be welcomed into the world by parents who are ready to provide them with the love, care, and nurture we want for every child in this country. More children will grow up in two-parent, married families or other fully supportive and stable circumstances; there will be less poverty, a lighter tax burden, less stress on families, and stronger communities. And there will be far less need for abortion.

THE NATIONAL CAMPAIGN TO PREVENT TEEN AND UNPLANNED PREGNANCY is dedicated to reducing teenage pregnancy. Their research argues that teens face significant consequences if they have unplanned pregnancy.

Simon Duncan, Claire Alexander, and Rosalind Edwards

What's the Problem with Teenage Parents?

[**W**]hy is there such an invested need in presenting an unremittingly negative image of young parents, and what does this say about the values placed on family and the role of paid work in twenty-first-century Britain? How—and why—have policy makers and news makers got the story about teenage parents so wrong?

New Labour and Teenage Parenting: An Economic or Moral Agenda?

2010 marks the year by which New Labour pledged to halve the number of pregnancies for under-eighteen-year-olds in the UK. The government's ten year Teenage Pregnancy Strategy was launched in 1999 in a report from the Social Exclusion Unit (SEU), then at the heart of government in Cabinet Office and itself resulting from a putative 'underclass unit' set up by Peter Mandelson, then Minister without Portfolio, in 1997. The report, which has set the framework for government policy since then, saw teenage pregnancy as a major social and economic problem, where Britain did much worse than other west European countries. Or as Tony Blair, then Prime Minister, put it, in his forward to the Social Exclusion Unit report:

> Some of these teenagers, and some of their children, live happy and fulfilled lives. But far too many do not. Teenage mothers are less likely to finish their education, less likely to find a good job, and more likely to end up both as single parents and bringing up their children in poverty. The children themselves run a much greater risk of poor health, and have a much higher chance of becoming teenage mothers themselves. Our failure to tackle this problem has cost the teenagers, their children and the country dear.

The SEU report identified the causes of this problem as low expectations and ignorance among teenagers, and mixed messages from the media. While the SEU report made clear a strong relationship between teenage pregnancy and social disadvantage, this association was downplayed either as cause or remedy, rather young parenting was seen to strongly reinforce disadvantage. And the way out was through a dual goal of prevention and direction—to reduce the number of under-eighteen pregnancies by half, and increase the number of teenage parents entering education, training, or employment to sixty per cent.

The heady political symbolism and mobilisation created by the media's moral panic reinforced the need for government to be seen to tackle what was already identified as a problem for 'teenagers, their children and the country.' All this was underlined by contrasting national teenage birth rates or, as Tony Blair put it in his forward to SEU's 1999 document, Britain's 'shameful record.' British rates remained among the highest in the 28 OECD developed countries (30 per 1000 in 1998, compared to 10 or less in Germany, France, Scandinavia and the Netherlands). Only the USA at 52.1, and more marginally Canada and New Zealand, had higher rates. This comparative failure has an important policy impact, as suggested by the highlighting of international comparisons in most government and policy reports. For while the UK seemed to be 'stuck,' as the SEU put it, the experience of western Europe implied that teenage pregnancy and parenting, perceived as a difficult social problem, was nonetheless amenable to policy solution. Underlying this comparison is an issue around economic, as well as social, competition—how can Britain compete with an inadequate workforce, where teenage pregnancy supposedly restricts educational achievement and employment participation.

This international comparative lesson was emphasised by the appreciation that local rates also vary widely across Britain; it is not just young women who are poorer that are more likely to become pregnant, and least likely to use abortion to resolve pregnancy—they also live in poorer areas. In contrast, some richer areas in Britain have teenage abortion and pregnancy rates more like supposed European exemplars such as The Netherlands. The 'problem' of teenage pregnancy was ripe for intervention by a reforming new government.

Hence the New Labour government rolled out its teenage pregnancy strategy from 1999 onwards, originally under the direction of a Ministerial Task Force, and co-ordinated by the Teenage Pregnancy Unit (TPU). Starting in 2001, each top tier local authority had an agreed teenage pregnancy strategy to reach local 2010 targets around the desired national average. Each local strategy was led by a Teenage Pregnancy Coordinator, working with a Teenage Pregnancy Partnership Board, and supported by a Local Implementation Grant. These local Strategies were supported and performance managed by a Regional Teenage Pregnancy Coordinator, based in the regional government office. Local indicators, such as levels of conceptions in targeted age groups, availability and use of services, and health outcomes, were devised to help monitor progress towards achieving these targets. In line with government objectives for 'joined-up' approaches to service and policy development, work locally was intended to proceed in conjunction with other national government initiatives such as Sure Start, Sure Start Plus and the Children's Fund, and other national government departments were expected actively to support the strategy. In this way the TPU would hopefully reach the two main targets, as set by the Social Exclusion Unit—to halve the under—eighteen teenage conception rate by 2010 and to substantially increase the participation of teenage parents in education, training or employment.

This is an impressive machinery. But the 'low expectations' explanation—which points towards tackling social disadvantage—seems to have been neglected. Rather, policy in practice focused on the 'ignorance' explanation—British youth were seen as deficient in their sexual health knowledge, poor users of contraception, shy about sex, and wary about accessing services. Perhaps this focus was the more appealing when current policy thinking tends to stress individual behaviour and motivations, rather than structural influences on behaviour, like social disadvantage. Certainly, on a relatively low budget (the initial TPU budget was only £60 million) it might have been here that the policy implementers hoped for 'quick wins,' when taking on social disadvantage would cost a lot more and take a lot longer. Policy then ended up pathologising teenage pregnancy and childrearing, when it was seen to arise from 'inappropriate motivations, ignorance and sexual embarrassment,' rather than supporting the positive features of parenting.

How has this approach endured the experience of implementation? The Department for Communities, Schools, and Families report *Teenage Parents: the next steps* was to give new guidance to local authorities and primary care trusts given the previous eight years experience. The report recognises failures in reaching the desired targets—the reduction rate in teenage births was only 11.8% over the period, rather than approaching the desired 50% by 2010; similarly only about 30% of teenage mothers were in employment, education and training (EET), rather than 60%. Hence the need for a 'refreshed strategy' as the report's introduction puts it. There was also a whole battery of research produced since the SEU's original 1999 report, which as a whole pointed to a substantial gap between policy and experience, indicating both that the outcomes for teenage parents were not as dire as assumed and that young parenting encapsulated many positive features as well as problems. This includes research reviewed, or directly commissioned, by the TPU itself. But despite recognition of 'What teenage mothers and young fathers say' in the new 2007 report (in its chapter four), the existing two-track approach remained. Teenage parenting was as a problem in and of itself and should be cut, and the further need was to integrate remaining young parents into a productive workforce. 'Refreshed' was more about changing the implementation channels from specialised services into mainstream midwifery and health visiting services, Children's Centres, and Youth Support Services.

The report bases the essential continuation of the two-track approach on its enumeration of the disadvantaged characteristics of teenage mothers, and the poor outcomes they—and their children—experience, using a whole range of social and economic indicators. There are a number of key features that can be identified in this policy portrait of teenage parenthood, and that echo the media and political representations discussed above. First there is the clear gendering of this discourse, with the focus being primarily on young mothers, while young fathers play a very secondary role. This links into an assumed conflation between young motherhood (where many will live with partners or grandparents, and others will have 'live apart together' relationships') and single motherhood. Second, there is the insistence on the negative consequences of teenage pregnancy on both the mother and child, in which health, emotional and economic 'wellbeing' are taken as the key problem areas (and largely seen as interchangeable). Third, there is the emphasis on prevention of pregnancy rather than support for teenage parents—and in the 2007 report, rather chilling, concern to prevent further pregnancies for young mothers (for some young mothers, especially those with partners, would like to reach a desired family size). Fourth, is the conflation of socio-economic deprivation with teenage pregnancy, the implication being that teenage pregnancy is a cause of poverty. The report asserts that these poor outcomes are partially independent of wider factors of social deprivation and rather points to 'the lifestyles and behaviour of teenage mothers' as contributory factors. Fifth, there is the 'classing' of the issue, with teenage pregnancy linked to specific socio-economic groupings, and their associated problems, in particular the low levels of labour market participation. Sixth, there is the insistence on education, training and paid employment as the sole legitimate pathway to social inclusion and to ameliorating the negative effects of young parenthood.

Hence Beverley Hughes, then Minister for Children, Young People, and Families, wrote in her forward to the 2007 report that:

> Children born to teenage mothers are more likely to live in deprived areas, do less well at school, and disengage from learning early—all of which are risk factors for teenage pregnancy and other poor outcomes.

Equally, one could write that teenage mothers commonly show resilience and motivation, and become more socially connected and purposeful, where pregnancy usually marks a turning point for the better, become more likely to take up education and employment, and do no worse—and often better—than their social peers once pre-existing disadvantage is allowed for. This contrast is the terrain of this book.

The Myth of the Teenage Pregnancy Epidemic

The perceived social threat from teenage parenting is buttressed by a negative public consensus around teenage conception and pregnancy itself. This consensus assumes that teenage pregnancy is increasing rapidly, that this increase is particularly marked among younger teenagers, that all teenage pregnancies are unplanned, that all these unplanned conceptions are unwanted, and that new teenage mothers are inevitably also single mothers without stable relationships with partners. All these assumptions are unfounded, but all serve to bolster the negative evaluation of subsequent teenage parenting, and hence the nature of the policy response.

Newspaper headlines frequently announce 'soaring' teenage birth rates, creating an 'epidemic' of births to teenagers. Indeed as many as 81% of respondents to a

2008 Ipsos MORI poll thought that teenage pregnancy was increasing, while about a quarter of the 16–24 age group thought that 40% of 15–17 year-old girls became parents each year. In fact there have been substantial declines in both birth rates and absolute numbers of births to teenagers since the 1960s and early 1970s (see Table 1). By 2007 only 11.4% of conceptions were to women aged under 20, with an even smaller share of births—6.4%. In addition few teenage mothers are under 16, only around 6% in 2006, accounting for just 0.9% of all births in Britain by 2007, while around 80% of teenage mothers were 18 or 19 years-old. Overall, teenage birth rates are now at around the same level as in the 1950s, that supposed 'golden age' of family.

What *is* different is that in the 1950s and 1960s, the majority of teenage parents married—although many seem to have been hastily enforced 'shotgun marriages,' notorious for high rates of dysfunctionality and breakdown. In addition, probably around 20% of the children were adopted shortly after birth. In contrast, by the 2001 census only 9% of teenage parents were married; although around

Table 1

Live Births and Birth Rates for Women Under 20, 1951–2008

	Numbers of live births	Birth rate per 1000 women aged 15–19
1951	29,111	21.3
1956	37,938	27.3
1961	59,786	37.3
1966	66,746	47.9
1971	82,641	50.6
1976	54,500	29.8
1981	60,800	30.9
1986	57,406	30.1
1991	52,396	33.1
1996	44,667	30.0
2001	44,189	28.0
2004	45,028	26.9
2005	44,830	26.3
2006	45,509	26.6
2007	44,805	26.0
2008	44,683	see note

Sources: ONS Birth Statistics, Health Statistics Quarterly.

Note: 2008 birth rate not available at time of press.

30% cohabited; in addition, around another quarter jointly registered the birth with the father at another address—which suggests some continuing parental relationship on the 'living apart together' (or LAT) model. There are now very few adoptions of teenage mothers' children. These trends away from marriage, and towards unmarried cohabitation and 'living apart together' reflect those for the population as a whole, especially among younger age groups. Thus in 2006, around 0.5% of all 18–24 year-olds in Britain were married, with 12% cohabiting, while as many as 35% were in 'living apart together' partner relationships.

Whatever the level of teenage pregnancy, it is assumed in the public and media discourse that all teenage pregnancies are unplanned, that all unplanned conceptions are unwanted, and that most result from ignorance if not wilful immorality. Certainly the Social Exclusion Unit's framework 1999 report identified 'ignorance'—the 'lack of accurate knowledge about contraception, STIs (sexually transmitted infections), what to expect in relationships and what it means to be a parent' as major cause of teenage pregnancy. This is repeated in succeeding policy and guidance documents. But there is little support for the assumption that teenage parents are particularly ignorant about sex, contraception, and parenting, that low levels of knowledge 'cause' teenage pregnancy, or that increased knowledge reduces pregnancy. It is hard to find young mothers who become pregnant due to ignorance about sex and contraception. Similarly, a meta-analysis of preventative strategies focusing on sex education, and improved access to advice and contraceptive services, concluded that this did not reduce unintended pregnancies among young women aged between 11–18.

Indeed, a significant minority of teenage mothers, and fathers, positively plan for pregnancy. Some are hoping for birthing success after an earlier miscarriage, others in this group, especially those with partners, plan for subsequent children so as to complete their desired family size and hence 'build' a family. Many other teenage parents are 'positively ambivalent' towards childbirth—that is, they do not actually plan it but would quite like a baby and do not use contraception for that reason. For most teenage parents, pregnancy may well be 'unplanned,' but then so are many, if not most, pregnancies for all women—the very idea of 'planning pregnancy' is something of a grey area to say the least. Few teenage mothers, it seems, regret early childbirth, as many of the succeeding chapters show. As with other women 'unplanned' pregnancy does not necessarily mean 'unwanted' pregnancy for teenage parents. Or, as Germaine Greer put it: 'We have 39,000 unwanted pregnancies a year unwanted by the Government that is. No one is speaking for the mums.'

This set of policy and public assumptions is the starting point for Pam Alldred and Miriam David in their examination on the role and importance of education in young mothers' lives, and on their gendered expectations regarding parenthood. For their research shows how the values and priorities expressed by young mothers do not fit comfortably within the model presented in the Teenage Pregnancy Strategy (TPS), nor with many of the values assumed in, or explicitly asserted by, the TPS. In particular, the chapter questions the assumptions that early mothering is undesirable or aberrant; that education or training in the child's early years is desirable or even accessible to young mothers; and that either 'parenting' or 'studying' can be assumed to be gender-neutral activities. The logic the authors find at work in the young women's lives in their study seems to reflect the dominant values in their community and this logic questions the link between teenage pregnancy and social exclusion asserted in government policy. Similarly; in chapter three, Jan Macvarish and Jenny Billings discuss how the teenage mothers in their study, living in Kent, made moral and thoughtful decisions about contraception, proceeding with their pregnancy, and engagement with health and welfare services. Rather than suffering 'broken' family circumstances, teenage parents were often embedded in networks of support, and were optimistic that parenthood would shift them onto a positive life trajectory.

Statistical Outcomes—Social Disadvantage Versus Teenage Mothering

The influential UNICEF report *Teenage Births in Rich Nations* claims that:

> giving birth as a teenager is believed to be bad for the young mother because the statistics suggest that she is much more likely to drop out of school, to have low or no qualifications, to be unemployed or low paid, to grow up without a father, to become a victim of neglect and abuse, to do less well at school, to become involved in crime, use drugs and alcohol.

But in fact the statistics show nothing of the sort—if we deal with the errors committed by statements like these. For the statement does not compare like with like in reaching its 'much more likely' attribution of statistical causation; ascribing causal effects to teenage motherhood is pretty meaningless if we compare teenage mothers with all mothers, rather than those of a similar background. Rather, if we wish to measure the statistical effect of teenage motherhood (and then go on to ascribe a social effect, which is not necessarily the same thing), we need to control for variation in other variables, so that we do compare like with like. In more formal terms, statistical analysis needs to control for 'selection effects:' This is a variant of the correlation problem so beloved in statistical textbooks. Variable X may be highly correlated with 'dependent' variable Y, but this does not mean that X causes Y; rather both may be caused by an unacknowledged variable A. In this case, becoming a young mother may not cause the poor outcomes—in terms of education, employment, and income—experienced by many teenage mothers; rather, both young motherhood, and poor outcomes, may be caused by pre-pregnancy social disadvantage. In this sense, social disadvantage may 'select' particular young women, and men, to become teenage parents, and this disadvantage will continue post pregnancy. Teenage parenting may therefore be a part of social disadvantage, rather than its cause. But if statistical studies do not control for these selection effects, then they will not be able to recognise this.

In fact, there has been a tradition of statistical studies which do try to take account of these selection effects. Some researchers devised 'natural experiments' where selection effects would be better controlled, such as comparisons between cousins whose mothers were sisters, between sisters, or between twin sisters (only one of whom was a teenage mother), and between teenage mothers and other women who had conceived as a teenager but miscarried (who presumably would have gone on to become mothers). This type of research began in the USA, and found that the social outcome effects of mother's age at birth were very small, or as Saul Hoffman put it in his systematic review of the US research 'often essentially zero.' Indeed, by their mid/late twenties, teenage mothers in the USA did better than miscarrying teenagers with regard to employment and income and this meant, ironically, that government spending would have increased if they had not become young mothers.

The UK-based studies available at the time the 1999 SEU report was produced did not take this 'natural experiment' approach to controlling selection effects, and instead relied on more general statistical controls of social background, like educational level, socio-economic status, housing type, and so on. Although they also concluded that much of the adverse social conditions linked with teenage parenting were associated with pre-pregnancy social disadvantage, this is perhaps why they nevertheless came to more ambivalent conclusions about the social effect of teenage pregnancy in itself. Since the publication of the SEU report, however, a number of British studies have taken up the 'natural experiment' approach, with the same results as in the USA. John Ermisch and David Pevalin, using the British Cohort Study to assess differences between miscarrying and successful teenage pregnancies, found that teen birth has little impact upon qualifications, employment or earnings by thirty years of age. While teenage mothers' partners were more likely to be poorly qualified or unemployed, and this then impacted on the mothers,' and their children's, standard of living, this is also akin to a selection effect. In itself, age of birth has little effect. A complementary study using British Household Panel data to follow teenage mothers over time came to similar conclusions, as does a study by Denise Hawkes on twins, where only one became a teenage mother. Finally, Karen Robson and Richard Berthoud used the Labour Force Survey to assess the link between high rates of poverty and high rates of teenage fertility among minority ethnic groups, particularly for the extreme case of Pakistanis and Bangladeshis where both variables are particularly high. They concluded that teen birth has little effect on future poverty, and does not lead to any further disadvantage beyond that experienced by the ethnic group as a whole.

In chapter four, Denise Hawkes follows this work in providing a wide-ranging statistical review of the life experiences and circumstances of teenage mothers and their children in Britain, compared with other mothers, based on the Millennium Cohort Study. She uses three indicative sets of statistical analyses to examine: (1) life course experience for mothers prior to the birth of the first child, (2) the early life circumstances of children at nine-months, and (3) health, cognitive, and behavioural outcomes for children at ages three and five. The first set of analyses, confirming earlier statistical studies, shows that teenage motherhood is really a symptom of a disadvantaged life course rather than the cause of it. The second set shows that those children with teenage mothers are indeed born into families experiencing multiple disadvantages. However, it is not the mother's age at first birth which is the main driver of these disadvantages—rather, it is the prior disadvantages experienced by the young mothers during their own childhoods. Again, this finding substantiates earlier research. The final set of statistical analyses takes comparison into a new area, and show that having a teenage mother does not significantly affect the chances of a pre-school child experiencing poor health, and makes little difference to how children score on cognitive tests. There is some difference for a few behavioural indices, but this largely disappears once prior life disadvantage is accounted for.

Hawkes notes that the starting point for most policy interventions around teenage parenthood is that the root of the problem is that the mother is a teenager—but her statistical analyses find that being a teenage mother does not in itself lead to poorer outcomes either for the mothers themselves or their children. Rather teenage motherhood often signals a life of exposure, for both mothers and children, to a range of social and economic disadvantages. She concludes that these results suggest a shift in government policy away from incidence of teenage motherhood itself, and a refocusing on the social and economic causes of teenage motherhood. What is more this sort of policy would be sensible because the factors associated with becoming a teenage mother appear to be the same factors as those influencing the life chances of their children.

Perhaps there can never be an accurate statistical measurement of the 'effect' of teenage motherhood, in the sense of finding some ultimate truth. Nonetheless, this statistical research tradition shows that—in these outcome terms—teenage childbearing in itself can be seen as only a minor social problem. It is not the teenage bit which is particularly important in these terms, but rather it is social and economic disadvantage which produce poor outcomes. In so far as teenage mothers are over-represented among the disadvantaged, this is because of their 'selection' through pre-existing disadvantage. A policy focus on being a teenage mother can only approach this wider problem of social disadvantage obliquely. Or as Hoffmann concluded for the USA, this sort of statistical study 'no longer supports the notion that teenage childbearing is a devastating event' and 'casts considerable doubt on the received wisdom about the consequences of teenage childbearing.'

Qualitative Accounts of Agency— Young Parents' Values and Experiences

What about the mothers and fathers themselves? A tradition of small-scale qualitative research focuses on their actual understandings and experiences of becoming a parent. In this way, qualitative research can help explain just why the statistical studies find that age of pregnancy has little effect on social outcomes, and may actually make things better. While Hilary Graham and Elizabeth McDermott see quantitative and qualitative research as contradictory (the former seeing teenage motherhood as a route to social exclusion, the latter as an act of social inclusion), this contradiction perhaps relates more to the way these results have been framed, interpreted and used within opposing discourses, rather than to the findings themselves. Instead, we can profitably see quantitative and qualitative studies as complementary in providing, on the

one hand, extensive evidence about overall social patterns and, on the other, intensive evidence on the social processes that create these patterns.

What these qualitative studies find is that many mothers express positive attitudes to motherhood, and describe how motherhood has made them feel stronger, more competent, more connected to family and society, and more responsible. Resilience in the face of constraints and stigma, based on a belief in the moral worth of being a mother, is one overriding theme. For some, this has given the impetus to change direction, or build on existing resources, so as to take up education, training, and employment. There has been less research on young fathers, but what there has been tends to contradict the 'feckless' assumption. Like teenage mothers, most of the fathers are already socially disadvantaged, and it does not appear that fathering will in itself make this any worse. But, also like teen mothers, most express positive feelings about the child and want to be good fathers. Most contributed maintenance in some way, and many were actively involved in childcare (this varies by age, with the youngest least likely to be involved). And, like teenage mothers, there is some evidence that successful fathering could be a positive turning point in young men's lives. In fact, it was an invisibility to professionals, as well as housing problems, which often excluded them from the parenting they desired. Again, like teen mothers, young fathers may be less of a social threat, more of a social possibility.

That teenage motherhood has a positive side is an enduring finding over time in this research tradition. Nearly two decades ago, the study by Ann Phoenix of teenage mothers in London, in the mid-1980s, found that most of the mothers and their children were faring well. Most (and their male partners) had already done badly in the educational and employment systems, and it did not seem that early motherhood had caused this or that deferring motherhood would have made much difference. Rather, if anything, motherhood was something of a turning point which 'spurred some women on' into education and employment. Contributions to this edited collection testify that, two decades later, this more positive picture remains pertinent.

While Phoenix's research prefigures the statistical 'natural experiments,' it remains unacknowledged in that tradition, and does not feature in the SEU 1999 framework report. The positive side to research findings about teenage mothering seems to be regularly disregarded in the more official literature, even when government commissions the research. Recent examples include TPU commissioned research on teenage mothers in rural and seaside 'hotspots', and on teenage mothers and education. The former noted how for some young women, motherhood: 'increased their self-esteem and enhanced their lives, providing a sense of security and stability in lives characterised by transience, detachment and low economic aspirations', while the TPU's own evidence showed that having a child provides motivation for young mothers to aspire to new educational and employment goals.

That teenage parenting can have many positive sides is a theme that reappears in most of the chapters in this book. In chapter five, Eleanor Formby, Julia Hirst, and Jenny Owen provide a compelling illustration across three generational cohorts of teenage parents from Sheffield and Doncaster. Having a baby as a teenager did not necessarily predict adversity, and the problems experienced arose more from the particular social and economic circumstances the mothers and fathers found themselves in, rather than the age at which pregnancy occurred. For mothers, difficulties in accessing appropriate housing was a major problem, while fathers recounted their sense of exclusion or marginalisation from the processes of antenatal care, childbirth, and postnatal care. While the mothers and fathers in the sample had not planned pregnancy, all recounted their pleasure at having a baby and never regretted the decision to continue with the pregnancy. Parents across all generations and social classes spoke of their parenting in positive terms, even if early parenthood for the mothers (but not the fathers) was accompanied by a sense of 'loss' of teenage life. All made explicit references to the positive 'turning-point' offered by pregnancy: the opportunity to make new plans, including the beginnings of a strong family unit or renewed efforts to gain qualifications and secure more certain futures. Despite the pleasure and pride that all participants described, stigma was also a feature of parenting that each generation, but mostly mothers, highlighted. Hence, living in a community where young parents were not unusual was cited as hugely influential, contrasting to the isolation experienced by some older and middle generation mothers who lived in middle-class communities where young parenthood was less visible. This theme is continued in chapter six by Ann McNulty. Exploring three generations of related young mothers down the generations in particular families, in the northeast of England, she challenges ideas about intergenerational transmission of low aspirations, and shows how each generation of young mothers in a family wanted to achieve, and wanted their daughters to achieve, in education and employment. Unmet expectations in relation to career options were more a matter of the (often declining) economic circumstances in their localities, rather than any culture of low aspiration. The chapter also notes the

marked shift, over recent decades, towards a negative conceptualisation of young motherhood.

This positive theme is replicated in other national contexts. Lee Smith-Battle's research in the USA is paradigmatic. She followed a small, diverse group of teenage mothers over 8 years, finding that many described mothering as a powerful catalyst for becoming more mature, and for redirecting their lives in positive ways. Mothering often 'anchors the self, fosters a sense of purpose and meaning, reweaves connections, and provides a new sense of future.' Indeed, two of the themes identified in a metasynthesis of US qualitative studies of teenage mothers undertaken during the 1990s are 'Motherhood as positively transforming' and 'Baby as stabilising influence.'

In this way, qualitative research can explain the patterns found by extensive statistical studies; they suggest just why teenage parenting does not produce particularly poor outcomes, and can sometimes make things better for young people. In addition, the qualitative research can go further in explaining the processes involved in teenage parenting just because it allows more attention to context and diversity—usually stripped out by extensive studies in their concentration on average measurement. This is not just a qualification to the statistical results, whereby teenage parents' experiences can be shown to vary significantly in different social groups and geographical places. For this also takes us to a vital 'missing link, and a key to understanding the agency of teenage parents—the life worlds in which they live. Becoming a teenage mother, and it seems a father, can make reasonable sense in the particular life worlds inhabited by some groups of young women and men. Recently, Rachel Thomson has conceptualised this as the 'economy of values' particular to different communities, and earlier Ann Phoenix found that early motherhood was common, and normally uncensured, in the social networks inhabited by the working-class teenage mothers in her 1980's London sample. Smith-Battle shows much the same for the USA; early motherhood often made sense in terms of local constitutions of opportunity, constraint, and social practice.

In chapter seven, we discuss our own research findings, from a small sample in Bradford, that teenage parents saw themselves unexceptionally as 'just a mother or a father' like any other. They were motivated to achieve well in education and employment so as to provide a stable future for their children, while at the same time they lived in communities where family and parenting was placed centrally as a form of local inclusion and social participation. The case of the two Asian mothers, who were married, is an indicative example. In this way, ethnicity, as well as class, shaped expectations around motherhood. The young mothers and fathers in the sample spoke of their positive experience and the ways in which having children had given them a sense of responsibility and adult status. The teenage mothers in the study were little different from many other mothers who morally and socially prioritise motherhood, not employment. It is not that the young mothers rejected education and employment; rather, self-esteem and identity are centred round motherhood; paid work was important more as a secondary and supportive part of life. While they faced many struggles, these were often linked to problems of wider social disadvantage, and they themselves strongly challenged the idea that these were related to their position as *young* parents. They resisted being characterised solely as a teenage mother or father and saw themselves as having multiple roles and identities, as individuals, partners, workers, students.

In chapter eight, Jenny Owen and colleagues develop this theme with respect to ethnicity. Drawing on a study of teenage mothers in Bradford, Sheffield, and three London boroughs, they examine in depth the transition to motherhood by young minority ethnic mothers. This reveals the strengths that these mothers draw on to deal with double-faceted prejudice—based on age and race/ethnicity—and their determination to make something of their own and their children's lives. However, at the same time many of the experiences of these young mothers are 'strikingly unremarkable': like older mothers, they are proud of their children; they aim to put them first; and they encounter familiar dilemmas in reconciling 'care' commitments with making a living and reaching accommodations with partners and other family members. This adds further weight to the general argument that 'teenage parents' should not be described as a homogenous group somehow separate from other mothers.

Conclusions: Experience v Policy?

The evidence substantiated in the chapters which follow shows that teenage childbirth does not often result from ignorance or low expectations, it is rarely a catastrophe for young women, and that teenage parenting does not particularly cause poor outcomes for mothers and their children. Expectations of motherhood can be high and parenting can be a positive experience for many young men and women. Furthermore, becoming a teenage parent can make good sense in the particular life worlds inhabited by some groups of young women and men. Policies about teenage parenting, however,

assume the opposite. Unfortunately, this also means that policy will be misdirected in its aims, use inappropriate instruments, and may be unhelpful to many teenage parents.

This brings us to the last question posed by the 'problem' of teenage parenting. Why then, is there such a yawning gulf between policy assumptions and the experiences of its subjects? And why does policy seem so resistant to evidence? This is the subject of our concluding chapter nine; the way forward, we claim, necessitates a 'smashing' of the policy making mould maintained by the 'epistemic community' existing around teenage parenting. We refer here to a network of professionals and policymakers with a shared set of normative, analytical and causal beliefs, with an agreed, shared and self-reinforcing knowledge base, and a common set of interests. Parameters of preferred policy models and narratives of cause and effect are set, to the exclusion of other ideas and information, even if those other data are more representative of everyday reality. The impetus is to retain these dominant and agreed conceptions in developing (further) policies, protecting them not only from critical scrutiny but even from recognising the existence of challenging alternative scenarios. Researchers working outside of these favoured models, with messages at odds with current policy directions, are unlikely to be heard or, if heard, considered relevant.

In this way, a monochrome, negative, stereotype of teenage parents and parenting has become embedded in policy, bolstered by shared assumptions about social participation and the nature of social mobility, and by neo-liberal ideas about individual choice and rationality. Ideas about what is 'rational' are integrally linked to what is held to be socially acceptable, which in turn is regarded as a universal 'common sense' applicable in all contexts, rather than being rooted in the specific perspectives of a particular classed and gendered group of people who have the ability to judge others and place them as outside of rationality. In the case of teenage mothers and fathers, they are envisaged as ignorant, immoral or both because they have deviated from the cost-benefit calculative, future-oriented planned pathway of life. As other chapters show, this thinking is at odds with the complex reality of young mothers' and fathers' understandings and motivations, and yet is unequivocally accepted as an accurate portrayal. And all this, we suggest, is underlain by idealisations of children and childhood, where teenage parents, and mothers especially, are regarded as taking on the 'adult' responsibilities of parenthood before they have undergone the necessary sloughing off of the immaturity of childhood. They are (almost) children who have disrupted the regulation represented by the boundaries of adulthood and childhood, embodying the breakdown of social order and the nation's moral turpitude.

The question remains of how to move on. On the basis of the evidence presented in this book, we suggest there needs to be a refocus on the value of parenthood in itself, both socially and for individuals. For teenage parents, this might focus on the positive experience of becoming a mother and father, and on young parents' own resilience and strengths. Education and employment for young parents should be recognised as a components of parenting (which would also include 'full-time' mothering at home), rather than as a return to individualised rational economic planning where children are seen as an obstacle. Policy may also be better directed at improving employment for young people as a whole in declining labour markets, and regenerating disadvantaged neighbourhoods, rather than targeting teenage parenting in itself. Teenage parenting might then be approached as a way through and out of disadvantage, given its positive potential, rather than a confirmation of it. It could be seen as more opportunity than catastrophe. Certainly stigmatising policies directed at the assumed ignorance and inadequacy of teenagers will be inappropriate.

Simon Duncan, Claire Alexander, and Rosalind Edwards have their chapter on teen pregnancy and parenting. This chapter, which takes a global perspective by looking at another Western society, England, argues that teenage pregnancy and parenting is not a problem.

EXPLORING THE ISSUE

Are Teenagers Too Young to Become Parents?

Critical Thinking and Reflection

1. Can you identify the emotional, moral, intellectual, and social components in the National Campaign's argument?
2. Can you identify the emotional, moral, intellectual, and social components in Duncan, Alexander and Edward's argument?
3. Can you identify your own emotional, moral, intellectual, and social responses to this issue?
4. What are some similarities and differences between your responses and the authors'?

Is There Common Ground?

Virtually everyone will agree that the outcome that they want is for (a) teens to make decisions about their sexual behavior that are consistent with their long-term goals and (b) children of teen parents to be raised with opportunities to achieve their American dream. What needs to be done to ensure that? Do we need to take a look at how we prepare teens with sexuality education? Should the approach we take be abstinence-only education? Should it be comprehensive sexuality education? What role does it play to help teens identify their long-term goals? When teens have children, what sort of role does family and society play in providing that young child with a social safety net? Is that solely the responsibility of the teen parent(s)? Or is there a larger societal responsibility at play?

Additional Resources

Bilingual site for teenage parents:

www.teenageparent.org/

American Academy of Pediatrics:

www.healthychildren.org/English/ages-stages/
teen/dating-sex/pages/Teen-Parents.aspx?
nfstatus=401&nftoken=00000000-0000-0000-0000-
000000000000&nfstatusdescription=ERROR%3a+
No+local+token

TeenPregnancy.com provides advice:

www.teenpregnancy.com/

About.com on teen pregnancy:

pregnancy.about.com/od/teenpregnancy/a/
Teen-Pregnancy.htm

Internet References . . .

American Family Association

www.afa.net

Focus on the Family

www.focusonthefamily.com

Planned Parenthood

www.plannedparenthood.org/

The National Campaign to Prevent Teen Pregnancy

www.thenationalcampaign.org/

Selected, Edited, and with Issue Framing Material by:
Don Dyson, *Widener University*

ISSUE

Is Polyamory a Good Alternative for Relationships and Families?

YES: Elisabeth Sheff, from "What You Can Learn from Polyamory," *Greater Good* (2017)

NO: Alan J. Hawkins, Betsy VanDenBerghe, and Lynae Barlow, from "The New Math of 'Consensual Nonmonogamy'," *National Review* (2017)

Learning Outcomes

After reading this issue, you will be able to:

- Define polyamory.
- Compare and contrast the concepts of jealousy and compersion.
- Analyze the pros and cons of polyamorous relationships.

ISSUE SUMMARY

YES: Elisabeth Sheff, PhD, CASA, CSE is an educational consultant and expert witness serving sexual and gender minorities. She is the author of The Polyamorists Next Door and When Someone You Love Is Polyamorous, as well as numerous academic and legal articles about polyamory, gender, families, and sexual minorities. Sheff presents evidence that the basic tenets of polyamory are not only healthy, but can teach monogamists skills for healthier relationships.

NO: Alan J. Hawkins is a professor and Lynae Barlow an undergraduate student in the Brigham Young University School of Family Life. Betsy VanDenBerghe is a writer based in Salt Lake City. Hawkins and VanDenBerghe are the authors of the National Marriage Project report "Facilitating Forever." Hawkins, Barlow, and VanDenBerghe argue that power dynamics, individual suffering, and preservation of family norms are all key reasons why polyamory is untenable.

P olyamory is a relationship style that has existed for thousands of years, yet it is one that is often misunderstood and misrepresented. At its core, polyamory involves the formation and maintenance of intimate and often sexual relationships beyond what is considered the "traditional" paradigm of relationships. When most folks think of intimate and romantic relationships, they immediately picture two people committed to one another and to the tradition of monogamy. Polyamory expands the relationship cluster beyond a dyad and allows for more than two people to be included.

Polyamory is not the same thing as "swinging" or having an open relationship. In those instances, the sexual connections that people make outside of a dyad are usually casual. It is also not the same thing as "cheating," which includes some form of deception or breaking of a vow or promise. In polyamorous experiences, there is usually some level of commitment made between all of the people involved in the relationship. As a result, there is also a commitment to honesty and communication that sets these relationships apart from those that involve cheating.

There are a lot of ways that people form polyamorous relationships. In some cases, there is a primary couple that includes romantic and sexual relationships with others who might be considered "secondary" partners. In others, three or more people might form a relationship together as a family unit.

In all polyamorous relating, there is a commitment to open and honest communication, and there is usually a set of agreements that guide the ways in which people relate. These agreements are negotiated, and at times renegotiated to allow for each of the people involved to get their individual wants and needs met.

One of the issues that often arises when people consider the idea of polyamory is the issue of jealousy. At its heart, jealousy is the feeling that someone else is getting something that I think I should have. This perspective, when it comes to relationships, is based in the concept that love is a finite resource. It is like a pie. If my partner is giving their love to someone else, then I must be getting less, and that is not okay. That person is getting a piece of the pie that should be mine, and now there is less pie for me. Polyamory argues that love is an infinite resource. As such, when my partner gives love to someone else, it results in more love. It does not diminish their love for me or rob me of love that I should be receiving.

Polyamory also includes the concept of compersion. Compersion is defined as the genuine feeling of joy that one gets when they see someone they love enjoying something that they love. Most of us have seen this in action when we see a loved one open a present that they really appreciate, experience achieving a longstanding goal, or simply watch them laugh with abandon. Polyamorous couples extend that feeling into knowing that their partner is enjoying love, sex, and relationships that make them feel happy and whole. They also appreciate the freedom to pursue and be celebrated for doing the same for themselves.

In the past few years, more and more young people have been embracing the idea that non-monogamous and polyamorous relationships may be an option for the ways that they organize their lives. In a 2016 poll by YouGov.com, 32% of those polled between the ages of 18 and 29 reported that they would be okay with non-monogamous relationships under some circumstances. In those polled between the ages of 30 and 44, the percentage rose slightly to 34. This shows higher rates of acceptance than any generation before them. For many, this has caused alarm.

There are a great many people who believe that healthy, monogamous marriages are the cornerstone of a civilized nation. In fact, they argue, polyamorous relationships threaten the well-being of society and children. For some, this argument is based in their religious beliefs. For others it is based in long-standing tradition. In either case, they argue that monogamy with and fidelity to one person is essential to a healthy and long-lasting relationship.

For others, the argument is less moralistic and more practical. While love might not be a finite resource, time is. There are only so many hours in a day, days in a week, etc. As a result, polyamorists must carve out time in their lives to meet the emotional and physical needs of more than one partner. In a world that is as busy and hectic as ours, many people find it difficult to crave out the time for career, children, and partners. Adding multiple partners into that equation creates the need to share what limited time one already has. And while being jealous about love might be managed in a polyamorous relationship, being jealous about the amount of time that other partners receive is a different thing entirely.

In addition to time, many folks see the limited resource of emotional and physical energy as another reason why polyamory doesn't work. At the end of a long and difficult day at work, coming home to the emotional support of a partner can be a relief. Having more than one partner who can support you in those times seems like a great idea. But when you reverse that, and come home after a long and difficult day to two or even three partners who need your support and care, the experience can be overwhelming.

Finally, some argue, that no matter the level of commitment and compersion, inevitably polyamory results in difficult and hurt feelings. If there is the opportunity for more love in a polyamorous relationship, then there is equal opportunity for more hurt. And complicating the already complicated landscape of relationships is a recipe for disaster.

As you read through these competing articles, ask yourself a few questions:

- Is the idea of multiple partners appealing to me?
- Do I have the communication skills to make something like that work?
- How do my personal values influence my thinking in this area?

YES

Elisabeth Sheff

What You Can Learn from Polyamory

A 20-year study of consensually non-monogamous adults reveals seven lessons for anyone who wants to keep love alive.

Do You Hope to Love One Person for the Rest of Your Life?

As romantic as that goal may sound, not everyone shares it. With economic, social, and health changes leading to much longer lifespans—and more control over fertility and childbearing—our attitudes towards monogamy have changed significantly. Divorce has become commonplace, and many people have embraced serial monogamy, forming one relationship at a time, falling in love and splitting up, and then doing it all over again.

But there's an alternative: polyamory, a form of consensual non-monogamy that emphasizes emotional and sexual intimacy with multiple partners simultaneously, ideally with the knowledge of all parties involved.

I studied polyamorous families with children for a period of 20 years, and I discovered their relationships can be intense, complicated—and fulfilling.

I also found that polyamorists have developed a set of relationship practices that can serve as lessons to people in monogamous relationships. Divorced parents and others in blended families may find them especially relevant, because they offer insights into dealing with challenging family communication among multiple adults and co-parents.

Polyamory isn't for everyone, but here are seven lessons from polyamorous families that anyone might find helpful.

1. Spread Needs Around

Expecting one person to meet all of your needs—companionship, support, co-parent, best friend, lover, therapist, housekeeper, paycheck, whatever—puts a tremendous amount of pressure on that relationship.

In their quest to maintain sexual and emotional fidelity, some monogamous relationships prioritize the couple

ahead of other social connections. When this focus reduces other sources of support, it can lead to isolation—and the resulting demands can be too much for many relationships to bear.

By and large, that's not the case for polyamorous people. Indeed, my study participants mentioned this as one of the primary benefits of being polyamorous: being able to get more of their needs met by spreading them out among multiple people. Sometimes they were lovers, or sometimes friends, family members, and ex-partners. The important thing is not the sexual connection, but the ability to seek and establish mutually supportive relationships beyond your partner. Allowing partners to form a range of relationships with friends and support circles can make life much easier for everyone.

This process can also be good for children. "It gives my children a sense of community," said Emmanuella Ruiz, one of my study participants. She continues:

> They don't have cousins or the typical biological extended family. But they have a big, happy, productive, healthy family nonetheless, and it is a chosen family. They know each person's relationship to them the same way they would know if they were first or second cousins, aunts, or uncles.

2. Don't Leave Too Soon

In serious relationships, giving up without trying hard to work things out can mean prematurely ending a good relationship that is simply having a difficult period. This is true for people in monogamous and serial-monogamous relationships, of course, which are more likely to last when both people put a lot of effort into the maintenance and sustenance of the relationship.

This article originally appeared on Greater Good, the online magazine of the Greater Good Science Center at UC Berkeley. Read more at greatergood.berkeley.edu.

But polyamorous relationship require even more of this kind of work, because of their complexity. My participants report developing the skill to stay with a difficult conversation, even if it is uncomfortable. As one study participant, Morgan Majek, told me about moving from monogamy to polyamory with her husband, Carl:

> It really opened up communication between us. Because we've been together for nine years and that was my biggest complaint about him was you don't talk to me... So it created pain, but it really just helped us to learn how to be completely honest and communicate. And so it benefited us.

People in polyamorous relationships are also more likely to seek support from others, something that could benefit and sustain serial monogamous relationships as well. When things get rocky, we're prone to hide the trouble from friends and family. Polyamorists suggest an alternative: reach out to friends and community members for sympathy, support, and advice. Getting professional counseling or relationship coaching can be tremendously helpful in dealing with concrete issues and establishing patterns for communication that can help deal with other matters that arise over time.

3. Don't Stay Too Long

In what can be a delicate balancing act, polyamorous people find that it is important not to drag things out until the bitter end, when partners have been so awful to each other that they simply must run away.

Instead, polyamorists suggest that it is better to recognize and accept when people have grown apart or are not working well together, and then change—not necessarily end—the relationship. "I am not best buddies with all my exes," said study participant Gabrielle. But she doesn't think of many of her "former lovers" as exes at all.

> We were lovers and now we're friends, and ex just seems kind of a weird way to think of someone I'm close to and care about. The real difference here, I think, is that the changes in relationship tended to have a much more gentle evolution rather than "official" breakups.

As a group, polyamorists don't see families as "broken" or "failed" because the adults changed the nature of their relationship. People can choose to view their relationships as good for the time. When needs change and so does the relationship, it does not have to be seen as a failure, and no one has to bear blame. From this perspective, gracefully ending or transitioning to a different kind of relationship can be a celebration of a new phase instead of a catastrophe.

4. Be Flexible and Allow for Change

Polyamorous people sustain their relationships through these changes in part by being willing to try new things. (This may also be because there are so few role models for consensually non-monogamous relationships that polyamorous people are usually making it up as they go along.) If the relationship isn't working, then trying something else can be quite effective for both polyamorous and monogamous people.

This can mean shifting expectations and letting go of former patterns, which can be both invigorating and frightening. Adjusting in response to changing circumstances allows families to be resilient, and polyamorous families must routinely adapt to new familial and emotional configurations as they accommodate multiple partners. To manage their unconventional family lives, polyamorous families try new things, reconfigure their relationships or interactions, and remain open to alternatives.

"I guess I'm not necessarily what you would call normal, but who cares?" said Mina Amore, the teenage child of one couple I interviewed. "Normal is boring."

With their many well-established roles and ingrained traditional expectations, people in monogamous relationships can find it more difficult to challenge entrenched patterns and do something completely different. Polyamorists often get help negotiating the changes by reaching out to trusted friends, a counselor, relationship coach, or even a mediator—change is easier when you have a team.

5. Support Personal Growth

Polyamory is emotionally challenging, no question. Jealousy, insecurity, and other negative emotions are all a part of any romantic relationship. Instead of trying to avoid painful emotions, however, polyamorists try to face them head on.

People in long-term polyamorous relationships say that a combination of introspection and candid communication is the route to managing potentially challenging or painful feelings. Having to face their self-doubts, question their own motives, and consider their own boundaries often forces poly people to either get to know themselves—or to quit polyamory.

Encouraging—or even allowing—a partner to explore personal growth can be difficult and frightening. What if they change so much in their growth that they no longer want to be in the relationship? That's a possibility polyamorists try to face. "One of the main advantages is knowing you have choices," says Marcus Amore, Mina's dad. Polyamorous people often emphasize the important role that choice plays in their relationships, and explain how they continually woo and lavish their long-term partners with affection and attention to foster the kind of loving environment that they choose to stay in, year after year.

Suppressing a partner to keep them from outgrowing their current relationship does not tend to work well as a long-term strategy because it fosters resentment and rebellion. That's a lesson for monogamous people—to allow their mates to grow, and to pursue their own path.

6. De-emphasize Sexuality

Even though most people associate polyamorous relationships with sex, polyamorists frequently de-emphasize sexuality to help reconfigure and cope with change.

Emotional attachment is the glue that holds families together anyway, and while sex is good and helps people feel connected, it is not enough by itself to sustain a long-term relationship. Polyamory emphasizes that the end of sex does not have to mean end of relationship. Remaining friends is a real choice, and especially important when people have had children together. Children do not care if their parents have sex, and in fact would much rather not hear about it or think of their parents as sexual beings.

Instead, de-emphasizing sexuality can allow family members to focus on cooperative co-parenting and remaining on positive terms. When people have treated each other with respect and allowed themselves to change, or leave a relationship that is no longer working before they do terrible things to each other, it makes it much more reasonable to actually co-parent or even be cordial to each other.

Another important element of de-emphasizing sexuality is the tremendous importance polyamorous folks often attach to their friendships and chosen-family relationships. Emotional connections with intimates do not rely on physical sexuality. Monogamous people can also establish deep friendships that provide support, emotional intimacy, and meet needs.

7. Communicate Honestly and Often

Polyamorous people put a lot of emphasis on communication as a way to build intimacy, explore boundaries, negotiate agreements, and share feelings. Telling the truth is paramount to this process, as honesty forms the basis for trust. Trust helps people feel safe, which in turn builds intimacy, and (ideally) communication creates a positive feedback loop within the relationship.

Monogamous relationships have many social rules that structure the way partners are supposed to interact. Some of these rules encourage people to tell each other small lies to smooth over possibly difficult or hurtful situations. While diplomatic phrasing and empathy are important for compassionate relationships, these small lies that start out protecting feelings sometimes grow into much larger or more systemic patterns of deception. Both deceit and attack are corrosive to intimacy, because they undermine trust and feelings of closeness and safety.

If you want to be close to your partner, tell the truth and create a compassionate emotional environment that is safe for them to tell you the truth as well. Gentle honesty may break well-established monogamous rules about hiding things from a spouse, but the outcomes of greater trust and intimacy can be well worth it!

Elisabeth Sheff, PhD, CASA, CSE is an educational consultant and expert witness serving sexual and gender minorities. She is the author of *The Polyamorists Next Door* and When *Someone You Love Is Polyamorous*, as well as numerous academic and legal articles about polyamory, gender, families, and sexual minorities.

Alan J. Hawkins, Betsy VanDenBerghe, and Lynae Barlow  **NO**

The New Math of 'Consensual Nonmonogamy'

Journalists and academics are ignoring polyamory's dark implications.

The equation starts out simply enough: 2+2+1=5. Julie and Joe are married, and so are William and Anna, but not Sayulita, all panelists appearing on a New York Times video called "Married, Dating Other People and Happy." Giggling like teenagers over liaisons that evoke a galactic system in which lovers, less significant partners, other couples, and asteroidal hook-ups orbit a foundational marriage, the panelists describe their journeys into "ethical nonmonogamy" — ethical because it's consensual.

Julie informed her husband, Joe, that she had become emotionally attached to another man and would stay only if they opened the marriage. Joe decided "she has that right." And from there the math gets fuzzier and the variables harder to track. Another married couple becomes involved when Julie dates William. But then Julie and William break up, William's wife Anna falls for Joe, and after that Anna realizes she also loves Julie. Meanwhile, William sleeps with Sayulita, who realizes she's attracted to Anna. After which the addition and subtraction morph into multiplication as panel members, amid more nervous laughter, explain that Julie currently dates three other couples, Sayulita sleeps with three men and three women, and William and Anna have a hard time putting a numerical value on just how many they're seeing.

The giggling abates when a yearning emerges, several times, for a simpler equation. Joe admits he still gets jealous of certain lovers, tries to find ways to "make *us* feel special," and inquires whether Julie would "give up all those other people" if asked, to which she replies no "every time." Sayulita voices deep fears of not having a "nesting partner, like these two couples," a reality impeding her hopes for "having a family, having a home together."

Welcome to Consensual Nonmonogamy, or CNM, as it has come to be known, not just within the purview of the New York Times' explorations of modern romance but also within mainstream scholarly circles. With roots in progressive social science and jurisprudence, CNM scholarship now proclaims that open relationships have all the same benefits that monogamous ones do. Employing weak methods, researchers shrug off the dangerous ramifications for individuals and families involved in CNM to promote a relational math so complex that few, if any, couples have the wherewithal to solve the equation.

To be sure, the sky isn't falling yet. Nine-tenths of American adults affirm the principle of marital monogamy. Overwhelmingly, the institution of marriage evokes theological, cultural, and artistic imperatives, like cleaving together to become one flesh, forsaking all others, and uniting Elizabeths and Darcys in satisfying finales.

But such abiding communal convictions gradually dissolve when popular and scholarly conversations put those expecting commitment and fidelity on the defensive. It is worth responding to those determined to upend the crucial institution of marriage, an institution that orders individual and collective lives.

Academic Exploration, Empirical Weaknesses

Unlike the "compulsory monogamy" of traditional marriage, consensual nonmonogamy involves having more than one sexual partner or romantic relationship at the same time. And unlike polygamy, CNM advances a libertine sexual ethic, with its roots in the 1960s free-love movement and feminist ideology, encompassing a smorgasbord of practices from one-night stands to bounded polyamorous systems of couples to a dizzying array of primary partners and secondary lovers.

No more than 10 percent of all couples engage in CNM, with marital CNM certainly much lower, unlikely more than 1–2 percent. Sexual orientation plays into these data, with bisexuals significantly overrepresented in polyamorous relationships. Gay married men seem most open to nonmonogamy in both theory and practice, while lesbian spouses tend toward monogamy despite more theoretical openness to CNM.

> The eager tone that popular media exude toward CNM represents more of prurience than prognosis.

For heterosexual couples, a dogged preference for monogamy empirically shows itself again and again. For instance, Penn State sociologists, mining a high-quality national data set, found that, on a scale from 1 to 10 rating how crucial fidelity is to a successful marriage, young women's average score was 9.8 and young men's average was 9.7. Recent national polling shows that more than 90 percent of Americans say that extramarital sex is morally wrong, a figure higher than that found in the prestigious General Social Survey, which currently finds that 76 percent of Americans view extramarital sex as "always wrong." This figure barely moves for the youngest generation, confirming that 21st-century attitudes about marital fidelity lean more puritanical than progressive.

Thus the eager tone that popular media exude toward CNM represents more of prurience than prognosis. A more even-keeled investigatory tone might be expected in scholarly circles, but instead, a breathless embrace of CNM pervades even highly respected journals. Perspectives on Psychological Science recently featured an extraordinarily long treatment of heterosexual CNM. The piece's authors, a team of CNM researchers, began by decrying "the presumed superiority of monogamy" and unsurprisingly concluded that CNM relationships display "equally positive relational outcomes" relative to monogamous ones.

The weaknesses of this team's study mirror the deficiencies of CNM research in general, beginning with a tendency to employ small, nonrepresentative samples. Finding participants through websites that cater to CNM or other sexual-interest groups ensures that researchers end up with participants who affirm adventurous sexual lives. Nearly all studies involve only self-reported responses, blatantly risking "affirmation bias." Moreover, the interviews usually involve just one partner, ignoring the other, who might reveal a more begrudging agreement than the term mutual implies. And despite three decades of scholarship on CNM, little research follows CNM individuals over time to observe long-term patterns and impacts, a hallmark of mature social science. Moreover, marital and non-marital CNM are seldom distinguished in this body of research, despite real differences between them. Curiously, the word children, surely an important theoretical, practical, and ethical consideration, rarely emerges in the writing.

Despite these ongoing weaknesses, the aforementioned team of enthusiastic CNM researchers declares that "no definitive evidence [exists] that tips the scale strongly in favor of monogamy [over CNM]" on a variety of outcomes. While acknowledging some weaknesses in the research, they argue that these flaws should not impede a social movement to accept CNM, in the same way that shortcomings in the research on same-sex couples became irrelevant to the cause of same-sex-marriage recognition.

Just as disturbing, prominent scholars outside the CNM vanguard find the lure of easy answers contagious. In psychology and management professor Eli Finkel's recent magnum opus, The All-or-Nothing Marriage, he recommends CNM as one remedy to the contemporary dilemma of expecting much more of marriage than it can realistically deliver. Partners' differences in sexual needs, he reasons, can be handled by loosening the reins of monogamy.

The influential sociologist Judith Stacey puts it most bluntly in her recent book Unhitched: "Monogamy is not natural or even possible for everyone. . . . Sexual variation, on the other hand, is natural and should be no cause for distress." Calling efforts to strengthen marriage "a quixotic effort to plant durable domestic turf in desire's rocky soil," Stacey condemns humanity's long-term obsession with monogamy as "unattainable and, in my view, uninspiring." Yet she and other academic CNM advocates can't completely shake off the vestigial need for some semblance of fidelity, so Stacey artistically advocates "vows of fidelity to whatever principles of intimacy and commitment [people choose] to negotiate and renegotiate among themselves."

> 'Is our culture ready for the heretic notion that a relationship could be reinforced by fluid boundaries, rather than destroyed?'

Though more nuanced than Stacey, Esther Perel, the renowned psychotherapist and bestselling author who explores the tensions between sexual freedom and relational security, also embraces CNM. In her newest book, The State of Affairs: Rethinking Infidelity, Perel maintains that "the polyamorous experiment is a natural offshoot of the societal trend toward greater personal license and self-expression" and asks, "Is our culture ready for the heretic notion that a relationship could be reinforced by fluid boundaries, rather than destroyed?"

While Perel encourages her readers "to be unafraid to challenge sexual and emotional correctness," legal scholars set their sights beyond social acceptance of CNM, with one legal academic hypothesizing that "expanding the ways we can come together to form intimate relationships will lead to stronger family bonds, fewer divorces, and more tolerance." After all, she continues, perhaps sensing the need to bolster this logic, full knowledge and consent might somehow result in less hurt, fewer divorces, and fewer fractured families. Echoing language in the U.S. Supreme Court decision that legalized same-sex marriage, other legal scholars call for recognizing multi-party marriage, arguing that it offers polyamorists protection from "mononormativity" that transmits "dignitary harm" and unjust discrimination toward a sexual minority.

Peeking Under the Sheets

Both academics and journalists portray CNM in almost uniformly bright colors. But in some venues the veneer over CNM lifts, revealing the heavy demands, psychological contortions, and thorny day-to-day challenges involved. Polyamorists' own comments in online forums, and in some published stories, surface the unbalanced math of CNM. These relationships require much more work and skill than keeping one marriage satisfying. 1+2 (or 3 or 5 or 7) turns out to be a far more daunting function than 1+1.

CNM is supposed to be the perfect solution to a variety of problems. Sexual needs not being met? Add a couple more lovers for fulfillment. Scared of monogamous boredom? Go ahead and explore exciting new relationships. Bisexual and unwilling to select one gender for life? Choose both. Struggling to remain faithful to a spouse you love and don't want to hurt? Redefine cheating.

What's not to like about these creative solutions? Let us count the ways, citing the grievances of CNM participants themselves. Time management, for one, constitutes an enormous burden. Even polyamory promoter Franklin Veaux admits that relationships require "a certain amount of 'alone time,' and . . . having two partners can mean having less time to spend with each of them." One husband concedes that "sometimes I find myself longing for my partner to be monogamous with me. . . . On off or down days, I really start to want for us to be together without polyamory." Another bemoans his wife's distractions with emails and texts from her other relationships "that can pull [her] from our moments. There is a third person in our relationship who is pervasively there and not there."

Resource issues rear their complex heads as well. Are finances to be shared with other partners? Who pays for expensive dates or anniversary trips? Who does the household chores? These can be hard questions for a monogamous couple; they are far harder in a polyamorous relationship.

One married couple's experience demonstrated how these issues can proliferate. The couple became involved with a vulnerable woman recovering from a divorce. But when the woman recovered thanks to the couple's financial and emotional help, she began exploring a new relationship — much to the chagrin of the couple. They felt used, wanting to be consulted about "how quickly and to what extent any new partnerships formed."

Additionally, regarding the "consent" that CNM advocates tout, what happens when one partner holds more power or leverage because he or she makes more money, is more attractive, is better at initiating new relationships, or just has a higher sex drive? Does an unemployed or introverted full-time homemaker, dependent on a financially successful, extroverted, and sexually adventurous spouse, truly have much leverage when her or his partner asks to open a marriage?

For hydra-like complications such as these, CNM advocates return to their core axiom: skilled, frequent, open communication — a feat important to all relationships, no doubt, but required in spades for CNM practitioners. Tristan Taormino, author of Opening Up: A Guide to Creating and Sustaining Open Relationships, recommends focusing constantly on the heavy-duty dialoguing of negotiated boundaries, parenting, and time management. While these areas may sound like familiar conversational territory for any couple, those with multiple partners no longer have trail markers and must create paths out of unmapped terrain. How do children fit in? Who disciplines them? How many sexual encounters is each spouse allowed with secondary partners? Now that we mention it, what are the rules about sexual hygiene? And who gets whom for Valentine's Day? Even more important, who gets to be involved in deciding these issues, just the primary partners, or secondary ones of a certain order or duration?

CNM is about freedom, not boundaries, so any borders must be permeable, bendable, and governed by frequent renegotiations.

Again, in theory, all these conversations would lead to mutually agreed solutions — albeit with continually evolving sets of rules. CNM is about freedom, not boundaries, so any borders must be permeable, bendable, and governed by frequent renegotiations requiring inordinate amounts of time and energy. Even an effusive New York Times story acknowledges that CNM depends on its participants' having few work and time impediments that could interfere with never-ending rapprochement. Aspirin, anyone?

Yet even enthusiasts with enough disposable time and income to deal with polyamory's complexities might want to consider the emotional downsides. One polyamorist woman describes the continual dialoguing as "gut-wrenching and sob-inducing. I remember listening to him speak and feeling like my heart was being pulled slowly out of my chest." While journalists extol the sense of adventure polyamorists discover in taking on new identities with different lovers, some survivors undergo a complete identity crisis. "I lost myself. . . . No, it would be more accurate to say that I demolished myself," says a woman who dealt with intense cognitive dissonance when dating a man whose wife allowed extramarital relationships but put "a long list of limitations" on them. She told herself, "just want something else, feel something else, BE SOMEONE ELSE." Another casualty realized that "I no longer could be the man I was. Experiencing consensual nonmonogamy was not simply changing how I viewed my sex life: it changed how I viewed humanity."

Cultural Ramifications of the New Math

The personal suffering of individuals involved in consensual nonmonogamy constitutes reason enough to resist the normalization of open relationships, but the preservation of marital norms remains a paramount consideration as well. If proponents of legal recognitions for CNM have their way, the choice of monogamy will get harder. "Anti-discrimination protections for polyamory," writes a legal scholar, "may have the incidental beneficial effect of encouraging those who desire to live the overtly non-monogamous lifestyle . . . but who previously did not have the courage to do so." Monogamy, once the expectation, becomes a negotiated clause harder to ask for,

let alone expect, putting old-school monogamists into a defensive crouch.

Much as those hoping to save sex for marriage became too outnumbered to expect abstinence in today's dating world, those who expect marital fealty could find their assumptions regarded as not only passé, but selfish. In her sympathetic New York Times exploration, Susan Dominus hints at the superiority of CNM couples not just interested in more sex, but "more interested in people, more willing to tolerate the inevitable unpacking conversations, the gentle making of amends, the late-night breakdowns and emotional work of recommitting to and delighting each other." Dominus goes on to second-guess her ick-factor instincts while watching a wife nuzzle a lover in the presence of her husband and child, lauding not only the "generosity" of the husband's attitude in comparison with "my own limitations," but also the brave wives willing to "risk so much on behalf of their sexual happiness."

> Accept the petition, or endure the likelihood that your spouse pursues the openness unilaterally or terminates the marriage.

And so a new paradigm emerges. Complain or act jealous and you become the bad guy in the new CNM model, which elevates a generous willingness to share a spouse with others as the ultimate marital virtue. Meanwhile, a double bind materializes for the petitioned partner: accept the petition, or endure the likelihood that your spouse pursues the openness unilaterally or terminates the marriage. One spouse trailblazing and the other tagging along thus equates to "mutual consent."

This potential zeitgeist harms even decidedly monogamous couples, who are left behind, plodding the prosaic plains of everyday marital life, having to resist fantasizing about a similar adventure for themselves. Certainly part of what helps married couples maintain their vows of fidelity is that everyone else is supposed to abide by the same rules. When prominent voices urge tolerance of rule-breaking, affirm visionary liberation, reject the oppression of mononormativity, and enshrine bold relational explorations in law, then even stuffy traditionalists will entertain alternatives. And because mutual consent is a bit of a squishy concept in CNM, cheating becomes just a matter of degree, no longer a fixed boundary. For example, Dominus discovers that her lead couples, Daniel and Elizabeth (and Daniel's out-of-state lover) and Joseph and Joseph's wife, all know about each other . . . except for Joseph's wife, and that's why Joseph won't be available for the interview.

Academic and pop-culture narratives gloss over the fact that CNM fundamentally alters a core element of marriage: making a choice to give up some choices, as prominent relationship scholar Scott Stanley puts it. Interestingly, some wounded CNM warriors use words like "trapped" to describe a situation they entered seeking liberation, an irony that strangely sheds light on the paradox of monogamous marital freedom. Stanley argues that the fences of marriage foster an intimacy unavailable in any less committed relationship, creating a place so secure and mutually beneficial that couples, like Adam and Eve, can experience emotional and physical nakedness and be "not ashamed." Hence the wise wedding vow to "forsake all others."

ALAN J. HAWKINS is a professor and **LYNAE BARLOW** an undergraduate student in the Brigham Young University School of Family Life. **BETSY VANDENBERGHE** is a writer based in Salt Lake City. Hawkins and VanDenBerghe are the authors of the National Marriage Project report "Facilitating Forever."

EXPLORING THE ISSUE

Is Polyamory a Good Alternative for Relationships and Families?

Critical Thinking and Reflection

1. Can you identify the emotional, moral, intellectual, and social components in Sheff's argument?
2. Can you identify the emotional, moral, intellectual, and social components in Hawkins, Barlow and VanDenBerghe's argument?
3. Can you identify the emotional, moral, intellectual, and social responses that you have to this issue?
4. What are some similarities and differences between your responses and those of the authors?

Is There Common Ground?

Most people would argue that there is value in close, loving relationships. In fact, research supports that there are both emotional and physical benefits to being closely connected to others. Where people disagree is in the types of relationships that are best to meet these needs. For some, the abundance of love that polyamory offers is an obvious choice. For others, the potential for hurt as well as their moral teachings say that monogamous relationships are better suited to meet those needs. When considering what types of relationships are best, it is important to consider both the benefits and costs of each type of relationship for each individual. Is the burden of monogamy going to result in dishonesty and cheating? Is the potential for jealousy and hurt too much to risk? In either case, are the needs of everyone within the relationship being honestly communicated and fully met?

Additional Resources

Scheff, E. (2016). When Someone You Love Is Polyamorous: Understanding Poly People and Relationships. Thorntree Press: Portland.

Barker, M. (2013). Rewriting the Rules: An Integrative Guide to Love, Sex and Relationships. Routledge: New York.

Scheff, E. (2014). The Polyamorists Next Door: Inside Multiple-Partner Relationships and Families. Rowman and Littlefield: Lanham, MD.

Internet References . . .

Loving More

https://www.lovingmorenonprofit.org/

National Coalition for Sexual Freedom: What Psychology Professionals Should Know About Polyamory

https://ncsfreedom.org/images/stories/pdfs/KAP/2010_poly_web.pdf

Polyamory Weekly

http://polyweekly.libsyn.org/

Selected, Edited, and with Issue Framing Material by:
Don Dyson, *Widener University*

ISSUE

Should Same-sex Adoption Be Legal?

YES: Elizabeth A. Harris, from "Same-Sex Parents Still Face Legal Complications," *The New York Times* (2017)

NO: Jules Gomes, from "Is Gay Adoption Wrong? The Children Say Yes," *Anglican Ink* (2017)

Learning Outcomes
After reading this issue, you will be able to: • Identify the challenges faced by same-gender couples wanting to adopt children. • Explain the research findings regarding same-sex adoption. • Articulate the arguments on both sides of the issue.

ISSUE SUMMARY

YES: Elizabeth Harris has been a culture reporter at *The New York Times* since 2009. In her tenure at the times, she has written from a variety of positions on issues from real estate to education foreign affairs. Harris argues that although same-sex adoption is legal in most cases, that there are state-by-state laws that challenge potential parents, and a shifting legal landscape that can result in a parent being a legal stranger to their own child simply by driving across a state line.

NO: Jules Gomes writes for The Anglican Ink, a publication of Anglican Television Ministries in Milford, Connecticut. Gomes reports on a study conducted in the United Kingdom by Robert Oscar Lopez and Brittany Klein titled: Jepthah's Children: the innocent casualties of same sex adoption. In his article, Gomes argues that bearing children is not a right, but a responsibility and a gift. He states that gay or lesbian adults should sacrifice their homosexuality and raise a child in a home with both a husband and wife (for the good of the child) or sacrifice their desire to have children.

In previous issues of *Taking Sides: Family and Personal Relationships*, the issue of marriage equality was explored. In essence, the question asked was whether or not someone should be able to marry the person of their own choosing regardless of the gender of their beloved.

The issue of marriage equity can be traced back to the 1970s, with varying degrees of intensity from that time until 2015. That year, the Supreme Court of the United States ruled in Obergefell v. Hodges that the Due Process and Equal Protection clauses of the Constitution upheld the fundamental right of same-sex couples to marry and to receive all of the benefits and responsibilities associated with that union. With that ruling, marriage equality was established in all 50 states and all territories of the United States.

With the ruling by the Supreme Court, adoption for same-sex couples became legal in all 50 states, with Mississippi being the lone holdout until a federal judge struck down their objection citing the Supreme Court ruling. The social battles around the issue of sexual orientation did not stop there, however. Now, one of the biggest hurdles to same-sex adoption sits in the hands of individual social workers practicing in the field of foster care.

Recent research from the U.S. Department of Health and Human Services, Adoption and Foster Care Analysis Reporting System (AFCARS) identifies that of the approximately half a million children in the foster care system in the United States, 100,000 are in need of adoption into safe, loving and permanent homes. Even in the face of this great need, however, some social workers in the field express concern about the "goodness of fit" for children in same-sex families. As they balance the experiences of trauma that these children have experienced, they worry about whether or not the children in their care will suffer additional social and emotional difficulty if adopted by same-sex people.

Socially, they express concern about whether or not children will be able to navigate both the stigma of foster care involvement as well as the potential added stigma of being raised in a household with two moms or two dads. Emotionally, they are concerned about whether or not these children will suffer without the example of both a mother and a father in their household. Single people who are gay, lesbian, or bisexual amplify their concerns when they consider adoption. In this instance, the stereotypes about the unrestrained sexual lives of gay men and bisexual people as well as the relationship enmeshment and instability of lesbians inform their concerns.

Despite the National Association of Social Workers (NASW) supporting lesbian, gay, bisexual, and transgender (LGBT) affirming legislation related to adoption, foster care, and parental rights as well as their Code of Ethics supporting LGBT people, some social workers continue to allow their personal biases inform their everyday practice. They are supported in these beliefs by many religious organizations that fight in social and political arenas to support a return to the traditional family and the values that once dominated this debate.

Within these arguments, the focus is usually placed on the well-being of the child. The concerns are presented as protecting children from harm. In this case, the argument is bolstered by the belief that children in foster care have already suffered harm, and are therefore in need of additional consideration.

One of the arguments used by some in this debate is that children raised by gay or lesbian people will experience confusion about their own sexuality and gender roles. They worry that having a homosexual or bisexual parent might lead children to identify themselves as homosexual or bisexual or that the gender nonconformity of some lesbian and gay people will lead to gender confusion in their children. The counter-point to this argument, however, is that gay, lesbian, and bisexual people have been raised by gender-conforming heterosexual parents for millennia and that has not resulted in them identifying as heterosexual.

Consider as part of this argument the reality that somewhere between 6 and 14 million children in the United States have a gay or lesbian parent, although they may not be residing with that parent. In addition, between 8 and 10 million children in the United States are being raised in gay and lesbian households. In reality, same-sex parenting is already happening at a large, national scale. The majority of these situations involve blended families, situations in which biological children were born to people who were previously in heterosexual relationships. Those that do not are often the result of reproductive technologies like In-Vitro Fertilization and surrogate pregnancies.

One of the compelling arguments on the side of supporting same-sex parenting is the reality that for same-sex couples, the decision to have a child is almost always intentional. Unlike heterosexual or mixed-gender couples, same-sex couples do not find themselves in the situation of having to navigate an unexpected pregnancy. As a result, they argue, the children that they choose (either through biological or adoptive means) are always entering into homes where there has been intentional discussion and preparation regarding parenting. In this way, it can be argued, same-sex couples offer children an advantage.

Contextualizing this debate in the available research is an important consideration. A number of studies have been done that compare the social and emotional health of children raised by same-sex couples. In each, to date, the research supports that there is no significant difference between the health and well-being of children raised by other-gender parents and those raised by same-sex parents. While there has been some criticism of this research for being inherently biased, and conducted by individuals and organizations with political or social agendas, large-scale longitudinal studies with very strict protocols have also been done. These studies seem to support the findings of the smaller and earlier studies. There is no difference in life outcomes for children raised in either type of family.

As you read the articles in this unit, consider some questions about your own values and beliefs. What do you think is most important in raising healthy and happy children? Is parenting a right or a privilege? Do the rights of parents supersede what you think is in the best interest of children?

YES ◁

Elizabeth A. Harris

Same-Sex Parents Still Face Legal Complications

At gay pride marches around the country this month, there will be celebrations of marriage, a national right that, at just two years old, feels freshly exuberant to many lesbian, gay, bisexual and transgender Americans.

But while questions of marriage are largely settled, same-sex couples who choose to have children still face a patchwork of laws around the country that define who is and who can be a parent. This introduces a rash of complications about where L.G.B.T.Q. couples may want to live and how they form their families, an array of uncertainties straight couples do not have to think about.

"There are very different laws from state to state in terms of how parents are protected, especially if they're unmarried," said Cathy Sakimura, deputy director and family law director at the National Center for Lesbian Rights. "You can be completely respected and protected as a family in one state and be a complete legal stranger to your children in another. To know that you could drive into another state and not be considered a parent anymore, that's a pretty terrifying situation."

Adoption laws, for example, can be extremely contradictory. In some states, like Maryland and Massachusetts, adoption agencies are expressly prohibited from discriminating based on sexual orientation. At the same time, other states, like South Dakota, have laws that create religious exemptions for adoption providers, allowing agencies to refuse to place children in circumstances that violate the groups' religious beliefs.

Alan Solano, a state senator in South Dakota, sponsored his state's adoption legislation. He said he was concerned that if those groups were forced to let certain families adopt, they might get out of the adoption business entirely, shrinking the number of placement agencies in the state.

"I wanted to ensure that we have the greatest number of providers that are working on placing children," Mr. Solano said. "I'm not coming out and saying that somebody in the L.G.B.T. community should not be eligible for getting a child placed with them. What I hope is that we have organizations out there that are ready and willing to assist them in doing these adoptions."

But as a practical matter, lawyers who specialize in L.G.B.T.Q. family law say that in some areas, religiously affiliated adoption organizations are the only ones within a reasonable distance. Moreover, they say, such laws harm children who need homes by narrowing the pool of people who can adopt them, and they are discriminatory.

"There is a very serious hurt caused when you're told, 'No, we don't serve your kind here,' and I think that gets lost in the public discourse a lot," said Susan Sommer, director of constitutional litigation for Lambda Legal. "There's just this narrative that absolutely ignores, and almost dehumanizes, L.G.B.T. people. They're missing from the equation here."

There are a number of laws that can affect L.G.B.T.Q. families, from restrictions on surrogacy to custody, and the landscape is constantly shifting.

Within a single state, there can be layers of befuddling complexity, with certain rules in place that help gay families and others that restrict them. But even in states that tend to have friendly laws, life is more complicated for gay parents.

Alice Eisenberg and Anna Wolk live in Brooklyn, and they decided together to get pregnant. Ms. Eisenberg carried the child, and Ms. Wolk was an equal partner every step of the way. For legal reasons, the couple was married before their daughter, Olympia Bruce Lavender Wolk, was born, and both parents' names are on the birth certificate.

Nonetheless, they are in the middle of doing a second-parent adoption.

The process varies from state to state — some states do not have them at all, instead offering stepparent adoptions — but in New York, the process is lengthy and complicated. Ms. Wolk must be fingerprinted and provide every address where she has lived, down to the month, going back decades. A social worker must do a home visit with the couple. The whole process will cost them about $4,000, they said, and could take a year to complete.

"We won marriage, and people thought the fight was over," Ms. Eisenberg said. "But having to adopt your own child feels way more invasive, upsetting, disturbing."

The Supreme Court has ruled that an adoption in one state must be honored in another, so even if a nonbiological parent is on the birth certificate — a right that stems from a recognition of the couple's marriage — L.G.B.T.Q. family law experts strongly recommend an adoption, or some kind of judicial decree as the strongest protection.

"It seems both insulting and ridiculous," said Ms. Sommer of Lambda Legal. "But sadly, the reality is, if you can manage it, you should do it."

After all, what if something happens to the biological parent, and their family members want custody of the child? While traveling internationally, parental rights that stem from a judicial order are more likely to be respected than rights that come from being married if a country does not recognize your marriage. And if a couple breaks up, lawyers say that without an adoption, the nonbiological parent may have to spend hundreds of thousands of dollars in court to establish the right to custody.

"We don't know which policies will continue on," said Diana M. Adams, who owns an L.G.B.T.Q. family-law firm in New York City. "You'll always be safer in more-conservative states and more-conservative countries if parentage is reliant on an adoption rather than on same-sex marriage."

For many couples, that uncertainty is the most compelling reason to do a second-parent adoption, to head off problems they cannot foresee.

"We're still coming from a place of fear about it," Ms. Wolk said. "I don't feel like right now we're going to get into trouble not having completed it, but you never know what's going to get overturned tomorrow."

The political climate has made many people especially nervous, lawyers say. Alana Chazan has a family law practice in Los Angeles, and she said that the busiest day of her career was Nov. 9, 2016, the day after Donald J. Trump was elected president.

"I have been telling people for years: Do a second-parent adoption, do a second-parent adoption, do a second-parent adoption," she said. With the Supreme Court's Obergefell v. Hodges decision in 2015 that made gay marriage legal nationwide, an expansion of parenting laws in California, and a feeling that the country was marching toward acceptance, Ms. Chazan said, many people seemed to think it would not be necessary.

"It was almost as though they thought I was scamming them as a lawyer, that I was just trying to take their money," she said. "But no. With the election of Trump, a lot of people got that."

When a second-parent adoption is finally complete, it can be a relief — but Ms. Wolk and Ms. Eisenberg said that when they leave the courthouse with their adoption decree, they have no plans to celebrate.

"I'm not going out to lunch to celebrate this," Ms. Eisenberg said. "This feels like something, as a movement of queer people, we should be rallying against."

ELIZABETH A. HARRIS is a culture reporter at *The New York Times*.

Jules Gomes

Is Gay Adoption Wrong?
The Children Say Yes

Hollywood did not invent the genre of horror. If you want to read a really grotesque horror story turn to the biblical Book of Judges and read the story of a judge named Jephthah, who is a bastard born of a whore. We do not know if Jephthah has a wife, but he has a daughter. Jephthah may have adopted her after kidnapping her from a village he raided.

The story climaxes with Jephthah vowing to sacrifice whoever comes forth from the doors of his house to meet him, should God grant him victory over Israel's enemies. Israel wins. Jephthah returns home and watches with horror as his daughter emerges from his house to welcome him.

Jephthah is the antithesis of a parent: he sacrifices an innocent child to placate his perverse beliefs. Parents sacrifice their ambitions and desires for their sake of their children. Jephthah sacrifices his child to satisfy his vainglorious ambitions and selfish desires. You could say the Jephthah syndrome defines the modern approach to child-rearing.

Dr Spock's revolution has proved to be short-lived. His ideas about childcare – persuading parents to be more flexible, responsive and affectionate with their children – no longer hold sway. Today children's needs come a definite second to parents' rights either to have them or to offload them. Mention Dr Bowlby's groundbreaking research on the baby's prior need for maternal attachment and expect to be told that a baby is capable of multiple attachments and substitute figures will do.

The evidence of the impact of maternal deprivation on babies has not changed – indeed findings mount on anxiety and heightened cortisol levels – but ideology about women's rights has. The logic of feminism, that children's needs can be subordinated to adult rights, is obvious. Once it is OK for daycare or fathers to substitute for mothers, so it becomes OK for anyone, regardless of whether or not they, as individuals, are indeed the best substitute (often granny) that can be found, in terms of meeting the child's needs.

Children raised by same-sex couples are now comparing their experience of gay adoption to Jephthah's story in the recent study Jephthah's Children: The Innocent Casualties of Same-Sex Parenting. Their revelations would have been deserving of attention even had not the tragedy of toddler Elsie, who was taken away from her family by social services, given to a gay couple for adoption and murdered by one of her adoptive dad, Matthew Scully-Hicks, hit the headlines.

Jephthah's daughter was an adult when she fulfilled her father's bizarre vow. Elsie was 18 months old when she died from Scully-Hicks's abuse resulting in broken ribs, a broken leg, bleeding on the brain and a fractured skull. Jephthah 'tore his clothes' with penitence when he saw the consequences of his behaviour. Remorseless Scully-Hicks referred to Elsie as 'Satan dressed up in a Babygro.'

The Book of Judges condemns Jephthah's behaviour and his society in the refrain, 'In those days there was no king in Israel. Everyone did what was right in his own eyes.' Social services and judges in our society commend gay adoption as a matter of gay rights and not as a response to children's needs.

Social services, so reluctant to remove Elsie from Scully-Hicks, did not hesitate in the case of a Christian heterosexual couple, Vincent and Pauline Matherick, who had fostered 28 children. Officials took from them an 11-year-old boy the couple were fostering because they'd refused to teach him about homosexuality. But in Elsie's case, social workers were terrified of questioning the dominant orthodoxy that same-sex couples make equally good or better parents.

This myth is based on 'fake research'. Nevertheless, it is a fiction that is leading to a boom in gay adoption, which has increased ever since it was allowed in Labour's 2002 Adoption Act. Numbers have risen further since same-sex marriage was introduced in England and Wales in 2014.

Same-sex couples now make up a record one in seven of the total approved to adopt children. Meanwhile, adoption by heterosexual couples has dropped 12 per cent this year.

In 2014, Simon Crouch, himself a gay parent, conducted a landmark study at the University of Melbourne influencing policy on gay adoption. The Washington Post sensationalised the study, declaring that 'children of same-sex couples are happier and healthier than peers'. Crouch claimed that his study on 315 mostly lesbian couples was the largest of its kind, despite serious methodological flaws including using a self-selected 'convenience sample' where the respondents knew the purpose of the survey, and thus the political and social importance of the results, before they were asked to participate.

By contrast, researchers Robert Oscar Lopez and Brittany Klein, editors of Jephthah's Children, draw on the first-hand experiences of scores of children (now adults) who were adopted by gay couples.

Lopez, who was gay and is now married to a woman, narrates his upbringing by two lesbians. 'We hear that gay couples have loving homes and they love their children,' he writes. 'I don't buy that because I think love means you sacrifice for the other person rather than expect the other person to sacrifice for you. If you are gay and love a child, you either sacrifice your gayness and raise the child in a home with both mother and father, or you sacrifice your dream of parenthood so the child can be adopted by a home with a mother and father.'

Children adopted by gay couples are raised in a culture that is 'highly specific and fraught with problems,' he writes, where 'adults have higher rates of depression, anxiety, eating disorders, sexually transmitted diseases including HIV/AIDS, domestic violence, sexual assault, and suicidal ideation'. He calls gay adoption 'systematic child abuse'.

Klein, who was also brought up by a lesbian couple, tackles the thorny issue of gays and surrogacy. 'How did parenthood become a right?' she asks. 'This is not about what goes on between two adults. This is a whole country becoming complicit in making women breeder livestock to meet the whims of a group of men and then denying children created as saleable goods the basic right to a mother and father . . . A child deserves a mother and a father. This is a basic human right. Parenthood is not a right . . . No homophobia in the world even competes with this socially accepted dehumanisation of children.'

Advocates for gay parenting are creating a system where children belong to adults who want them, not adults who conceived them, the researchers argue.

Klein is begging society to listen to today's Jephthah's daughters and sons. 'There are many of us out in the world. Our parents used us as little display objects. We existed only to make our parents look good – living, breathing political statements. We existed to feed the insatiable egos that were our parents. Does that sound like a happy childhood?'

As a researcher she puts her finger on a raw methodological nerve. 'Don't ask the six-year-old if she or he is happy. The toddlers have been trained to speak like a pet bird. They live in fear of what a parent will do if they dare to make the parent look bad. Don't go by the dog and pony show at the Pride Parade. Ask us, those of us who broke away from the culture that we grew up in. We will tell you.'

Academic research must start to reconsider the children just as John Bowlby did when he brought attention to the long-term effect on children of separation anxiety – from his study of children brutally separated them from their natural parents during the war.

Klein writes: 'History will be a harsh taskmaster. Children grow up. Trendy social causes are often revealed as bad ideas. I can say honestly that I don't know a single one of us – those raised in gay and lesbian households – who is going to tell you they have had anything even remotely related to a happy childhood. How could we? We were just pawns. We existed only as a mirror, and there were not enough mirrors in the world to satisfy them.'

Homosexual parenting is not a matter of right. Nor is being a parent a right. It is a gift and a duty. But as in the days of the Book of Judges, there are no moral absolutes in our society today. Everyone does and can do what is right in his or her own eyes. Elsie is dead. Jephthah lives on. And that is wrong.

JULES GOMES is a journalist and academic. He writes for *The Conservative Woman* and is the religious affairs correspondent for *Virtue Online*.

EXPLORING THE ISSUE

Should Same-sex Adoption Be Legal?

Critical Thinking and Reflection

1. Can you identify the emotional, moral, intellectual, and social components in Harris' argument?
2. Can you identify the emotional, moral, intellectual, and social components in Gomes' argument?
3. Can you identify your own emotional, moral, intellectual, and social reactions related to this issue?
4. What are some similarities and differences between your answers and the authors?

Is There Common Ground?

For both sides of this argument, the heart of the issue is the well-being of children. Both sides believe that they have a responsibility to look out for the interests of the children in these situations. On one side, folks are making the argument that being in loving, caring, and permanent homes where support and concern are present is a far better option for children than the foster care system. On the other side, folks argue that children who have already experienced the trauma of the loss of their biological parents need to have an extra layer of protection, which includes protection from lifestyles that are alternative and additional experiences of bullying and harassment. Although their core values of the protection and care of vulnerable children are similar, the ways that they translate those values are clearly influenced by other values and beliefs.

Additional Resources

Goldberg, A. E. (2010). *Lesbian and Gay Parents and Their Children: Research on the Family Life Cycle*. American Psychological Association: Washinton, DC.

Parr, T. (2010). *The Family Book*. Hachette Book Group: New York.

Sember, B. (2006). *Gay & Lesbian Parenting Choices: From Adopting or Using a Surrogate to Choosing the Perfect Father*. The Career Press: Franklin Lakes, NY.

Internet References . . .

Gay Parent Magazine

https://www.gayparentmag.com/adoption-foster-care-resources

Lifelong Adoptions

https://www.lifelongadoptions.com/lgbt-adoption-resources/lgbt-adoption-articles

National Clearinghouse on Child Abuse and Neglect Information: National Adoption Information Clearinghouse

https://www.childwelfare.gov/pubPDFs/f_gay.pdf

Selected, Edited, and with Issue Framing Material by:
Don Dyson, *Widener University*

ISSUE

Does Having a Transgender Parent Hurt Children?

YES: Brynn Tannehill, from "Here's What It's Really Like Having a Transgender Parent," *TheHuffingtonPost.com, Inc.* (2016)

NO: Caitlin White, "A Void Wider Than Gender: Here's What My Life has Been Like Since My Father Came Out as Trans," *Vice* (2015)

Learning Outcomes
After reading this issue, you will be able to:
• Identify three challenges that a child with a transgender parent might experience.
• Compare and contrast the experience of someone who learned of their parent's transition early in life versus later.
• Identify the ways that societal expectations of gender can be damaging to transgender people.

ISSUE SUMMARY

YES: Brynn Tannehill graduated from the Naval Academy with a BS in computer science in 1997. She earned her Naval Aviator wings in 1999 and served as a campaign analyst while deployed overseas. In 2008, Brynn earned an MS in Operations Research from the Air Force Institute of Technology and transferred from active duty to the Naval Reserves. In 2008, Brynn began working as a senior defense research scientist in private industry. She left the drilling reserves and began transition in 2010. Since then she has written for *OutServe magazine*, The New Civil Rights Movement, and Queer Mental Health as a blogger and featured columnist. Brynn presents the first-person narrative of her 8th-grade daughter about what it is like to have a transgender parent.

NO: Caitlin White is a writer in Brooklyn, New York, and a regular contributor to *Brooklyn Magazine*. Caitlin writes poignantly about the challenges she experienced when her parent came out to her as transgender. While an advocate of trans people, she writes about the difficulties faced by a child whose parent changes their gender identity.

In order to consider a question about transgender parents, it is first necessary to have a basic understanding of the concepts of gender and transgender. With that understanding, you will be able to consider some of the complex issues that arise when thinking about issues that affect people who have a transgender experience. While the description below is not comprehensive (which would result in this introduction taking up pages and pages of the text), it should provide a basic understanding that can inform your thinking.

To begin, it is important to differentiate between biological sex (which is a function of hormones, chromosomes, and genitals) and gender (which is a complex combination of societal expectations that are based upon people's beliefs about who people are or should be as a result of their biological sex).

Biological sex is a category into which people are placed, usually by a doctor, by the time that they are born. In most cases, when a person is pregnant, the first question that is asked of the parent is, "Is it a boy or a girl?" In this case, the question comes from a desire to know about the anatomy of the child. Will it be born with a penis or a vulva? Biological sex is more complex that genital anatomy and can include many combinations of hormones, chromosomes, and genital configurations. Most common is a combination of those factors that result in a child being assigned male or female, with males having a combination of factors that result in genitals that include a penis and females having a combination of factors that result in a vulva. There are some combinations of hormones, chromosomes, and genital configurations that result in a condition that doctors refer to as intersex. While this may be an experience about which you may have some curiosity, it is outside of the scope of this discussion. I have provided a resource at the end of this chapter for folks who would like to know more.

Gender is what people want to do with the knowledge that they have (or think that they have) about a baby's biology. They want to know if they should buy blue or pink onesies as gifts for the baby shower. Gender is grounded in what people believe about the appropriate roles and expectations that they should have for a person. You can see this not only in the ways that people think about clothing, but also in the ways that they describe people of different genders. Girls are sugar and spice and everything nice. Boys are snakes and snails and puppy dog tails.

Research tells us that around the age of three, children have internalized enough of the messages about boys and girls that they develop an internal sense of who they are, either a boy or a girl. That internal sense of who they are is often referred to as someone's gender identity. Research also tells us that once someone has established a stable gender identity, that it is not possible to change that understanding.

It is important to understand that the construct of gender is a powerful force in contemporary culture. The stores that you shop in are divided into departments by gender. The bathrooms you use are divided by gender. Many religious practices are divided by gender. Our social world is very invested in a traditional understanding of gender, and culturally we are very adamant that people perform the roles that we have identified for them based upon which gender category we believe they fit into. In fact, people actively police one another if folks engage in behaviors that are not considered appropriate for the gender box that we believe they do or should fit into. We do this when we tell boys not to cry, to "man up", to be strong. For girls, we do this when we tell them to be nice, to smile, to cooperate. We see this in gendered professions (doctors and nurses) as well as in gendered ways of relating (girls are emotional; boys are stoic).

Complicating this discussion is the reality that current U.S. culture largely thinks about gender using a binary system. People are girls or boys, one or the other. In the last decade, a more complex, and some argue more accurate was of identifying gender arose. In this conception of gender, there are more categories that exist. These include genderqueer, gender nonbinary, gender non-conforming, and others. Again, explaining this in detail would make this introduction too long to be helpful, but I have included a resource for those of you who are interested in learning more.

For the sake of this discussion, consider the ideas of biological sex and gender identity. For people who have a transgender experience, there are important ways in which their gender identity does not match their biological sex. Who they are at their core in regards to gender does not fit the gender box that society wants them to fit into based on their biological sex. In many cases, this causes a great deal of anxiety and grief.

The anxiety and grief do not come from an internal place of mental illness, however. The challenges that transgender people experience come largely from the experience of being forced by their surroundings to conform to society's gender roles. They experience humiliation and shame from their families, who often try to "fix" their gender atypical interests. They experience bullying and violence when they make attempts to be themselves because they dare to engage in behaviors that are not "appropriate" for the box that have been forced into. As they grow into adulthood they often keep their internal struggle a secret, fearing the loss of family and friends if their secret was known. In some cases, they get married to people in order to fulfill the expectations of an unforgiving society.

When people who are transgender do tell others about their difference, they often experience humiliation, loss, and violence. For trans people of color, the likelihood of experiencing violence increases significantly. In the vast majority of cases, transgender people face an overwhelming battle in their attempt to be true to who they know they are.

In this chapter, we take a look at the experience of children who have transgender parents. Rather than exploring this issue from the lens of medicine or research, I am asking you to explore this concept from the personal accounts of two real people. Both of them have parents who are transgender. Both of them know about their parents' trans experience. Both of them love their trans parent.

As you read the articles, consider a few questions: How does each person think about their parent? What life experiences have informed how they feel? Where do some of their struggles come from? Do their words offer you any insight into their parent's experiences with being transgender?

YES ↵

Brynn Tannehill

Here's What It's REALLY Like Having A Transgender Parent

An 8th grader shares her personal experiences.

Katherine, aka "Honey Badger" is on the right. Mom is trying to contain Liam, and Maddy is on the left with Kyra.

A while back I ran across an article by a woman who had a transgender parent and still hasn't forgiven them for transitioning, decades after their death. She keeps trying to tell the world how having a parent that is transgender is just terrible, and that people should be legally prohibited from transitioning because won't someone PLEASE think of the children! She also runs a reparative therapy organization promoted by the Family Research Council, an anti-LGBT hate group. But, you know, details.

This article came up over dinner, and our 8th grade daughter was mortified. She asked me if she could write about her own experiences with a transgender parent to give people a perspective that isn't based on the presumption that transgender people are somehow broken, sinful, and in need of fixing. This is what she had to say.

How a can child have a good family life if one of their parents is forced to constantly lie to them while hating themselves for being different? This may seem like an odd situation to be in, but many transgender parents face this problem. My name is Kate "Honey Badger" Tannehill and I have a transgender parent.

My siblings and I chose the name Maddy when "Dad" was transitioning. Maddy is a combination of Mom and Daddy. We chose this new name for three reasons. The first being it would be confusing having two heads sticking out of doors every time we yell "MOM!" down the hall. Secondly it would feel wrong calling our parent "Dad" as she wore a skirt and makeup. Lastly we chose this name because we found it ironic because "Dad" (pre-transition) was often sad or upset. After her transition she became much nicer though.

People sometimes ask me "Weren't you confused?" or "Were you surprised?" or the best one of all, "I don't think I could have gone through that. You poor thing you were so young." It didn't really affect me or surprise me. My sister and I would play games where one of us would be the prince and one of us would be the princess so being someone of the opposite gender than the one you were born in wasn't new territory. My sister and I at the time didn't fully grasp the situation but we weren't as affected by it as people think. It just was what it was.

I remember talking to Maddy one night in the car as she drove me home from dance class. She started crying because she felt so awful about lying to us kids for all those years. I just told her that I was thankful that she was finally being honest. Then told her to pay attention to the road because there was traffic, but my point still stands.

My parents brought me to some of their therapy sessions after I started claiming that Maddy was my Aunt when people started asking who this new woman was who was picking me up from dance. However I only used the excuse of her being my Aunt with adults. With people who were my own age I was completely honest. When kids started asking about Maddy volunteering at the after school running club I told them the whole story. To be honest I hated the running club, mostly because I prefer binge watching Netflix and eating pizza rather than running half a mile.

Life now is good, if not your average suburban life. I get decent grades in school and am part of the after school theater club. I have fun with my friends after school sometimes, we typically walk across the road and hang out at Starbucks or the fro-yo place. My life isn't boring but it's not worth making a drama series about either.

Maddy's coming out has helped me become a more open and accepting person. As my parents and I can attest to, I am a Hufflepuff. (For all the people reading this who aren't avid Harry Potter fans, Hufflepuffs are people who are willing to accept people as they are regardless of how they were born.) Maddy has also given me a more in depth view of the LGBT community from meeting allies and other members of the community (who also happen to be Maddy's friends). Her friends have always been really nice to me and have always been willing to talk to me like a grown-up, unlike a lot of other adults I know. I'm not saying that everyone who is LGBT is kind, but they have all been willing to treat me the way I want to be treated.

All together I feel that Maddy's transition was good for the family as a whole. Don't get me wrong, my parents annoy me to no end, but the ways they irritate me are the usual reasons why you would expect a teenager to be mad at her parents. My reasons for annoyance vary from being forced to clean my room to folding laundry, to insisting I be nice to my sister. Worst of all is how they're always embarrassing me in front of my friends.

I know one day we will have to answer my younger brother's questions as to why he has two moms. He was less than a year old when Maddy transitioned. I just hope when he asks these questions it is in a future where being transgender, or having a transgender parent, is no big deal.

BRYNN TANNEHILL graduated from the Naval Academy with a BS in computer science in 1997. She earned her Naval Aviator wings in 1999 and did four overseas deployments. In 2008, Brynn earned an MS in Operations Research from the Air Force Institute of Technology and began working as a senior defense research scientist in private industry. She began transitioning in 2010. Since then she has written for the New York Times, Slate, Salon, Huffington Post, The Advocate, LGBTQ Nation, and USA Today as a blogger and featured columnist. Her first book, *Everything You Ever Wanted to Know About Trans* (*But Were Afraid to Ask)* was published in 2018. She lives with her wife Janis and their three children in Northern Virginia.

Caitlin White  **NO**

A Void Wider Than Gender

Here's what my life has been like since my father came out as trans.

"For all intents and purposes, Cait, I identify as a woman."

We were sitting around the barbecue on old flimsy lawn chairs perched on the blacktop of my long driveway, the one my grandpa poured with my dad when they built this house in the mid 90s. I was home from Brooklyn, visiting my parents in the sleepy wine-country town in Oregon where I grew up. I had been fired the week before and hoped home would be a solace. I wasn't even in Oregon to visit my parents—I'd come back for the wedding of my high school best friend. I'd come to my hometown for one day so my parents could meet my new boyfriend, the first serious one I'd had. They'd taken us from winery to winery, eager to impress my guest. He was there, inside, passed out on the couch from too much wine. I had drunk enough to be nearly blacked out myself.

My mother and sister already knew. My dad hadn't told me or my brothers yet since we lived farther away on the East Coast and were rarely home. We'd spent the evening barbecuing, like we always did, when my dad came out to me as transgender. It was the worst moment of my life so far.

I've been winding my anger up inside like an old pocket watch ever since. I was angry that in 25 years I'd never known the true self of someone I loved so much. I was angry, too, that my dad wasn't him, my father, but a specter; an idea of a man, a summation of guesses, an empty mask. I refused to fully accept the assertion, even as *"This is why"* tiles began falling into place in my memory, spelling out the truth like a demented Scrabble game. *"This is why dad cries all the time." "This is why dad is suicidal and constantly depressed." "This is why dad has disordered eating." "This is why my expectations about men are always tragically off."* A woman for a father? The irony of it is almost Shakespearean: the hyper-conservative man

of the church, secretly wrestling with fluidity of gender, a truth that flew in the face of those beliefs. What kind of person can make a whole self up? What was it like to feel like you had to?

My father is a former Christian preacher, worship leader, and staunchly conservative blog reader. Especially after 9/11, my dad would come straight home from work and read political updates on conservative sites until my bedtime. My parents' beat-up van still has a Bush/Cheney bumper sticker on it. The man who raised me was abusive, manipulative, and selfish, plagued by rampant insecurities and narcissism. There was no disagreeing with my father's political or religious views. Ever. There was no sparing of the proverbial rod of punishment in our house either. Actually, belts were more common than rods. As an adult, when I make a mistake my first reaction is still a rush of fear that I will be punished somehow. My father's punishments were physically abusive, but I think the emotional abuse hurt much more. I struggle daily with fear that I will be belittled or mocked for my opinions, especially dissenting ones. But I love my dad so much. I did whatever I could to never disappoint my father. Anything that fell outside of the ridiculously narrow spectrum of appropriate sexuality was a sin, so I dutifully attended purity retreats as a pre-teen. I remember meekly signing my commitment to abstain from sex of any kind until marriage. I didn't think I even had a choice, really.

After college, I finally began to think for myself about many of the beliefs my parents held, but it's hard to shake the commandments of childhood. My gut instinct when it comes to expressing my sexuality, or even supporting liberal political views, is still guilt. Sometimes, I get jealous of my friends who grew up with the freedom to explore their own beliefs. I was denied that. I felt a hyper-specific, steely anger that my dad had been grappling internally with aspects of these doctrines all along, even while foisting them on me and my siblings. Even while I felt I could never tell my dad any of my own real feelings about issues like this. I already supported LGBT people before my dad came out. (Currently, my parents attend a church that supports the LGBT community. Many factions of Christianity, too, are self-correcting to embrace all gender identities.)

. . .

"Language is important. Using accurate terminology is the first step toward creating a respectful story about transgender people."

Though it's been almost two years since that night, I often still feel trapped there. No, I'm not OK, but thank you for asking. It will not be fine. The formative man in my life was, in actuality, a woman. My dad isn't here anymore. I miss that man so much sometimes I don't want to be here either. I wonder what she will be like, even as she emerges. You're losing someone. You're gaining someone. It's messy. There's no right or wrong way to feel. Supporters of the transgender community, very well-meaning allies, will tell me I'm misgendering my father—the most fundamental masculine figure in my life for nearly 30 years—if I slip and say *he* instead of *she*. I have the right to take time, to hurt, and work through this. Sometimes I still say *he*. It will never be hateful; it's only habit. There's a difference between swapping out pronouns for trans public figures and grappling with the gender-flipped identity of your most prominent male figure. I say *she* whenever I remember to. I forget most often when I'm talking to my siblings. We have a shared memory of the man who raised us.

I support my father's transition, but I am still grieving. Not only do I not have a dad now, in reality, I never had one. Though I am peripheral to the transgender identity, I'm not peripheral to the consequences of being raised by someone who hates themselves. I grew up thinking it was normal to despise your own body. I was not immune to the intense dysphoria that was passed down, imbued in me by a person trapped between two genders. What I cannot get back is the chance to grow up without a suicidal streak that suggested this life was not enough—nothing would ever be enough. That void is deep and wide, wider than gender. I am not ready for this strange woman to come into my heart and replace my dad. I am not ready to admit that they are one and the same.

There's no road map for what I should do next. Mostly, I feel alone. I grieve. I am questioning nearly 30 years of memories. Are those years lost or just murky? Why didn't I figure it out? This endless parsing of the past is its own kind of grief. I thought if I tried hard enough I could write or say something that would make this anger go away. I thought if I went through enough drafts of my story I'd land on the one that paints me as the Ideal Daughter struggling with this awkward, bungled burden. No one in this essay is a hero. It's just me in my weird universe, watching my father slip away, a strange woman looming on the horizon.

There's a difference between endorsing something in an abstract sense and having it presented to you unflinchingly. And as much as you want the people you love the most to be happy, it doesn't make it easier to reconcile. I support transgender rights. I miss my dad. I still feel angry. Those are the three things I feel deepest on most days, and they're not contradictory. This essay is only one moment, a Polaroid maybe, but I desperately need this snapshot to make it through. Maybe you need it too.

. . .

"You still have two parents who love you; you should feel lucky."

I kept the knowledge secret for months, even from my own brothers, as I was requested to do. My father couldn't bear to tell his sons, thinking their devastation would stem from another place more directly related to their conceptions of manhood. I still urged their inclusion. How could our family move on and accept this new gender identity without full disclosure? Splintering us into factions felt unfair. Later, over Christmas, they learned of the situation in calm, quiet, and sober family conversations. I envied them for this.

After they knew, I finally told a friend. Then, emboldened, I told another. The second one was the doozy. I fell to pieces at how others knowing made it real—my life reflected in empathetic eyes that actually understood the cost of this.

Since I know you'll ask, my mother is staying. People seem to think that is a noble deed. There's no essay on how much I want my mother to leave. I wish so much that she'd go discover what kind of life she might really like to have, like my father finally will. If you asked a different question, I could tell you how I feel this decision to be her final prison: another sacrifice she's made in a long line of things given up to make her husband happy, to make us kids happy. She'd always put herself last while fielding my dad's mood swings, raising four kids, and working night jobs so we could pay our mortgage. Is she doing this out of duty, or is it what she really wants? I'm not sure she's even asked herself that.

I want to tell you about my father getting her ID checked at the store by bitter, leering clerks. I want to tell you about my dad claiming to understand the crushing weight of the patriarchy, something this person had previously enforced in my life for decades. I'm just not sure that's true. Her understanding of those gendered forces will always be different from mine. For instance, I do not understand the vitriol she will face for the rest of her life. I do not know the full scope of the dysphoria she was born with and bore for 50 years. But I watched my dad relegate me, my sister, and my mother to strictly traditional gender roles for my entire life. We did the dishes while the boys watched sports. We weren't allowed to date, but my brothers could. Could she ever understand the contradictions that she dictated? I thought it was a man I resented all along. Imagine my surprise.

No one really wants to cope with the tangled web of pronouns, psychology, and taboo that a transgender father brings along with it. It's hard work. It's cumbersome. Even if they do care, there's no script for their terrified sympathy. They especially do not want to hear me describe how I felt that first night (not again) sobbing in my car, my body wracked with tears until I puked, gazing up at the looming mess of this. Of all the things I'd believed and supported because my father wanted me to, this was the one that felt like too much. A final straw. It felt like the one thing that all those other convictions had been a distraction from or a cover for.

My father's transition took a toll on my relationship too. The night my dad came out, I dragged my boyfriend to the car and drove him down the deserted back road where I'd always taken my small-town pain. I couldn't stop crying as I told him the news. He sat bleary-eyed and drunk beside me, already backing away: I should reach out to my siblings instead of him, he said. I remember weeks down the line, realizing he had no real grasp of the fundamental nature of the transgender experience. Still, it's not like he didn't try. I remember the nights when he'd wake up to my crying and comfort me, hold me until he fell back asleep. I would not fall asleep. I would watch him and think about how much I loved him, how very unlikely it was that our fledgling relationship could stand all this. We started drifting. I was unable to be any sort of partner to him. I was a walking wound. He began spending more time at the office, at the bar, anywhere but with me, perpetually at home, glued to my mascara-blackened pillow. I still blame my dad for thrusting a psychological earthquake into my relationship. I saw it as another casualty of my father's war with herself. I will never get my first love back: an exacting price from an exacting process.

While my world unspooled and the cornerstone of my family unit disintegrated, my friends defected, too. They opted for the less emotional—less dramatic, they'll say—choice in the breakup. I didn't know how to deal with losing my first love, not on top of coping with my dad's transition, but mostly because of it. I still don't. You could say it is going poorly. People began lying so they didn't have to deal with me. The ultimate, deafening conclusion is that my pain doesn't matter. Not to the people I thought loved me, and certainly not to society. Former friends still insist on greeting me cheerily when I see them at social functions, but months ago, when I was barely holding on, they denied my desperate requests for a drink, a hug, a text. Eventually, I learned to stop asking. Small pockets of people knowing about the situation had other consequences. My boundaries were often violated. Most hurtful was the uninvited confidant who pretended I shared the situation with them when I hadn't. Probably a well-intentioned effort at empathy, but loaded with the unsettling, disorienting tell that those who do know discussed this behind your back with third parties. Of course they did. It is a grief too big to be private, but that does not make it feel public.

This is an issue people don't want to be involved in, not really. People don't know how to respond because the emphasis in these situations is never on the family as a whole but on the individual, the "hero." I must be a relentless ally, simply because everyone else, detached from nearly three decades of family dynamics, perceives that to be the only proper response. Do I want my father to be happy? You're goddamn right I do. The slightest smirk, slur, or sideways glance toward anyone in any stage of transition induces a hurricane of rage in the very center of my body. When it recedes, I am still there, in the center of what remains a lonely and devastated place.

. . .

"I'm nothing if I can't be me. If I can't be true to myself, they don't mean anything."

We are in the midst of a breakthrough moment for transgender identity. In 2013, Laverne Cox portrayed a transgender woman on the incredibly popular show *Orange Is the New Black*. It was one of the show's major plot lines for the first season. It was also the first time I had really considered the trans identity. Cox is a beautiful and strong trans woman whom I admire for her intersectionality and capacity for love. She was on the cover of *Time* magazine at the end of last year, keeping her chin up. She is a force of good in the world. Chelsea Manning is a US soldier who entered the public eye for disclosing military secrets, and after these charges revealed her gender identity as a woman, her experience shed light on the difficult, tenuous relationship trans and LGBT people have with our military community. Laura Jane Grace of Against Me! publicly transitioned and then wrote a powerful album about it with the no-holds-barred title *Transgender Dysphoria Blues*. You have no idea how many enthusiastic straight people and trans allies have asked me if I've watched *Transparent* yet. For the record, I have not. I'm proud that a daughter shared her story, but why cast a cis man to portray a trans woman? Difficult plot lines usually aren't as moving or poignant if you're currently living them.

Last fall, the suicide of a **young trans teen named Leelah Alcorn** became a flashpoint for religious disavowal of transgender existence. Leelah's suicide note is heartbreaking, but what's worse, it's merely one life we've lost to the insidious force of suicide that claims countless trans lives every year. We lose an actual countless number of trans and gender-nonconforming lives because so many of their deaths go unreported. Many are homeless. Many are teens. Few are as beautiful as Laverne Cox or Caitlyn Jenner. We have a long way to go.

Jenner's *Vanity Fair* cover story was, in its own way, a triumph. I applaud her. Many people are happy to send a few positive tweets when someone with **every resource imaginable** comes out in a glamorous cover shoot. But the transition process is not all **"be free now pretty bird"** tweets, though the strength it took for Kendall Jenner to write that floors me. Transitioning does not occur in the space of two-hour interviews or a smoldering magazine cover. That is what no one gets. No one seems to really consider the toll that hiding your true identity might take on the individual.

Gender dysphoria manifests itself in certain ways long before a person begins their transition. My father was not well. Her suicidal thoughts, blue-black depression, and eating disorders haunted my childhood. There is no space on a *Vanity Fair* cover for my abuse. Do you know how hard it is to even admit the word *abuse*? The shame it carries is outweighed only by my fear of how deeply that word will cut. There's no easy way to explain how much more I need to say this then, to voice what I endured at the hands of this secret. I do not need you to tell me how you are awed by Caitlyn's beauty. I do not find your memes funny. So many of these "advocates" would probably laugh and squirm if they saw me standing on the street next to my father. Is there room anywhere in the world for my disgust at your flimsy, myopic support?

Personally, watching the spectacle of Caitlyn's Jenner's transition while still privately coping with my own father's process is the hardest thing yet. My name itself is caught up in the relentless Kardashian current. Jenner and I now share a name—I'm Caitlin with an "i," she's Caitlyn with a "y." Someone else **cheerily wrote about sharing this name for** the *New York Times*, but it

has been a hard coincidence for me. Worse than what feels like disingenuous support is the certain subset of people who won't stop hacking Caitlyn's *Vanity Fair* cover to bits, sneering and simpering even if no hate speech is technically uttered. As they say her name it rings in my ears as mine. It rings in my ears as hate speech against my father. I left work early the day the cover broke in a state of near-collapse. Thankfully, I have sensitive and caring bosses who support me. I am one of the lucky ones. Learn. Be kind. That is how you support transgender people and those of us who love them, who are hurt by careless, smirking asides and salacious gossip. Their surgeries are not headlines. Their bodies are not punchlines.

Now that my name is caught up in part of the Kardashian's narrative, it gets harder to distinguish between me and them. That Kim, Khloé, and Kourtney—and Kylie and Kendall, especially—might feel this same anger, hurt, and confusion is comforting. That they broadcasted none of it was helpful for everyone but me and other children of transgender parents. God fucking bless Khloé for being the only one who was **honest about her anger** when Caitlyn wasn't candid with them about the pace or nature of her transition. That is the only thing I saw in those episodes that I identified with. Maybe that, and a shot of Kendall curled up on the couch, her face an impassive mask, looking slowly and quietly around the room at her father and her sisters.

Peripherally, that Kanye West is one of Caitlyn's strongest proponents in this narrative is incredibly comforting. He is my favorite creative being on the planet. That Kanye has pondered the same situation I am facing and come down firmly in absolute support of Caitlyn is a soothing joy, unlike anything I've felt thus far. If Kanye loves Caitlyn, he would love my dad. This love is a counterweight to the hate and fear my father will face for the rest of her life. This is how your support for transgender people matters; it expands outward in waves.

. . .

"What if you allow yourself to call it abuse, then what? It doesn't change anything, it doesn't undo anything, doesn't make you a better or worse person, nor dad."

What will happen if I speak? Will my anger and grief be my sin? I have every right to love this person and grieve my father's vaporization at the same time. I can challenge the abuse I faced without vilifying a new woman, wobbly-kneed in identity. There are layers of hurt here the Jenner-Kardashian saga makes no attempt to capture. Then again, that anyone **should begrudge the Jenner**

children their privacy on this matter infuriates me. There is no winning. Perhaps my grief is not in the best interest of the cause. Some days I am too exhausted to care about the cause.

I need a venue for telling my father I love her, but things have to change beyond gender for this relationship to be repaired. It's not all different immediately. She has a new name, different hair, but the same patterns exist even under those new clothes. The removal of a mask also lets me finally see the mask and the psyche behind it.

My father is transitioning, and I am trying to grasp the decades of emotional and physical abuse that stemmed from her severe depression and buried dysphoria. This is the part that is much harder to cope with than any concept of gender. Her abusive patterns developed long before I was born, when her own mother belittled and destroyed her emotional health, grieving the loss of an infant son born before this child. It is OK that I am struggling to accept my father's new identity, especially since her fight against it has been hurting me my whole life.

Throughout it all, there were bursts of the human she wished to be—pure, sensitive, even understanding—but only within certain parameters. Her imagination is endless, her joy can be infectious, and sometimes I'm overwhelmed by her compassion for others. But it can all turn to anger and hatefulness so quickly. It's hard to feel safe around a person like that. It's hard to heal around a person like that. We haven't spoken in months, but that does not mean I don't love my father. Transgender people are not making a choice. I have watched this person struggle for decades to be happy. I have seen her balk at her failure to do so, one part bewildered and one part simply wearied of the attempts. Now, finally, I see her. She seems happy.

My mom asked me to write this essay anonymously or not at all. But I am not anonymous. I am Caitlin. I have lived with anonymous pain and grief for two years. She said she does not think it is anyone's business. That cannot be the case as we move through the current political climate and this volatile revolution in the way transgender people are represented in society. Today, I am coming out too: My father is living openly as a transgender woman. I want to live openly as her daughter. This is not something I am ashamed of or a secret I have to keep hidden away. I am tired of listening to people's disrespectful, ignorant opinions and saying nothing. I want people to know why this issue carries specific urgency for me. I am proud to be part of the greater trans community of supporters and allies, even as I continue to struggle with how those things might manifest themselves. If no one speaks about this experience, whether it is transgender people themselves or their families, how will others learn? It is everyone's business to educate themselves and to make this conversation happen at a national and global level.

Supporting the transgender people in your life does not mean pretending they are perfect, flawless beings. They are not heroes or angels. They are humans. The utter loss of experience—a childhood, an entire life as their affirmed gender identity—is heartbreaking for transgender people. Many try to deny them their true existence or any existence at all. They are crushed and coerced into fragile shells of experience they do not wish to embody. No one understands what it feels like to be so hurt by this person, to be devastated by your own grief, and still wish you had the capability to give them everything they want. I see now that most of my father's decisions as a parent were guided by fear. Now that I know the root of that terror was to be discovered or found out, I don't feel as betrayed by it. I can redirect some of my anger toward the world that made her feel the need to stay hidden. I see stories of five-year-old children allowed to embrace their true gender identities, and I mourn for the little girl my father never got to be.

I cry for all the dresses and makeup and jewelry my dad lost in that first half a century on earth. Then I cry because I realize I'll never see my dad again in any of the slacks and dress shirts I so carefully helped pick out at Nordstrom. And then, sometimes, I find a way to ruefully laugh at how much my dad always loved shopping more than anyone else in our family besides me. If you can't find the humor in a situation like this, you won't be able to survive it. The moments when I can laugh at the absurdity of gender as a concept at all are the best—the moments when I wish I could throw her a coming-out party instead of dwelling in grief. These moments are few and far between in the darkness of my grief—desolate stars—but they are there. They exist. This is exactly how grief works. This is exactly how healing works and life works. Everything is dark, and then a tiny happiness emerges out of nowhere when you thought it never possibly could.

. . .

"Loving transgender people is a revolutionary act."

I am writing this because I found nothing like it. I am writing something that didn't exist for me. It is the hardest thing I have ever written. For those reading this who are in similar circumstances, know this: Even if it seems like no one stands by you, reaches out, or wants to hear you as a valid and unique human, you can make it through. At least I have to keep believing you can. Even if it means you lose people you love along the way. This is an essay to say that your weird, horrible, secret life is good and worth having. This is an essay for the ones who convinced me of that fact—the ones who refused to stop loving me no matter how far toward dark and destructive my grief took me. Here's an essay to thank the one who held me while I sobbed over a man who wouldn't—or wasn't big enough—to hold me through this. For the one who looked me dead in the eye and told me to stop being a slob and get my apartment together for my own good. Or the one who made me dinner once a week and listened to me leech pain when I couldn't bear to hold it all alone. This is for my friend who made me feel brave and supported enough to publish my thoughts somewhere besides Tumblr. For my sister, who carried my father's secret and supported her many months before I knew and is the strongest woman I know. For my brother, who proves that good men do exist. And ever for her, my dad, whom I love despite, because, and through it all—even if we are never perfect.

If you feel like there is no one else, that is not true. Those who don't support you through transition or gender exploration or abuse recovery or therapy are the only thing not worth having in your life. Your life is worth having. Your life is precious and rare. This experience has taught you deep things about the world others will never know—that is where beauty lives. You don't have to hide. Even when you face negativity and hate, your freedom will make you feel more powerful than any persecution. You can stay standing. I will stand next to you. Compassion will find you; maybe we will find it together. Keep going. Gender is a social construct, and social constructs fade. They always have. Your happiness will not. In all your various states and non-gorgeous attempts at happiness, you are beautiful to me. It took my everything to write this. Take your everything and write more. If my voice exists, then so does yours.

CAITLIN WHITE is a writer in Brooklyn, New York, and a regular contributor to *Brooklyn Magazine*.

EXPLORING THE ISSUE

Does Having a Transgender Parent Hurt Children?

Critical Thinking and Reflection

1. Can you identify the emotional, moral, intellectual, and social components in Brynn's argument?
2. Can you identify the emotional, moral, intellectual, and social components in Caitlin's argument?
3. Can you identify your own emotional, moral, intellectual, and social responses to this argument?
4. What are some similarities and differences between your responses and the authors?

Is There Common Ground?

There are a number of things that both of these authors have in common. The first, is that they love their parent. Although the experiences of one author include a great deal of pain that was passed on from her parent's own experience of pain, the love that she has for the person she knew as her father is still present. The second is that both support transgender people beyond their own parent. Neither argument is a challenge to the right of each person to be authentic in their own skin. Also shared between the two is the belief that the problems that trans people experience are the result of societal pressures to conform to binary gendered expectations. Perhaps if there was less pressure for people to fit into narrow boxes of male and female, perhaps if we were able to disconnect our social expectations of others from their biological sex, more people would be able to authentically express themselves in their lives and there would be less violence in the world.

Additional Resources

Green, E.R. & Maurer, L. (2015). *The Teaching Transgender Toolkit: A Facilitator's Guide to Increasing Knowledge, Reducing Prejudice and Building Skills*. Out for Health & Planned Parenthood of the Southern Finger Lakes: Ithaca, NY.

Rudacille, D. (2006). *The Riddle of Gender*. Random House: New York.

Stryker, S. (2008). *Transgender History*. Seal Press/Hachette Book Group: New York.

Internet References . . .

Gender Spectrum

www.genderspectrum.org

Human Rights Campaign

https://www.hrc.org/explore/topic/transgender?utm_
source=GS&utm_medium=AD&utm_campaign=
BPI-HRC-Grant&utm_content=276042104804&utm_
term=what%20is%20transgender&gclid=
EAlaIQobChMImY_N2fXR3gIV0IuGCh0mHwyh
EAAYASAAEgI4FfD_BwE

Intersex Society of North America

http://www.isna.org/

National Center for Transgender Equity

https://transequality.org

Unit 2

UNIT

Contemporary Issues in Relationships

*A*s human beings, we spend a great deal of our lives seeking out, engaging in, and maintaining intimate relationships. In a culture dominated by Disney expectations of finding our soulmate and spending the rest of our lives in wedded bliss, we frequently crash into challenges that force us to reconsider that expectation. This unit explores some of the controversial issues that affect our romantic relationships.

Selected, Edited, and with Issue Framing Material by:
Don Dyson, *Widener University*

ISSUE

Is Cybersex "Cheating"?

YES: Susan A. Milstein, from "Virtual Liaisons: Cybersex Is Cheating," Original essay written for this volume (2009)

NO: Crystal Bedley, from "Virtual Reality: Cybersex Is Not Cheating," Original essay written for this volume (2009)

Learning Outcomes

After reading this issue, you will be able to:

- Identify the major arguments made for and against whether cybersex is cheating.
- Compare and contrast the competing arguments made for and against cybsersex as cheating in this issue.
- Evaluate the implications of cybersex on the impact this has on dating, marriage, and other intimate relationships.

ISSUE SUMMARY

YES: Susan Milstein is a Certified Health Education Specialist and a Certified Sexuality Educator. She is an Associate Professor in the Department of Health Enhancement at Montgomery College in Maryland, as well as the Lead Consultant for Milstein Health Consulting. Milstein contends that while it is diffcult to create a universal definition of cheating, the majority of people feel that cybersex outside of a primary relationship is cheating.

NO: Crystal Bedley argues that the anonymous nature of cybersex means that it is not cheating.

What is your definition of infidelity? Does it include flirting? Phone sex? Sexting? If you are in a committed relationship, does your significant other have the same definition? Too often, couples fail to have this conversation. In the event that this conversation occurs, they may find that they have significantly different definitions of what is monogamy as well as what is infidelity. This divergence in definitions can lead to significant conflict within a relationship. The differences may very well be vast without even raising the topic of cybersex.

Infidelity is a common occurrence in American society. Most people know more than one person who has been unfaithful. National headlines are full of famous Americans who had been unfaithful to their spouses: Eliot Spitzer, John Edwards, A-Rod, Tiger Woods, and Peter Cook, Christie Brinkley's former husband. All of these cases involved real life, in-person affairs.

However, cybersex is creating new types of headlines among the powerful. A conservative Congressman from Florida was caught sending sexually explicit text messages to teenage pages working in Washington, DC. A couple of years later, a liberal Congressman from New York was caught sending similar photos, but these were to young women on Twitter. For both men, the scandal destroyed their political careers. While this case did not involve the question of whether this was cheating, it raised a national dialogue regarding the expected norms related to virtual sex.

Infidelity dates as far back in human history as marriage. Sometimes infidelity is sanctioned by society or the spouse, but it is typically forbidden. Infidelity can lead to marital breakups, creating great stress and instability in people's lives. It is highly unlikely for in-person infidelity to guarantee anonymity.

Cyberspace has fundamentally altered the landscape for meeting others, particularly for anonymous sexual encounters. Now without leaving one's home, with minimal risk of meeting someone one knows, a person can have written, spoken, or streaming video cybersex with different people at any time. Indeed, one can log on at any time and find a significant number of people looking to meet someone.

In fact, there is not even a need to be yourself. Online, people change their hair color, height, weight, eye color, sexual history, age, race, and gender. It is possible to have cybersex with a level of anonymity that cannot be realized in person. One can live out their sexual fantasies without fear of rejection from someone they care about, or even know who they are. With the opportunity for sexually explicit virtual meetings, the personal risk of being identified recedes.

Cybersex has created a new dimension, a potential form of twenty-first-century infidelity, depending on one's definition of infidelity. This is new terrain that presents a unique set of challenges. The lines of what is cheating may be difficult to draw with new technology. Even if you determine that certain scenarios are off limits, temptation to stray is virtually omnipresent when in the privacy of your own residence.

Before reading this issue, write down your definition of infidelity. Include a definition of what types of cybersex, if any, you regard as being unfaithful. Does anything on your list surprise you? While reading, examine the ways in which the authors' assessment compares and contrasts with your values. What are some ways in which your beliefs were supported? What are some of the ways in which they were challenged? In addition, what are the generational differences, if any, of views of cybersex and infidelity?

Have you ever hid something from your significant other that you feared would make him or her jealous? Maybe texting an ex? Visiting a strip club? Going out to a platonic dinner with someone you find attractive? While none of these incidents are physical sexual encounters with another person, many people will conceal these encounters out of fear that their significant other will regard them as being unfaithful in their relationship. Each incident described has some degree of emotional or physical interaction. In contrast, cybersex can be nonphysical and anonymous. Facing reduced risks for exposure and regular access to virtual sexual encounters, cybersex creates a new set of boundaries to be negotiated in a relationship.

Cybersex potentially changes the ways in which trust is extended within a relationship. While access to anonymous sexual encounters may be a threatening prospect to many, there is a fundamental question which needs to be asked and evaluated that has not changed despite the virtual world of sexual relations: What is a healthy relationship?

Write down what you consider to be the most important qualities of a healthy relationship. Then rank how important the different qualities are. This should provide a larger perspective related to cybersex and infidelity. Whether the Internet exists or not, the qualities of healthy relationships should remain constant.

Once you have identified your views about sexual infidelity and cybersex, are you ready to talk about your criteria with a significant other? How might you respond to answers that may differ from yours? Specifically, weigh whether or not you can negotiate if you have decidedly different values related to cybersex and infidelity. How much are you willing to compromise your beliefs? What are your expectations related to how your significant other will compromise his or her beliefs?

If you are in a relationship that lacks equality or fails to communicate respectfully, you may find that this conversation is difficult to have. If you are in a relationship of equality and mutual respect, this conversation is far easier, provided that you and your partner feel comfortable having frank conversations about sexuality. Keep in mind that it is normal to struggle when having frank conversations about sexuality. It might be a good idea to acknowledge that at the start of such a conversation and not to be too hard on yourself if the conversation is challenging.

Melanie Davis, an expert on communicating about sexuality within families and relationships, advises that a person do the following in starting this conversation: "The first thing is for the person who wants to bring up the conversation to define the purpose of the conversation. It is just curiosity, or is there some sort of fear? Or is there a need to disclose something? That can help you get into the right frame of mind. If you think your partner is cheating on you, it might come across as accusing the person, and that is never an effective way to start a conversation. The other thing to consider is where you're going to have the conversation. It is probably not a conversation you want to have in the middle of a crowded restaurant. If you fear what will be disclosed, you might want to have the conversation in the presence of a counselor or a therapist who can help guide the conversation."

Davis adds, "Sometimes you just want to test the waters conversationally. A good way to do that is to remark about a TV show or an article that you read, something that can get you to that topic of conversation in a neutral way."

Once these conversations begin, you may find that they are likely to get easier, provided you have a cooperative and supportive partner. If these conversations cannot occur, it may not be surprising if people get hurt when they lack a full understanding of each other's boundaries and their rationale behind them.

YES

Susan A. Milstein

Virtual Liaisons: Cybersex Is Cheating

Consider the following behaviors: flirting with a coworker, engaging in intimate phone calls or sending love letters to someone other than your partner, looking at sexually explicit images while masturbating, having a one-night stand. Would any of these behaviors be cheating?

You may have answered "yes" to none, some, or all of these behaviors, whereas your partner's answers may have been very different. For this reason, defining cheating can be difficult. Many couples may never take the time to sit down and discuss what behaviors they consider to be cheating but feel betrayed nonetheless when certain lines are crossed. The lines of what is considered cheating may become even more blurred when the actions in question take place online.

Enter the world of cybersex.

What Is Cybersex?

There is no single definition of cybersex. It is a broad term that may be used to encompass a variety of behaviors, including different methods of communication that happen online like love letter e-mails or instant messages. Sex, Etc. (http://www.sexetc.org/) defines cybersex as "Sexual encounters that take place entirely via the Internet." This would include going on a virtual "date" in a chat room that may involve one or both people masturbating in real life. These dates may happen simply by typing on a keyboard, or they may include the use of webcams and microphones.

Meeting for cybersex can take place in a multitude of places, including chat rooms, inside online games like World of Warcaft, or inside the virtual world of Second Life. Thanks to webcams, Skype, and Googlechat, you don't necessarily need a specific site like a chat room to meet—you just need the time, the technology, and another person. The definition of cybersex will continue to evolve as technology changes, and for some, the new definition will include the use of teledildonics.

For some people, the use of teledildonics with a person other than a significant other crosses yet another boundary in the world of cybersex and infidelity.

So, What Is Cheating?

Many of us associate sexual infidelity with the word "cheating." It involves having sexual contact with someone other than your partner. How much sexual contact is required for it to be cheating will vary from one person's definition to another. It may extend beyond sexual intercourse to include oral sex or kissing, but regardless of how much contact is involved, most of us usually think of something physical when we think of cheating. But, there's more to it than that. Online or offline, cheating on a significant other may involve physical acts, which is called sexual infidelity, or it may involve emotional infidelity (Whisman & Wagers, 2005).

Emotional infidelity occurs when someone is spending time with, giving attention to, or falling in love with someone other than their partner (Shackelford, LeBlanc, and Drass, 2000; Whitty and Quigley, 2008). Regardless of whether it is emotional or sexual infidelity, violating the bounds of one's relationship can lead to anger, jealousy, hurt, resentment, and potentially the ending of the relationship.

Subotnik and Harris (2005) describe four different types of affairs one might see in offline relationships. The first type is the serial affair, where there are a string of one-night stands or affairs that lack both an emotional connection and commitment. The second type of affair is the fling, which can be seen in one-night stands. The other two types of affairs are the romantic love affair and the long-term affair. These two affairs are similar in that there is a deep emotional component to each. One thing that differentiates these two affairs is the amount of time that is invested in each. All of these types of affairs can be carried out online through cybersex, and like offline affairs, they can have a tremendous negative impact on relationships.

Then there's the emotional affair, or what Glass and Staeheli (2003) describe as the "extramarital emotional involvement" (p. 35). This emotional involvement consists of three components: emotional intimacy, secrecy, and sexual chemistry. All three of these components may happen during cybersex, whether it's a one-time "date" in a chat room or an affair which is taking place solely online.

As with offline affairs, relationships where cybersex has occurred face many challenges. The affair may lead to conflict and a decision to separate or divorce as a result of the online cheating (Docan-Morgan and Docan, 2007; Schneider, 2000; Young, Griffin-Shelley, Cooper, O'Mara, and Buchanan, 2000). The partner who was cheated on may feel a host of emotions, including betrayal, abandonment, and shame (Schneider, 2000). Part of the healing process for the partner who was cheated on through cybersex involves learning to cope with what happened and trying to find closure (Maheu and Subotnik, 2001).

Cybersex and Cheating

Research is showing that people do believe that cybersex is cheating and that it can have a negative impact on relationships. One study found that 33 percent of respondents felt that cybersex of any kind was cheating. If certain circumstances occurred, for instance, the use of webcams, or having cybersex repeatedly with the same person, then the number increased to 58 percent (McKenna, Green, and Smith, 2001).

One researcher, Monica Whitty, has completed a number of studies looking at which specific cybersex behaviors people believe constitute infidelity. What she has not been able to do is come up with one list of cybersex behaviors that everyone agrees is cheating. But this is to be expected. If you look back at the behaviors at the beginning of this article, you'll see why one list of "cheating behaviors" will probably never exist for cybersex or for offline behaviors. What her research has shown is that there are many who believe that cybersex is infidelity and that it can have just as much of a negative impact on a relationship as cheating that is done offline (Whitty, 2003, 2005).

The research previously mentioned was done using respondents' opinions based on hypothetical situations. It would be easy to say that what someone says in a hypothetical situation may be different from what that person would say if faced with the same situation in real life. This may be true in that people who have found out that their partners had been engaging in cybersex might be more likely to say that they feel like they were cheated on.

When looking at studies that involved people who had direct experience with cybersex, you can see the negative impact that it has on people and their relationships. One study found that the offline partners of those engaging in cybersex reported feeling hurt, abandoned, and betrayed (Schneider, 2000). In another study, one-quarter of the people surveyed who were engaging in cybersex admitted that it had affected their primary relationship (Underwood and Findlay, 2004).

Given the findings of these studies, it should come as no surprise that therapists are seeing the impact of cybersex among their clients. In one study, a majority of marriage and family therapists reported having clients where cybersex was a problem, and 16 percent of the therapists reported that cybersex was the primary reason why the couple was in therapy (Goldberg, Peterson, Rosen, and Sara, 2008). And this is just the beginning, as the number of people affected seems to be increasing. In the two years prior to the survey, more than half of the therapists said their cybersex caseload had increased (Goldberg, Peterson, Rosen, and Sara, 2008).

Cybersex Is Cheating

We know that people who are involved in committed relationships are having cybersex. In a survey done in 1998, almost 85 percent of people who reported that they were engaging in online sexual activity were either married or in a committed relationship (Maheu and Subotnik, 2001).

We also know that cybersex is viewed by many as cheating and that it can have the same long-term negative impact on relationships that offline infidelity has.

So what's the bottom line? If what one person is doing is going outside the bounds of his or her relationship, then it's cheating, and it doesn't matter if it's in a hotel room or a chat room.

References

T. Docan-Morgan and C. A. Docan, "Internet Infidelity: Double Standards and the Differing Views of Women and Men," *Communication Quarterly* (vol. 55, no. 3, 2007).

S. P. Glass and J. C. Staeheli, *"Not 'Just Friends.' Rebuilding Trust and Recovering Your Sanity after Infidelity* (New York: Free Press, 2003).

P. D. Goldberg, B. D. Peterson, K. H. Rosen, and M. L. Sara, "Cybersex: The Impact of a Contemporary Problem on the Practices of Marriage and Family Therapists," *Journal of Marital and Family Therapy* (vol. 34, no. 4, 2008).

M. M. Maheu, and R. B. Subotnik, *Infidelity in the Internet. Virtual Relationships and Real Betrayal* (Naperville, IL: Sourcebooks, Inc., 2001).

K. Y. A. McKenna, A. S. Green, and P. K. Smith, "Demarginalizing the Sexual Self," *The Journal of Sex Research* (vol. 38, no. 4, 2001).

J. P. Schneider, "Effects of Cybersex Addiction on the Family: Results of a Survey," *Sexual Addiction & Compulsivity* (vol. 7, 2000).

Sex, Etc., "Cyber Sex" (n.d.). Retrieved March 15, 2009, from http://www.sexetc.org/glossary/1148.

T. K. Shackelford, G. J. LeBlanc, and E. Drass, "Emotional Reactions to Infidelity," *Cognition & Emotion* (vol. 14, no. 5, 2000).

R. B. Subotnik and G. G. Harris, "*Surviving Infidelity. Making Decisions, Recovering from the Pain* (Avon, MA: Adams Media, 2005).

H. Underwood and B. Findlay, "Internet Relationships and Their Impact on Primary Relationships," *Behaviour Change* (vol. 21, no. 2, 2004).

M. A. Whisman and T. P. Wagers, "Assessing Relationship Betrayals," *Journal of Clinical Psychology* (vol. 61, no. 11, 2005).

M. T. Whitty, "Pushing the Wrong Buttons: Men's and Women's Attitudes toward Online and Offline Infidelity," *CyberPsychology and Behavior* (vol. 6, no. 6, 2003).

——— "The Realness of Cybercheating. Men's and Women's Representations of Unfaithful Internet Relationships," *Social Science Computer Review* (vol. 23, no. 1, 2005).

M. T. Whitty and L-L. Quigley, "Emotional and Sexual Infidelity Offline and in Cyberspace," *Journal of Marriage and Family Therapy* (vol. 34, no. 4, 2008).

K. S. Young, E. Griffin-Shelley, A. Cooper, J. O'Mara, and J. Buchanan, "Online Infidelity: A New Dimension in Couple Relationships with Implications for Evaluation and Treatment," *Sexual Addiction & Compulsivity* (vol. 7, 2000).

Susan A. Milstein, PhD, is a Master Certified Health Education Specialist and a Certified Sexuality Educator. She is a Professor in the Department of Health Enhancement, Exercise Science and Physical Education at the Rockville Campus of Montgomery College in Maryland. Milstein contends that while it is difficult to create a universal definition of cheating, the majority of people feel that cybersex outside of a primary relationship is cheating.

Crystal Bedley

Virtual Reality: Cybersex Is Not Cheating

As the Internet continues to expand and evolve, so do the possibilities for engaging in sexual encounters online. From chat rooms, to social networking sites, to virtual boy/girlfriends, new technologies are shaping the ways in which desires can be explored and indulged. Couples must navigate these new technologies to determine the role(s) that virtual encounters may or may not play in their relationships. Some people might enjoy engaging in cybersex, whereas their partners may not; some couples may enjoy engaging in cybersex together, whereas others may not. To understand whether a particular cybersex act is a form of cheating, therefore, one must take into account the nature of the relationship. Ultimately, whether cybersex is a form of cheating depends largely on both the interpersonal dynamics of the couple *and* the intentions and perceptions of the cybersex participant.

The term "interpersonal dynamics" refers to the nature of the relationship between the two romantic partners. More specifically, interpersonal dynamics shape how partners come to agree or disagree about the meanings of particular acts (e.g., whether cybersex is a form of cheating). Importantly, the ways in which couples negotiate their relationships, especially when each partner has different expectations, shape how both partners will interpret particular behaviors. For example, few people would argue that, if both partners agree to participate in cybersex together, that their shared action is a form of cheating. Moreover, if one partner communicates to the other partner that she or he would like to engage in cybersex and the other partner consents, then most would agree that the partners are being faithful to one another. Each of these examples demonstrates how the interpersonal dynamics of the couple determine whether cybersex is cheating. The ways partners choose to communicate with one another and the decisions they reach are critical for understanding whether cybersex is cheating or an expression of sexual desires. If both partners share an understanding of cybersex as an expression of sexual desire that does not constitute cheating, then it is clear that cybersex is not cheating. By the same token, if both partners believe the

act of cybersex is cheating, then there is no reason to draw a different conclusion.

In contrast, if a partner deceives the other partner in order to engage in cybersex, one could argue that in this context, cybersex is an act of infidelity. Because relationships are built on mutual trust (among other factors), deception not only serves to destabilize the relationship but also becomes the framework for interpreting the cybersex act as an act of cheating. Importantly, recent research suggests that deception and emotional unavailability are primary reasons why partners view cybersex as equivalent to adultery (Schneider, 2003). In these cases, it is clearer that cybersex is an act of infidelity.

Although there are a variety of ways to engage in cybersex, when it comes to interpreting cybersex as cheating, traditionally the virtual form of the sex act is often inconsequential, trumped by the emotional toll paid by the partners involved in the relationship. Consider the following example:

> Shannon and Kendall are in a long-term committed relationship. Neither partner has been physically or emotionally intimate with anyone outside of the relationship. One day, Kendall decides to participate in a mutual masturbation session with an anonymous person he meets in a chat room. Minutes later, Shannon walks into Kendall's office and witnesses the masturbation session. Devastated by what she sees, Shannon feels that Kendall has cheated. From Shannon's perspective, Kendall's online session is a form of cheating because of the sexual intimacy Kendall shared with the other person. From Kendall's perspective, Shannon is overreacting. Kendall believes that because cybersex does not involve physical contact, it is not cheating. So, Kendall views the cybersex act as a way of exploring one's fantasies in a safe environment.

This scenario illustrates the notion that the same act (in this case, the act of participating in a mutual masturbation session) can be interpreted in different and sometimes conflicting ways. For this reason, I argue that the individual perceptions of each partner are important to understanding whether cybersex should be considered cheating. The expression "individual perceptions" refers to the beliefs and/or attitudes of a person, which shape how the individual will interpret a particular behavior. Unlike interpersonal dynamics, which involve a negotiated agreement (or disagreement) about the meanings attributed to particular acts, individual perceptions are those beliefs held by each individual about the meanings attributed to particular acts, *regardless* of the beliefs of one's partner. To clarify the distinction between individual perceptions and interpersonal dynamics using the current example, it is clear that Kendall's individual perception is that the cybersex act is not a form of cheating, whereas Shannon's perception is that it is cheating. The interpersonal dynamics of the couple can be described as a disagreement over the cybersex act because each partner's perceptions are at odds with the other's.

Because partners can have differing perceptions of the same act, it is critical to also consider each partner's perception of cybersex to understand whether the cybersex is a form of infidelity. On the one hand, let's assume that Shannon is not emotionally hurt by the act of masturbation alone, but rather is hurt that Kendall transgressed upon an important moral boundary in their relationship; namely, that partners are to remain sexually faithful to one another. On the other hand, Kendall does not see cybersex as cheating because the cybersex was used only to facilitate masturbation. Because masturbation has never been considered an act of cheating throughout the course of their relationship, Kendall believes that cybersex is merely another form of masturbation. Therefore, Kendall's perception of cybersex as masturbation reinforces the belief that Kendall is remaining sexually faithful to Shannon. Undoubtedly, Shannon and Kendall have differing views about the same act. If Shannon and Kendall cannot come to an agreement about whether or not the online mutual masturbation session was indeed an act of cheating, then whose perception helps us to best understand whether this act of cybersex is a form of cheating?

Traditionally, the perceptions of the partner not involved in the act of cybersex determine whether the act is considered cheating. In other words, if the partner not involved in the act of cybersex believes cybersex is cheating, then it is cheating.

But why should the perceptions of the partner prevail over the perceptions of the cybersex participant? The short answer is that they should not. Instead, whether an act of cybersex is cheating depends primarily not only on the intentions of the person who engages in cybersex but also on how this person perceives the cybersex act. I am arguing that rather than privilege the perceptions of the person not directly involved in the cybersex act, one must focus instead on the cybersex participant. Specifically, it is important to take into account both the intentions *and* perceptions of the cybersex participant in order to determine whether an act of cybersex is a form of infidelity.

To demonstrate the significance of one's intention in relation to the cybersex act, it is helpful to think about the following contrasting examples. In the first example, the cybersex participant intends to seek sexual and/or emotional pleasure from a person who is outside the participant's relationship. The person may feel guilty for engaging in cybersex because she believes that she is being unfaithful given the nature of the cybersex encounter (e.g., cybersex acts that foster emotional and/or sexual intimacy). In this case, because the cybersex participant's intentions and perceptions of her behavior are adulterous, then this act should be interpreted as cheating. Even if a cybersex encounter does not begin with adulterous intentions, if the cybersex participant's intentions and/or perceptions of the act change during the course of the encounter, then the act could still be considered cheating. For many cybersex participants, however, this is not the reality of their experience. To state this point differently, many people who engage in cybersex do not engage in cybersex in order to cheat on their partners. Because people often do not engage in cybersex to harm their relationship, it is important to consider other intention/perception understandings of the cybersex act.

Now consider the case of a person who engages in cybersex with the sole intention of having an orgasm. It is important to point out that this person is not engaging in deceptive behavior in order to take part in the cybersex act. In this case, the cybersex participant is not looking to create an emotional connection with another person but instead is seeking out a stimulating aid for the purpose of masturbating. This person could choose to watch a pornographic movie, for instance, but instead chooses a chat room for arousal. In fact, an in-depth interview study of cybersex participants found that these participants often "equated participation in chat rooms with watching a movie or reading a novel" (Mileham, 2007, p. 16). Therefore, not only does the person involved in the cybersex act intend to engage in masturbation (a sexual act that is not generally considered to be a form of cheating), his perception of the experience is the same. Specifically, the cybersex participant perceives the cybersex act as an act of masturbation, not infidelity. From this perspective, I argue that the cybersex participant did not cheat on his partner because he did not intend to cheat, nor did he perceive the act as cheating.

For those who still remain skeptical as to whether cybersex is cheating, it is critical to understand the implications of this position. If someone believes that, although the cybersex participant thinks he is simply masturbating, he is actually cheating on his partner, then where can we draw the distinction between other forms of masturbation and cheating? Is the person who masturbates to a racy magazine cheating on her partner? Moreover, how do we make sense of situations where a person's mind wanders during sex? Is one cheating if he thinks of someone other than his partner during sex? Clearly, neither of these cases seems to constitute cheating. Skeptics must be aware that if the intentions and the perceptions of the cybersex participant are overlooked, then a variety of sex acts should also be considered alternative forms of cheating. Yet, if these masturbatory acts were all considered cheating, many of us would have to acknowledge that we've cheated on our partners!

By privileging the perceived "victim's" individual perceptions of the cybersex act above the intentions and perceptions of the cybersex participant, one is more likely to conclude that cybersex is cheating. It has been my aim to question this traditional bias to suggest that many of the acts typically considered cheating are vastly more complicated. By highlighting the intentions and perceptions of the cybersex participant, it becomes clear that many cybersex acts are not necessarily acts of infidelity. Often, cybersex is used to sexually enrich the lives of those who take part, which can ultimately benefit a relationship rather than destroy it.

References

B. L. A. Mileham, "Online Infidelity in Internet Chat Rooms: An Ethnographic Exploration," *Computers in Human Behavior* (vol. 23, 2007), 11–13.

J. Schneider, "The Impact of Compulsive Cybersex Behaviours on the Family," *Sexual and Relationship Therapy* (vol. 18, no. 3, 2003), 329–354.

CRYSTAL BEDLEY holds an MA in Sociology and is currently a Doctoral Student in Sociology at Rutgers University. Bedley has developed and taught interdisciplinary courses on the topics of the research process, methodology and graduate education preparation. Bedley argues that the anonymous nature of cybersex means that it is not cheating.

EXPLORING THE ISSUE

Is Cybersex "Cheating"?

Critical Thinking and Reflection

1. Can you identify the emotional, moral, intellectual, and social components in Milstein's argument?
2. Can you identify the emotional, moral, intellectual, and social components in Bedley's argument?
3. Can you identify your own emotional, moral, intellectual, and social responses to this issue?
4. What are some similarities and differences between your responses and the authors'?

Is There Common Ground?

The truth is that couples may often disagree in many ways over what constitutes cheating. There is a long list of questions that will elicit different answers from individuals. Is kissing someone else cheating? Does talking with your ex constitute cheating? How about dinner with your ex? Getting a lap dance from at a strip club? Getting a lap dance at a party? Looking at pornography? A lack of understanding of your partner's definition of monogamy can lead to serious problems in a relationship. Refer to the advice of Melanie Davis in the Introduction to this section and work on communicating openly and honestly within relationships.

Additional Resources

The following Web sites examine the question as to whether cybersex is cheating:

http://marriage.families.com/blog/is-cybersex-cheating#

www.lovematters.info/cybersex-cheating-does-it-count

www.ivillage.com/cybersex-really-cheating-0/4-n-282345

Internet References . . .

Organizations exist online solely to classify cybersex as an addiction—or to encourage cybersex. Those results are either one-sided or not the right fit for this section.

To learn more, please Google, "Is Cybersex Cheating?" and a wide array of articles will be available for further study.

Selected, Edited, and with Issue Framing Material by:
Don Dyson, *Widener University*

ISSUE

Is Hookup Culture on College Campuses Bad for Heterosexual Girls?

YES: **Amy Julia Becker,** from "Hookup Culture Is Good for Women, and Other Feminist Myths," *Christianity Today* (2012)

NO: **Timaree Schmidt**, from "Hookup Culture Can Help Build Stronger Relationships," Original essay written for this volume (2014)

Learning Outcomes
After reading this issue, you will be able to:
• Summarize competing arguments related to hookup culture.
• Evaluate the gender imbalance of this debate and why there is particular focus on the impact on women.
• Evaluate the long-term implications of sexual decision-making in college.

ISSUE SUMMARY

YES: Amy Julia Becker argues that hookup culture demeans women. From a Christian perspective, she argues that sex leads to greater life fulfillment when removed from the hookup culture.

NO: Timaree Schmidt argues that hookup culture is nothing new and that it can be healthy for people to have different sexual experiences.

Sexual activity occurs on college campuses, and it sometimes occurs with high frequency. Larger schools allow a level of anonymity that students would never have experienced in high school. Sometimes sexual activity is in the context of a long-term, committed relationship. Other times it is in the context of a one-night stand.

Who benefits from a one-night stand? Is it wrong to want one? Is it wrong to enjoy it? Should there be a different answer for males or females, and for heterosexual, gay, lesbian, or bisexual individuals?

Hooking up in college is not something new. However, there are some newer trends in higher education. For example, women are attending in much larger numbers than men. Some colleges have 60 percent or more female students. Add a few other variables to this: (a) most studies show a higher proportion of gay men versus lesbians in the general population; and (b) some men are already in committed relationships at school or at home. On many college campuses, if a woman is looking for a long-term heterosexual relationship, she is finding that the odds are stacked in the men's favor.

What about the women who are not looking for a long-term relationship? What about the pre-med student who does not want a relationship to tie her down when she is ready to leave for medical school? Or the woman who believes that college is the right time to experiment? One college student recently posted many of her sexual experiences online and wrote, "I turn 20 in two weeks. I feel like I should be making a lot more mistakes right now."

Why does this discussion so often focus on the impact on women? There is often an assumption that men prefer hookup culture and women prefer relationships.

The theory goes that women are joining hookup culture at their own expense to please men.

How much is hookup culture today different from generations past? Does it diminish a woman's chances of being in a relationship?

Of course the major point of college is the education that is received there. Yet during our time in colleges, relationships are formed, sometimes long-term, and hookups occur. One mother wrote an open letter to the young women attending Princeton University telling them that they would never again be in such a large pool of marriageable, impressive men. They should be using this opportunity to find a husband rather than engage in hookup culture.

Why do women hookup? Is it because they like sex? Or is it because they want to please men? What about when they keep hooking up with the same person, known as friends with benefits? Are they keeping the relationship light to please a man?

We are in an era today in which there is a sex-positive feminism that is captured by *Sex and the City, Girls*, Christina Aguilera, and many others. Do these media depictions of sex-positive women capture a real demographic in American society? If so, how big is it? How overestimated or underestimated is it?

The truth is that during college we learn a great deal more than what comes from the instruction of our professors and the words in our books. We learn a great deal about relationships from the people around us. The general culture influences how the people around us act.

The articles in this essay help us take a better look at the case for or against the impact of hookup culture on heterosexual girls.

YES

Amy Julia Becker

Hookup Culture Is Good for Women, and Other Feminist Myths

According to *Atlantic* essayist Hanna Rosin, we should celebrate that young women are now acting as sexually selfish as their male counterparts.

Pornography. Casual sex. Crude jokes about sex. Hooking up with no strings attached.

Hanna Rosin's most recent *Atlantic* article, "Boys on the Side," describes highly intelligent, career-oriented women engaging in all of these behaviors with a mere shrug of the shoulders. In the minds of many driven young women on college campuses across the country, sexual promiscuity doesn't harm anyone. Hooking up has become the new sexual norm for young adults, and according to this norm, students shy away from committed relationships and instead enjoy one-time sexual encounters with no expectation of further intimacy. And, Rosin argues, the sexual liberation of the 1960s that led to the more recent "hookup culture" on college campuses is good for women—it allows women to enjoy casual sex without being "tied down" by serious commitment.

Rosin initially substantiates this claim through interviews with her subjects. Most women who are engaging in the hookup culture report that they don't want to return to the days of chastity belts or even more traditional dating, and Rosin takes these positive reports as evidence that the hookup culture is not only here to stay but is also good for the women involved. She provides no evidence, however, that women who hookup a lot during their early 20s go on to lead fulfilling lives, and she doesn't offer a counterpoint of women who have opted out of hooking up. Furthermore, Rosin offers a few statistics to demonstrate positive trends nationwide when it comes to sexual mores. The rate of teenage girls having sex has declined from 37 to 27 percent in the past 25 years, for instance. And the rate of rape and sexual assault against females has declined by 70 percent nationally since 1993. Both of these numbers demonstrate significant progress for women. Whether or not the positive statistics correlate to the rise of the hookup culture, however, remains unclear.

Rosin's stance on hookup culture hinges on two assumptions. First, she assumes that economic productivity and personal independence are the twin goals of every modern person. Feminists shouldn't decry the advent of the hookup culture, she argues, because it "is too bound up with everything that's fabulous about being a young woman in 2012—the freedom, the confidence, the knowledge that you can always depend on yourself." Moreover, "[the hookup culture] is not a place where they drown . . . unlike women in earlier ages, they have more-important things on their minds, such as good grades and internships and job interviews and a financial future of their own." Intimacy, family, and community might be desirable, but only after a woman has established herself as an independent financial entity.

Second, though I suspect she would disagree with me here, Rosin's argument assumes that for women to "arrive," they must become *just like men*. She describes sexually aggressive women at a business-school party as ones who "had learned to keep pace with the boys," and later as ones who were "behaving exactly like frat boys." Instead of challenging male behavior that demeans women (and men), Rosin capitulates to it. Instead of arguing for men and women to change culture in such a way that the responsibility for pregnancy and childrearing falls on the shoulders of both parents, she simply heralds women's ability to avoid pregnancy through birth control and abortion. And instead of promoting an understanding of human flourishing that includes relationships with trust, responsibility, and love, she succumbs to a truncated and depleted view of humanity that esteems individual work as the highest goal and self-serving love as the highest love.

From a Christian perspective, it's easy to critique Rosin's argument, one that she explores in her new book, *The End of Men* (a review of which *Christianity Today* will publish online in the coming weeks). Even if they don't always heed it in practice, Christians at least acknowledge the truth and goodness of the biblical view of human sexuality—that both men and women will honor God and find personal fulfillment in engaging in a sexual relationship with one other person within the covenant of marriage. Christians understand relationships as the core of our humanity, beginning with God's relationship within the Trinity, and extending to humans, who are invited into relationship with God but also into interdependent relationships with one another. Marriage, children, and community are viewed not as problems to be delayed until a career is in place, but rather as blessings to be received. And Christians understand love as, at its core, self-sacrificial, modeled after the love of Christ offered to us on the cross.

In Rosin's view, "Feminist progress right now largely depends on the existence of the hookup culture." But women can continue to find their rightful roles in the workplace and within the home without succumbing to the lie that a fulfilling life is one in which financial independence and self-sufficiency are the primary goals.

Instead of assuming that women must become just like the traditional norm of sexually active men, the gospel offers a transformative vision of humanity. And it isn't a picture of the 1950s housewife either. It's a picture that challenges notions of traditional masculinity and femininity, including, but not limited to, the sexual norms for both. Yes, it's a picture that calls for chastity for both men and women outside of marriage. But it's also a picture that holds forth the possibility not of sexual liberation, but of true freedom.

Christians have done plenty of finger-wagging about the state of our nation's sexual culture, for the same reasons that Rosin extols it. But Rosin's posture, and the norm it extols, calls for more than rebuke. Christians have an opportunity to offer a different understanding not only of sex, but of what it means to know abiding joy and peace as a full human being. Let's make sure we can both articulate and live that understanding of sex and humanity in a world starving for true fulfillment.

Amy Julia Becker focuses her writing on faith, family, disability, and ethics. She is identified as a Christian theological conservative and also socially liberal.

Timaree Schmit

Hookup Culture Can Help Build Stronger Relationships

Hookup Culture, if such a thing exists, provides opportunities for young people to be more contemplative and communicative about sexuality, fostering a climate that encourages collaborative, consensual sexual behavior over transactional or predatory behavior. It also holds the possibility of freeing women and men from constraints of traditional gender expectations.

Is Hookup Culture Real?

When a young person says that he or she "hooked up with" someone, this should prompt more questions than commentary. After all, there is no strict definition of the term or even a majority opinion on what, specifically, must happen for a "hook up" to have occurred. Among college students, the phrase can indicate anything from prolonged kissing to oral, vaginal and anal sex. While common, the term is often too vague to be useful.

Researcher Amanda Holman uses the term hookups to refer to sexual behavior that takes place without the expectation of commitment. This is often purported to represent a fundamental change in the dating and sexual patterns of young people from previous generations. However, a comparison of responses to the General Social Survey from 1988–1996 and those of 2002–2010 failed to find evidence this is true. Sociologists Martin Monto and Anna Carey's research found "no evidence that there has been a sea change in the sexual behavior of college students or that there has been a liberalization of attitudes towards sexuality." They found a greater percentage of current college students indicate that they have had sex with a friend within the last year (68% versus 56%) and a larger number report having had sexual activity with a casual partner (44% compared to 34.5%). This degree of change indicates that casual sex was already a common experience and that a significant portion of the population does not engage in commitment-less hookups.

Instead, Hookup Culture is largely a matter of change in conversations about sexual behaviors. Students are more likely to talk with peers about experiences, but use non-specific terms like "hookup" to describe what happened. This intentional vagueness serves several functions. It can retain privacy, diminish embarrassment associated with using more technical or degrading terminology, or deliberately give the impression that a greater or smaller variety of sexual acts occurred.

There is not much research, about whether most young people approve of Hookup Culture or think it is harmless. Qualitative interviews about hooking up find experiences may range from entirely satisfying to devastating. Additionally, there continue to be different social acceptance levels for males and females in terms of frequency of casual sex and number of partners. While traditional sexual gender norms are expanding for both men and women, many of the stigmas and expectations remain. Males are more likely than females to receive social encouragement to seek sexual pleasure, engage in sexual activity without intimacy or commitment and to be sexually involved with multiple partners.

Social Desirability Bias is a major issue when researching sexual behaviors, as respondents often feel pressure to appear 'normal' among their peers or to align their answers with personal ideals about how much and what kind of sex is OK to have. Perhaps young people now, especially young women, are simply more willing to acknowledge sexual activity that occurs outside of a serious relationship than in previous decades. Holman also suggests that young men now may feel pressured to over-report their experiences, thinking that their peers are engaging in more casual sex than they really are. She argues that the vagueness of the term "hookup" cultivates misperceptions about how much sex young people are having, giving the false impression that committed relationships are no longer the most common context for sexual activity.

What is Wrong with Hookup Culture?

Many discussions about hooking up focus on whether or not it's healthy for young people to have more casual sexual encounters. Some emphasize that Hookup Culture is a result of independent, career-oriented women feeling free to express their sexual desires and seek physical satisfaction without commitment in the way that only men were previously able to do. Others express concern that a climate that encourages strings-free sex will make it harder for young adults to build respectful and loving committed relationships or to say "no" to sex without facing social disapproval.

As for the first claim, longitudinal studies are not yet possible about how Hookup Culture affects women later in life, their relationship outcomes, satisfaction and sense of self. As for the latter claims, we have no evidence either. In fact, rates of sexual assault have dropped dramatically since the 1970s, with evidence that enthusiastic sexual consent may be viewed as more important now than in previous generations. Assessing whether intimacy in relationships is harmed by hooking up is made extra complicated by the variety of other variables of modern life, including: the ubiquity of social media, online dating, and a growing body of research that shows social isolation has increased for all demographics of Americans over the last two decades.

What Might be Right about Hookup Culture

Among the few facts we can ascertain about Hookup Culture, there are positive signs. Any deconstruction of traditional sexual mores bodes well for those who have been historically subjugated by them. For young women, the probability of negative consequences for engaging in premarital sexual behavior is reduced, including: harassment, ostracism, and the perception that she is no longer marriageable. As marriage becomes less and less vital for a woman's survival and sense of self, Hookup Culture enables those women who want to remain single to do so without sacrificing sexual pleasure, an optional luxury long granted to men.

Hookup Culture also supports the "queering" of restrictive sexual norms. Queer Theory aims to deconstruct restrictive essentialist ideas about men, women and sexual identities. Traditional sexual norms divide identities and behaviors categorically: man and woman, straight and gay, good and bad. Through a queer lens, sexuality is viewed as fluid and existing on a continuum, rather than in dichotomous boxes. According to both feminist and queer thought, someone's sex or gender shouldn't limit their behavioral choices. Since Hookup Culture subverts traditional sexual norms, it serves as a de facto "queering." As it expands the parameters of what is possible sexually, it holds the possibility of adding to the liberation of gay, lesbian and bisexual individuals. For those who are oppressed by a system that says sex is only appropriate for a husband and wife, any opportunity to reexamine these beliefs may hold promise.

Finally, Hookup Culture prioritizes sexual pleasure. Traditional sexual norms emphasize male sexual prowess and female sexual purity. These ideas put unrealistic expectations on young men and discourage them from expressing doubt or seeking information about what is pleasurable to female partners. Females, in contrast, are discouraged from demonstrating familiarity with their turn-ons, or expressing sexual desires. This results in a cycle of sexual encounters where men feel uncomfortable asking for direction and females are unable to ask for what they want. Even in the context of long-term relationships, partners may fear communicating uncommon desires out of fear of rejection or upending stability. The commitment-free nature of a hookup allows for partners to express their sexual needs without fear of judgment or compromising the relationship. Within Hookup Culture, individuals may experience a greater variety of partners and sexual acts, possibly introducing them to a diverse array of sexual pleasures that they can integrate into any future sexual interactions, including those in committed situations. Some authors have described this experimental process as helpful "practice" for more significant relationships.

A young person may choose to stop having sexual relations with a partner who is selfish, unwilling to learn, or otherwise unsatisfying, and focus their energies on partners who are more giving and open to experience. A selfish lover may find their reputation disqualifies them with other possible partners. This encourages a culture of reciprocal, mutually pleasurable sexual experiences.

Hookup Culture will never be acceptable to those who espouse the belief that sex is only appropriate between committed partners. However, there is little evidence that those people will have to change to accommodate those who do not share this belief. The possibility of Hookup Culture is not a replacement of traditional norms, but the addition of new norms with different values.

TIMAREE SCHMIT runs a sex-positive podcast and blogs under the title *Sex with Timaree*. She possesses a doctorate in human sexuality from Widener University.

EXPLORING THE ISSUE

Is Hookup Culture on College Campuses Bad for Heterosexual Girls?

Critical Thinking and Reflection

1. Can you identify the emotional, moral, intellectual, and social components in Becker's argument?
2. Can you identify the emotional, moral, intellectual, and social components in Schmit's argument?
3. Can you identify your own emotional, moral, intellectual, and social responses to this issue?
4. What are some similarities and differences between your responses and the authors'?

Is There Common Ground?

Both authors have opposite views regarding the impact of hookup culture on college campus. However, both, to a certain degree, have the same goal: they want young women to do what is in their best interest. Of course one argument is secular and one is non-secular. Beyond that, there are other reasons that are not necessarily anchored in religious faith: transmission of sexually transmitted diseases, finding the right partner, and other goals. What sort of sexuality education can occur on campus—or off campus—that can help students make sexual decisions that are consistent with their best interest and long-term goals?

Additional Resources

Kathleen A. Bogle, *Hooking Up: Sex, Dating, and Relationships on Campus* (2008)

Donna Freitas, *The End of Sex: How Hookup Culture Is Leaving a Generation Unhappy, Unfulfilled, and Confused about Intimacy* (2013)

Laura Stepp, Sessions, *Unhooked: How Young Women Pursue Sex, Delay Love and Lose at Both* (2008)

Internet References . . .

American Psychological Association

www.apa.org/monitor/2013/02/ce-corner.aspx

Bacchus Network

www.bacchusnetwork.org

P.S. I Love You

https://psiloveyou.xyz/hookup-culture-is-ruining-everything-7ed4b64d8c64

Harvard Political Review

http://harvardpolitics.com/harvard/hookup-culture/

Boys on the Side (The Atlantic)

https://www.theatlantic.com/magazine/archive/2012/09/boys-on-the-side/309062/

Selected, Edited, and with Issue Framing Material by:
Don Dyson, *Widener University*

ISSUE

Are Open Relationships Healthy?

YES: Donald Dyson, from "Seeing Relationships Through a Wider Lens: Open Relationships as a Healthy Option," Original essay written for this volume (2009)

NO: Stanley Kurtz, from "Here Come the Brides: Plural Marriage Is Waiting in the Wings," *The Weekly Standard* (2005)

Learning Outcomes

After reading this issue, you will be able to:

- Identify the major arguments made for and against open relationships.
- Compare and contrast the competing arguments made for and against open relationships in this issue.
- Evaluate the implications of open relationships on the stability of marriage and the larger fabric of American society.

ISSUE SUMMARY

YES: Donald Dyson is assistant professor of human sexuality education at Widener University and the national co-chair of the conference for the American Association of Sexuality Educators, Counselors, and Therapists. Dyson argues that there are essential qualities of a healthy relationship and that an open relationship can be successful.

NO: Stanley Kurtz, a writer and senior fellow at the Ethics and Public Policy Center, argues that allowing same-sex marriage will create a slippery slope, eventually leading to plural marriages. Kurtz contends that such marriages prove destructive to the institution of marriage itself.

During the nineteenth century, the U.S. Congress outlawed polygamy. Although all citizens of the United States were affected by this, the intent was to target members of the Church of Latter-Day Saints, otherwise known as Mormons. In fact, in order for Utah to join the union, the state first had to adopt anti-polygamy laws.

In the late 1870s, George Reynolds, a Mormon resident of Utah, was arrested for having multiple wives. He was convicted and sentenced to two years in prison and was fined $200. Reynolds challenged his conviction, and the case, *Reynolds v. United States,* reached the Supreme Court of the United States.

The Court ruled to uphold anti-polygamy and anti-bigamy laws, stating: "Polygamy has always been odious among the northern and western nations of Europe,

and, until the establishment of the Mormon Church, was almost exclusively a feature of the life of Asiatic and of African people."

The bizarre, and frankly racist, choice of words in the Supreme Court opinion seemingly blames people of color, who were largely banned from the Mormon Church at that time, for white, Mormon polygamy. Aside from this language, this decision provides case law in addition to already existing statutory law stating that there is no right to plural marriages.

Although polygamy is illegal in the United States today, sex outside of a primary relationship—including sex outside marriage—occurs to a significant degree. Over the course of a heterosexual marriage, an estimated 24 percent of husbands and 18 percent of wives have sex outside marriage. The temptation to have sex outside marriage is clearly significant, and the practice is fairly common. These statistics reflect the frequency of sex outside marriage *without* the permission of one's spouse.

The difference between infidelity and an open relationship is that in an open relationship, sex occurs outside the marriage or relationship with the consent of one's partner or spouse. Open relationships have been referred to as wife swapping, swinging, and "the lifestyle." "Wife swapping" is perhaps the most misappropriated phrase. First, it implies that all open relationships are inherently heterosexual. Second, it indicates that men possess the power and that women are commodities being traded.

Heterosexual women in open relationships are often in high demand. Women in such relationships often find that they have a significant amount of power. In fact, in some relationships, the man might push to experiment with swinging, only to find that he does not care for it after seeing how sought-after his partner is by other men.

It is a challenge to find open relationships represented positively in television or film. A number of major American cities have swingers clubs that typically cater to heterosexual couples and single women. Due to the stigma associated with open relationships, most people within them work to conceal this from friends, family, and acquaintances.

Although open relationships exist, the majority of Americans believe that sex outside marriage is morally wrong and destructive. These individuals typically regard sexual intimacy and emotional intimacy as inseparable. They will often voice concerns that open relationships are bound to threaten the stability of a person's marriage or committed relationship.

When reading these articles, give some thought to historical factors that influence sexual morality today. Examine how your value system affects your reaction to these articles.

Sometimes the concept of open relationships is addressed in a cursory way by the popular media:

- On one episode of the sitcom *King of Queens,* Doug and Carrie, a married couple featured in the show, both agree that they can have sex outside their marriage with their dream person if the opportunity arises. They have to tell each other who that person is. Carrie shares first, disclosing a famous celebrity. Doug agrees to her choice, then shares his choice: a woman he works with. Amid laughter, Carrie refuses to accept his choice.
- On an episode of the cable series *Entourage,* Vincent Chase, a fictional Hollywood star, meets a woman in public and has sex with her in a nearby hotel room. He asks her whether they can see each other again. She explains she is engaged and can only do this once. She and her fiance both have a list of famous people they are allowed to have sex with.

Despite these examples from popular television shows, monogamy is treated as such a universal value that a significant number of readers may have never heard of polyamory or open relationships before reading this issue. What are some of the reasons that people are hesitant to discuss alternatives to monogamy? What is the impact, positive or negative, of this silence on individual relationships?

Aside from the diverse views of polyamory espoused by Dyson and Kurtz, this issue exposes fundamentally different philosophies. Dyson argues that open relationships can be positive. The argument portrays the impact of open relationships as self-contained to the individuals involved rather than assuming that such an arrangement will have a single, universal impact on all relationships. In contrast, Kurtz contends that any redefinition of marriage will be the start of a slippery slope that will ultimately affect everyone by causing the institution of marriage itself to disintegrate.

What do their views reveal about their position on the Political Ideology Continuum examined in the Introduction to this book? How do your views on this topic compare and contrast with other relationship issues raised in this book? The truth is that many people in open relationships are traditionally conservative, and many people committed to lifetime monogamy are quite liberal.

Regardless of the conclusion that you reach, this issue should help readers understand that one cannot make an assumption that relationship monogamy is a universal value. It is well advised for the reader to talk with a significant other at some point about his or her views on monogamy and relationships.

YES

Donald Dyson

Seeing Relationships Through a Wider Lens: Open Relationships as a Healthy Option

Introduction: The Current Cultural Context for Relationships

There are many ways in which human beings have learned to organize their daily relationships. People sometimes have family with whom they are very close; they have layers of social circles in which they operate, have friends, good friends, and intimate friends (some of whom may also be lovers). People have lovers and spouses; they have husbands and wives; they have partners and playmates. Each of these relationships involves a unique level of intimacy, the level of which is usually determined by the unique natures of the individuals involved.

Often, when people think of ideal relationship structures, they initially think of the types of relationships with which they are most familiar, or to which they have been most exposed. In Western cultures such as the United States, that relationship structure is most often a heterosexual, monogamous, married couple. In fact, so strong is the bias toward this one type of relationship structure, the questions of multiple partners or alternatives to monogamy are rarely discussed or considered.

Pile on top of this unquestioned assumption the cultural and clinical bias we see attached to sexual activity outside a monogamous pair bond. When one even considers sex with someone other than a primary partner, immediately the words "infidelity" and "cheating" spring to mind. Connected to those words are the culturally constructed ways in which people are supposed to respond to such things: anger, jealousy, hurt, rage. Indeed, such behaviors have many iconic images attached to them, including throwing a partner's belongings onto the front yard or cutting the partner's face out of pictures from a photo album.

Almost never does one instantly consider the possibility that the couple has agreed to a relationship style different from the monogamous monopoly. In the Clinton/ Lewinsky scandal of the 1990s, in which Hillary Clinton was seen by some as a devoted wife who "stood by her man," and by others as a weak woman who should have divorced her husband for cheating on her—few considered the possibility that then-President Clinton and his wife might have had a different relationship style. Instead, people wondered why Mrs. Clinton remained with her spouse and conjectured that the president must have been a sex addict of some sort. This type of knee-jerk reaction clearly illustrates the monogamist (assuming that everyone is or should be monogamous) cultural bias in which we now live.

Add to this the prevailing cultural myth of "The One." This myth creates the expectation that somewhere, out there in the wide world, there is just one special person (think of the idea of a "soulmate") that is waiting for each of us. That person will meet all of our emotional, physical, intellectual, social, and sexual needs. That person will be the "yin" to our "yang." That one special person will become a person's "better half." That one individual, somewhere out there in the world, will "complete" another person. With every Disney movie supporting this romanticized ideal, how can we, as a culture, *not* believe that such a "One" exists?

Consider, then, where this leaves us. We are culturally programmed to consider only traditional, pair-bonded relationships that without question include sexual monogamy. We are taught that the proper definition of sex outside a committed relationship is cheating and it should be punished, or at least pathologized. We are brainwashed with the myth of "The One"; taught to believe that we must find that person within the billions of people in the wide world. In essence, people today are taught from early childhood to hold the highest of standards for potential partners, believing that this special person must be everything to them. Is it any wonder that the divorce statistics for traditional marriage relationships are so high?

An original essay written for this volume. Copyright ©2009 by Donald A. Dyson, Ph.D. Reprinted by permission.

One Possible Scenario: Consider This

The author's first experience with a couple who had an open relationship was in meeting a heterosexual married couple in their 60s. After a 30-year relationship, when they were in their 50s, the wife in the couple was diagnosed with a degenerative illness—one they were told would result in a loss of sensation in her sexual organs. In addition, the medicine that she took to slow the progression would result in a decrease in her interest in sex. Given this inevitability, the couple looked for viable alternatives. Neither wanted to end their marriage; they were both still very much in love. They also continued to enjoy an active sex life, which was very important to both of them.

How could they resolve their dilemma? Was the wife to ask the husband to give up sex entirely for the rest of his life? Was the husband to foreswear sexual activity of any kind out of a grand gesture for his wife—a promise that would have been ripe for building resentment and bitterness?

This couple chose to open their relationship. The result was wonderful for both of them. They continued to be happy for 10 years after, and may still be enjoying the love they have nurtured for decades.

Alternatives: What Options Exist?

In reality, there are many "lifestyles" that people have adopted and adapted over time to suit their intimacy needs. In his 1985 work, Dr. William R. Stayton identified 17 different types of relationships. These included traditional monogamy, serial monogamy, singlehood, single parenthood, child-free marriage, polyamory, polyfidelity, open marriage, group marriage, swinging, synergamy, communal living, cohabitation/trial marriage, family clusters, secret affairs, celibate monogamy, and lifelong celibacy/chastity.

Of those 17, polyamory, polyfidelity, open marriage, group marriage, swinging, synergamy, family clusters, and secret affairs are relevant to this discussion. Briefly:

- "Polyamory" is a general term often used to describe all forms of multipartner relating.
- Polyfidelity is a form of group relationship where all the members agree to be faithful within their group and commit to exist as a family.
- Open marriage is when the primary couple agrees to engage in sexual activities with others outside the dyad. In these situations, couples usually make agreements that dictate the nature of relationships and sexual activities that would be deemed acceptable outside the primary relationship.
- Group marriage usually includes three or more people who agree to "marry" each other.

- Swinging is often a couple's experience and includes the practice of having sexual relationships with others, sometimes in groups, and is founded upon responsible, consensual sexual relating.
- Synergamy is when one or both people involved in a couple have an additional intimate relationship outside that pair. This arrangement often includes the establishment of more than one household and the full involvement of the individual in more than one family system.
- Family clusters include multiple family systems that are interdependent in social, relational, financial, and sometimes sexual functioning.

Secret affairs are relevant here because it is this type of "open relationship" that is most practiced in our current cultural milieu. Current statistics estimate that between 45 and 50 percent of married women and between 50 and 60 percent of married men engage in extramarital sex at some point during their relationships (Atwood and Schwartz, 2002). Although this type of relationship is the most common, it is also the most damaging. It is estimated that 60 to 65 percent of divorces result from secret affairs. In addition, the betrayal of trust, the lack of communication, and the resulting deceptions are often considered to be the most harmful outcomes of these experiences.

The Argument: Why Are Open Relationships Healthy?

With all of these options giving context to the argument, it must be acknowledged that no matter the specifics of the lifestyle or relationship choice, it is the practice of a relationship that makes any of them healthy or unhealthy. It is the behavior of the people involved that has the greatest effect on the relative healthiness of any given relationship style.

Whether checking dating and relationship Web sites, looking through marriage encounter brochures, perusing the outlines of pre-cana marriage classes, or flipping through the pages of *The Complete Idiot's Guide to a Healthy Relationship* (Kuriansky, 2001), each source includes three basic requirements for healthy and long-lasting relationships: trust, honesty, and communication. Although some sources include additional components, the universality of these three is striking.

Let us consider these three in reverse order, beginning with communication. The skills of good communication are the stuff of workshops, lesson plans, relationship and marriage seminars, and countless books and articles. These skills include using direct language, "I" statements, and active listening, among others. What is critically important here, though, is that these skills are not dependent on the type of relationship in which they are used. The same skills work effectively in conversations with one's parents, one's coworkers, and with one's sexual and relationship partners.

Good communication in open relationships is no different from good communication in monogamous ones. Instead, because of the many complexities inherent in dyadic communication, including significant others, those complexities increase exponentially. As a result of this explosion, open relationships might offer individuals increased opportunities for intimacy, as well as challenges to honing their communication skills.

Add to these multiple complexities the sensitive nature of the topics about which the individuals involved are communicating. Conversations are occurring about intimacy needs, sexual desires and fantasies, and personal preferences, as well as limitations, jealousy, attraction, and so much more. Many couples never brave these waters. For people involved in open relationships, they are necessary and sometimes daily conversations.

This level of communication leads directly into the next aspect of healthy relationships: honesty. As individuals broach subjects such as sexual desires, jealousies, and possibilities, the need for and reliance upon honesty increases. In the context of loving relationships, people can begin to express not only the ways that they feel fulfilled by a partner, but also the wants and needs that they are experiencing that are not being met by their primary partner. They can be honest about their sexual and emotional attractions to others. These are topics that are often avoided by other couples for fear of hurting one another or for fear of reprisals for having these types of feelings.

In this way, the honesty required within open relationships can be a very healthy benefit to the relationship overall. Secret keeping and lying take energy. So does honest communication . . .

Finally, the practice of open and honest communication requires a significant degree of vulnerability. As individuals express their wants and needs, their often secret desires and attractions, and their jealousy or fears of loss, the resulting vulnerability is incredibly acute. When this vulnerability is met with equal honesty and care, and when good communication is present and practiced, the result is a significant increase in trust and intimacy between the partners.

Trust, or the reliance upon the strength, integrity, ability, and surety of a person, is certainly a cornerstone of healthy relationships. It is usually built, bit by bit, within the shared experiences of vulnerability and care experienced by people within their relationships. In the context of open relationships, this trust is discussed, explored, and tested in ways that many in monogamous relationships never openly experience. As people practice honesty in their relationships, discuss sexual boundaries and limitations, acknowledge and explore their own desires, and allow their partners to do the same, that trust can increase, and the bonds between people can become stronger.

Summary

No type of relationship, in and of itself, is inherently or unequivocally healthy or unhealthy. It is the practice of relationships that give them their subjective qualification. Healthy relationships require effective, open communication; honesty; and trust. Open relationships can, indeed, be characterized by all of those things, thus characterizing them as healthy.

In addition, open relationships may offer some specific benefits. They can release individuals and relationships from the unspoken specter of monogamy. That is not to say that couples who discuss alternative relationship structures and choose monogamy are less healthy or self-aware. Instead, it demonstrates that the discussion and intentional choices related to monogamy are opportunities for growth and increased intimacy.

Open relationships also have the power to allow individuals to be less "perfect" within their relationships and more human in their strengths and shortcomings. The pressure to be someone's "everything" and the resulting disappointment and resentment when that individual falls short of those expectations have surely been the demise of many potentially wonderful relationships. Exploring options for individuals to have their wants and needs met outside a dyadic relationship might well be the healthiest thing within a given relationship.

As people express their intimacy needs, their sexual fantasies, and their desires, they practice honesty in ways that many others never do. This exploration and reflection allow individuals to build increased levels of sexual awareness and self-awareness that have the potential to benefit not only themselves, but also all of their current and future partners.

And finally, open relationships by necessity include the constant practice of good communication skills. The opportunities to practice talking about all aspects of the relationship increase skills that are easily transferable to other situations. Healthy and honest communication is a benefit to every relationship. Open relationships are not a paradigm to be compared and contrasted with traditional monogamous ones. Instead, they are a paradigm all their own and should be measured against standards for good relationships, not monogamy.

For more information about open relationships, consider *Loving More: The Polyfidelity Primer,* by Ryam Nearing (PEP Publishing, 1992) or *The Ethical Slut,* by Dossie Easton and Catherine A. Liszt (Greenery Press, 1998).

References

J. D. Atwood and L. Schwartz, "Cyber-Sex: The New Affair Treatment Considerations," *Journal of Couple and Relationship Therapy* (vol. 1, no. 3, 2002).

J. Kuriansky, *The Complete Idiot's Guide to Healthy Relationships,* 2d ed. (Fort Smith, AZ: Alpha Books, 2001).

W. R. Stayton, "Alternative Lifestyles: Marital Options," in D. C. Goldberg and P. J. Fink, eds., *Contemporary Marriage: Special Issues in Couples Therapy* (Homewood, IL: Dorsey, 1985).

DONALD DYSON is associate dean of School of Human Service Professions, director of Center for Human Sexuality Studies, and associate professor at Widener University and the national cochair of the conference for the American Association of Sexuality Educators, Counselors and Therapists. Dyson argues that there are essential qualities of a healthy relationship and that an open relationship can be successful.

Stanley Kurtz

 **NO**

Here Come the Brides: Plural Marriage Is Waiting in the Wings

On September 23, 2005, the 46-year-old Victor de Bruijn and his 31-year-old wife of eight years, Bianca, presented themselves to a notary public in the small Dutch border town of Roosendaal. And they brought a friend. Dressed in wedding clothes, Victor and Bianca de Bruijn were formally united with a bridally bedecked Mirjam Geven, a recently divorced 35-year-old whom they'd met several years previously through an Internet chatroom. As the notary validated a *samenlevingscontract,* or "cohabitation contract," the three exchanged rings, held a wedding feast, and departed for their honeymoon.

When Mirjam Geven first met Victor and Bianca de Bruijn, she was married. Yet after several meetings between Mirjam, her then-husband, and the De Bruijns, Mirjam left her spouse and moved in with Victor and Bianca. The threesome bought a bigger bed, while Mirjam and her husband divorced. Although neither Mirjam nor Bianca had had a prior relationship with a woman, each had believed for years that she was bisexual. Victor, who describes himself as "100 percent heterosexual," attributes the trio's success to his wives' bisexuality, which he says has the effect of preventing jealousy.

The De Bruijns' triple union caused a sensation in the Netherlands, drawing coverage from television, radio, and the press. With TV cameras and reporters crowding in, the wedding celebration turned into something of a media circus. Halfway through the festivities, the trio had to appoint one of their guests as a press liaison. The local paper ran several stories on the triple marriage, one devoted entirely to the media madhouse.

News of the Dutch three-way wedding filtered into the United States through a September 26 report by Paul Belien, on his Brussels Journal website. The story spread through the conservative side of the Internet like wildfire, raising a chorus of "I told you so's" from bloggers who'd long warned of a slippery slope from gay marriage to polygamy.

Meanwhile, gay marriage advocates scrambled to put out the fire. M.V. Lee Badgett, an economist at the University of Massachusetts, Amherst, and research director of the Institute for Gay and Lesbian Strategic Studies, told a sympathetic website, "This [Brussels Journal] article is ridiculous. Don't be fooled—Dutch law does not allow polygamy." Badgett suggested that Paul Belien had deliberately mistranslated the Dutch word for "cohabitation contract" as "civil union," or even "marriage," so as to leave the false impression that the triple union had more legal weight than it did. Prominent gay-marriage advocate Evan Wolfson, executive director of Freedom to Marry, offered up a detailed legal account of Dutch cohabitation contracts, treating them as a matter of minor significance, in no way comparable to state-recognized registered partnerships.

In short, while the Dutch triple wedding set the conservative blogosphere ablaze with warnings, same-sex marriage advocates dismissed the story as a silly stunt with absolutely no implications for the gay marriage debate. And how did America's mainstream media adjudicate the radically different responses of same-sex marriage advocates and opponents to events in the Netherlands? By ignoring the entire affair.

Yet there is a story here. And it's bigger than even those chortling conservative websites claim. While Victor, Bianca, and Mirjam are joined by a private cohabitation contract rather than a state-registered partnership or a full-fledged marriage, their union has already made serious legal, political, and cultural waves in the Netherlands. To observers on both sides of the Dutch gay marriage debate, the De Bruijns' triple wedding is an unmistakable step down the road to legalized group marriage.

More important, the De Bruijn wedding reveals a heretofore hidden dimension of the gay marriage phenomenon. The De Bruijns' triple marriage is a bisexual marriage. And, increasingly, bisexuality is emerging as a reason why legalized gay marriage is likely to result in legalized group marriage. If every sexual orientation has a right to construct its own form of marriage, then more changes are surely due. For what gay marriage is to homosexuality, group marriage is to bisexuality. The De Bruijn trio is the tip-off to the fact that a connection between bisexuality and the drive for multipartner marriage has been developing for some time.

As American gay-marriage advocates were quick to point out, the cohabitation contract that joined Victor, Bianca, and Mirjam carries fewer legal implications and less status than either a registered partnership or a marriage—and Dutch trios are still barred from the latter two forms of union. Yet the use of a cohabitation contract for a triple wedding is a step in the direction of group marriage. The conservative and religious Dutch paper *Reformatorisch Dagblad* reports that this was the first known occurrence in the Netherlands of a cohabitation contract between a married couple and their common girlfriend. . . .

So the use of cohabitation contracts was an important step along the road to same-sex marriage in the Netherlands. And the link between gay marriage and the De Bruijns' triple contract was immediately recognized by the Dutch. The story in *Reformatorisch Dagblad* quoted J.W.A. van Dommelen, an attorney opposed to the De Bruijn union, who warned that the path from same-sex cohabitation contracts to same-sex marriage was about to be retraced in the matter of group marriage.

Van Dommelen also noted that legal complications would flow from the overlap between a two-party marriage and a three-party cohabitation contract. The rights and obligations that exist in Dutch marriages and Dutch cohabitation contracts are not identical, and it's unclear which arrangement would take precedence in case of a conflict. "The structure is completely gone," said Van Dommelen, as he called on the Dutch minister of justice to set up a working group to reconcile the conflicting claims of dual marriages and multipartner cohabitation contracts. Of course, simply by harmonizing the conflicting claims of dual marriages and triple cohabitation contracts, that working group would be taking yet another "small step" along the road to legal recognition for group marriage in the Netherlands.

The slippery-slope implications of the triple cohabitation contract were immediately evident to the SGP, a small religious party that played a leading role in the failed battle to preserve the traditional definition of marriage in the Netherlands. SGP member of parliament Kees van der Staaij noted the substantial overlap between marriage rights and the rights embodied in cohabitation contracts. Calling the triple cohabitation contract a back-door route to legalized polygamy, Van der Staaij sent a series of formal queries to Justice Minister Piet Hein Donner, asking him to dissolve the De Bruijn contract and to bar more than two persons from entering into cohabitation contracts in the future.

The justice minister's answers to these queries represent yet another small step—actually several small steps—toward legal and cultural recognition for group marriage in the Netherlands. To begin with, Donner reaffirmed the legality of multipartner cohabitation contracts and pointedly refused to consider any attempt to ban such contracts in the future. Donner also went so far as to assert that contracts regulating multipartner cohabitation can fulfill "a useful regulating function" (also translatable as "a useful structuring role"). In other words, Donner has articulated the rudiments of a "conservative case for group marriage."

The SGP responded angrily to Donner's declarations. In the eyes of this small religious party, Donner had effectively introduced a form of legal group marriage to the Netherlands. A party spokesman warned of an impending legal mess—especially if the De Bruijn trio, or others like them, have children. The SGP plans to raise its objections again when parliament considers the justice department's budget.

It's not surprising that the first English-language report was a bit unclear as to the precise legal status and significance of the triple Dutch union. The Dutch themselves are confused about it. One of the articles from which Paul Belien drew his original report is careful to distinguish between formal marriage and the cohabitation contract actually signed by Victor, Bianca, and Mirjam. Yet the very same article says that Victor now "officially" has "two wives."

Even Dutch liberals acknowledge the implications of the De Bruijn wedding. Jan Martens, a reporter and opinion columnist for *BN/DeStem*, the local paper in Roosendaal, wrote an opinion piece mocking opposition to group marriage by religious parties like the SGP. Noting the substantial overlap between cohabitation contracts and marriage, Martens said he agreed with the SGP that the De Bruijn triple union amounts to a "short-cut to polygamy." Yet Martens emphasized that he "couldn't care less if you have two, three, four, or sixty-nine wives or husbands."

Minority religious parties and their newspapers excepted, this mixture of approval and indifference seems to be the mainstream Dutch reaction so far. Not only has Justice Minister Donner articulated the beginnings of a conservative case for group marriage, but Green Party spokesman Femke Halsema, a key backer of gay marriage, has affirmed her party's support for the recognition of multipartner unions. The public has not been inclined to protest these developments, and the De Bruijn trio have been welcomed by their neighbors. . . .

When it comes to marriage, culture shapes law. (It's a two-way street, of course. Law also influences culture.) After all, Dutch same-sex marriage advocates still celebrate the foundational role of symbolic gay marriage registries in the early 1990s. Although these had absolutely no legal status, the publicity and sympathy they generated are now widely recognized as keys to the success of the Dutch campaign for legal same-sex unions and ultimately marriage. How odd, then, that American gay-marriage advocates should respond to the triple Dutch wedding with hair-splitting legal discourses, while ignoring the Dutch media frenzy and subsequent signs of cultural acceptance—for a union with far more legal substance than Holland's first symbolic gay marriages. Despite the denials of gay-marriage advocates, in both legal and cultural terms, Victor, Bianca, and Mirjam's triple union is a serious move toward legalized group marriage in the Netherlands.

Given the stir in Holland, it's remarkable that not a single American mainstream media outlet carried a story on the triple Dutch wedding. Of course the media were all over the Dutch gay marriage story when they thought the experiment had been a success. In late 2003 and early 2004, in the wake of the Supreme Court's *Lawrence v. Texas* decision, which ruled sodomy laws unconstitutional, and looming gay marriage in Massachusetts, several American papers carried reports from the Netherlands. The common theme was that Holland had experienced no ill effects from gay marriage, and that the issue was no longer contentious. . . .

Although the triple Dutch union has been loosely styled "polygamy," it's actually a sterling example of polyamory. Polyamorists practice "responsible nonmonogamy"—open, loving, and stable relationships among more than two people (see "Beyond Gay Marriage: The Road to Polyamory," *The Weekly Standard,* August 4/August 11, 2003). Polygamous marriages among fundamentalist Mormons or Muslims don't depend on a blending of heterosexuality and bisexuality. Yet that combination perfectly embodies the spirit of polyamory. And polyamorists don't limit themselves to unions of one man and several women. One woman and two men, full-fledged group marriage, a stable couple openly engaging in additional shifting or stable relationships—indeed, almost any combination of partner-number and sexual orientation is possible in a polyamorous sexual grouping.

Polyamorists would call the De Bruijn union a "triad." In a polyamorous triad, all three partners are sexually connected. This contrasts with a three-person "V," in which only one of the partners (called the "hinge" or "pivot") has a sexual relationship with the other two. So the bisexuality of Bianca and Mirjam classifies the De Bruijn union as a polyamorous bisexual triad. In another sense, the De Bruijn marriage is also a gay marriage. The Bianca-Mirjam component of the union is gay, and legalized gay marriage in

Holland has clearly helped make the idea of a legally recognized bisexual triad thinkable. . . .

The germ of an organized effort to legalize polyamory in the United States can be found in the Unitarian Church. Although few realize it, the Unitarian Church, headquartered in Boston, played a critical role in the legalization of same-sex marriage in Massachusetts. Julie and Hillary Goodridge, lead plaintiffs in *Goodridge v. Department of Public Health,* were married at the headquarters of the Unitarian Universalists in a ceremony presided over by the Reverend William G. Sinkford, president of the Unitarian Universalist Association. Hillary Goodridge is program director of the Unitarian Universalist Funding Program. And Unitarian churches in Massachusetts played a key role in the struggle over gay marriage, with sermons, activism, and eventually with marriage ceremonies for same-sex couples. Choosing a strongly church-affiliated couple like the Goodridges as lead plaintiffs was an important part of the winning strategy in the *Goodridge* case.

It's a matter of interest, therefore, that an organization to promote public acceptance of polyamory has been formed in association with the Unitarian Church. Unitarian Universalists for Polyamory Awareness (UUPA) was established in the summer of 1999. At the time, the news media in Boston carried reports from neighboring Vermont, where the soon-to-be-famous civil unions case was about to be decided. And the echo effect of the gay marriage battle on the polyamory movement goes back even further. The first informal Unitarian polyamory discussion group gathered in Hawaii in 1994, in the wake of the first state supreme court decision favorable to same-sex marriage in the United States.

"Our vision," says UUPA's website, "is for Unitarian Universalism to become the first poly-welcoming mainstream religious denomination." Those familiar with Unitarianism's role in the legalization of gay marriage understand the legal-political strategy implicit in that statement. UUPA's political goals are spelled out by Harlan White, a physician and leading UUPA activist, on the society's website. Invoking the trial of April Divilbiss, the first American polyamorist to confront the courts, White says, "We are concerned that we may become the center of the next great social justice firestorm in America."

White maintains that American polyamorists are growing in number. An exact count is impossible, since polyamory is still surrounded by secrecy. Polyamorists depend on the Internet to connect. Even so, says White, "attendance at conferences is up, email lists and websites are proliferating, and poly support groups are growing in number and size." As for the Unitarian polyamorists, their email list has several hundred subscribers, and the group has put on well-attended workshops at Unitarian General Assemblies since 2002. And although the number of open polyamorists is limited, some Unitarian ministers already perform "joining ceremonies" for polyamorous families. . . .

Shortly after the second article appeared, UUA president Sinkford circulated a statement among Unitarians acknowledging that press interest in Unitarian polyamory had "generated a great deal of anxiety" among the church's leadership. "Many of us are concerned that such press coverage might impair our ability to witness effectively for our core justice commitments." Sinkford appeared to be expressing a concern that had been stated more baldly in the original *Chronicle* article. According to the *Chronicle*, many of the students and faculty at the Unitarians' key west-coast seminary, Starr King School for the Ministry, in Berkeley, see the polyamory movement as a threat to the struggle for same-sex marriage.

In other words, Unitarians understand that moving too swiftly or openly to legitimize polyamory could validate the slippery-slope argument against same-sex marriage. So with news coverage prematurely blowing the cover off the Unitarians' long-term plan to legalize polyamory, President Sinkford took steps to hold UUPA at arm's length. Sinkford issued a public "clarification" that distanced the church from any formal endorsement of polyamory, yet also left room for the UUPA to remain a "related organization." . . .

The other fascinating angle in the *San Francisco Chronicle*'s coverage of the Unitarian polyamorists was the prominence of bisexuality. Most members of UUPA are either bisexual or heterosexual. One polyamorist minister who had recently come out to his congregation as a bisexual treated polyamory and bisexuality synonymously. "Our denomination has been welcoming to gays and lesbians and transgendered people," he said. "Bisexuals have not received the recognition they deserve." In other words, anything less than formal church recognition of polyamory is discrimination against bisexuals.

Two developing lines of legal argument may someday bring about state recognition for polyamorous marriage: the argument from polyamory, and the argument from bisexuality. In a 2004 law review article, Elizabeth F. Emens, of the University of Chicago Law School, offers the argument from polyamory (see "Monogamy's Law: Compulsory Monogamy and Polyamorous Existence," *New York University Review of Law & Social Change*). Polyamory is more than the mere practice of multiple sexual partnership, says Emens. Polyamory is also a disposition, broadly analogous to the disposition toward homosexuality. Insofar as laws of marriage, partnership, or housing

discriminate against polyamorous partnerships, maintains Emens, they place unfair burdens on people with "poly" dispositions. Emens takes her cue here from the polyamorists themselves, who talk about their "poly" inclinations the way gays talk about homosexuality. For example, polyamorists debate whether to keep their poly dispositions "in the closet" or to "come out."

Emens's case for a poly disposition was inspired by the radical lesbian thinker Adrienne Rich, who famously put forward a "continuum model" of lesbianism. Rich argued that all women, lesbian-identified or not, are in some sense lesbians. If women could just discover where they fall on the "lesbian continuum," then even those women who remain heterosexually identified would abandon any prejudice against homosexuality.

Following Rich, Emens argues that all of us have a bit of "poly" inside. By discovering and accepting our own desires for multiple sexual partners, then even those who remain monogamous would abandon their prejudice against polyamorists. Of course, some people fall at the extreme ends of these continuums. Some folks are intensely monogamous, for example. But by the same token, others are intensely polyamorous. Whether for biological or cultural reasons, says Emens, some folks simply cannot live happily without multiple simultaneous sexual partners. And for those people, Emens argues, our current system of marriage is every bit as unjust as it is for homosexuals. . . .

The second legal strategy available to the polyamorists is the argument from bisexuality. No need here to validate anything as novel-sounding as a "polyamorous disposition." A case for polyamory can easily be built on the more venerable orientation of bisexuality. While no legal scholar has offered such a case, the groundwork is being laid by Kenji Yoshino, a professor at Yale Law School and deputy dean for intellectual life.

Yoshino's 2000 *Stanford Law Review* article "The Epistemic Contract of Bisexual Erasure" has a bewildering title but a fascinating thesis. Yoshino argues that bisexuality is far more prevalent than is usually recognized. The relative invisibility of bisexuality, says Yoshino, can be attributed to the mutual interest of heterosexuals and homosexuals in minimizing its significance. But according to Yoshino, the bisexuality movement is on the rise and bound to become more visible, with potentially major consequences for the law and politics of sexual orientation.

Defining bisexuality as a "more than incidental desire" for partners of both sexes, Yoshino examines the best available academic studies on sexual orientation and finds that each of them estimates the number of bisexuals as equivalent to, or greater than, the number of homosexuals. Up to now, the number of people who actively think of themselves as bisexuals has been much smaller than the number who've shown a "more than incidental" desire for partners of both sexes. But that, argues Yoshino, is because both heterosexuals and homosexuals have an interest in convincing bisexuals that they've got to make an all-or-nothing choice between heterosexuality and homosexuality.

Heterosexuals, for example, have an interest in preserving norms of monogamy, and bisexuality "destabilizes" norms of monogamy. Homosexuals, notes Yoshino, have an interest in defending the notion of an immutable homosexual orientation, since that is often the key to persuading a court that they have suffered discrimination. And homosexuals, adds Yoshino, have an interest in maximizing the number of people in their movement. For all these reasons and more, Yoshino argues, the cultural space in which bisexuals might embrace and acknowledge their own sexual identity has been minimized. Yoshino goes on to highlight the considerable evidence for the recent emergence of bisexuality as a movement, and predicts that in our current cultural climate—and given the numerical potential—bisexuality activism will continue to grow.

In addition to establishing the numerical and political significance of bisexuality, Yoshino lays down an argument that could easily be deployed to legalize polyamory: "To the extent that bisexuals are not permitted to express their dual desires, they might fairly characterize themselves as harmed." Yet Yoshino does not lay out a bisexual defense of polyamory. Instead Yoshino attacks—rightly—the stereotype that treats all bisexuals as nonmonogamous. Yet the same research that establishes the monogamous preferences of many bisexuals also confirms that bisexuals tend toward nonmonogamy at substantially higher rates than homosexuals. (See Paula C. Rust, "Monogamy and Polyamory: Relationship Issues for Bisexuals," in Firestein, ed., *Bisexuality: The Psychology and Politics of an Invisible Minority*.) That fact could easily be turned by a bisexuality rights movement into an argument for legalized polyamory. . . .

In 2004, the *Journal of Bisexuality* published a special double issue on polyamory, also released as the book *Plural Loves: Designs for Bi and Poly Living*. It's clear from *Plural Loves* that the polyamory movement now serves as the de facto political arm of the bisexual liberation struggle. As one contributor notes, "the large number of bi people in the poly movement provides evidence that bisexuality is one of the major driving forces behind polyamory. In other words, polyamory was created and spread partly to satisfy the need for bisexual relationship structures. . . . [T]he majority of poly activists are also bisexual. . . . Poly activism is bi activism. . . . The bi/poly dynamic has the potential to move both communities towards a point of culture-wide visibility, which is a necessary step on the road to acceptance."

Clearly, visibility and acceptance are on the rise. This past summer, the *Baltimore Sun* featured a long, friendly article on the polyamorists' national conference, held in Maryland. In September, the *New York Times* ran a long personal account of (heterosexual) polyamory in the Sunday Styles section. But the real uptick in public bisexuality/polyamory began with the October 2005 release in New York of the documentary *Three of Hearts: A Postmodern Family.*

Three of Hearts is the story of the real-life 13-year relationship of two men and a woman. Together for several years in a gay relationship, two bisexual-leaning men meet a woman and create a threesome that produces two children, one by each man. Although the woman marries one of the men, the entire threesome has a commitment ceremony. The movie records the trio's eventual breakup, yet the film's website notes their ongoing commitment to the view that "family is anything we want to create." . . .

Of course, many argue that true bisexuality does not exist. In this view— held by a variety of people, from some psychiatrists to certain pro-gay-marriage activists— everyone is either heterosexual or homosexual. From this perspective, so-called bisexuals are either in confused transition from heterosexuality to homosexuality, or simply lying about their supposedly dual sexual inclinations. Alternatively, it's sometimes said that while female bisexuality does exist, male bisexuality does not. A recent and controversial study reported on by the *New York Times* in July 2005 claimed to show that truly bisexual attraction in men might not exist.

Whatever view we take of these medical/psychiatric/philosophical controversies, it is a fact that a bi/poly rights movement exists and is growing. Whether Koen Brand and Bianca and Mirjam de Bruijn are "authentic" bisexuals or "just fooling themselves," they are clearly capable of sustaining polyamorous bisexual V's and triads for long enough to make serious political demands. *Three of Hearts* raises questions about whether the two men in the triangle are bisexual or simply confused gays. But with two children, a 13-year relationship, and at one time at least a clear desire for legal-ceremonial confirmation, the *Three of Hearts* trio is a harbinger of demands for legal group marriage. Public interest in the De Bruijn triangle has already raised the visibility and acceptance of polyamorous bisexuality in the Netherlands. For legal-political purposes, acceptance is what matters. And given Yoshino's numerical analysis, the growth potential for self-identifying bisexuals is substantial.

Americans today respond to gay and bisexual friends and family members in a variety of ways. Despite stereotypical accusations of "homophobia," the traditionally religious generally offer a mixture of compassion and concern. Many other Americans, conservative and liberal alike, are happy to extend friendship, understanding, and acceptance to gay and bisexual relatives and acquaintances. This heightened social tolerance is a good thing. Yet somehow the idea has taken hold that tolerance for sexual minorities requires a radical remake of the institution of marriage. That is a mistake.

The fundamental purpose of marriage is to encourage mothers and fathers to stay bound as a family for the sake of their children. Our liberalized modern marriage system is far from perfect, and certainly doesn't always succeed in keeping parents together while their children are young. Yet often it does. Unfortunately, once we radically redefine marriage in an effort to solve the problems of adults, the institution is destined to be shattered by a cacophony of grown-up demands.

The De Bruijn trio, Koen Brand, the Unitarian Universalists for Polyamory Awareness, the legal arguments of Elizabeth Emens and Kenji Yoshino, and the bisexual/polyamory movement in general have been launched into action by the successes of the campaign for gay marriage. In a sense, though, these innovators have jumped too soon. They've shown us today—well before same-sex marriage has triumphed nationwide—what would emerge in its aftermath.

Liberals may now put behind-the-scenes pressure on the Dutch government to keep the lid on legalized polyamory for as long as the matter of gay marriage is still unsettled. The Unitarian polyamorists, already conflicted about how much recognition to demand while the gay marriage battle is unresolved, may be driven further underground. But let there be no mistake about what will happen should same-sex marriage be fully legalized in the United States. At that point, if bisexual activists haven't already launched a serious campaign for legalized polyamory, they will go public. It took four years after the full legalization of gay marriage in the Netherlands for the first polyamory test case to emerge. With a far larger and more organized polyamory movement in America, it might not take even that long after the nationalization of gay marriage in the United States.

It's easy to imagine that, in a world where gay marriage was common and fully accepted, a serious campaign to legalize polyamorous unions would succeed—especially a campaign spearheaded by an organized bisexual-rights movement. Yet win or lose, the culture of marriage will be battered for years by the debate. Just as we're now continually reminded that not all married couples have children, we'll someday be endlessly told that not all marriages are monogamous (nor all monogamists married). For a second time, the fuzziness and imperfection found in every real-world social institution will be contorted into a rationale for reforming marriage out of existence.

STANLEY KURTZ is a writer and senior fellow at the Ethics and Public Policy Center. Kurtz is a key contributor to American public debates and has written on issues for various journals, particularly National Review Online. Kurtz argues that allowing for same-sex marriage will create a slippery slope, eventually leading to plural marriages. Kurtz contends that such marriages prove destructive to the institution of marriage itself.

EXPLORING THE ISSUE

Are Open Relationships Healthy?

Critical Thinking and Reflection

1. Can you identify the emotional, moral, intellectual, and social components in Dyson's argument?
2. Can you identify the emotional, moral, intellectual, and social components in Kurtz's argument?
3. Can you identify your own emotional, moral, intellectual, and social responses to this issue?
4. What are some similarities and differences between your responses and the authors'?

Is There Common Ground?

What is your response to Dyson's argument that the impact depends on the individual relationship? What is your response to Kurtz's argument that same-sex marriage will lead to polyamory? Is the progression as inevitable as he contends? What are some other factors that influence your views related to monogamy and polyamory?

This issue specifically asks whether open relationships are healthy. Is there a universal definition for what is emotionally healthy regarding sexual partners? Specifically, is monogamy a universal value that should be practiced in all relationships? Is polyamory a universal value that should be practiced in all relationships? What, if anything, would you regard as a standard relationship model that all couples should aspire to? Is sex outside marriage cheating if your spouse approves of it? Most importantly in seeking common

ground, what kind of communication is necessary to ensure that people are being honest about their feelings?

Additional Resources

Polyamory Forum:

www.polyamory.com/forum/

Xeromag presents Polyamory 101:

www.xeromag.com/fvpoly.html

The Daily Beast reports on polyamory:

www.thedailybeast.com/newsweek/2009/07/28/only-you-and-you-and-you.html

Alternatives to Marriage Project presents polyamory:

www.unmarried.org/polyamory.html

Internet References . . .

Categories of Poly Resources

www.polyamory.org/SF/groups.html

Patheos: Strategies for Open Relationships

www.patheos.com/Resources/Additional-Resources/Bouquet-of-Lovers.html

WebMD: Open Marriages

www.webmd.com/sex-relationships/features/the-truth-about-open-marriage

Unit 3

Contemporary Issues in Parenting

*A*sk any new parent. There are few things in life about which people have more opinions that the right way to parent a child. And folks seem to believe that every parent wants (or needs) to know not only what they should do as they raise their child, but also the places where they are getting it wrong. "I blame the parents" is frequently heard whenever a child acts in a way that crosses someone's expectation for appropriate behavior. In fact, there are myriad ways to raise a healthy child. In each parent's story, though, there are moments of crisis in which they must face challenging choices. This unit explores some of the challenges that parents face as they navigate the minefields of childrearing.

Selected, Edited, and with Issue Framing Material by:
Don Dyson, *Widener University*

ISSUE

Do Parents Have the Right to Deny Their Children Lifesaving Medical Care Due to Their Religious Convictions?

YES: Calvin P. Johnson, from "Closing Statement for Parents: In Re the Matter of the Welfare of the Child of Colleen and Anthony Hauser," Minnesota, District Court, Fifth Judicial District (2009)

NO: John R. Rodenberg, from "Opinion of the Court: In the Matter of the Welfare of the Child of Colleen and Anthony Hauser," Minnesota, District Court, Fifth Judicial District (2009)

Learning Outcomes

After reading this issue, you will be able to:

- Identify the major arguments made for and against parents denying their child lifesaving medical treatment.
- Compare and contrast the competing arguments made for and against parents denying their child lifesaving medical treatment in this issue.
- Evaluate the implications of parents denying their child life saving medical treatment on children's health as well as religious liberty.

ISSUE SUMMARY

YES: Calvin P. Johnson, Esq., is the attorney for the parents, Colleen and Anthony Hauser. Johnson argues that the government forcing medical care for the Hauser child violates his religious liberty and is abusive to this child.

NO: John R. Rodenberg is the District Court judge in this case. Rodenberg argues that all parties are acting out of convictions for the best interest of the child. He also argues that the state has a compelling interest to act against Hauser's religious views for medical care since the child is only thirteen years old.

The use of chemotherapy as a cancer treatment dates back to the early twentieth century. It was designed as the use of chemicals to treat disease. In 1935, the National Cancer Institute was set up and provided an organized system for screening drugs that treated cancer. However, the level of toxicity of the drugs proved to be a challenge for wider use of this treatment.

During World War II, it was noted that when troops were exposed to sulfur mustards due to an accidental spill, more purposeful research occurred to better understand the impact of these chemicals on things like cancer.

While initially highly controversial, attempts to treat cancer with chemotherapy would enjoy wide levels of support over the coming decades. Within the past couple of decades, it has become a highly regarded method for treating cancer.

Christian Scientists have received a considerable amount of attention for refusing medical care for themselves and their children, sometimes for even life-threatening illnesses such as cancer. Generally speaking, many Christian scientists are expected to heal themselves through prayer of minor sicknesses such as the cold and flu as well as life-threatening conditions such as cancer. However, if a child dies as a result of his or her parents denying their child life saving medical care, then the parents are sometimes charged and prosecuted.

Although Christian Scientists receive perhaps the highest profile for this belief, they are by no means the only religion that subscribes to such a belief. The Nemenhah and

Indigenous Traditional Organization, also known as the Oklevueha Native American church of Nemenhah, was established by self-determination in 2002. They describe themselves as a "restoration of the Pre-Colonial and Pre-Conquest Nomadic Indigenous People which inhabited parts of Central America, North America, the Pacific Islands, Japan, Korea, China, and Tibet anciently." Their Web site states that they focus on "the Healing of the Body Physical, the Body Familial, the Body Societal and the Whole Earth." The Nemenhah are committed to natural healing.

The Nemenhah Constitution states the following:

- We believe in miracles, such as cures, healings, prophecies, visions . . . and that it is the right of all people to heal and be healed without restriction from any earthly government, for natural medicine and natural modalities of healing are gifts of the Creator.
- The Sacred Sahaptan Healing Way is that body of knowledge which is compiled into a uniform curriculum for the systematic training and education of the Medicine Men and Medicine Women of the Band. It is the criteria by which Band Adoption is entered into and the basis and foundation of this spiritual and physical ceremonies.
- Article Fifteen: The right of community members to choose their method and kind of medicine shall not be denied or abridged in any way and the councils shall not enact any counsel that shall place one profession or modality of medicine over any other, except when such professions or modalities tend to render a person unable to earn a living, or when they threaten to do so.

Clearly, this religion possesses the basic tenet that they have their own rights to determine the best course for healing when sick. That course includes a denial of intervention for modern Western remedies.

The First Amendment to the U.S. Constitution says, "Congress shall make no law respecting an establishment of religion, or prohibiting the free exercise thereof." The First Amendment provides us with this right, known as the Free Exercise Clause, as one that is so important that it is often referred to as a fundamental right.

What sort of limitations do we place on fundamental rights? Should we allow human sacrifice? Use of drugs? Wearing a weapon such as a knife, which also has strong religious significance in some cultures, in schools? Opting out of a class at school because a child feels that it violates his or her religious convictions?

In short, we are attempting to determine when there is a compelling state interest to intervene. In the case of the Hausers, which is explored in this chapter, the question is how do we protect a child with cancer. The Hausers argued in court that they should be free to intervene as they wish with their son's cancer. Their son had Hodgkin's lymphoma. His story would generate national headlines.

Doctors argued that with proper medical treatment, Daniel had a 90% chance of survival. Without the treatment, he would have only a 5% chance of survival. The Hausers, who belong to the Nemenhah faith, believe that their son is a medicine man and can best determine his path in healing his body and spirit.

The judge ruled that Daniel had to get chemotherapy. As a result, Daniel's mother took him and fled.

Jeffrey Toobin, CNN senior legal analyst, says that the state must intervene: "Virtually all the time the court says that what this mother is doing, while we sympathize with her pain, this is child abuse. He is a minor. He is not qualified to make the decision for himself. This is what it means to be a minor: other people make your decisions for you. This is the same thing as if he got hit by a car, blocking the ambulance. If need be, they have to take the kid away, strap him down, and apply chemotherapy. . . . It's life or death."

After Daniel and his mother fled, Daniel was eventually returned after almost one week on the run. The parents consented to have their son undergo his chemotherapy treatment.

The doctors treating Daniel received mail from all over the country, ranging from those who believe in natural medicine to anti-abortion activists to conspiracy theorists. One opponent of the medical intervention created a Web site of a needle being injected into a monkey and said that doctors were "dripping poison into yet another child."

Daniel did not have a positive reaction to the chemotherapy, explained a family spokesman: "Danny has had a horrible day, he's felt terrible all day long. He's not happy. The doctor changed the number of chemotherapy drugs in the protocol submitted to the court. Danny is not tolerating the drugs well and has been vomiting all day. He is understandably angry and depressed about being forced to go through the ravages of chemotherapy again."

Daniel Hauser's lymphoma went into remission after his radiation treatment. Although his doctors credit the radiation, the Hausers credit Daniel's good diet.

In this issue, you have excerpts from the primary sources from the court case, representing both sides. You can determine the reasoning of the Hausers, as well as the court, in informing your decision.

YES

Calvin P. Johnson

Closing Statement for Parents: In Re the Matter of the Welfare of the Child of Colleen and Anthony Hauser

Respondents, Colleen and Anthony Hauser, submit this legal memorandum in support of their closing arguments in this matter.

Thank you to all, with your words of encouragement. And thank you to those on the other side, for genuinely believing in their position.

Most importantly, I thank Danny Hauser, a true Medicine man. This thirteen-year-old young man has turned this community upside down and inside out. A world is listening.

I respectfully submit that he is one of the more powerful medicine men around.

Danny is a Medicine man by virtue of his ranking as a male in the family. That is contained in the Nemenhah Constitution that you could not understand. It is written in clear language.

This Court has always held, from day one, to the steadfast principle of protecting our children. We do not harm our children. We do not torture our children.

Yet the path advocated by the State is one of torture and criminal action.

There is a reason why 91% of the oncologists on staff at McGill Cancer Centre in Montreal do not take chemotherapy or allow their family members to take it for cancer treatment. It's too toxic, and not effective. This is exactly as the standard of medical care advocated and pronounced by Dr. Shealy.

This matter has been pummeled to death with the percentage of a 90% cure rate. And yet we come to find that a cure rate can be defined as "tumor shrinkage" but not the elimination of cancer, at all. In fact, given the statistics as provided to this Court, and demonstrated by a reputable, peer-reviewed, journal (*Clinical Oncology*, 2004; 16:549–560.), the real rate of survival hovers around 35–40%.

Apparently, if a study predicts a 6% success rate, and they achieve 12%, the cancer industry reports that as a 50% increase in their success rates. It is unconscionable that the absolute numbers were not given to the Hausers in this particular matter. It is unconscionable that the cancer industry would perpetrate a number that does not stand up to actual fact. And it is unconscionable that we had to enter into an emotional issue when the true issue is the care of a thirteen-year-old young man, and the ability of that young man and his parents to realistically assess their best survival rates from reputable, peer-reviewed medical journals, before making their decision.

To condense the posture of this case, it looks like this:

A doctor went to a state official and said we have a 90% chance that this young man is going to die if he does not use my product.

By legal definition, if you use the product, it constitutes felony assault, and may very well constitute torture, when you force the use of the product against the will of the victim.

It will seriously damage the largest component of this young man's body: his immune system.

It may kill him.

Without question, it will cause serious disfigurement, including the fact that there will probably be no progeny of this thirteen-year-old young man.

It will cost $92,900 just for the first round of chemotherapeutic agents and initial testing, and we will apply it five to six more times.

We cannot tell you the manner in which we can do this against the will of the child.

When we promise a 90% cure rate, that really only amounts to 40.3%, as measured by the best statistics available from our very own peer-reviewed medical journals.

We will not rebut a very prominent surgeon's opinion that chemotherapy constitutes torture.

We will make this application five or six more times, over the course of six months.

If the young man is still alive after that time, we will apply radiation to him.

United States District Court, Minnesota, Fifth Judicial District, 2009.

We will do this against his religious beliefs, and we will try to convince the Court that his religion is not his.

Further, we will make sure that you cannot consider any other modes or options for health treatment, because they are not approved by a "standard of care" that does nothing to address this soul's individual consciousness.

If I brought a client in front of this Court and asked for permission to do this, you would look at me and ask that I be locked up, not just my client. If we would make a proposal to exercise torture on any of the detainees at Guantanamo, in the same measure as advocated by the doctors in this case, our country's reputation would be in a shambles. It is too easy to fall prey to that 90% number. This is a real case, involving real issues, and involving freedom of consciousness.

The Hausers . . . have integrated a process of pH-balanced therapy that is and has been accepted in much of the world. This water machine that Danny told the Court (Kangen water) is found in practically every major hospital in Japan.

We have long known the history of the pH balance. After World War II, the only survivors of Hiroshima and Nagasaki were the Japanese monks who focused on a diet of miso soup and short-grained brown rice, a pH-balanced diet. They lived. The others died horrible deaths.

It is entirely fitting that Japan would be a leader in this "standard of care." It would be a shame to preclude a modality of healing for a thirteen-year-old because we determined it is more fitting to torture and to assault the juvenile, with poisons he does not want.

The point is simple: the Hausers have elected forms of alternative healthcare that they believe to be more effective and more beneficial than those recommended by the cancer industry.

This trial is the act of two loving parents who will go to any length to save their child from assault and torture.

This Court has a long and strong history of protecting children. Now is the time to do so, according to the dictates of Danny and his family's consciousness and spiritual being. The fact remains, that there are an abundance of scientifically proven, medical therapies available for Danny. If this Court wants to intervene, consistent with their conscious and religious beliefs, It must follow the reasonable path of healing as articulated by our evidence.

The Guardian Ad Litem takes no consideration of the spiritual path chosen by the parties. Nor does she give any power of the parents to help with the spiritual education of their son.

What is without question is the verification of Danny's status as a member of the Nemenhah band. This has not been refuted.

What is without question is that we, even the Guardian Ad Litem, must allow Danny's conscience to worship God as he sees fit. His conscience shall not be infringed. She cannot infringe upon it now. Nor shall she control or interfere with his right of conscience. Nor can the State. The State is attempting to do so, by their act.

We qualify our "liberty of conscience" in that we cannot exercise acts of licentiousness or justify practices inconsistent with the peace or safety of the State. We do not assault our children. We do not torture the juveniles of this state. We are a bright and shining beacon for freedom and justice for the rest of the world.

We come to understand that healing is more than just a physical act of the administration of drugs or chemicals. It begins at the deep level of Soul, and continues through the mind, emotional and physicals bodies.

The confidence of healing is of paramount concern. Danny holds this confidence, and is self-sufficient in his understanding of healing. He is self-actualized, and not in that group of 99.2% of those people who will die in the next fifteen years, from their beliefs.

What has happened is, by his very acts and deeds, Danny has become a torch bearer of an important message: the people of this state have the right to chose their own reasonable medical modality. We have the ability to go beyond those standards established by the courts, and the medical "religion," and to go beyond the "standard of care" advocated and compelled upon all doctors in this state.

We heard the testimony of Dr. Bostrom, who indicated that Danny could be part of a study.

It is entirely reasonable for parents to reject experimentation upon their son, especially when his life is on the line.

It is ironic that the parents have to fight for their right not to have radiation on Danny, and yet, by the flip of a coin, if Danny is selected in one of the factions of the study group, he won't get radiation.

Finally, before you get to the heart of my legal argument, I would ask the court to consider the definition of a medicine man. Again, like all these computer people, I go to Wikipedia for a first review.

Medicine man, Role in Native Society:

"The primary function of these 'medicine elders' is to secure the health of the spiritual world, including the Great Spirit, for the benefit of the entire community. Sometimes the help sought may be for the sake of healing disease, sometimes it may be for the sake of healing the psyche, sometimes the goal is to promote harmony between human groups or between humans and nature."

I realize that Ms. Oliver doesn't know what a Medicine man looks like. In seeing and understanding the changes brought about by this thirteen-year-old young man, we are coming to understand what a Medicine man does.

We are moving into a new arena of consciousness. We are rejecting a modality of treatment that is assaultive and torturous. We are relying upon our bodies to do what the good Lord intended: to heal.

Legal Argument as Applied from the Facts

The Guardian Ad Litem's Testimony Constitutes an Impermissible Imposition of a Religious Test

Religious freedoms are constitutionally protected by both the United States Bill of Rights, as well as by our Minnesota Constitution. Specifically, these documents state:

U.S. Bill of Rights: Amendment I

Congress shall make no law respecting an establishment of religion, or prohibiting the free exercise thereof; or abridging the freedom of speech, or of the press; or the right of the people peaceably to assemble, and to petition the Government for a redress of grievances.

Minnesota State Constitution: Article I, Bill of Rights

Sec. 16. Freedom of conscience; no preference to be given to any religious establishment or mode of worship. The enumeration of rights in this constitution shall not deny or impair others retained by and inherent in the people. The right of every man to worship God according to the dictates of his own conscience shall never be infringed; nor shall any man be compelled to attend, erect or support any place of worship, or to maintain any religious or ecclesiastical ministry, against his consent; nor shall any control of or interference with the rights of conscience be permitted, or any preference be given by law to any religious establishment or mode of worship; but the liberty of conscience hereby secured shall not be so construed as to excuse acts of licentiousness or justify practices inconsistent with the peace or safety of the state, nor shall any money be drawn from the treasury for the benefit of any religious societies or religious or theological seminaries.

Sec. 17. Religious tests and property qualifications prohibited. No religious test or amount of property shall be required as a qualification for any office of public trust in the state. No religious test or amount of property shall be required as a qualification of any voter at any election in this state; nor shall any person be rendered incompetent to give evidence in any court of law or equity in consequence of his opinion upon the subject of religion.

"Religious liberty is a precious right," *State v. Hershberger* (Minn. 1990). The people of this state have always cherished religious liberty, and the high importance of protecting this right is demonstrated by its treatment in our constitution, where it appears even before any reference to the formation of a government. *State by Cooper v. French* (Minn. 1990). The Minnesota Supreme Court has consistently held that article I, section 16 of the Minnesota Constitution affords greater protection against governmental action affecting religious liberties than the First Amendment of the federal constitution. "Whereas the first amendment establishes a limit on government action at the point of *prohibiting* the exercise of religion, section 16 precludes even an *infringement* on or an *interference* with religious freedom," *Hershberger*. Thus, government action that is permissible under the federal constitution because it does not prohibit religious practices but merely infringes on or interferes with religious practices may nonetheless violate the Minnesota Constitution.

Minnesota courts employ a heightened "compelling state interest balancing test" when determining whether a challenged law infringes on or interferes with religious practices. The test has four prongs: (1) whether the objector's beliefs are sincerely held; (2) whether the state regulation burdens the exercise of religious beliefs; (3) whether the state interest in the regulation is overriding or compelling; and (4) whether the state regulation uses the least restrictive means.

As the Court will recall, the Guardian Ad Litem had stipulated to the genuineness of both the parents' and Daniel's religious beliefs. However, during trial, the Guardian Ad Litem broke her word when said she was now challenging the agreed-upon Pre-Trial Stipulation. Mr. and Mrs. Hauser have been prejudiced, because they were not adequately informed that this would be an issue for trial. In fact, they were told the opposite.

As argued in Respondents' previous Memorandum, parents have a significant interest in establishing a spiritual path for their child. The State may not come in and qualify that path. To do so violates State and Federal Constitutional Protections.

The qualification by the Guardian Ad Litem is limited in this situation. While she indicated that she read the Constitution of the Nemenhah Spiritual Path, she testified that she did not understand it. She further testified that she did not see any of the principals embodied in the way of life of the Hausers. She could not tell the Court why Danny is a medicine man.

On the contrary, the Hausers have demonstrated an ability to walk their path in all aspects of their lives. They will do no harm. They eat food from the land, not polluted by pesticides and herbicides. They use oils, herbs, and other remedies to promote and maintain healthy bodies. They act as a harmonious family together.

In the present case, Danny's Guardian Ad Litem has attempted to qualify his membership and beliefs in the Nemenhah spiritual path. Her doing so constitutes an impermissible religious test, in violation of both the Federal and Minnesota Constitutions. There is no evidence contradicting Danny's beliefs in the Nemenhah faith or its spiritual path, or that these beliefs are anything but sincere. Certainly, the interference that is being advocated in this case, that of forcing Danny to undergo chemotherapy when such treatment is in direct violation of these religious beliefs burdens Danny's exercise of his religious beliefs. The state has failed to demonstrate a compelling interest in this matter that would justify imposition of the propounded medical treatment in violation of Danny's religious beliefs.

CALVIN P. JOHNSON, ESQ., of the Calvin P. Johnson Law Firm, is the attorney for the parents, Colleen and Anthony Hauser. Johnson argues that the government forcing medical care for Hauser violates his religious liberty and is abusive to this child.

John R. Rodenberg  **NO**

Opinion of the Court: In the Matter of the Welfare of the Child of Colleen and Anthony Hauser

The Court is today determining that the Petition alleging Daniel Hauser to be a child in need of protection or services has been proven by clear and convincing evidence. The Court is also concluding that the State of Minnesota, through Brown County Family Services ("BCFS"), has demonstrated a compelling state interest in the life and welfare of Daniel sufficient to override the fundamental constitutional rights of both the parents and Daniel to the free exercise of religion and the due process right of the parents to direct the religious and other upbringing of their child.

This much is certain and the Court so finds: All of the actions of the parties which bring this matter before the Court have been done in good faith. The parents, Daniel, the treating doctors, the child welfare agency, the Brown County Attorney and the Guardian ad Litem have at all times acted in good faith herein.

. . .

Daniel Hauser is currently 13 years of age. He has been diagnosed as suffering from nodular sclerosing Hodgkin's disease, stage IIB. The Hauser family's local family practice doctor, Dr. Joyce, correctly identified on January 21, 2009 that "lymphoma certainly seems likely" when Daniel presented with a persistent cough, fatigue, swollen lymph nodes and other symptoms. Dr. Joyce made a referral to oncology specialists at Children's Hospitals. The diagnosis was made there and it was determined that the cancer was readily treatable by therapies including chemotherapy.

Daniel's mother consented to the administration of the recommended chemotherapy beginning on February 5, 2009. The gravity and imminence of Daniel's situation limited the available options. Mrs. Hauser effectively consented to the initiation of chemotherapy after being adequately informed of her rights as Daniel's parent.

Daniel's lymphoma responded well to the initial round of chemotherapy.

Unfortunately Daniel also had adverse side effects to the administration of chemotherapy. While this was not unusual, both Daniel and his parents were justifiably quite concerned. The parents, acting in absolute parental good faith, chose to seek out a second opinion and consulted with Mayo Clinic. Mayo Clinic doctors concurred with the earlier medical advice. The parents, again in complete good faith, sought a third medical opinion, this time from the University of Minnesota Hospitals. Again, the recommendation was that the additional course of chemotherapy should be undertaken.

The doctors at these facilities, which are among the finest available in this part of the country, agree that Daniel has a very good chance of a complete recovery with additional chemotherapy and possibly radiation. Estimates of complete 5-year remission with this course range from 80% to 95%. These doctors are also in agreement that Daniel has very little chance of surviving 5 years without the prescribed course of treatment. If the mediastinal tumor were to increase in size and become resistant to chemotherapy, as all of these doctors opine that it will without the prescribed treatment, the long-term prospects for Daniel decrease significantly, even if the chemotherapy is resumed in the future.

The family has also consulted with Dr. Kotulski, an osteopathic physician practicing in Mankato, Minnesota. Dr. Kotulski agrees with the recommended chemotherapy. The Hauser family's local doctor, Dr. Joyce, also agrees with the recommendations of the oncologists.

In short, five (5) different medical doctors, three (3) of whom specialize in pediatric oncology, have all agreed upon the necessary medical care for Daniel.

There were several experts testifying at trial who believe in alternatives to chemotherapy for treatment of some cancers in some instances. However, there was absolutely no evidence presented at trial from any health care practitioner who has examined Daniel and who recommends any course of treatment different than that prescribed by the oncologists and medical doctors. The evidence is uncontroverted that Hodgkin's lymphoma, stage IIB, is best treated by chemotherapy and possible later radiation.

The family has a genuine and strong belief in the benefits of holistic medicine and, specifically, in Nemenhah. Nemenhah is based upon Native American healing practices. Daniel is deemed to be a "medicine man" by Nemenhah and does not wish to receive any additional chemotherapy.

Daniel Hauser is an extremely polite and pleasant young man. While he is 13 years of age, Daniel is unable to read. He does not know what the term "elder" means, although he claims to be one. He knows he is a medicine man under Nemenhah teachings, but is unable to identify how he became a medicine man or what teachings he has had to master to become one. He believes in the principle of "do no harm" and attributes his belief to Nemenhah teachings. He lacks the ability to give informed consent to medical procedures.

The doctors who have filed reports with Brown County concerning Daniel and who testified in this case have acted in conformity with their duties under well-established Minnesota statutory law. Brown County has properly brought this matter before the Court for determination and has filed a Petition with the Court as it is authorized to do by [law]. The parents and Daniel have properly asserted their positions in the matter in a very orderly and respectful fashion, with the capable assistance of counsel. The Guardian ad Litem, whose role it is to advocate for the best interests of a child claimed to be in need of protection or services, has carefully considered the matter and has expressed her opinions as to the child's best interests consistent with her obligation to the Court.

There are sharp differences in the positions of the parties.

The Hauser family members have a constitutional right to freedom of belief. The parents also have a right to parent their child that is based in the Due Process Clause of the United States Constitution. These constitutional freedoms can be overcome only upon a showing of a compelling state interest.

Correspondingly, there can scarcely be imagined a governmental interest more compelling than protecting the life of a child.

Minnesota has a long-standing statutory requirement that parents must provide "necessary medical care" for a child and providing that "complementary and alternative health care" is not sufficient. Multiple Minnesota statutes so provide. The legislature has also mandated by statute that both medical providers and "complementary and alternative practitioners" must report to child welfare authorities any situation in which a child is not being provided with "necessary medical care."

As applied to this case, Minnesota's statutory provisions have an effect upon the religious practices of the Hauser family. The mother asserts that a core tenet of Nemenhah is "first do no harm." The mother asserts that God intends that the body should be healed the natural way and that chemotherapy and radiation are poisons. Daniel also professes to the primacy of the "do no harm" tenet.

Under the relevant authorities and as applied to the facts in this case, Brown County has demonstrated a compelling state interest in seeing to it that Daniel's prospects for life are maximized by his being found in need to protection or services. The parents are free to provide Daniel with complementary or alternative therapies, but under Minnesota law, as applied here consistent with both federal and state constitutions, the parents must provide "necessary medical care" to Daniel.

As set forth below, the Court is intending to leave Daniel in the custody of his parents and to allow the parents the maximum legally-permissible range of choices for treatment of Daniel. Daniel loves his parents and they love him. He should remain with them as long as he receives treatment complying with the minimum standards of parental care provided by Minnesota law.

The issue in this case is not whether the State of Minnesota should have enacted the law as it did. The Court is obligated to apply the law as it is written unless to do so would violate a constitutional right. Settled state and federal case law establish that the State of Minnesota may constitutionally intervene in the present matter.

Surely many will think that the law should be different. With issues as sensitive as these, there are bound to be strong feelings both ways about what the law should be. To the extent that the parties involved in this case and members of the public in general believe that [the Minnesota law] or any other statute should be revisited, those arguments are properly made to the Minnesota Legislature. The Court is resolving this matter solely with reference to the relevant legal authorities, and not based upon the Court's personal opinion with regard to what Minnesota substantive law should be. The only personal observation the Court makes is this: If the Minnesota Legislature ever reconsiders the relevant statutes, I am confident that I join all of the others involved in this matter in hoping, and indeed in praying, that Daniel Hauser lives to testify at that hearing.

. . .

Conclusions of Law

- Daniel Hauser is a child in need of protection or services within the meaning of [Minnesota law].

- The parents and Daniel have made their arguments with respect to the free exercise clause of the First Amendment to the United States Constitution. "Congress shall make no law respecting an establishment of religion, or prohibiting the free exercise thereof; or abridging the freedom of speech, or of the press; or the right of the people peaceably to assemble, and to petition the Government for a redress of grievances." The Minnesota Constitution also contains a provision relating to religious liberty. "The right of every man to worship God according to the dictates of his own conscience shall never be infringed . . . nor shall any control of or interference with the rights of conscience be permitted. . . ." This provision of the Minnesota Constitution affords greater protection for religious liberties against governmental action than the first amendment of the federal constitution. The Court is analyzing the free exercise claim under both provisions. In that that state constitution affords greater protection to the free exercise of religion and imposes a higher standard in order to justify any state action the impinges upon the free exercise of religion and conscience, it follows that if Brown County is able to satisfy the requirements of the Minnesota Constitution in this matter, then it will also have satisfied the requirements of the federal constitution.

· · ·

- The State of Minnesota has legislatively determined that ensuring that children receive necessary medical care is very important state interest. This state interest is also reflected in the requirement imposed upon both medical doctors and practitioners of complimentary or alternative therapies to report to child welfare agencies any failure to provide "necessary medical care."
- The law does not condone the injury of children, nor will it accommodate danger for children. The welfare of children is a matter of paramount concern. The power of the courts to protect children is now exercised by the state as an attribute of its sovereignty. The state as *parens patriae* has authority to assume parental authority over a child who because of misfortune or helplessness is unable to properly care for himself.
- *Wisconsin v. Yoder* (1972) involved Amish parents who refused to send their children to school past the 8th grade. The Amish claimed that the compulsory attendance statute encroached on their rights and the rights of their children to the free exercise of the religious beliefs they and their forbears had adhered to for almost three centuries. The U.S. Supreme Court wrote that: "In evaluating those claims we must be careful to determine whether the Amish religious

faith and their mode of life are, as they claim, inseparable and interdependent. A way of life, however virtuous and admirable, may not be interposed as a barrier to reasonable state regulation of education if it is based on purely secular considerations; to have the protection of the Religion Clauses, the claims must be rooted in religious belief." Wisconsin argued that its interest in its system of compulsory education was compelling, such that even the established religious practices of the Amish needed to give way. Wisconsin argued that its system of compulsory education prepared children to participate in our political system so as to preserve freedom and independence and also that education prepares individuals to be self-reliant and self-sufficient participants in society. The U.S. Supreme Court accepted those propositions but determined that the State had not made a sufficient showing to justify the severe interference with religious freedom entailed by compulsory education, in light of evidence that the Amish were a successful, though nonconventional, society in America. Wisconsin also asserted a *parens patriae* interest in the well-being and educational opportunities of Amish children. The Supreme Court wrote that: "if the State is empowered, as *parens patriae* to 'save' a child from himself or his Amish parents by requiring an additional two years of compulsory formal high school education, the State will in large measure influence, if not determine, the religious future of the child. When the interests of parenthood are combined with a free exercise claim of the nature revealed by this record, more than merely a 'reasonable relation to some purpose within the competency of the State' is required to sustain the validity of the State's requirement under the First Amendment. To be sure, the power of the parent, even when linked to a free exercise claim, may be subject to limitation . . . if it appears that parental decisions will jeopardize the health or safety of the children, or have a potential for significant social burdens." (bolding added). The Supreme Court determined that "the record strongly indicated that accommodating the religious objections of the Amish by forgoing one, or at most two, additional years of compulsory education will not impair the physical or mental health of the child. . . ."
- Minnesota courts have enunciated and applied a balancing test, balancing the state's interest in cases such as this against the actor's free-exercise interest in religious-based conduct. Where it is undisputed that the religious belief is sincerely held and that the religious belief would be burdened by the proposed regulation, the

balancing test requires proof of a compelling state interest. Minnesota has a compelling interest in protecting the welfare of children. A parent may exercise genuinely held religious beliefs; but the resulting conduct, though motivated by religious belief, must yield when—judged by accepted medical practice—it jeopardizes the life of a child. Religious practices must bend to the state's interest in protecting the welfare of a child whenever the child might die without the intervention of conventional medicine. This is settled Minnesota law.

- In *Hofbauer v. Saratoga County Department of Social Services* (N.Y. App. 1979), a case similar to this matter, a county filed a petition to have an eight-year-old child, who was suffering from Hodgkin's Disease, adjudged to be a child neglected by his parents. The parents were not following the treating physician's recommendations for radiation and chemotherapy, but instead entrusted the child to the care of a duly licensed physician advocating nutritional or metabolic therapies, including laetrile injections. The New York appellate court held that the decision as to whether the parents were providing adequate medical care must be "whether the parents, once having sought accredited medical assistance and having been made aware of the seriousness of their child's affliction and the possibility of cure if a certain mode of treatment is undertaken, have provided for their child a treatment which is recommended by their physician and which has not been totally rejected by all responsible medical authority."

- The present situation is *unlike* that in the Hoffbauer case. There, a medical authority was monitoring the treatment. If there were to be a medically approved way to treat Daniel's Hodgkin's lymphoma different than what the five different medical/osteopathic doctors have thus far opined, then the parents here would be free to pursue such an option under the statute. Where there is unanimity of medical opinion and where the matter is an important one of life and death, the State has a compelling State interest sufficient to overcome the parents' Free Exercise and Due Process rights.

- The Court's resolution of the issue presented is limited to the specific factual situation present. What is not before the Court in this matter is the issue of whether there would ever be the case of an older or particularly mature minor who expresses a position opposed to medical treatment and who might therefore have a constitutional right to direct his or her own treatment contrary to what is "medically necessary." This matter, as more fully described above, involves a 13-year-old child who has only a rudimentary understanding at best of the risks and benefits of chemotherapy. He genuinely opposes the imposition of chemotherapy. However, he does not believe he is ill currently. The fact is that he is very ill currently. He has Hodgkin's lymphoma which is apparently not in remission from the available evidence. In this case, the state has a compelling state interest sufficient to override the minor's genuine opposition. . . .

JOHN R. RODENBERG is the District Court Judge in this case. Rodenberg argues that all parties are acting out of convictions for the best interest of the child. He also argues that the state has a compelling interest to act against Hauser's religious views for medical care since the child is only 13 years old.

EXPLORING THE ISSUE

Do Parents Have the Right to Deny Their Children Lifesaving Medical Care Due to Their Religious Convictions?

Critical Thinking and Reflection

1. Can you identify the emotional, moral, intellectual, and social components in Johnson's argument?
2. Can you identify the emotional, moral, intellectual, and social components in Rodenberg's argument?
3. Can you identify your own emotional, moral, intellectual, and social responses to this issue?
4. What are some similarities and differences between your responses and the authors'?

Is There Common Ground?

Even the judge in this case acknowledged that everyone involved was looking out for the best interest of Daniel Hauser. The right to express our religion is a fundamental right that enjoys wide protection in our society. At the same time, protecting the health and welfare of children is critical in any caring society. How much power should be ceded to medical professionals? Although the state did not support the position of Daniel's parents, what might have caused a different outcome? What if Daniel's illness were not fatal? In what circumstances, if any, would you let parents' decision-making rights supersede the states decision based on the testimony of medical professionals?

Additional Resources

Nemenah and Traditional Indigenous Organization:

www.nemenhah.org/

Christian Science:

http://christianscience.com/

Washington Post article about prayer and healing:

www.washingtonpost.com/wp-dyn/content/ article/2006/03/23/AR2006032302177.html

Healing Scripture:

http://healingscripture.com/

Religious tolerance and medical care:

www.religioustolerance.org/medical1.htm

Internet References . . .

American Bar Association: Rights of Children Regarding Medical Treatment

www.americanbar.org/newsletter/publications/ gp_solo_magazine_home/gp_solo_magazine_index/ medicaltreatment.html

Attorney Supporting Parents' Rights

www.robertslaw.org/refuse-medical-treatment.htm

University of Illinois Chicago School of Medicine: Ethics in Clerkships

www.uic.edu/depts/mcam/ethics/refusal.htm

Selected, Edited, and with Issue Framing Material by:
Don Dyson, *Widener University*

ISSUE

Is Internet Pornography Harmful to Teenagers?

YES: Wayne Grinwis, from "Is Pornography Harmful to Teenagers? Yes!" Original essay written for this volume (2009)

NO: Justin A. Sitron, from "Why Porn Is Not Harmful to Teens," Original essay written for this volume (2009)

Learning Outcomes

After reading this issue, you will be able to:

- Identify critical research about the impact of pornography on teens.
- Compare and contrast interpretations of research in determining how to help teens develop in a way that is consistent with being sexually healthy.
- Evaluate the unique role of the Internet and pornography on teens.

ISSUE SUMMARY

YES: Wayne Grinwis has been a Sexual Health Educator for Planned Parenthood for 15 years. He is also Adjunct Professor in the Department of Health at West Chester University. Grinwis credits Andrea Daniels for help with this article. Grinwis argues that pornography is all right for adults, but for teenagers, it can create unrealistic expectations about sex, provide a negative and inaccurate sexuality education, and increase sexual violence against women.

NO: Justin Sitron is an Assistant Professor of Education at Widener University. Sitron argues that pornography has no negative impact on teenagers and, in fact, has potential benefits. Sitron contends that Internet pornography can be helpful in providing teens an opportunity to see real bodies, a chance to learn about sex from seeing rather than doing, and an open door for communication with parents.

The First Amendment to the U.S. Constitution states, "Congress shall make no laws . . . abridging the freedom of speech." While this amendment is written as an absolute, there are limitations to speech that are known as unprotected speech, including libel, slander, seditious speech, and obscenity. It is the latter form of unprotected speech that is the focus of this issue, as obscenity is often used as synonymous with pornography. For many children, the Internet has allowed greater access to pornography than ever before.

In the United States, federal censorship of obscene materials began with the Tariff Act of 1842. While prosecutions were initially limited, the American middle class grew following the Civil War. Many social reformers believed that America too often failed to apply proper moral values, thus leading to social problems. Anti-vice societies were formed and worked to create laws regarding labor, prison reform, temperance, welfare, and obscenity. By 1873, America had a federal anti-obscenity law, often referred to as the Comstock Law.

During this time, anti-obscenity laws were designed to protect three groups who were considered to be particularly vulnerable, which included women, the lower classes, and children. Today, women and the so-called lower classes are not considered groups that deserve legal protections, though the primary audience for pornographic pictures and films today is men.

A challenge that has existed regarding censorship has been to determine specifically what is obscenity. In 1973, The Supreme Court of the United States provided the following standard for evaluating whether materials are pornographic in the case of *Miller v. California*:

1. That the average person, applying contemporary standards, would find a work, taken as a whole, appeals to the prurient interest;
2. Whether the work depicts or describes, in a patently offensive way, sexual conduct specifically defined to be offensive and "hard core" by the applicable state law;
3. That the work, taken as a whole, lacks serious literary, artistic, political, or scientific value.

Therefore, there exists a legal standard of how to define pornography and legal precedent that pornography is regarded as unprotected speech. In addition, there is legal precedent that children do not have the right to have access to pornography. As a result, the federal government sought to create new censorship policies in the face of children's access to pornography online.

Congress passed and President Clinton signed into law both the Communications Decency Act of 1996 and the Child Online Protection Act of 1998. Each of these laws was struck down by the Supreme Court. The Supreme Court did not challenge the fact that pornography can be censored for children. However, there was no mechanism to limit children's access to online pornography without also limiting adult access to pornography. When censoring unprotected speech, in this case children's access to pornography, laws cannot be so broad that they also censor protected speech, in this case adults' access to pornography.

With limited means for government censorship, controlling access to pornography becomes almost entirely the domain of parents and children. The access to sexually explicit materials that exists is unprecedented in human history. Children today have more access to sexually produced materials than ever before. Previously, parents were urged to leave their computer in a common, public space in their house. Today, however, few families buy desktop computers, opting instead for a portable laptop which can be privately used more easily. In fact, many children access the Internet whenever they want, wherever they want, via their iPhone or another portable device.

This issue examines the debate over the impact of pornography on teenagers. The conclusions that one reaches should have significant implications in what teenagers should be taught by their parents about pornography.

Pornography is one of the most controversial issues addressed in this volume. What are some of the ways in which these articles reinforced your value system? What are some of the ways in which these articles challenged your value system? How did it feel when your value system was challenged?

In some sections of this issue, Grinwis and Sitron addressed the same issue but cited different research, therefore reaching different conclusions. For example, Grinwis stated that pornography can lead to sexual violence, in part by citing research published by the National Online Resource Center on Violence Against Women. In contrast, Sitron argued that the research is divided but that a meta-analysis published in the *Annual Review of Sex Research* found no association between pornography and "high levels of sexual aggression." What are some ways that you can examine these resources to determine which research you think is accurate?

Students may find important research topics raised in this issue. That can include topics that were specifically examined in this issue as well as other issues not specifically examined. What are some related topics that are important to address?

For example, Sitron's article cites the significant amount of amateur pornography uploaded onto the Internet when he addresses the diversity of body images available online. A separate issue to consider, particularly for young people, are issues of consent for uploading photographs and video online. One significant technological difference for teenagers today as compared to generations past involves the degree of access to photo and video cameras. Some questions that can be considered are the following:

- What are some of the ways, if any, that teenagers today feel pressure to photograph and record themselves hooking up?
- How does seeing amateur pornography online influence discussions or actual behavior with teenagers about recording themselves when hooking up?
- How can teenagers ensure that their pictures or video will never be posted online without their consent?
- Have teenagers had experiences being recorded without first giving consent?
- Does consent to be recorded mean that there is consent to show the footage to others?
- Sometimes amateur footage is seen by millions of people. How might seeing amateur pornography

featuring people one meets in their everyday lives possibly affect their college admissions? College scholarships? Job prospects? Familial relationships?

- In short, what are the rights of people featured in amateur pornography available online?

Beyond these questions, middle school and high school students need to know that some teenagers are being prosecuted for creating child pornography when recording themselves engaged in sexual activities before they have reached the age of 18. Crimes that teenagers are charged with can range from public indecency to the creation of child pornography, possession of child pornography, and distribution of child pornography. Some of these young people have been convicted of felonies, sentenced to long prison terms, and will be required to register as sex offenders after their release.

Today, teenagers have not just access to pornography but also the ability to create pornography with greater ease than ever before. While it is important to research the impact of viewing pornography on teenagers, it is also necessary to conduct more research to better understand the ways in which the creation of amateur pornography may be affecting the young people involved.

YES

Wayne Grinwis

Is Pornography Harmful to Teenagers?

There are some who would argue that pornography has no acceptable audience or any valid place, even for entertainment purposes, in a healthy relationship. In this mindset, pornography might even be considered harmful and its effects wide-reaching enough to encapsulate every age group who may be attracted to the lure of a little adult fantasy. High school students, grandparents, Baby Boomers, Gen Xers—all would fall victim to its inappropriate ideals if we were to place a general label of "harmful"—a sort of "Mr. Yuck" sticker for grown-ups, if you will—onto pornography. I am unable to do such a thing. In the right setting and with the right frame of mind, pornography can be a pleasurable addition to an adult individual's or couple's sexual life.

When speaking of teenagers, however, the term *harmful* may well apply. Without the proper maturity and level of experience, navigating through the very adult world of relationships and sex, most teens simply do not possess the necessary tools needed for their first foray into fantasy, and many of the themes found in a good deal of easily accessible pornography may actually be harmful to their adolescent development.

Access to Pornography

Before we can examine pornography's harmful effects on teenagers, we must first discuss the specifics of what pornography actually is. Former Supreme Court Justice Potter Stewart said, in discussing a potential definition of pornography, "I know it when I see it" (*Jacobellis v. Ohio*, 1964). That statement, albeit somewhat glib, brings to mind a serious thought: In the high-tech, ever-evolving cyber-realm that young people today inhabit, they are inundated with more varied forms of pornography than ever before, stumbling upon sites that they probably shouldn't and gaining access to those deemed "adult-only" by easily tiptoeing around safeguards as flimsy as a few keystrokes and the honor system.

In the past, teens had to seek out pornography by obtaining and viewing magazines (*Playboy* and *Hustler* are among the more tame periodicals), locating old VHS films or DVDs not hidden quite carefully enough in their own homes, or watching soft-core versions of these films on cable (good 'ol' "Skinemax"—an informal reference to occasional late-night viewing opportunities on Cinemax—has long been a favorite). However, tech-savvy young people have more opportunities than ever before to satisfy their sensual cravings. In recent years, pornographic-like activity has been added to some video games (*Grand Theft Auto,* one of the most popular video games among this demographic, is rife with sexual content), and then, of course, there is the ever-pervasive Internet, which, to many teens, is just as tangible a home as the concrete structures they inhabit with their family members. Although the one-time estimate that over 80 percent of Internet sites are pornographic was proven false (Godwin, 2003), recent estimates are that 12 percent of all Web sites are porn and that a quarter of all search engine requests are for porn (Ropelato, 2003). Even if someone were trying to avoid this type of explicit sexual material, it would only be the über-diligent who would succeed in avoiding pornography on the Internet, and it is important to note that not all teenage exposure to pornography is intentional; contact may be unintended—stumbled upon when receiving emails advertising porn sites or even through the simple act of employing an Internet search (Bryan, 2009). For those who do take the time to seek out pornography, their fingers don't have far to travel on their computer keyboards. From things as basic as still pictures to home videos of sexual encounters, from monthly subscription services to "fetish" sites, thousands upon thousands of hours of porn can easily be found online.

It is true that most adult sites stipulate that a viewer must be "18 to enter;" however, age is often established by a simple mouse click stating that the visitor is, indeed, the required age or by asking the visitor to enter in his or her birthdate. Young people can handle the simple math of subtracting a few years from the date on which they were born in order to appear age-appropriate for viewing.

Now that we have determined the ease with which pornography can be viewed and before we begin to examine the harmful effects of pornography on teenagers, we must first establish the gender of which we speak. Do we mean male teens or female? The simple answer is both. Although teens actively seeking out and viewing pornography are predominantly male, girls are also affected by the messages boys receive.

But all of this—the pervasive and easily accessible nature of pornography—is not in and of itself proof positive of its harmful nature when speaking in terms of teens. We must now begin to dig deeper to unearth the negative effects that exposure to an adult-oriented fantasy world has upon adolescent development by examining pornography's fostering of unrealistic expectations when it comes to sexual encounters and body image, its role as an unqualified sexuality educator, and its bent toward violence.

Unrealistic Expectations

How many times has this happened to you? You're in your office making copies, perhaps scantily clad and probably glistening a little from the heat of the copier, and in walks a very attractive member of the opposite sex, who immediately begins complimenting your body and undressing you. Moments later, you are in the throes of passion, with the copier working overtime capturing fantasy, flipbook-worthy images of all that is happening on it.

This has never happened to you? Then clearly you are not living in the world of pornography.

Most teenagers lack the abstract processing skills that advise them that the incidents and images displayed in pornography are not representative of most adults' sex lives. Teens exposed to what the pornography industry and, indeed, its consumers ordain as "sexy" or "passionate" or "hot," and who lack the aforementioned skills, eventually begin to think that the sexual acts displayed are necessary to have the desired adjectives listed above become attributes of their own lives.

This is especially true when it comes to body image. Average people, who are endowed in a very average way, are not typically stars of the pornographic industry, or at least not pre-surgical alteration. As teenagers watch pornography, they cannot help but make comparisons to the unrealistic images they see and, consequently, may begin to find themselves and perhaps their own partners less attractive. As if being a teenager and dealing with hormonal changes and body image insecurities weren't difficult enough, now teenagers are comparing pornographic superstars to their own developing young bodies and those of their partners.

However, it is not body image alone that suffers through the consumption of pornography. Often a teen's view of the sex act itself becomes skewed in an unrealistic

and unhealthy way, especially when pornography becomes the educator through which he or she learns about sex.

Pornography as Education

Where do young people actually learn to have sex? Comprehensive sexuality education, although widely favored in this country (despite the current trend of abstinence-only education), doesn't include demonstrations or lessons on how to engage in the act of having sex. Likewise, most parents surely don't advise their children on the virtues and techniques of making love. When people lose their virginity, one hopes the experience will happen with a partner whom they are able to feel comfortable with and who will accept their genuine selves. In an ideal situation, one inexperienced partner should be able to say to the other: "I don't really know what I'm doing!" However, sad truth though it may be, that is not usually the case. Many times, people lose their virginity with someone they've just met, or when they've been drinking or using drugs, or with someone they care about but with whom they aren't completely intimate—in other words, not someone with whom they can allow themselves to be completely vulnerable. That leaves pornography as the most viable sexual education tool.

We've already established that pornography sets up unrealistic expectations, and that most certainly poses a problem when people are modeling their sex life after knowledge—albeit knowledge that has no basis in reality—gleaned from pornography and when they lack any other alternative. But consider the advantages film has over real life. What appears to the viewer as a 15-minute sexual encounter may have taken eight hours to film, incorporated multiple camera angles to find the best view of the bodies, and required extensive editing in order to make it work—all advantages that the fantasy world of pornography has over typical sexual experiences.

This leads us to our last concern: Besides the unrealistic expectations created by viewing and utilizing pornography, even inadvertently, as an educational tool, the simple, yet serious fact is that pornography can contribute to greater acceptance of sexual violence. This is because much of pornography is based around images and incidents that are degrading toward women, exhibit misogynistic attitudes, and largely focus on the pleasure of the male as its utmost goal.

Sexual Violence

Pornography is rarely about love, intimacy, tenderness, and affection. It is about sex. People don't view pornography to feel closer to themselves or their partner emotionally. They view it for the purpose of arousal and, often, use it as an impetus for masturbation or intercourse. As previously stated, viewers of pornography are predominantly male, and because of this and of its aforementioned purpose, pornography often objectifies women—props who become a means to an end, with an end most likely translating into male orgasm.

In much of the pornographic world, women are there to serve men and to be dominated by them, the ideas of sexual arousal and power becoming intertwined in a way that can be processed cognitively by an adult, but not by a teenager whose emotions and hormones so often overrule any rational thought (Peter and Valkenburg, 2007). Think of the underlying meaning of a porn staple, "the money shot," where the male subject in a pornographic film ejaculates onto his partner, expressing his regard for her with an action devoid of any feeling or affection. If this doesn't model the idea that women are objects, then what does?

The fact is, young men who view pornography are more likely to have negative perceptions of women and be more accepting of violence toward them (Jensen and Okrina, 2004). This is not to say that all men who view pornography will engage in an act of sexual assault, but viewing pornography certainly contributes to a misogynistic culture, a culture where men feel entitled to view and treat women as sexual objects, and in that type of culture, men are more inclined to take advantage of women and, indeed, have an easier time justifying sexual violence.

Although adult men may have the internal processing skills to understand that what they see in porn is not an accurate portrayal of how men should treat women, teenage boys often have not developed that capacity. When they continually see a man belittle a woman in pornography—either emotionally or physically—they view that attitude as acceptable. This is especially true if young men view porn with their friends, as the pack mentality increases the support for this notion—further proof that no good can come of inappropriate sexual content coupled with immaturity.

Conclusion

A healthy sexual appetite is normal and can be expressed in myriad ways. For adults, viewing pornography with a partner can be a fun and "inspiring" experience, but it requires maturity to keep it in the proper context.

Though youth has its advantages, it also has its limitations. Young men and women who are just beginning to develop as sexual beings should take care to learn from examples of loving, mature, and healthy relationships. Pornography does not provide the proper model for any of these and is more likely to prove harmful to teens than advantageous in any way. A healthy sex life is not teeming with unrealistic expectations or fraught with an underlying sense of violence or disrespect. Teenagers whose sexual education is informed through the dark, sensual world of pornography are sure to come to the opposite conclusion, and their relationships will only suffer because of it.

References

C. Bryan, "Adolescence, Pornography, and Harm," *Trends and Issues in Crime and Criminal Justice* (vol. 368, 2009).

M. Godwin, *Cyber Rights: Defending Free Speech in the Digital Age* (Cambridge, MA: MIT Press, 2003).

Jacobellis v. Ohio, 378 U.S. 184, 197 (1964).

R. Jensen and D. Okrina, *Pornography and Sexual Violence* (2004). Retrieved March 14, 2009, from National Online Resource Center on Violence Against Women, http://new.vawnet.org/Assoc_Files_VAWnet/AR_Porn AndSV.pdf.

J. Peter and P. M. Valkenburg, "Adolescents' Exposure to a Sexualized Media Environment and Their Notions of Women as Sex Objects," *Sex Roles* (vol. 56, 2007).

J. Ropelato, *Internet Pornography Statistics* (2003). Retrieved March 22, 2009, from Top Ten Reviews, http://www.internet-filter-review.toptenreviews.com/internet-pornography-statistics.html.

WAYNE GRINWIS has been a Sexual Health Educator for Planned Parenthood for almost 20 years. He is also Adjunct Professor in the Department of Health at West Chester University. Grinwis credits Andrea Daniels for help with this article. Grinwis argues that pornography is all right for adults, but for teenagers it can create unrealistic expectations about sex, provide a negative and inaccurate sexuality education, and increase sexual violence against women.

Justin A. Sitron

 **NO**

Why Porn Is Not Harmful to Teens

The question about whether pornography is harmful is something that has been on the minds of researchers, parents, and others for decades (Malamuth, Addison, and Koss, 2000). Since the invention of the Internet, the question has become more and more popular, as access to pornography has become as easy as pressing the keys on a keyboard and clicking a mouse. While years ago most people had to go to a bookstore, video store, or adult sex shop to access pornography, now one does not even need to leave one's home or even pay for it. With much more explicit cable television programming and the advent of the Internet, accessing pornography for teens is as easy as finding out the answers to a question on their geography homework (and, the teens might say, infinitely more interesting!). Some researchers even have shown that some youth who access porn do so unintentionally (Sabina, Wolak, and Finkelhor, 2008; Ybarra and Mitchell, 2005).

The question about whether pornography is harmful, dangerous, or leads to aggressive sexual behavior has been studied in adults with varying results (e.g., Fukui and Westmore, 1994; Kutchinsky, 1991). Quite simply, some researchers have found that it makes men more aggressive, whereas others find that it does not. Malamuth, Addison, and Koss (2000) conclude in their meta-analysis of such studies that ". . . for the majority of American men, pornography exposure (even at the highest levels assessed here) is not associated with high levels of sexual aggression" (p. 85). So why the big concern about teens having access to porn?

While in recent years there is growing interest in the effects of online pornography on youth, there has been little research done to date (Sabina, Wolak, and Finkelhor, 2008). In maintaining my position that porn is not harmful to people—teen and adult alike—I need to describe the context in which pornography exists. By and large, the opposing viewpoint—that pornography is harmful to teens—comes from a place of fear; fear of sex and sexual pleasure that has been a part of American society since before the word "American" even existed (Klein, 2006).

The sexual value system that prevails in the United States sees sex as St. Augustine of Hippo saw it after his conversion from a period of lust and sexual promiscuity to a Christian man of high morals—sexual behaviors are only appropriate between a man and a woman, within the confines of marriage, and for procreative purposes. This same value system is one that leaves out something that has become a part of American mainstream media in recent years with sex therapists and relationship counselors on America's talk shows, like *Oprah, Tyra Banks,* and *Dr. Phil,* among others, as well as the nightly news: sexual pleasure. Sexual pleasure is a part of pornography, whether it is something that filmmakers aim to represent on the screen or it is being experienced by pornography's viewers. It is a part of sexual expression and sexual behaviors. If it were not, our culture would not be spending as much time discussing it—and certainly nowhere nearly as much money on it—as it does.

In a society that values sex for reproduction rather than for sexual pleasure and an individual's right to ecstasy and self-fulfillment, the very idea that our teenagers might be experiencing pleasure or witnessing others doing so incites an even more pronounced fear. Certainly, these fearful individuals speculate, indulgent pleasure can only have one outcome—danger or harm. Therefore, the idea of consuming pornography is reserved for the lowest members of society—criminals, perverts, sex maniacs, and so on. Those who aim for achieving the greater good by being successful in our careers, raising families, and experiencing a sense of spiritual satisfaction wouldn't allow ourselves to stoop to self-satisfying physical pleasure. It is far too much of a distraction, and therefore not valued.

Varying media, when relating stories about the Internet, frequently discuss either the wealth of information that it offers or the dangers of its use. Sutter (2000) connects the statements I make above with a recurring fear of humanity since its very first scholars: "The furor over Internet pornography follows the classic pattern of moral panic throughout the ages. From Plato's concerns regarding the 'dramatic poets' effects on the young to the 1980s 'video nasties' scare, to screen violence and internet pornography in the 1990s and beyond: the contexts change but the arguments are consistent" (p. 338). So, I ask that we reconsider the question and begin to explore the panic from a new angle: an angle that begs us to ask what the harmful effects of the panic itself may be.

The panic in which our society engages around the harmfulness of pornography, as I mentioned before, is about the assumption that sexual pleasure is harmful and therefore something from which teens must be protected. Consider this short scenario:

> A parent and 10-year-old child are sitting around the living room, and perhaps the child is sitting on the floor playing with a toy while the parent is flipping through prime-time television. After flipping through the channels, the parent decides on a favorite love story. Although the story itself is over the child's head, the child is otherwise occupied. As the story progresses, the child begins to watch and ends up captivated until the parent switches the channel, which sparks protest in the child because the story was so engaging. The parent's response is, "Go back to playing with your toys, I want to watch something else." What sparked the change of channel? The two main characters engaged in a kiss that transformed into the removal of clothing and rolling in the sheets. No nudity. No words between the characters of any kind, just a romantic ballad in the background and two people beginning to kiss passionately and remove clothing.

Although the child in the story objects to the channel being changed, the parent does nothing to engage the child in a discussion about why the channel was changed or what was going on in the story before the flick of the remote. The message that is entirely implicit in this situation is that kissing and the touching of naked bodies between two adults is not something a child should see. If something suitable for prime-time television is too harmful for children, the mainstream thinking would certainly hold that pornography is harmful as well, if not more so.

I disagree. I posit here that there are benefits to teens watching pornography: (1) Internet pornography offers teens an opportunity to see real bodies; (2) pornography offers an opportunity for teens to learn by watching rather than by doing; and (3) pornography opens doors for communication.

Internet Pornography Offers Teens an Opportunity to See Real Bodies

The days of pornography being only accessible in commercially produced formats (DVD, VHS, film, etc.) are gone. Such content has been described by researchers as being responsible for promoting artificial and unrealistic body types in women and men alike. Certainly, this is not a phenomenon left to the pornography industry alone; producers of mainstream film, television, and video all contribute to the perpetuation of unrealistic body types as more beautiful than that of the average viewer. Why, then, should pornography be held to a higher standard than any other type of media?

On the Internet, there is a multitude of sites where Internet users can generate their own original video content and post it on Web sites for others to see. A visitor to sites like XTube.com and Bigbeautifulwomen.com can see a variety of different film clips that include a diversity of body types, sexual orientations, gender, body hair levels, and sexual behaviors ranging from the most mainstream to fetishes. Such a site can build a sense of self-esteem for individuals who might never have seen other people whose nude bodies are like their own.

Pornography Offers an Opportunity for Teens to Learn by Watching Rather Than by Doing

Howard Gardner's (1983) theory of multiple intelligences, which articulates the varying ways in which people express their learning styles, has had a great impact on the ways in which educators approach teaching students. Two of the intelligence styles are kinesthetic, which learns best by physically doing and/or handling something, and visual, which prefers seeing. Teens who match either of these two learning styles may be able to use pornography as a substitute for actual sexual behaviors. Although the kinesthetic learners might be motivated naturally to engage in sex, they may find watching it or masturbating while watching it to be a learning experience. They can understand what they do and don't find arousing; they can learn about their own bodies and what feels and does not feel good. Pornography, and any sexually explicit material for that matter, can actually serve as an excellent teaching tool. Considering that no one has ever gotten pregnant or acquired a sexually transmitted infection from masturbation, one might go so far as to argue that teens who view porn might be able to maintain a decision to remain abstinent longer than teens who do not.

In addition to pornography serving as a tool for varied learning styles, it also serves as a medium through which to portray sexual behaviors. There are few educational venues for teens to see sex in this way. Sexuality, as it is taught in schools, is taught very much separate from the rest of the human body, often even in a different set of classes from other body parts and their functions. Sexual health and reproduction are usually a stand-alone unit in a health class or biology class. The focus of such education is on how the parts work, what their purpose is (procreation), and how to avoid disease. So, although the body parts (uterus, vagina, ovaries, penis, testicles, prostate, etc.) are explained, and often their functions described, all of it is done as if they are detached organs from the rest of the body and without discussion of pleasure.

From a learning standpoint, adolescents and teens are concrete learners—they must have very specific, straightforward examples to support teaching in order for that teaching to resonate. Talking hypothetically about sexual behaviors is often much more challenging for a teenager to understand than seeing an actual representation of it. Pornography provides teens with that representation.

Pornography Opens Doors for Communication

Finally, pornography offers us, as adults, an opportunity to engage young people in conversations about sexuality. If we engage in conversations with young people about sexuality, sexual bodies, and sexual pleasure, we provide teens with valuable lessons. Pornography as a medium, therefore, becomes neutral, neither good nor bad. It is merely another teachable moment for educators and parents alike.

Realistically speaking, the context in which pornography is viewed is the complicated and potentially troubling component. Sure, some pornography depicts stereotypical sexual behaviors, unrealistic body types, and even behaviors that some perceive to be violent or degrading, but this all presents just as many challenges for teens as it does for adults. Viewing pornography, if not done critically and with discussion, may leave the viewer with misconceived notions of sexual behavior and pleasure. The problems with pornography are cultural and social and can be further understood and framed appropriately with teens only if adults are willing to engage teens in a discussion—a discussion that may even include watching pornography together. Adults sometimes expect that they can control their children's lives, their exposure to the world, and their behaviors. The reality is that while many parents take action to censor their children's Internet access, friends, and media viewing, children who aim to find pornography will always be able to do so. In addition, as mentioned earlier, even children who do not aim to

find or view pornography sometimes come upon it unwittingly. The irony of the situation is that enough studies have been done to demonstrate that adolescents and children are sexual, whether alone or with someone else, and even without engaging in sexual behavior, they have fantasies and think about it. As most adults who work with children and teens will tell you, when adults are not present, sex is something teens talk about.

If adults and children don't discuss sex and sexuality, then where are the models for adults to discuss it as well? Pornography, whether viewed in secret, in groups, or with adults present, opens the door for young people to talk about sex and their feelings about it and to find out what important adults in their lives think about it. Pornography presents an opportunity to raise many questions, if the questions are allowed to be asked. Openly discussing sexuality can bring a lot of potential benefits to teens as they age. To consider the ramifications of a culture where sex is taboo, one only needs to read through a chapter in a text on the treatment of sexual dysfunctions. So many of the problems that adults face with the expression of their sexuality have their roots in their lives as children, teenagers, and young adults—times in their lives when sex was not discussed openly, positively, or in constructive ways. Rather than predispose our teens to a future with sexual dysfunction and a fear of finding support around their sexuality, why not begin conversations about sex when young people naturally want to have them?

If our answer to the question posed as the title of this section—Is viewing pornography harmful to teens?—is "yes," we begin on a misguided, thorny path of protecting children and teens from pornography, sexual pleasure, and sex in general by shutting and locking the doors to learning and communication. On the other hand, if the answer is "no," doors open to begin a dialogue about pornography, its use, misuse, benefits, and detriments, and an invaluable conversation can begin between adults and children about healthy sexual expression.

References

A. Fukui and B. Westmore, "To See or Not to See: The Debate over Pornography and Its Relationship to Sexual Aggression," *Australian and New Zealand Journal of Psychiatry* (vol. 28, 1994).

M. Klein, *America's War on Sex* (New York: Praeger Publishers: 2006).

B. Kutchinsky, "Pornography and Rape: Theory and Practice? Evidence from Crime Data in Four Countries Where Pornography Is Easily Accessible," *International Journal of Law and Psychiatry* (vol. 14, 1991).

N. M. Malamuth, T. Addison, and M. Koss, "Pornography and Sexual Aggression: Are There Reliable Effects and Can We Understand Them?" *Annual Review of Sex Research* (vol. 11, 2000).

C. Sabina, J. Wolak, and D. Finkelhor, "The Nature and Dynamics of Internet Pornography Exposure for Youth," *CyberPsychology & Behavior* (vol. 11, 2008).

G. Sutter, "'Nothing New Under the Sun': Old Fears and New Media," *International Journal of Law and Information Technology* (vol. 8, 2000).

M. L. Ybarra and K. J. Mitchell, "Exposure to Internet Pornography Among Children and Adolescents: A National Survey," *CyberPsychology & Behavior* (vol. 8, 2005).

JUSTIN A. SITRON is an Assistant Professor and Director of PhD Programs at Widener University. Sitron argues that pornography has no negative impact on teenagers and, in fact, has potential benefits. Sitron contends that Internet pornography can be helpful in providing teens an opportunity to see real bodies, a chance to learn about sex from seeing rather than doing, and an open door for communication with parents.

EXPLORING THE ISSUE

Is Internet Pornography Harmful to Teenagers?

Critical Thinking and Reflection

1. Can you identify the emotional, moral, intellectual, and social components in Grinwis' argument?
2. Can you identify the emotional, moral, intellectual, and social components in Sitron's argument?
3. Can you identify your own emotional, moral, intellectual, and social responses to this issue?
4. What are some similarities and differences between your responses and the authors'?

Is There Common Ground?

While the authors may disagree over the impact of pornography, they both would probably agree about the potential dangers of recording and posting teens' own sexual behaviors. We have seen some cases of teens committing suicide after sexually explicit video of them has been posted online. What are some things that can occur to create a generation of more sexually literate teenagers who make decisions that are consistent with their long-term goals? What responsibilities do families have to teach their children about creating sexually explicit videos? What responsibilities do schools have to teach children about creating sexually explicit videos?

Additional Resources

C. Bryan, "Adolescence, Pornography, and Harm," *Trends and Issues in Crime and Criminal Justice* (vol. 368, 2009)

M. Godwin, *Cyber Rights: Defending Free Speech in the Digital Age* (MIT Press, 2003). *Jacobellis v. Ohio*, 378 U.S. 184, 197 (1964)

R. Jensen and D. Okrina, *Pornography and Sexual Violence* (2004). Retrieved March 14, 2009. Accessible online at National Online Resource Center on Violence Against Women, http://new.vawnet.org/Assoc_Files_VAWnet/AR_PornAndSV.pdf

L. Margolies, *Teens and Internet Pornography* (2010). Psych Central. Retrieved September 4, 2011. Accessible online at http://psychcentral.com/lib/2010/teens-and-internet-pornography.

Optenet. More than one third of Web pages are pornographic [Press release]. (2010). Retrieved September 10, 2010. Accessible online at www.optenet.com/en-us/new.asp?id=270

J. Peter and P. M. Valkenburg, "Adolescents' Exposure to a Sexualized Media Environment and Their Notions of Women as Sex Objects," *Sex Roles* (vol. 56, 2007).

Internet References . . .

Googling this tends to result in sites supporting Internet pornography. To read more, search this under the "news" section of your favorite search engine.

Selected, Edited, and with Issue Framing Material by:
Don Dyson, *Widener University*

ISSUE

Should There Be Harsh Penalties for Teens Sexting?

YES: Lisa E. Soronen, Nicole Vitale, and Karen A. Haase, from "Sexting at School: Lessons Learned the Hard Way," *National School Boards Association, Inquiry & Analysis* (2010)

NO: Julie Hilden, from "How Should Teens' 'Sexting'—The Sending of Revealing Photos—Be Regulated?" *Findlaw.com* (2009)

Learning Outcomes

After reading this issue, you will be able to:

- Identify arguments made for and against taking teen sexting seriously.
- Compare and contrast the major arguments cited and analysis used in examining penalties for teen sexting.
- Evaluate the ways in which teen sexting affects the lives of teens who participate.

ISSUE SUMMARY

YES: Lisa E. Soronen, Nicole Vitale, and Karen A. Haase are writing on legal issues for the National School Boards Association. This article encourages administrators to hand over cell phone sexting cases to the appropriate law enforcement agencies.

NO: Julie Hilden is a graduate of Harvard College and Yale Law School. A former clerk for Supreme Court Justice Stephen Breyer, she has more recently appeared on *Good Morning America,* Court TV, CNN, and NPR. Hilden argues that harsh penalties are extreme and unjust.

Sexting—the slang term for the use of a cell phone or other similar electronic device to distribute pictures or video of sexually explicit images. It can also refer to text messages of a sexually charged nature.

We know that teens participate in a significant amount of interaction electronically. In 2010, the average American teen, ages 13–17, sent 3,339 texts per month. This can be difficult for adults to understand, as they only send and receive approximately 10 text messages per day. As a result, a decidedly different level of communication occurs among teens while sending text messages.

Why do teens sext? Are the reasons similar? How often does it occur?

According to the National Campaign to Prevent Teen and Unplanned Pregnancy, this is how many teens ages 13–19 are engaging in sending or posting nude or sem-inude pictures or videos of themselves:

20 percent of teens overall

18 percent of teen boys

22 percent of teen girls

11 percent of young teen girls (ages 13–16)

How many teens are sending or posting sexually suggestive messages?

39 percent of all teens.

36 percent of teen girls.

40 percent of teen boys.

48 percent of teens say they have received such messages.

What accounts for the differences that we see in gender? Why are some teens not engaging in such behavior? Lack of technology? Personal morals? Lack of a trusted person to send such messages to? Once someone presses Send, these images can go anywhere, but who are the pictures, photos, and videos initially being sent to?

71 percent of girls and 67 percent of guys who have sent such images have directed them to their boyfriend or girlfriend.

21 percent of girls and 39 percent of boys have sent them to someone they wanted to hook up with or date.

15 percent have sent them to someone they only met online.

Do they understand the risks? They appear to. Over 70 percent of teens know that sending and posting such photos, videos, or messages "can have serious negative consequences."

Of course the biggest fear that most people have is that a person will share these images with others. How often does that occur?

44 percent of boys and girls say it is common for sexually explicit text messages to be shared with others.

36 percent of girls and 39 percent of boys say it is common for nude or seminude photos to be shared.

Does sexting affect their lives? Many say that it does. For example, 22 percent of teens say that they are more forward and aggressive via electronic communication than in real life; and 38 percent say it makes dating or hooking up more likely. In fact, 29 percent say that sending such messages means you are "expected" to date or hook up.

If that is the impact, what is the motivation? Over 60 percent say it is to be "fun or flirtatious." Over half of girls who send sexually explicit messages or photos were giving their significant other a "sexy present." Almost half sent them in response to something they had received. Even 40 percent of girls say that they sent such messages as a joke. One-third of girls do so to "feel sexy."

What about pressure from their peers? Fifty-one percent of girls say they send such messages due to pressure from a guy. Only 18 percent of teen boys report that pressure from a female. Close to one out of four teens post sexually explicit messages, photos, or videos as a result of being pressured by their friends.

If sexting is so common, what are some helpful guidelines to keep in mind when doing so? According to the National Campaign to Prevent Teen and Unplanned Pregnancy, these five steps should occur before pressing the Send button:

1. **Don't assume that anything you send or post will remain private.** Your messages and images will get passed around, even if you think they won't.
2. **There is no changing your mind in cyberspace—anything you send or post will never truly go away.** Something that seems fun and flirty on a whim will never really die. Potential employers, college recruiters, teachers, coaches, and parents, friends, enemies, strangers, and others may be able to find your past posts, even after you have deleted them.
3. **Don't give in to the pressure to do something that makes you uncomfortable, even in cyberspace.** Peer pressure is major motivation for sexting—a very bad motivation.
4. **Consider the recipient's reaction.** Not everyone will take the messages as you intend. For example, 40 percent of teen girls have sent a sexually explicit message as a joke, but 29 percent of boys take it as a sign that she wants to hook up or date.
5. **Nothing is truly anonymous.** Even if you think you are anonymous online, it may be easier to find you than you realize. Many people learn this the hard way when they think what they are doing will occur without their true identity ever being revealed.

It is not just teens. According to the American Association of Retired Persons (AARP), sexting is up among senior citizens. Relationship coach Susan Blake explains that seniors engage in sexting because they "want sexual activity. They want to flirt. It makes them feel healthy and young."

One senior citizen says that she likes to send sexually explicit messages because she feels that she has a "naughty secret. If you're sitting in a restaurant waiting for your food, you can just talk dirty to someone, and no one knows what you're doing. I would rather talk on the phone. But I'm also comfortable with hiding behind texting if I want to say something dirty."

However, senior citizens are not being charged with harsh penalties in response to their sexting. Teenagers, however, are sometimes finding that their lives will never be the same. Will harsh laws and a punishing adult reaction reduce the degree to which teens send sexually explicit messages? If not, what will?

In this issue, one side argues that schools need a harsh reaction to protect themselves. The opposing view is that we are being far too tough on teens with our treatment of them over sexting. See which argument you find most compelling.

YES

Lisa E. Soronen, Nicole Vitale, and Karen A. Haase

Sexting at School: Lessons Learned the Hard Way

A 16-year-old boy asks his 15-year-old girlfriend to send him a naked photo of herself. She does so via text message, thinking that the photo will remain private and will show him how much she cares about him. Three weeks later, the couple breaks up, and her boyfriend forwards the text message to his friends, who quickly spread the image throughout the school. The girl is teased for months afterward, her grades plummet, and the formerly sunny teen refuses to go to school or to socialize with other students.

As many school attorneys and administrators know, this case is far from isolated. "Sexting," the practice by which teens forward sexually explicit images of themselves or their peers via text messaging, has become increasingly common nationwide. According to a frequently cited survey from the National Campaign to Prevent Teen and Unplanned Pregnancy, one in five teens have sent or posted nude or seminude photos of themselves online or via text message. Twenty-two percent of teens have received a nude or semi-nude photo of someone else. The study found that while most of the images are exchanged between boyfriends or girlfriends, 15 percent of teens have forwarded images to someone they only know online.

The potential detrimental effects that sexting can have on students are vast. Educators, child psychologists, and prosecutors agree that most teens do not understand the implications that sexting may have on their futures. While sexting often originates as a private exchange between a teen and his or her love interest, relationships can quickly deteriorate. Before long, the seemingly private images can be distributed throughout the school. These incidents can be highly embarrassing for students and, in some extreme cases, can have deadly consequences. At least two female students have committed suicide after the sexually explicit photos of themselves sent to a boy were disseminated to classmates. As discussed below, criminal prosecution—including being required to register as a sex offender—is another possible long-term negative consequence of sexting.

This article discusses a number of legal and practical issues related to sexting in schools. Specifically, this article discusses searching cell phones, what steps administrators can and should take upon discovering sexting, anti-sexting policies, and preventing sexting through education.

Searching Cell Phones

School administrators typically find out about sexting through the rumor mill. Of course, the only way administrators can determine if sexting actually has happened and who is involved is to ask students or to "see for themselves." In the ideal world, students will readily admit to being involved in sexting upon being questioned by administrators. In the real world, administrators may feel they need to search cell phones as part of a sexting investigation. Depending on the facts, searching a student's cell phone without a warrant may violate the Fourth Amendment. Likewise, it is at least arguable that searching open text messages on a cell phone without consent violates the Stored Communications Act. To avoid Fourth Amendment and Stored Communications Act issues, school administrators may always seek consent of a student and his or her parents before searching a cell phone as part of a sexting investigation.

Fourth Amendment Concerns

The U.S. Supreme Court held in *New Jersey v. T.L.O.* that school officials may search students as long as the search is reasonable; that is, the search must be justified at its inception and reasonable in scope. According to the Court:

> Under ordinary circumstances, a search of a student by a teacher or other school official will be "justified at its inception" when there are

behavior, and administrators should follow abuse and neglect reporting statutes if they fear a parent's reaction might be violent.

Tell the Police

State law or school district policy may require school districts to report to the police certain crimes that have happened on school grounds. It may come as a surprise to school administrators that sexting in some states in some instances may be a crime. In fact, students in a number of states have been charged criminally and convicted of violating child pornography laws by sexting. For example, students likely could be prosecuted for sexting under Ohio's Illegal Use of Minor in Nudity-oriented Material or Performance statute, which prohibits "[p]hotograph[ing] any minor . . . in a state of nudity, or creat[ing], direct[ing], produc[ing], or transfer[ing] any material or performance that shows the minor in a state of nudity. . . ." Under the Ohio statute, it appears that both the girlfriend and the boyfriend from the example at the beginning of this article could be convicted. The girlfriend photographed herself nude and transferred the picture; the boyfriend further transferred the picture. The Ohio Legislature is considering adopting a statute specifically aimed at minors sexting.

Prosecutors across the country have taken various approaches to sexting. Parties who have been charged include the "victim," the recipient, and the disseminator. Prosecutors in some instances may not charge anyone at all or may recommend that those charged participate in a diversion program. Few reported cases discuss whether, and under what circumstances, students can be criminally prosecuted for sexting. . . . In this case, a school district discovered sexting and informed the district attorney. The parents of the girls depicted in the photographs successfully challenged the district attorney's threat to criminally prosecute them unless they participated in an education and counseling program. This case has been appealed to the Third Circuit.

District attorneys have been heavily criticized for prosecuting children engaged in sexting—particularly when the result is the child prosecuted being required to register as a sex offender. As one district attorney points out, child pornography laws were intended to prosecute child sexual predators, not minors who may not even know what child pornography is. Miller is a great example of backlash against district attorneys prosecuting sexting cases.

To respond to myriad concerns raised by sexting, in 2009, lawmakers in at least 11 states have introduced legislation addressing the issue, according to the National Conference of State Legislatures. At least two other states—Kentucky and Virginia—are expected to consider legislation in 2010. . . . To summarize, a number of states have adopted (Vermont, North Dakota) or proposed (Ohio, Pennsylvania) legislation that specifically addresses sexting as a crime separate from child pornography with lesser penalties. Other states have created (Nebraska) or proposed to create (New York) an affirmative defense to child pornography statutes for sexting in some circumstances. Two states have proposed to create (New Jersey, Pennsylvania) educational diversionary programs for students charged or convicted of sexting. Two other states (Colorado, Oregon) have amended their Internet sexual exploitation of a minor statutes to include texting. Finally, two states have proposed to educate students about sexting (New York, New Jersey).

Given that sexting is a new phenomenon and that most child pornography statutes were adopted before cell phones were widely used and sexting was a national problem, school attorneys in most instances will not be able to determine definitely whether a crime has been committed. For this reason, school districts are well-advised to inform the police of sexting so that they can conduct a criminal investigation. However, any school administrator who knows the facts of Miller v. Skumanick as described by the district court—where the district attorney threaten to charge the girls depicted in the photographs with felonies that could result in a long prison term, a permanent record, and registration as sex offenders—would think twice before telling the police about sexting. School administrators should not assume all district attorneys will prosecute all sexting cases or that school administrators will be unable to influence the district attorney. Sexting is a new crime. For this reason, many district attorneys likely would welcome input from school district officials on how to handle these cases. Particularly if the district is going to discipline the students involved, the district attorney may be amenable to not charging the students criminally depending on facts of the case.

It is always a good idea for school district officials to try to foster cooperation with local police and the prosecutors. The best time to approach the district attorney's office about this issue is before sexting occurs on campus and before a district attorney has had the chance to decide that prosecuting sexting cases will be the new "tough on crime" tactic. Likewise, part of building a good relationship with the district attorney's office may be asking for input on how the district should punish sexting and inviting the district attorney to participate in the district's sexting education and prevention efforts.

Report Sexting as Suspected Child Abuse and Neglect

A sexted image may constitute child abuse or neglect, depending on the state's definition of these terms and what is exactly depicted in the photograph. All states have child abuse and neglect reporting statutes which apply to school districts. Most, if not all, statutes include in the definition of child abuse and neglect sexual crimes against a child. For example, Virginia's definition of an abused or neglected child include one: "[w]hose parents or other person responsible for his care commits or allows to be committed any act of sexual exploitation or any sexual act upon a child in violation of the law." Virginia's Department of Social Services states that child abuse occurs when a parent: "[c]ommits or allows to be committed any illegal sexual act upon a child including incest, rape, fondling, indecent exposure, prostitution, or allows a child to be used in any sexually explicit visual material."

Ting-Yi Oei admitted that he did not think about the sexting incident in terms of whether it violated Virginia's child abuse and neglect reporting statute. It is unlikely Oei could have been successfully prosecuted under this statute for at least three reasons. First, he did not know the identity of the girl, though her identity was determined later. Second, he did not know she was only 16. Third, the circuit court ruled in Oei's possession of child pornography case that the picture was not "sexually explicit visual material." Had Oei known the girl's identity and age, and had the picture been more revealing, Oei likely would have had a reporting obligation under Virginia law.

In short, depending on the state's definition of abuse and neglect and depending on the visual depiction in the sexted photograph, school districts may have an obligation to report sexting under child abuse and neglect reporting statutes.

Minimize Exposure to Child Pornography Charges

School administrators should take steps to avoid being accused of possession of child pornography by prosecutors or disgruntled parents. This may simply involve turning over confiscated evidence of sexting to the police immediately. In fact, Oei may have avoided being charged altogether had he taken possession of the boy's phone and turned it over to the police promptly, like the school officials in Miller, instead of receiving and maintaining the photo on his own phone.

School administrators should also take steps to avoid charges of disseminating child pornography. As described later in this article, a lawsuit has been filed against a Washington state school district which rather cryptically accuses school officials of showing sexted photographs of a student to "other adults" in violation of Washington's dissemination of child pornography statute. The district denies doing so in its answer. Regardless of what actually happened in this case, it illustrates that a school administrator who discovers sexting should not share the images with other school employees much less non-employees.

The Utah legislature, likely in response to the Ting-Yi Oei incident, has passed a law to ensure that school employees and others cannot be liable "when reporting or preserving data" in a child pornography investigation. . . .

Discipline the Students Involved

As the case described below illustrates, school districts should consider disciplining all students involved in the sexting—the student featured in the image, students who received the image (unless they deleted it immediately), and students who disseminated the image—equally if possible.

The parents of a Washington state high school student are suing the school district for violating Washington's sexual equality statute for only punishing their daughter in a sexting incident. The parents admit in their complaint that their daughter took a naked picture of herself which was circulated among other students. The school district suspended her for one year from the cheer squad for violating the athletic code. Her parents alleged that the school district violated Washington's sexual equality statute by punishing only her and not the football players who possessed and viewed the picture of her. The school district responded that it did not discipline the football players because it did not know who sent, received, or forwarded the pictures. The daughter refused to tell the district because she did not "want to get anyone in trouble."

Whether the sexual equality claim is successful, plaintiffs do have a fair point that the boys who received and did not immediately delete the photograph of their daughter—or, worse yet, forwarded it—also should have received punishment. While a court likely will not be sympathetic to the daughter's refusal to inform the district of the football players who received and forwarded the picture of her, it likewise might not be sympathetic to the school district's failure to investigate further without her help.

Preventing Bullying and Harassment

Eighteen-year-old Jessica Logan committed suicide after being bullied and harassed after her ex-boyfriend forwarded to other students nude photos she took of herself and sent to him. Her parents are suing the school district, who was aware of the sexting, claiming that the district did not do enough to stop her from being harassed. Whether their claim against the district will be successful, it illustrates that districts should take measures to prevent harassment before and following a sexting incident.

Preventing bullying and harassment at school generally is a difficult task. At minimum, those involved in a sexting incident should be specifically instructed not to harass the "victims" of sexting. Likewise, before a sexting incident occurs, parents and school staff should be informed that sexting may occur, discipline will result, and harassment is prohibited. If an incident occurs, these messages might have to be reiterated. Finally, if harassment or bullying related to a sexting incident occurs, the district's anti-harassment/bullying policy should be followed and harassers should be disciplined.

Anti-sexting Policies

Adopting anti-sexting policies may be one approach school districts can take to prevent sexting. Obviously, no anti-sexting policy will stop sexting altogether, no matter how carefully written or widely circulated. However, an anti-sexting policy will put students and their parents on notice that sexting is unacceptable and has serious consequences.

School districts may take a variety of policy approaches to prevent sexting. Districts may revise existing policies addressing acceptable use, student codes of conduct, cell phones, harassment and bullying, or other similar subject areas, to prohibit sexting. School districts may ban cell phone use during school or cell phone possession at school altogether to prevent sexting. Some boards may decide that they need a separate policy addressing sexting.

Districts adopting a comprehensive anti-sexting policy should consider including the following elements. First, an anti-sexting policy should clearly state that the mere possession of sexually explicit digital pictures on any device is prohibited regardless of whether the state's child pornography law is violated. Second, the policy should state that all involved in sexting, unless they deleted images right away, will be punished. For example, student handbook language should prohibit "sending, sharing, viewing, or possessing pictures, text messages, emails, or other material of a sexual nature in electronic or any other form on a computer, cell phone, or other electronic device." Third, the policy should inform students that their parents and the police may be contacted and sexting may be reported as suspected child abuse or neglect. Fourth, the policy should put students on notice that administrators may search their cell phones if they have reasonable suspicion a student has been involved in sexting. Fifth, the consequences for sexting should be clearly stated but should include discretionary wording that allows administrators to adjust punishments up or down as appropriate. Finally, the policy should prohibit harassment and bullying related to sexting incidents and should punish nonconforming behavior.

Education as Prevention

Education professionals—including school lawyers—should make parents, staff, and students aware of the existence of and dangers of sexting. School districts should consider a variety of actions to raise awareness of and increase education about sexting. Districts may partner with other community organizations or public offices to provide staff trainings on bullying, cyber-bullying, and computer/Internet safety, including sexting and safety on social networking sites. This can include in-school assemblies for students, professional development for staff, training for school board members, distribution of school rules and policies through student handbooks, newsletters/correspondence to the community, meeting with parent groups, and resources on the school webpage and public forums.

Any education around sexting can and should be aimed at the whole community when possible. This means including students, board members, and staff as well as parents and community members. While the majority of recent press has involved middle and high school students, education regarding computer/Internet/technology safety should include younger children as appropriate. A variety of websites and documents provide information about sexting for students, parents, and educators.

Such exceptions might accord well with our sense of when sexting is really disturbing, and appropriately deemed a crime, and when it is better addressed (if at all) with non-criminal remedies such as school suspension, parental punishments, and the like. Notably, the ACLU, in the Pennsylvania case, has suggested that "sexting," in some cases, is not innocuous and may perhaps be penalized—but not through the criminal law.

The Tricky Issues of Consent That Sexting Raises, Especially with Respect to Forwarding

"Romeo and Juliet" exceptions in the sexting context probably will do more good than harm, in practice. But they will also have costs, if they are applied as bright-line rules.

That's because sexting is, in a way, more complicated than statutory rape. Statutory rape, by definition, comes out of a consensual act of sex; if it didn't, it would just be rape. The argument is that the young person's consent is not valid due to his or her immaturity, not that consent was not given. Thus, defining a crime as statutory rape moots out the consent issue. But often, the nature of sexting is intertwined with issues of consent and lack of consent that cannot be so easily put aside.

For instance, a 16-year-old sophomore girl might "sext" a nude photo she has taken of herself to her 18-year-old senior boyfriend, yet not intend that he share it with his 18-year-old friends. In my view, the girl's sexting the photo to the boyfriend would and should be immune from prosecution under a Romeo and Juliet exception—but one might argue that his forwarding of the photo to his same-age friends should not be immune (especially, but perhaps not only, if the girl did not consent to the forwarding). In other words, with respect to sexting, a pure age-based Romeo and Juliet exception, one that renders consent irrelevant, could be a refuge for scoundrels.

This example shows a strong tension between simple, bright-line age-based safe harbors for sexting, and a nuanced inquiry into whether the original "sexter" consented to forwarding. And there may be another nuance as well: Based on my admittedly limited knowledge as a member of Generation X and a viewer of the documentary *American Teen* (which covers a sexting story, among others), it seems to me that sexting in high school may be intimately bound up with issues of popularity, insecurity, and humiliation. And that explosive mix could lead to important and tricky issues regarding consent, particularly consent to forwarding.

For instance, a teen might authorize forwarding, but then later falsely claim that he or she did not consent, if the forwarding was accompanied by the forwarder's humiliating commentary on his or her body or if such commentary by recipients led to humiliation at school. Parental disapproval—or ignorance—of teen relationships could lead to lying, too. In addition, a good-looking teen could deem it cooler to pretend that he or she was not, in fact, the driving force ensuring that a particularly flattering and explicit photo of him or her had ended up being "sexted" to the whole school but was "shocked, shocked to discover" that this had occurred.

In sum, I suspect that there is a whole complex anthropology here that it will be difficult for adults to fully understand. High-school communities might have unspoken "default rules," such as: "You can forward, but only with the photographer's—or subject's—okay." Or, "You can forward, but only to our clique, not to outsiders."

It's worth considering here that the worst sexting abuses, among teenagers, might lead to a civil claim for intentional infliction of emotional distress, or to expulsion from school. In light of these possible remedies, as well as the chance that parents will take action, it's possible that Romeo and Juliet exceptions, although not ideal, might be good enough.

Such exceptions would still allow authorities to crack down on the 18-year-old senior who takes and "sexts" a photo of a 13-year-old eighth-grader, and who truly is engaging in child pornography. Yet these exceptions would also avoid imposing stiff criminal penalties on more-or-less same-age kids for what is, in essence, ugly immaturity, not crime. Alternatively, a compromise solution would create low-level misdemeanor offenses relating to sexting—offenses that would ensure that teenagers, who are often impulsive, could not ruin their lives with a single, ill-considered forward.

Julie Hilden is a graduate of Harvard College and Yale Law School. A former clerk for Supreme Court Justice Stephen Breyer, she has more recently appeared on *Good Morning America*, Court TV, CNN, and NPR. Hilden argues that harsh penalties are extreme and unjust.

EXPLORING THE ISSUE

Should There Be Harsh Penalties for Teens Sexting?

Critical Thinking and Reflection

1. Can you identify the emotional, moral, intellectual, and social components in Soronen, Vitale and Haase's argument?
2. Can you identify the emotional, moral, intellectual, and social components in Hilden's argument?
3. Can you identify your own emotional, moral, intellectual, and social responses to this issue?
4. What are some similarities and differences between your responses and the authors'?

Is There Common Ground?

No one wants to see teens feel humiliated as a result of sexting messages being shared, or even made public. Is the answer harsh penalties or education? Our laws are still evolving regarding how to respond to teen sexting. However, that shouldn't stop us from better educating children about digital citizenship. Are children receiving a proper education in this regard? Is this the job of schools? Parents? Places of worship? Can parents do a better job being aware of who their children are communicating with? Are there proper limits on electronic communication for children as they develop their digital citizenship skills? Should parents monitor what their children are posting? Do children know what their parents' expectations are of them online?

Additional Resources

Psychology Today on teens' sexting:

www.psychologytoday.com/blog/teen-angst/201103/
sexting-teens

ABC News and "Sexting Teens Going Too Far":

http://abcnews.go.com/Technology/WorldNews/
sexting-teens/story?id=6456834

Pew Internet and American Life Project and teens' sexting research:

www.pewinternet.org/Reports/2009/Teens-and-
Sexting.aspx

Safeteens.com provides sexting tips:

www.safeteens.com/teen-sexting-tips/

Internet References . . .

American Academy of Pediatrics: Talking to Kids and Teens about Social Media and Texting

www.aap.org/en-us/about-the-aap/aap-press-room/
news-features-and-safety-tips/pages/Talking-to-Kids-
and-Teens-About-Social-Media-and-Sexting.aspx

Momlogic: Teen Sexting

www.momlogic.com/resources/sexting.php

School Superintendent Association: Sexting

www.aasa.org/content.aspx?id=3390

Selected, Edited, and with Issue Framing Material by:
Don Dyson, *Widener University*

ISSUE

Is Traditional Masculinity Harmful to Boys and Men?

YES: Brianna Attard, from "Toxic Masculinity: How Our Current System of Gender Relations is Harmful to People," *The Sydney Feminists* (2017)

NO: Paul Nathanson, from "A Requiem for Manhood," *Australian Institute of Male Health and Studies* (2018)

Learning Outcomes

After reading this issue, you will be able to:

- Identify three components of traditional masculinity.
- Identify two ways that traditional masculinity may be difficult for men.
- Identify two ways that traditional masculinity may be helpful to men.

ISSUE SUMMARY

YES: Brianna Attard is a researcher and writer at The Sydney Feminists, Inc. She wrote her first article for TSF on toxic masculinity. Brianna enjoys volunteering and working for organizations that operate within a feminist framework. She outlines Toxic Masculinity and its impact on women, men, and interpersonal interactions.

NO: Paul Nathanson has a BA (art history), a BTh (Christian theology), an MLS (library service), an MA (religious studies), and a PhD (religious studies). Of particular interest to him is the surprisingly blurry relation between religion and secularity: how religion underlies seemingly secular phenomena such as popular movies and political ideologies. Nathanson argues, through the use of cinematic examples, that there is a need among men for creating identity through masculinity.

In the issue, "Does Having a Transgender Parent Hurt Children" in this work, we unpacked the difference between biological sex and gender. There, we identified that gender is a social construct and is a product of the expectations that we have as a culture for people to behave in particular ways based upon others' perceptions of their biological sex. These gendered roles are powerful influences in our culture.

In this issue, we will look further into gender to begin to examine the differences between the two boxes of gender that dominate the discussion: masculinity and femininity. To do this, there are a few things we need to understand about the ways in which masculinity and femininity operate. First, we need to understand that the concept of masculinity cannot exist without its opposite, femininity. In order for someone to behave in masculine ways, they must not behave in feminine ways. We need this dichotomy to make sense of the categories. One cannot exist without the other.

We also need to understand that the concepts of masculinity and femininity are not constants. They have changed over time. What we now consider to be masculine in the United States is grounded in Western European ideals that emerged in early-modern times. This idea emerged from ideals of individualism and personal agency that grew in Europe and were accompanied by capitalist and colonizing perspectives. People's success or failure became based in their individual traits, rather than in the success of their tribe or people. As a result, differentiation was made between traits that made one successful in this new environment and those that made someone unsuccessful. Thus, strength, power, and independence became markers for success, while weakness and dependence became things to be avoided. Because of the role of childbearing and rearing, women's value became decreased. Their dependence was seen as weakness and did not set them up for being successful at independent, capitalist ventures.

In this way, strong differentiations began to appear between what was considered masculine (strong, successful) and what was considered feminine (weak, emotional). In that social context, people started to ascribe certain attributes as masculine and others as feminine. This process continues today. Culturally, we continue to code things in our world as masculine or feminine, a process many refer to as gender coding.

Gender coding is the cultural practice of putting specific characteristics and ascribing them to the categories of either masculine or feminine. This happens all of the time, in many different ways. Consider the attributes of being physically strong, being loud or boisterous, being a leader, and being outspoken. Each one of these our culture puts into the category of masculine. Then consider the attributes of being gentle, nurturing, kind, or meek. Each of these our culture codes as feminine. And this process of gender coding has grown to include things as simple as color (pink and blue) and as complex as professions (nurses and doctors).

As we highlight those differences, we ascribe them value. Here is where the influence of sexism can be seen at work. In general, we have a tendency to value things that are masculine as positive, while ascribing a negative value to things considered feminine. We value stoicism in U.S. culture, seeing strength in the ability of people to hold their emotions at bay and respond to situations with cool dispassion. On the flip side, we devalue people who readily show their emotions. Stoicism has been coded as masculine. Emotionality has been coded as feminine. It is good to be strong, independent, and successful, and therefore masculine. It is bad to be considered weak, dependent, and unsuccessful, qualities that are ascribed to femininity. Gender coding, with the addition of sexism, creates the situation where masculinity becomes the ideal and femininity becomes devalued.

This value orientation has resulted in an extreme of masculinity often identified as hyper-masculinity. In order to be considered more powerful, more successful, more masculine, men started to move toward the extreme of the masculine ideal. In this process, they have turned away from gentleness, kindness, compassion—all feminine traits. Remember, that masculinity requires its opposite (femininity) to be understood. By moving away from all feminine-identified traits, men convince themselves that they are more powerful than their rivals. The more that they can move away from the feminine, the more access they will have to power and prestige.

One of the challenges of that stance is that in reality each person has attributes that are both traditionally masculine and traditionally feminine. All people experience emotion, for example, even though that trait is coded feminine. Most people are capable of being kind and nurturing, characteristics that are again coded as feminine. As a result, as men strive for masculinity they must bury those traits that are coded as feminine. If they do not, other men police them through ridicule and bullying. Don't be a wimp. Boys don't cry. Man up. Walk it off. This kind of policing occurs regularly and brutally in many spaces where men gather. Men respond to that pressure by hiding their feminine traits and emphasizing (and in some cases over-emphasizing) their masculine traits. As a result, they are prevented from exploring and expressing their whole selves.

To further complicate this process, the devaluing of what is feminine, and by association women as a whole, has resulted in such an intense level of misogyny (contempt for and prejudice against women). This process of hating women results in many men believing that they are superior to women, that women exist to meet their needs, and that they are less than men in many ways. This combination of valuing strength and power and devaluing women, some argue, is one of the dangerous roots of violence against women. If men fail to see women as fully equal human beings, they can more easily justify violence against them.

It is important to remember in this discussion that not all expressions of masculinity are physically violent toward women. Many men, in their understanding of masculinity as strength, see women as precious and valued. As a result, they encourage their nurturing side by identifying the role of caring for and protecting women. In this understanding, men see value in the feminine as a counterpoint to the masculinity of men. They believe that the balance of masculinity and femininity that is found in heterosexual pairings is a perfect balance for human interaction. Men protect and provide. Women nurture and care. In this way, each gendered experience completes the other in meaningful ways.

It is into this understanding of masculinity and femininity that the authors in this issue write. Specifically, they attempt to address the issue of the ways in which masculinity is coded, valued, and expressed in our culture and the effect that process has on boys and men who must contend with it.

As you read the articles, consider a few questions: What masculine qualities are part of who you are? What feminine qualities? How has your culture taught you how to think and feel about these different attributes? Do you think that there is a "right" way to express your varied traits? From where does that message about right and wrong arise?

YES

Brianna Attard

Toxic Masculinity: How Our Current System of Gender is Harmful to people

Toxic Masculinity

Toxic masculinity is a cultural script of acceptable behaviour for men. Harmful effects of toxic masculinity arise when men internalise stereotypes associated with masculinity that are inconsistent with their inner experience, desires and understanding (Pleck, 1981). Countering masculine ideals is difficult because socialisation of men to accept these norms is so insidious that many do not realise the expectations conferred by masculine ideology are completely arbitrary and unnecessary. Feminism is not only concerned with liberating women through broadening what they can achieve, but also with liberating men from restrictive ideals of manhood contained in toxic masculinity. Outside of feminist and psychological research, however, masculinity is not widely discussed. It has been acknowledged that masculinity is 'unmarked precisely as a factor of its privilege' (Puri, 2006; cited in Peretz, 2016). This means that masculinity is at the same time universal and invisible, making it difficult to recognise, critique and understand. As such, this paper aims to draw together findings from various researchers to explore the perpetuation of toxic masculinity throughout society and the ways in which it is harmful to people.

What is Toxic Masculinity?

Across many societies, the way we view gender and gender relations are governed by a masculine/feminine binary.[1] That is, women should be feminine and men should be masculine. Femininity refers to a possession of traits that are stereotypically associated with women. For example, they should be gentle, nurturing, empathetic and sexually chaste. Masculinity, on the other hand, refers to a possession of traits that are stereotypically associated with men. While there are a number of ways to express masculinity (known as 'multiple masculinities'), hegemonic masculinity is understood as the dominant form of masculinity across cultures (Connell, 1987). This masculinity contains a script of manhood that is governed by a rigorous set of unattainable standards including that men should be stoic, physically tough, competitive, successful, able to provide for others and sexually adept. A further problem with this dominant form of masculinity is that it reflects a white, heterosexual, middle class standard (Connell, 1987), thus being restrictive in relation to cultural background, sexuality and class.

It is this form of masculinity feminists are referring to when they speak of toxic masculinity. It is toxic because the standards of manhood that it prescribes are unattainable; the idea of manhood has been described as an 'elusive ideal' (Vandello & Cohen, 2008, p. 653). It is toxic because hegemonic masculinity itself is a cultural and structural ordering of the masculine/feminine binary that reinforces and 'institutionalises men's dominance over women' and men's dominance over each other (Connell, 1987, p. 185–186; cited in Bird, 1996). In relying on the masculine/feminine binary, hegemonic masculinity ignores and invisibilises those falling outside the binary. This maintains stigma around gender fluidity, gender non-conformity, bisexuality and people who are transgender or intersex.

In formulating the concept of hegemonic masculinity, Connell (1987) acknowledges micro interactions may differ significantly from this dominant form of masculinity. However, she proposes key aspects of social organisation at a structural level centres on the dominance of hegemonic masculinity over femininity and other masculinities (such as homosexual masculinity) (Connell, 1987). The systemic dominance of hegemonic masculinity is linked to the perpetuation of patriarchy as one of the prevailing social structures in modernity. Accordingly, the way in which hegemonic masculinity achieves its ascendancy is complex. Hegemonic masculinity is embedded in various institutions throughout society such as mass media, religious doctrine, the labour force, welfare and taxation (Douglas, 1993). The role media and popular culture play in its dominance will be discussed later in this paper.

How is it Harmful to People?

Toxic masculinity is one of the ways in which patriarchy is harmful to people. It facilitates what has been referred to as a 'triad of violence' (Kaufman, 1987 cited in Burrell, 2016). That is, men's violence against other men, against women and against themselves. Further, it impacts men's health, wellbeing and relationships (Brooks, 2010; Hayes & Mahalik, 2000; Lease, Çiftçi, Demir, & Boyraz, 2009 cited in Pietraszkiewicz, Kaufmann & Formanowicz, 2017). Accordingly, this section will explore the various ways hegemonic masculinity is detrimental to people.

Before doing so, it is first necessary to understand the social and cultural context that sustains toxic masculinity. The dominant form of masculinity is socially constructed and hence systemic. The social system that constructs and perpetuates toxic masculinity is patriarchy. Inherent in patriarchy is an expectation of behaviours, roles and values for men that are learned and passed down from one generation to the next through socialisation (Schumann, 2016). Thus, performing gender and gender relations in accordance with ideals of toxic masculinity is not the problem of a 'tiny number of bad men' (Flood, 2013). Rather, it is the problem of ordinary men who have been taught to be complicit in a system of social relations that benefits them whilst simultaneously suppressing others (Flood, 2013).

Men's Violence Against Other Men

Interpersonal violence between men is one of the ways toxic masculinity is harmful to men. Men are overwhelmingly the perpetrators of violence, both amongst themselves and against others (Flood, 2010; Burrell, 2016). However, this violence is not inevitable or biologically innate. Rather, it is the result of a complex interplay of 'cultural, ideological, economic, political and personal forces' (Douglas, 1993). Such violence arises out of commonly held versions of manhood that are reinforced at various levels of society (Jewkes, Flood and Lang, 2014). Accordingly, the way in which toxic masculinity can materialise as interpersonal violence is complex.

One explanation for the emergence of masculinity as violence is the performative nature of masculinity (Vandello & Cohen, 2008). Masculinity is a social and cultural construct that is not naturally attained upon maturation of boys to men, but requires constant performance in order to be earned and maintained (Gilmore, 1990; cited in Vandello & Cohen, 2008). Vandello and Cohen (2008) propose that men use violence against other men as a response to real or perceived threats to social standing in order to uphold stereotypical standards of manhood, such as physical toughness. The performance of masculinity is not peculiar, as the very nature of gender and gender expression is something society expects people to perform.[2] Hostile interpersonal behaviour is also understood as a projective psychological defence to the unattainability of masculinity (Mahalik, Cournoyer, DeFranc, Cherry & Napolitano, 1998 cited in Hayes & Mahalik, 2000). Toxic masculinity materialising as violence against other men evidences one of the ways in which it is harmful to men.

Homophobic Violence

An exploration of homophobic violence and violence against people with diverse sexual orientations and gender identities is illustrative of the way in which hegemonic masculinity dominates other expressions of masculinity and is therefore harmful to people. Homophobia is still rife across many societies and cultures. People who identify as LGBTIQ experience violence, harassment and bullying at rates higher than the general population (Australian Human Rights Commission, 2014). Ratele (2014) states that homophobic violence is a tool used to protect and maintain hegemonic masculinity. He reads homophobic violence as an expression of the frustration of the unattainability of hegemonic masculinity (Ratele, 2014). Homophobic violence allows the perpetrator to perform heterosexuality by distancing themselves from homosexuality as well as male expressions of femininity (Ratele, Shefer, Strebel and Fouten, 2010).

Further, people who are transgender experience even greater levels of physical and non-physical violence than people who are homosexual (Australian Human Rights Commission, 2014). This demonstrates a broader stigma around human experience that falls outside the narrow confines of the masculine/feminine binary. Homophobic and transphobic violence therefore exemplify how hegemonic masculinity is harmful to people and the way in which expressions of hegemonic masculinity serve to reinforce the binary of gender relations.

A review of perceptions of sexually assaulted male people further illuminates the dominance of hegemonic masculinity over homosexual masculinity. Davies and Rogers (2006) found that male people who had experienced rape and who are homosexual are judged to be more at fault than male people who had experienced rape and who are heterosexual (Davies & Rogers, 2006). Further, those who had experienced rape who are homosexual and also effeminate are judged to be more at fault than those who are homosexual but 'straight-acting' (Davies & Rogers, 2006, p. 375). These homophobic perceptions of rape and violence further elucidate hegemonic masculinity's dominance over subordinate masculinities and femininities and the harmful effects this dominance has on people.

Violence (Including Sexual Violence) Against Women

Toxic masculinity also contributes to men's violence against women. This is because violence against women arises out of norms within which men are socialised; the way men are taught to behave and the way men are taught to view women (Flood, 2013). It is not possible to explore the way in which hegemonic masculinity is linked to violence against women without acknowledging the widespread incidence of gender inequality and sexism across societies and cultures. Men's violence against women is inherently gendered for the fact that physical and sexual violence could be 'perpetrated by anyone, against anyone but are committed by men against women in uniquely systemic and structured ways' (Burrell, 2016, p. 70). This means gender, gender inequality, toxic masculinity and violence against women are 'inextricably linked' (Sharma & Das, 2016, p. 7).

A number of examples serve to explain these links. First, a global view of men's violence against women demonstrates that rates of violence are higher in societies with rigid constructions of the gender binary and strong policing of manhood (Flood, 2013). In societies with rigid gender roles, men are more likely to be career-focused while their female partners are more likely to take on the role of housekeepers, wives and mothers (Flood, 2013). The unpaid domestic labour performed by women in these societies perpetuates power imbalances as the female partner becomes economically dependent on her male partner. In fact, male economic dominance in the family sphere is one of the strongest predictors of violence against women (Heise, 1998 cited in Flood, 2013).

In following these rigid gender roles, women are also socialised to feel responsible for her male partner's emotional and sexual needs (Flood, 2013). Men's pressure and coercion of women into sex relies on the assumption that men are entitled to access women's bodies (Burrell, 2016; Flood, 2013). This male entitlement stems from the dominance of men over women inherent in patriarchal social relations and embedded in hegemonic masculinity. Accordingly, if a woman refuses to fulfil a man's emotional and sexual needs that he feels entitled to, performance of physical and sexual violence against women is used to maintain dominance. The impact of men's violence

against women is that it reinforces and maintains the dominance of hegemonic masculinity as well as unequal social relations.

The use of sexual violence and harassment against women as an expression of male-to-male solidarity is another example illustrating the link between gender, gender inequality, toxic masculinity and violence against women. Socialisation of boys and men in particular peer cultures 'foster and justify abuse' and promote violence against women (Flood, 2008, p. 342). Such peer cultures have been identified in male prisons, college fraternities, male rugby, the Royal Australian Navy and the Australian Defence Force (Thurston, 1996, Boswell and Spade, 1996, Muir and Seitz, 2004, Agostino, 1997 cited in Flood, 2008). They are also present in informal peer groups (Gardner, 1995 cited in Flood, 2013). Just as men's violence against other men arises out of the performative aspect of masculinity, men's physical and sexual violence against women is performative. This performance again serves the function of maintaining dominance of men and masculinity over women and femininity.

Specific aspects of these male-to-male peer cultures are characterised by various problematic behaviours and norms, which perpetuate toxic masculinity and violence against women. In particular, the boasting of a man's sexual exploits of women is an important aspect of male bonding across male social groups (Bird, 1996; Boswell and Spade, 1996 cited in Flood, 2008). Interviews with convicted rapists specifically elucidate this point (Scully, 1990 cited in Flood, 2013). Further, the policing of manhood in these peer cultures results in many men who have non-sexual relations with women being 'homosexualised and feminized' by other men (Flood, 2008, p. 245). Men's violence against women can also be practiced collectively (Flood, 2013). At its extreme; this is discernible through instances of gang rape but also includes street sexual harassment such as catcalling and wolf whistling and other more insidious forms of violence or harassment (Flood, 2013).

Without disregarding the validity of the adult industry and sex work as a legitimate form of work, Flood (2008) also points to some particularly problematic social practices that serve to consolidate male-to-male social bonds whilst simultaneously objectifying women. These include watching pornographic movies together, sharing sexually explicit content, harassing women on the street from their cars, going to strip shows and frequenting brothels together. Ultimately, many aspects of male homosociality reinforce ideals of manhood constructed by hegemonic masculinity.

These relations form the foundation on which violence and harassment against women can be reproduced.

Men's Violence Against Themselves: Male Suicide

Whilst more women attempt suicide each year, men are more likely to be successful in their attempts (Australian Bureau of Statistics, 2016; World Health Organization, 2015). This data adds further weight to the claim that toxic masculinity is harmful to men. A number of links can be drawn between hegemonic masculinity and suicide. First, adherence to stereotypically masculine traits such as emotional detachment, stoicism, risk-taking and sensation seeking can increase propensity for suicide amongst males. Further, toxic masculinity confers social roles that are difficult for most males to fulfil. Finally, hegemonic masculinity's dominance over other masculinities such as homosexual masculinity is linked to higher suicide rates amongst LGBTIQ populations than the general population.

Adherence to Stereotypically Masculine Traits and Suicide

As mentioned earlier, emotional detachment and stoicism are stereotypical traits associated with men through hegemonic masculinity. Bird (1996) found that the most highly stigmatized behaviours in male homosociality are those that are associated with expressions of intimacy, such as talking about feelings. Expressing feelings is something that is seen as feminine and weak and is therefore suppressed (Bird, 1996). In her interviews with men, Bird (1996) found that violating this social norm often results in ostracism from one's male social group. Conversely, suppression of emotion signifies strength, a trait associated with manhood. Suppressing emotions and feeling unable to seek help and support for their problems can increase a man's capability for suicide (Granato, Smith & Selwyn, 2014). This occurs because without help, those who adhere to masculine gender norms must cope by relying only on themselves, which leads to problems when self-reliance inevitably becomes an insufficient coping mechanism (Granato et al., 2014).

Other typical masculine behaviours include risk-taking and sensation seeking. These traits have been linked to the gender discrepancy in suicide rates as adherence to these norms results in higher pain tolerance and impulsivity, thus leading to an acquired capability for suicide (Alabas et al., 2012; Cazenave, Le Scanff, & Woodman, 2007; Öngen, 2007 cited in Granato, et al., 2014). Consequently, adherence to behavioural norms encapsulated in hegemonic masculinity is linked to higher rates of suicide amongst men.

Increased Capability for Suicide Through Expected Social Roles

Toxic masculinity is also linked to male suicide rates by presupposing social roles upon men that cannot be fulfilled. Two examples are illustrative of this idea. First, inherent in hegemonic masculinity is the idea that men should be able to provide for others. This aspiration is problematic, especially for men of a lower socioeconomic status (SES) (Jewkes et al., 2014). There is evidence of male suicide rates following a linear SES-suicide gradient, where suicide rates increase as SES decreases (Taylor, Page, Morrell, Harrison & Carter, 2005). The gradient remains the same even after controlling for demographic factors, country of birth and rurality (Taylor et al., 2005). Interestingly, the linear SES-suicide gradient is not evident in female suicide rates (Taylor et al., 2005).

Second, hegemonic masculinity places unachievable social roles upon men by expecting success in the delivery of their duties. As Douglas (1993) observes, the majority of the world's generals, admirals, bureaucrats and politicians are men. Men are also seen across many cultures as the head of the family (Douglas, 1993). While this confers a great amount of social power upon men, there is an expectation imparted by hegemonic masculinity that men cannot make mistakes in the delivery of their duties as heads of institutions and families (Vandello & Cohen, 2008). Due to the performative aspect of masculinity, a decreased sense of personhood and identity may arise if mistakes are made (Vandello & Cohen, 2008; Bird, 1996). The significant link between men and their value of power may compound feelings of failure (Pietraszkiewicz et al., 2017). Adherence to the masculine norm of success and power is not directly linked to suicide, but does promote exposure to painful life events, which increases capability for suicide amongst men (Granato et al., 2014). Ultimately, toxic masculinity's unachievable social roles lead to a range of harmful consequences for men, including an acquired capability for suicide.

Diverse Sexualities, Masculinities and Suicide

Finally, hegemonic masculinity is related to higher rates of suicide amongst people in the LGBTIQ population than in the general population (National LGBTI Health Alliance, 2016). As explained earlier, hegemonic masculinity exists relationally to subordinate masculinities and femininities, such as homosexual masculinity (Connell, 1987). Expressions of homosexuality or diverse sexuality therefore exist outside of the script of expected behaviour imparted by hegemonic masculinity. This is supported by the social and cultural norm that individuals of a social identity not encapsulated in the dominant ideology are not tolerated (World Health Organisation, 2009). Consequently, suicide rates amongst people who identify as LGBTIQ represent another problematic link between toxic masculinity and suicide.

Men's Health, Wellbeing and Relationships

Negative impacts on men's health, wellbeing and relationships arise as a result of internalising stereotyped masculine norms that they cannot achieve. The gender-role strain paradigm, developed by Pleck (1981), proposes that psychological strain arises when gender expectations are contradictory or unattainable. This psychological strain impacts on men's health, wellbeing and relationships in a number of ways. It has been linked to higher rates anxiety and depression (Cournoyer & Mahalik, 1995; Davis, 1998; Good & Mintz, 1990; Sharpe & Heppner, 1991; Simonsen, Blazina & Watkins, 2000 cited in Hayes & Mahalik, 2000) as well as alcohol abuse (Blazina & Watkins, 1996 cited in Hayes & Mahalik, 2000). It also inhibits men's likelihood to seek help and support in instances of ill-health (Courtenay, 2000).

Further, some men have expressed social discomfort caused by an inability to express affection or emotionality toward other men (Hayes & Mahalik, 2000). The consequence of this is twofold. First, men feel unable to express emotionality to other men. Second, men feel uncomfortable when other men are emotionally expressive toward them. This is perpetuates stoic behaviour, which is contained in the script of hegemonic masculinity, but is contradictory to true human experience.

Finally, conformity to hegemonic masculinity is linked to lower intimacy and lower relationship satisfaction, especially with women (Campbell & Snow, 1992; Cournoyer & Mahalik, 1995; Rochlen & Mahalik, 2004; Sharpe & Heppner, 1991; Sharpe, Heppner & Dixon, 1995 cited in Burn & Ward 2005). Restrictive emotionality contained in the script of hegemonic masculinity can lead to feelings of distance and a lack of understanding between partners (Burn & Ward, 2005). Accordingly, men's socialisation within the dominant masculine ideology can lead to gender-role strain, which has a number of harmful consequences on men's health, wellbeing and relationships.

Popular Media's Reinforcement of Toxic Masculinity

As noted earlier, the way in which hegemonic masculinity achieves its ascendency is complex. Ideals of manhood encapsulated in hegemonic masculinity are reinforced and perpetuated throughout societies and cultures at various levels. Because of its pervasiveness, the media's role in reinforcing toxic masculinity is particularly significant. As a powerful institution, the media is part of a broader, structural conditioning of boys and men. Analysis of the media in this context reveals how popular media and commercial pornography reinforce narrow archetypes of manhood. Further, the media's use of language invisibilises toxic masculinity's role in various phenomena.

Depictions of Men in Popular Media

Looking to depictions of men in popular media assists in understanding the dominant form of masculinity and the expectations it places upon men. The imagery and narratives of manhood presented by the media are widespread but extremely limited. Examples can be found in advertising, popular film, television and sports. These narratives are particularly restrictive in relation to men of colour.

Advertising reinforces problematic ideals of manhood to appeal men to certain products. One of the most pervasive advertising figures in the world is the Malboro Man (Jhally, 1999). He is a rugged individualist, keen for adventure and epitomises strength and prowess; encompassing many of the reductive attributes contained in hegemonic masculinity (Jhally, 1999; Connolly, 2011). Utilising the hyper-masculine image of the Malboro Man proved a successful way of distancing the product of filtered cigarettes from its previous perceptions of femininity (Connolly, 2011). More recent advertising of protein, strength and muscle-building products reproduce the idea that physical strength, size and muscularity are integral aspects of manhood.

In film and television, there is no shortage of imagery of violent men and sexualised violence against women. Various action films portray stoic and violent men as heroes (e.g. James Bond films, Rambo, Die Hard, Dirty Harry, recent portrayals of Batman). Further, the slasher film archetype includes scenes of girls undressing with provocative camera angles at the moment the woman is assaulted (Jhally, 1999). These films sexualise violence, thus presenting violence in a way that is enticing and exciting for heterosexual male viewers (Jhally, 1999).

Even romantic comedies have humourised men's violence against women. The film 'There's Something About Mary' portrays a woman being stalked by various different men, yet is presented as light-hearted and humorous, thus normalising men's violence against women (Jhally, 1999). Accordingly, advertising, film and television portray limited images of manhood, which reinforce narrow ideas of what it means to be a man.

Nonetheless, the portrayal of the hyper-masculine, violent male person is not limited to advertising, film and television. A glance at two prominent sporting events in 2017 shows how sporting culture is underpinned by ideals of toxic masculinity. First, the recent boxing match between Floyd Mayweather Junior and Conor McGregor involved months of widely publicised pre-match slurs between the contenders. This maintains the association between physical toughness, strength, violence and aggression inherent in toxic masculinity. Further, the 2017 Tour de France showed the daily winner of the jersey on a podium with women in little clothing applauding the man from either side. This scenario depicts an athletic sportsman being praised by beautiful women, maintaining the narrative that if a man is athletic, he will receive attention and praise from women. This reinforces the expectation that manhood requires physical prowess whilst simultaneously maintaining masculinity's dominance over femininity.

Hegemonic masculinity is particularly narrow in relation to men of colour. Popular media is problematic in relation to many cultures and backgrounds because it is a system monopolised by wealthy, white men (Jhally, 1999). Thus, most common representations of men in the media are that of white, middle-class, heterosexual men. When men of differing cultural backgrounds are included in popular media, the imagery and characterisation used to present them is reproduced in very distinct ways. For example, media depictions of men who are African-American are presented as hyper-masculine, and their bodies are often glamourised and sexualised.[3] The depiction of men of Latino backgrounds is often restricted to criminals (particularly drug criminals) or other tough and stoic characters (Jhally, 1999). Men from various Asian regions are often grouped together as martial artists or hyper-intelligent beings (Jhally, 1999). Interestingly though, the media presents violence as an inherent aspect of men across cultural backgrounds, which helps reinforce the link between violence and masculinity as a universal norm. In reproducing distinct imagery of men from differing cultural backgrounds, the media reinforces expectations of men of colour that are extremely narrow and thus harmful.

Depictions of Sexuality in Commercial Pornography

In discussing the media's reinforcement of toxic masculinity, the narratives presented in commercial pornography cannot be ignored. There is an increasingly widespread digital access to pornography for young boys and men. Data from Australia, the US and Sweden shows that pornography consumption is most common among young boys and men aged between 16 and 29 (Flood, 2010). Young men's consumption of pornography occurs in a context of limited formal sexual education (Gelder, 2002; cited in Flood, 2010a). Accordingly, commercial pornography is influential in shaping men's sexual practices and repertoires.

Commercial pornography reinforces the masculine/feminine binary by reproducing limited narratives about sexual practices. Commercial pornography is marketed to young, heterosexual men, thus primarily depicting heterosexual sex (Flood, 2010a). In commercial pornography, the woman is depicted as submissive whilst the man dictates and controls how the sex plays out (Mackinnon, 1983; Dines, 2010). The woman is often objectified as an instrument of male pleasure and feminine desire and pleasure is suppressed or presented only as supplementary to the narrative.

In addition, mainstream pornography reinforces myths on men's sexual adeptness, which is an integral aspect of manhood encapsulated in hegemonic masculinity. According to Brod (1990, cited in Flood, 2010a), these myths include that men are continually ready for sex, that people only experience sexual pleasure through genital stimulation and that there is a standard penis size. The limited sexual narratives have the effect of homogenizing men's sexual preferences through reinforcing what is acceptable sexual behaviour for a man (Brod, 1990; cited in Flood, 2010a). Therefore, mainstream pornography reinforces the ascendancy of masculinity over subordinate masculinities and femininity by presenting a narrow version of acceptable sexual practices, which centres on men's dominance and sexual adeptness.

Invisibility of Masculinity in the Media Through Language

The media uses language that degenders phenomena that occur in specifically gendered ways, such as men's widespread use of violence against women. This disguises the problematic influence of hegemonic masculinity. Using the passive voice and failing to report the true cause of the crime in discussing men's physical and sexual violence against women invisibilises male perpetrators and shifts the blame to female victims (Jhally, 1999). Examples include 'woman was raped', 'slain mother' or 'axe slashes family apart' (Gilmore, 2016; Gilmore 2016a). Using an active voice and representing the true cause of the crimes would lead these headlines to read 'man rapes woman', 'husband murders his wife' or 'man uses axe to slash family apart.' In contrasting the differences between possible ways of reporting, it is apparent how the influence of gender in violence is presented as unremarkable. Thus, the media's use of language disguises the influence of hegemonic masculinity in violence against women. In doing so, problems perpetuated by ascribing to the dominant masculinity are assumed normal.

Consequently, the media reinforces toxic masculinity not only by narrowly characterising men in advertising, film, television, sports and pornography, but also by disguising its influence in phenomenon that occurs in specifically gendered ways.

An Alternate Masculinity

Toxic masculinity is harmful to all people. However, because hegemonic masculinity is perpetuated by complex systems and structures that invisibilise its absurdity as normal and universal, hegemonic masculinity maintains its dominance. Men and boys are conditioned to accept the rigorous set of unattainable standards associated with manhood. At the same time, hegemonic masculinity ascribes men a superior place in society. This means hegemonic masculinity simultaneously benefits men by affording them structural power whilst also harming them and their structural subordinates of women and people with diverse sexualities and genders. Hence, what is needed is a broader understanding of the ways in which toxic masculinity is harmful to people. Attention must be brought to the daily politics of doing gender, to bring consciousness to the unlearning of what people assume normal expressions of self. Space must be created for men to express themselves as broadly and colourfully as possible (Ford, 2017). An alternative masculinity would socialise men to respect themselves and others, to express vulnerability and shame, to have no tolerance for objectifying and degrading language and behaviour toward non-men, to know that sexually aggressive behaviour reinforces power imbalances, to practice empathy and to know that they are still men when they assume these behaviours and characteristics. The socialisation of men into hegemonic

masculinity may be insidious, but social structures can be transformed.

. . .

References

Australian Bureau of Statistics, *3303.0 - Causes of Death, Australia, 2015*. (2016). *Australian Bureau of Statistics*. Retrieved 30 September 2017, from http://www.abs.gov.au/ausstats/abs@.nsf/Lookup/by%20Subject/3303.0~2015~Main%20Features~Australia's%20leading%20causes%20of%20death,%202015~3

Australian Human Rights Commission. (2014). *Face the Facts: Lesbian, Gay, Bisexual, Trans and Intersex People* (pp. 1–8). Sydney: Australian Human Rights Commission. Retrieved from https://www.humanrights.gov.au/education/face-facts/face-facts-lesbian-gay-bisexual-trans-and-intersex-people

Bird, S.R. (1996). 'Welcome to the men's club: Homosociality and the maintenance of hegemonic masculinity.' *Gender and Society*, 10(2), 120–132.

Burrell, S. R. (2016). 'The invisibility of men's – practices: Problem representations in British and Finnish social policy on men's violences against women.' *Graduate Journal of Social Science*, 12(3), 69–93.

Burn, S. M., & Ward, A. Z. (2005). 'Men's conformity to traditional masculinity and relationship satisfaction'. *Psychology of Men & Masculinity*, 6(4), 254–263.

Brod, H. (1990). Pornography and the alienation of male sexuality. In Hearn J. & Morgan D.H.J (Eds.) Men, Masculinities and Social Theory (pp. 124–139). Boston, London: Unwin Hyman.

Connell, R. (1987). *Gender and Power: Society, the Person, and Sexual Politics*. Stanford, CA: Stanford University Press.

Connolly, K. (2011). *Six ads that changed the way we think*. BBC News. Retrieved 30 September 2017, from http://www.bbc.com/news/world-us-canada-11963364

Courtenay, W. H. (2000). 'Constructions of masculinity and their influence on men's well-being: a theory of gender and health.' *Social Science & Medicine*, 50(10), 1385–1401.

Davies, M. & Rogers, P. (2006). 'Perceptions of male victims in depicted sexual assaults: A review of the literature.' *Aggression and Violent Behaviour*, 11, 367–377.

Dines, G. (2010). *Pornland: How Porn has Hijacked our Sexuality*. Boston, MA: Beacon Press.

Douglas, P. (1993). Men = Violence, a feminist perspective on dismantling the masculine equation. In *Second National Conference on Violence* (pp. 1–11). Canberra: Australian Institute of Criminology.

Flood, M. (2008). 'Men, sex and homosociality. How bonds between men shape their sexual relations with women'. *Men and Masculinities*, 10(3), 339–359.

Flood, M. (2010) *Where Men Stand: Men's roles in ending violence against women*. Sydney: White Ribbon Prevention Research Series, No. 2.

Flood, M. (2010a). Young men using pornography. In K. Boyle, *Everyday Pornography* (1st ed., pp. 164–178). London: Routledge.

Flood, M. (2013). Involving men in ending violence against women: Facing challenges and making change. In *Global to Local: Preventing Men's Violence against Women – Research, Policy and Practice in One Space*. Sydney: White Ribbon Foundation.

Ford, C. (2017). *The male victims of domestic violence we need to listen to. The Sydney Morning Herald*. Retrieved 13 October 2017, from http://www.smh.com.au/lifestyle/news-and-views/opinion/clementine-ford-the-male-victims-of-domestic-violence-we-need-to-listen-to-20170619-gwudzj.html

Foster, T. (2011). 'The sexual abuse of black men under American slavery.' *Journal of the History of Sexuality*, 20(3), 445–464.

Gilmore, J. (2016). *10 headlines about male violence that needed to be fixed in 2016. The Sydney Morning Herald*. Retrieved 30 September 2017, from http://www.smh.com.au/lifestyle/news-and-views/opinion/10-headlines-about-male-violence-that-needed-to-be-fixed-in-2016-20161211-gt8rve.html

Gilmore, J. (2016a). *Fixed it: why do headlines about violence focus on the victim rather than the perpetrator?. SBS*. Retrieved 30 September 2017, from http://www.sbs.com.au/news/thefeed/article/2016/08/08/fixed-it-why-do-headlines-about-violence-focus-victim-rather-perpetrator

Granato, S. L., Smith, P. N. & Selwyn, C. N. (2014). 'Acquired capability and masculine gender norm adherence: potential pathways to higher rates of male suicide'. *Psychology of Men and Masculinity*, 16(3), 246–254.

Hayes, J. A. & Mahalik. J. R. (2000). 'Gender role conflict and psychological distress in male counseling center clients'. *Psychology of Men and Masculinity*, 1(2), 116–125.

Jewkes, R., Flood, M. & Lang, J. (2014). 'From work with men and boys to changes of social norms and reduction of inequities in gender relations: a conceptual shift in prevention of violence against women and girls'. *The Lancet*, 385(9977), 1580–1589.

Jhally, S. (1999). *Tough Guise: Violence, Media and the Crisis in Masculinity*. United States of America: Media Education Foundation.

Levi-Strauss, C. (1973). 'Structuralism and ecology.' *Social Science Information*. 12(1), 7–23.

Mackinnon, C.A. (1983). 'Feminism, Marxism, method and the state: Toward feminist jurisprudence).' Signs, 8(4), 635–658.

National LGBTI Health Alliance, *Snapshot of Mental Health and Suicide Prevention Statistics for LGBTI People*. (2016) (pp. 1–14). Newtown. Retrieved from http://lgbtihealth.org.au/wp-content/uploads/2016/07/SNAPSHOT-Mental-Health-and-Suicide-Prevention-Outcomes-for-LGBTI-people-and-communities.pdf

Peretz, T. (2016). 'Why study men and masculinities? A theorized research review.' *Graduate Journal of Social Science*, 12(3), 30–43.

Pietraszkiewicz, A., Kaufmann, M. C. & Formanowicz. M. M. (2017). 'Masculinity ideology and subjective well-being in a sample of polish men and women.' *Polish Psychological Bulletin*, 48(1), 79–86.

Pleck, J. H. (1981). *The myth of masculinity*. Cambridge, MA: MIT Press.

Ratele, K. (2014). 'Hegemonic African masculinities and men's heterosexual lives: Some uses for homophobia.' *African Studies Review*, 57(2), 115–130.

Ratele, K., Shefer, T., Strebel, A. & Fouten, E. (2010). '"We do not cook, we only assist them': Constructions of hegemonic masculinity through gendered activity.' *Journal of Psychology in Africa*, 20(4), 557–568.

Schumann, D. (2016). 'Photo series: Making men and mankind'. *Graduate Journal of Social Science,* 12(3), 94–118.

Sharma, A. & Das, A. (2016). 'Editorial: Men, masculinities and violence.' *Journal of Social Science,* 12(3), 7–11.

Taylor, R., Page, A., Morrell. S., Harrison, J. & Carter, G. (2005). 'Mental health and socio-economic variations in Australian suicide'. *Social Science and Medicine,* 61, 1551–1559.

Vandello, J.A. & Cohen, D. (2008). 'Culture, gender, and men's intimate partner violence.' *Social and Personality Psychology Compass,* 2(2), 652–667.

World Health Organisation, (2009), *Violence prevention evidence: Changing cultural and social norms that support violence.* (1st ed., pp. 1–18). Geneva, Switzerland. Retrieved 30 September 2017, from

World Health Organization. (2015). *Suicide rates (per 100 000 population). World Health Organization.* Retrieved 30 September 2017, from http://www. who.int/gho/mental_health/suicide_rates_male_female/en/

Notes

1. Binaries inherently denote that one side is dominant (masculinity) and the other side is subordinate (femininity). Thus, it is important to note that traits associated with the masculine side of the binary are privileged throughout society (Levi-Strauss, 1973).

2. The way society expects people to perform their gender is problematic, especially for people who are gender diverse or non-binary.

3. The sexualisation of black male bodies has a particularly problematic historical context. Ownership and control of men (and women) of colour during slavery had their bodies being simultaneously viewed as beastly and unappealing on one hand, and hypersexual on the other (Foster, 2011).

BRIANNA ATTARD is a researcher and writer at The Sydney Feminists, Inc. She wrote her first article for TSF on toxic masculinity. Brianna enjoys volunteering and working for organizations that operate within a feminist framework.

Paul Nathanson  **NO**

A Requiem for Manhood

Yesterday was a fine spring day. On my way out for the afternoon, I saw some yellow tulips shyly lifting their heads to the sky and the first bright and feathery leaves unfolding on branches. And yet I spent the afternoon indoors at a movie. It's about the decline of manhood and therefore should be of great interest to everyone who cares about men. Here's a synopsis of *The Rider* (Chloé Zhao, 2018).

Its setting is a Lakota reservation in the "badlands" of North Dakota. Brady is a beautiful young man, who loves horses and can't imagine a life without caring for them and riding them. He lives in poverty with his retarded younger sister and widowed father. But Brady has a big problem, and it isn't poverty. It's the result of falling from his horse during a rodeo. Even with a metal plate in his skull, he still has seizures now and then. One symptom is his right hand, which clenches uncontrollably and makes it impossible for him to use the reins effectively while riding. For a while, Brady maintains the hope of recovering fully and makes a little money by taming the local wild horses. When that proves too difficult, he gets a menial job in the local supermarket. Nonetheless, he enjoys being with two friends and visiting a third friend in hospital. Lane has had a similar fall but been much more severely wounded. He can neither walk nor speak. But Brady's visits to the hospital always leave Lane more cheerful than he usually is. The great love of Brady's life is Apollo, however, his ill-fated horse, Eventually, Brady realizes that he will never be able to live his dream and enact his identity. His ultimate fate remains unknown as the closing credits roll.

The Lakota in this movie reveal deep ambivalence about their identity. On the one hand, they're Americans. They speak English (when they speak at all, which is not often) and have English names. Brady and his friends call themselves "cowboys" (certainly not "Indians"). As in "western" movies, they adopt "cowboy" costumes (notably big black or white hats), use saddles on their horses (instead of riding bare-back) and perform in "cowboy" rituals (such as rodeos). At dusk, sitting around campfires on grassy meadows and watching the sun dip below the long horizon, they play their guitars and sing "country" songs. These people are Christians, moreover, which is why Brady's mother lies in a graveyard with many crosses.

On the other hand, these people are unlike other Americans, even other western or poor Americans. They retain at least some sense that manhood was once a noble calling. (And I'm not referring merely to the poster in one scene that urges readers to believe that "the Lakota way is a good way.") Brady and the other men in this movie, for instance are capable of caring for each other and even of compassion. Brady loves his sister and acknowledges his need to protect her. His seemingly laissez-faire father sacrifices his own desires in order to buy a horse for his son and later shows up at the rodeo to cheer him on (after angrily warning Brady to heed a medical warning). Like many American men, it's true, these dudes have emotional lives that they express most intensely in gestures or even silence rather than words. In one scene, Brady weeps privately over his fate. In another scene, he and his friends hug each other. *Unlike* many other American men, though, these men are very careful about expressing one particular emotion. Of interest here is their passivity, which contrasts with the rage of many other poor communities. *Neither*, of course, is characteristic of a healthy collective identity. I'll return to that in a moment.

Historic versions of masculinity, including the traditional Lakota version, have become *vestigial*. The lives of Lakota men still revolve around horses, to be sure, but that very fact isolates them from modernity and makes them living anachronisms. These "riders" might sell a few horses to ranchers or tourists, for instance, but their only real opportunity to earn money is by performing at rodeos: modern rituals with nostalgic value but no economic (or military) value. These ceremonial events can no longer function as a coming-of-age ritual for boys, at any rate, because preparing for them doesn't equip them with the knowledge or skills that would ensure communal survival. (Rodeos are thus like the jousting tournaments in late-medieval Europe—that is, long after jousting had lost any relation to the dissolving feudal system. By that time, tournaments had come to focus on the preservation of aristocratic status, symbolically, at a time of increasing social mobility due to the revival of trade and commerce.) Consequently, the boys *remain boys*. As many people know by now, this is precisely the fate of so many boys in all modern, or postmodern, societies.

Not surprisingly, *The Rider* includes both explicit and implicit references to *death*. Brady visits his mother's grave in an early scene, for instance, where he prays to, for and somehow with her. Toward the end, moreover, Apollo is wounded and must be "put down." Brady says that his own fate would be the same as Apollo's if he had been a horse; being a man, he must (lamentably) live with his wounds no matter how crippling they are. And yet he clearly tries to kill himself by riding in another rodeo and thus rejecting the warnings of his physician. Other references to death, however, are implicit. The cinematography features North Dakota's beautiful landscape—flat, bleak and largely empty but also open to infinity both horizontally and vertically. (Could that suggest eternity as well? Possibly.) I found it distinctly sad. How long will this wilderness survive the onslaught of urbanization, industrialization—and now, judging from the garbage and abandoned machinery that litter parts of the cinematic landscape, de-industrialization? I found the background music equally beautiful and sad. It, too, is elegiac and almost funereal.

At the surface level, this movie is about the fate of one young man and his friends. At a deeper level, it's about the fate of all men on their tribal reservation. Every major character and almost every minor character, after all, is male. And at a still deeper level, it's about the fate of manhood in American society society. Instead of heaping shame and contempt on these faltering and vulnerable men and therefore on men in general, Chloe Zhao has written and directed what amounts to a *requiem* for manhood. Why would she choose to do so in the specific context of tribal men? It's because tribal societies have long been symbols for so many other Americans of decline, defeat, marginality and therefore of "death." Zhao refrains from reminding viewers of the many social problems that afflict these peoples (including those of the Pine Ridge Reservation, where she shot this movie with non-professional actors). Her goal is not to study this community, so *The Rider* is not (fortunately) a sociological or anthropological treatise on them in the cinematic form. Rather, her goal is to *mourn the decline and distortion* of masculine tradition in modern societies. The whole movie functions as an epitaph. I'm thinking of what Linda tells her son Biff in *Death of a Salesman*: "I don't say he's a great man. Willy Loman never made a lot of money. His name was never in the paper. He's not the finest character that ever lived. But he's a human being, and a terrible thing is happening to him. So attention must be paid. He's not to be allowed to fall into his grave like an old dog. Attention, attention must be finally paid to such a person."

Once upon a time, though, masculinity was *not* some historical anachronism or anthropological curiosity. It was a distinctive, necessary and publicly valued way of life. This morning, by chance, I watched an earlier cinematic exploration of manhood in trouble. In *The Best Years of Our Lives* (William Wyler, 1946), three soldiers return from combat in World War II and try to pick up their lives again but find that they have to start all over. Originally, this movie was Hollywood's attempt to comment on a current social problem: the re-integration of veterans after years of combat overseas. Watched now, though, after more than seventy years, *Best Years* is even more disturbing and more moving than it ever was.

Of the three returning soldiers, only one seems destined, at first, to succeed in peacetime. Before the war, Al had been a happily married man of the upper middle class. His wife and daughter greet him with joy. He can begin right away, therefore, to resume his old life. He steps back into his job at a bank. The war has not changed that. It has, however, changed Al. When another former soldier comes to his office and asks for a loan, Al is delighted to help him start a business—even though the younger man lacks collateral. Al's boss is less than pleased. He's interested only in making money on secure loans, not in rewarding patriotism or gambling on the youthful ambition that has made America the land of opportunity. But Al's wife does understand what the war has done to him and supports his idealism.

Before the war, Fred had been materialistic and hedonistic. Not surprisingly, he had married someone with the same outlook. But the war has changed him no less than Al. He returns with no money, no job and no idea of what would give meaning to his survival in combat. To make ends meet, he takes the only available job and becomes a soda jerk at the local drugstore. Trouble is, his wife wants only to live it up as if no war had intervened—and if not with Fred, then with some other man.

Before the war, Homer had been a happy-go-lucky boy whose thoughts about the future extended only to marrying the girl next door and living happily ever after. But the war has changed him even more than the others. Homer's hands have been burnt off in combat, leaving him with steel hooks to replace them. Although he has learned how to use these effectively, he has trouble adjusting to public curiosity and, even worse, pity from his girlfriend—even though she has both the undiminished love and the courage to marry him anyway.

All three men, as I say, have endured years of suffering as soldiers in wartime, the ultimate proving ground of *manhood* in their world. Each manages to re-invent himself as a *man* according to universally accepted virtues of *masculinity*, which they can re-affirm along with everyone else—*despite its heavy price*. These virtues include not only courage and self-sacrifice but also integrity, honesty, generosity, tenacity, compassion and faithfulness (virtues not limited to male people except for their particular manifestations in daily life). One scene is particularly moving in this respect. At the soda fountain, a cynical middle-aged man tells Homer that the war had been unnecessary—and so had the sacrifices of so many young men like Homer himself, who have ended up either dead or mutilated. Homer rejects this point of view as a matter of honor, and Fred, who overhears the conversation, comes to his aid by slugging the stranger (thus losing his lowly job at the soda fountain).

Best Years is not merely a sad story, not for me. As a refugee from the mid-twentieth-century, I allowed my eyes to linger on its costumes and sets. More important, I allowed my mind to explore its beliefs about how families and communities work, especially its beliefs about manhood. Those things came from another world, one that I had known intimately long ago. It was the world of my childhood, the one that my parents bequeathed to me with all of their love and hope. Nothing is left of it now, nothing but ruins—that is, relentless rage and pervasive cynicism. No wonder my dead parents continue to *haunt* me. You could say that I feel "nostalgic," but that word, despite its etymology, has come to connote something superficial, misguided or even shameful. What I am, truly, is intensely *homesick* (which says something about a man who was intensely unhappy as a child almost everywhere *but* at home). I want desperately to live once again in a world that, despite its terrible flaws (such as war, class conflict and racial segregation), made sense at least as a *shared and uniting ideal*. At home, I had both unconditional love and earned respect. More important, I understood that men and women actually needed and tried to support each other.

I feel now like Dorothy in *The Wizard of Oz*. Captured in a witch's gloomy castle, she looks into her captor's sinister crystal ball and sees the farm back in Kansas. Sick with worry, Auntie Em is calling out for her. In the gloomy castle, though, Dorothy looks around her in despair and says, "I'm frightened, Auntie Em, I'm frightened." And so am I but not only for myself. What, I ask over and over, am I doing here? How did we all get here? What went wrong? Is there really nothing left that's worth fighting or even dying for? Those are not only historical, anthropological,

psychological, political or even moral questions. Considering the rapid fragmentation of our society into a seething collection of polarized identity groups, these questions are also existential ones.

This brings me to what I've been saying for years about the problem of manhood today: the inability of men, at least so far, to create a *healthy identity* for themselves (as distinct from allowing women to create an unhealthy one for them). A healthy identity emerges from and fosters at least one *distinctive, necessary and publicly valued contribution* that men can make specifically *as men* to society. (Fatherhood is possibly the only, remaining source for a healthy collective identity, and that has already been trivialized and even demonized beyond recognition.) Failing to establish a healthy identity, more than a few men succumb to either passivity or rage—or both. This is true of more and more young men not only individually but also collectively. The statistics don't lie. Some boys and men abandon a society with no room for them *male people*; they give up, drop out or kill themselves. Others turn against society, believing that even a negative identity is better than no identity at all; they kill themselves, too, and sometimes (in the context of personal psychopathology) take others with them.

My point here is not merely to eulogize masculinity as I knew it in my own youth. That gender paradigm had its flaws, notably its association of maleness with what Warren Farrell calls "disposability." Being gay when homosexuality was considered either immoral or sick, moreover, I was a victim of both boys and girls who had no understanding of masculinity (or femininity) and therefore no way of placing conventional markers of gender within larger cultural, historical and moral contexts. They bullied me relentlessly because I was different from them in that way, but I could have been equally different in many other ways.

My point here really is, however, to assert that masculinity per se (not this or that version of it) is more than some arbitrary or oppressive "social construction," let alone one that originates in the sinister motivation of men to "dominate" women. If I'm correct, then we're not quite free to abandon it as a disease to be cured in accordance with this or that fashionable ideology. Rather, as I now see after many years of denial, masculinity of one kind or another is a universal feature of human societies (no matter how minimal any gender system might be in some cultures).

To put it bluntly, I don't believe that our society can continue to pathologize or demonize just about every feature of masculinity (or even maleness itself) without continuing to destroy the personal and collective identities of half the population.

I'll conclude with a sad comment on manhood in my own environment. Long ago and in a galaxy far away, the ideal Jewish man was (and still is in some communities) a Torah scholar. For *Life Is with People*, sociologists Mark Zborowski and Elizabeth Herzog interviewed Jewish women from pre-war Eastern Europe. Asked what made men look sexy, the women agreed that men should look pale and thin—as if they could afford to spend entire days in the synagogue praying and studying rabbinic commentaries on the Torah. Translated into secular terms, the ideal Jewish man became a doctor, a lawyer or an academic. Without the spiritual matrix, however, the Jewish ideal differed little from the ideals of many (but by no means all) other communities. It became a very effective way to climb out of poverty and rise in status. That worked for two or three generations, but it doesn't work so well now. Apart from the Hasidim, Jewish men today face the same problems as those of men in general, let alone Lakota men: cultural indifference, ideological hostility and, most important of all, vocational obsolescence. What replaced the traditional Jewish ideal animates bitterly satirical novels by authors such as Philip Roth and Mordecai Richler. No ideal of manhood, in short, has escaped erosion and distortion.

PAUL NATHANSON has a BA (art history), a BTh (Christian theology), an MLS (library service), an MA (religious studies), and a PhD (religious studies). Of particular interest to him is the surprisingly blurry relation between religion and secularity: how religion underlies seemingly secular phenomena such as popular movies and political ideologies.

EXPLORING THE ISSUE

Is Traditional Masculinity Harmful to Boys and Men?

Critical Thinking and Reflection

1. Can you identify the emotional, moral, intellectual, and social components in Brianna's argument?
2. Can you identify the emotional, moral, intellectual, and social components in Nathanson's argument?
3. Can you identify your own emotional, moral, intellectual, and social components responses to this article?
4. What are some similarities and differences between your responses and the authors?

Is There Common Ground?

In this issue, it may feel difficult to find common ground. That difficulty arises partially from the beliefs that being male and masculine are core and unchangeable traits, and that those traits are valued so highly by the culture. It is also difficult to help some men to see the challenges that traditional masculinity has created for them because they have invested a lifetime of denial into over-emphasizing their masculine traits and denying their femininity. To accept this argument would invalidate all of the effort and pain that they have invested into the process. Add to that the strict gender policing that happens among men, and encouraging one's own feminine traits becomes not just uncomfortable, but potentially dangerous. Where there may be common ground is among those from both sides of the argument that agree that violence against women is problematic and needs to be stopped. Here you may get buy-in from those men who see women as precious and in need of protection, but the trade-off for women is that this stance continues to frame women as weak and in need of the protection of men.

Additional Resources

Johnson, A.G. (2014). *The Gender Knot: Unraveling Our Patriarchal Legacy*. Temple University Press: Philadelphia.

Perry, G. (2017). *The Descent of Man*. Penguin Random House: New York.

Internet References . . .

The American Men's Studies Association

https://mensstudies.org/

The Good Men Project

https://goodmenproject.com/

Selected, Edited, and with Issue Framing Material by:
Don Dyson, *Widener University*

ISSUE

Should Parents Allow Puberty Blocking Hormones for Their Transgender Children?

YES: Jacqueline Ruttimann, from "Blocking Puberty in Transgender Youth," *Endocrine News* (2013)

NO: Michelle Cretella, from "I'm a Pediatrician: Here's What I Did When a Little Boy Patient Said He Was a Girl," *The Daily Signal* (2017)

Learning Outcomes

After reading this issue, you will be able to:

- Define transgender.
- Identify three challenges faced by transgender adolescents.
- Compare and contrast the approaches to helping transgender and gender non-conforming young people.

ISSUE SUMMARY

YES: Jacqueline Ruttimann is a freelance writer living in Chevy Chase, Maryland. She argues that pubertal blockers allow transgender youth to carefully consider transition and decreases the need for cross-sex hormones later in life, which results in fewer health risks for the individual.

NO: Michelle Cretella, MD, is the President of the American College of Pediatricians, a national organization of pediatricians and other health-care professionals dedicated to the health and well-being of children. She argues that no one is born transgender, and that "gender confused" children should be supported in their biological sex through puberty.

In the issue "Does Having a Transgender Parent Hurt Children" presented earlier in this book, we explored and explained the meaning of transgender and the various ways in which people navigate that experience. In this chapter, we are exploring the experience of being transgender in childhood and adolescence. Specifically, we are considering whether or not treatment at this age through the use of puberty blockers is a helpful strategy for families navigating this experience.

Current estimates of the adult population estimate that approximately 1.4 million people in the United States identify as transgender. Within that number, approximately 150,000 young people (between the ages of 13 and 17)

identify as transgender as well. What is not currently known is how many children below the age of 13 identify as trans. However, as cultural awareness and acceptance of trans identities and diversity grow, doctors are reporting an increase in the number of children who are identifying as a gender other than the one they were assigned at birth. Most of these doctors believe that this is because more parents are becoming accepting of gender nonconformity and are seeking help for their trans kids.

To frame this discussion, it is important to remember that research has said that by the age of three, most people have developed a strong internal sense of themselves as either a boy or a girl. This sense of self is informed by the child's internalizing of the gendered messages that they experience in their world combined with their internal sense of how they fit or don't fit into those gendered boxes. For many parents with transgender or gender non-conforming children, they remember clearly their young child's insistence that they were not the gender they were assigned at birth. Clear statements like, "I am not a boy, I'm a girl!" of "When am I going to grow a penis?" are part of the experience of these children. For other children, their gender is expressed with less certainty. But in most cases, their insistence on their gender difference is both persistent over time and pervasive through their entire experience of their world.

Also important in this discussion is identifying that for trans youth, the rates of depression and suicide are far above the average for cisgender (non-trans) youth. The depression is often the result of the rejection and bullying that they suffer as well as the ways in which their bodies change when they hit puberty. Puberty is the time at which secondary sex characteristics develop. For those whose biological sex is female, that includes the development of breasts and widening of the hips. For those whose biological sex is male, that includes the enlargement of the penis and the development of facial hair. Prior to puberty, children's bodies are somewhat androgynous, with the exception of their genitalia, and their biological sex can be masked by clothing and hairstyles. This allows trans youth to present themselves to the world in ways that feel more consistent with their internal gender identity. At puberty, however, trans youth often describe the feeling that their bodies are "betraying" them by developing in ways that are inconsistent with the gender they feel they are inside. This sense of betrayal can contribute to depression. Medical treatment for transgender children helps to alleviate this issue.

The medical protocols for treating transgender children include hormone blockers (that prevent the onset of puberty) as well as mental health screening and evaluation. The basic premise of delaying the onset of puberty is to give these young people a chance to do some evaluation with the help of their parents and mental health professionals. In essence, it buys trans youth some time to consider their options and make thoughtful and informed choices before they either continue on their trans journey or allow their bodies to develop in ways consistent with their biological sex. The hormone-blocking treatment is largely reversible, with the exception being that the treatment can interfere with calcium production and bone density, which can lead to osteoporosis later in life.

Often while undergoing this treatment, trans children spend their lives living as the gender that is consistent with their gender identity rather than their biological sex. This usually involves a change of name and coming out to people in their world, including teachers, peers, and other family members. At the conclusion of this treatment, they, along with their parents and doctors, make the decision to continue or to stop treatment.

Those who end hormone-blocking treatment and allow their bodies to develop without medical intervention are often identified as "desisters." After the conclusion of their mental health screening and evaluation and after a great deal of reflection and discussion, they make the choice to discontinue medical intervention and allow their bodies to develop without intervention.

For those who continue on their transgender journey, the next step in treatment is hormone therapy. In this phase, hormones are given to the young person so that their body develops in ways consistent with their gender identity. Gender affirming surgeries are never part of the medical protocol for children.

While this is considered the appropriate treatment for transgender children, there remains some controversy in the medical field about the use of hormone blockers. Much of the controversy arises from a study done in 2011. In that small, qualitative study, researchers identified that 85% of the trans identified young people involved desisted their belief that they were transgender. The desisters in this study identified changes in their environments, falling in love and other factors that influenced their decision to desist.

Although the study was very small (it had only 25 participants), some medical professionals who oppose treating trans children with hormone blockers use the argument that 85% of trans children are likely to desist. This number has become a rallying point for those who believe that the vast majority of children who present with a transgender identity will desist if allowed to experience puberty without any medical intervention.

It is into this challenging issue that the articles for this issue are written. As you read them, consider a few questions: Is the emotional well-being of a child a good reason to engage medical treatment at such a young age? Is it right to deny that treatment to parents and children who seek it out?

YES ↵

Jacqueline Ruttimann

Blocking Puberty In Transgender Youth

For as long as his parents could remember, 12-year-old Jack acted "female." He favored Barbies over Transformers, often wore his sister's underpants, and refused to use urinals.

Similarly, the mother of 14-year-old Janice cannot remember a time when her daughter did not dress androgynously—preferring short haircuts, boxer shorts, and extra-tight sports bras.

Like many young adolescents, Jack and Janice are uncomfortable with their bodies. However, their anguish runs a lot deeper. At 10, Jack attempted to leap out of a rapidly moving car. Janice has had repeated episodes of cutting herself with a razor blade.

Separate psychologists working with Jack and Janice confirmed that the teens have gender identity disorder (GID) and are possibly transgender, a catch-all phrase for individuals whose gender identity is different from their biological sex.

Increasingly, pediatricians and psychologists are challenged by cases like Jack's and Janice's in which kids want to be the opposite gender. It is an emotional and confusing time for the family and the children, who often are on the cusp of puberty at the very time they are rejecting their biological gender. One solution specialists recommend is puberty blockers, drugs that delay the onset of puberty and give the children time to sort out their gender identity.

"Pediatric endocrinologists are the only specialists who see children and adolescents who require pubertal blocking drugs in the course of regular practice," said Norman Spack, a pediatric endocrinologist at Boston Children's Hospital whose practice mainly focuses on transgender youth. "If they do not get involved in cases where they can be helpful, it is unlikely anyone else will."

In the course of their practices, pediatric endocrinologists typically use drugs that delay puberty, such as gonadotropin releasing hormone (GnRH) analogues, to treat conditions such as central precocious puberty and congenital adrenal hyperplasia. The drugs have a good track record, with 30 years of follow-up data showing them to be safe and effective. For transgender patients, the verdict is still out; as transgender patients enter adulthood, data are trickling in as to the benefits and risks of these drugs.

Deciding to treat with such drugs may not be an easy choice, Spack admitted. "It is difficult for pediatric endocrinologists to grasp the idea of treating a child who otherwise seems perfectly normal and may not reveal his/her mental suffering and risk of self-harm. It is all too easy to turn away referred patients with whom the physician has no prior relationship and whose condition may be considered psychiatric."

Gender fluidity is common among children, but it typically crystallizes during the teenage years. Among preadolescents who manifest GID traits, 80 percent will "desist" from being transgender before entering adolescence, according to Kenneth Zucker, Ph.D., of the University of Toronto. Half or more of the youths will go on to identify themselves as gay or lesbian.

Despite increased coverage in the popular press, the prevalence of transgenderism is quite low—about one in 10,000–30,000, according to the fourth edition of the American Psychiatric Association's Diagnostic and Statistical Manual of Mental Disorders (DSM IV).

In a recent commentary in Pediatrics, Walter J. Meyer III, a psychiatrist at the University of Texas Medical Branch in Galveston, Texas, whose practice includes young patients with gender identity issues, cautioned pediatricians not to be so quick to diagnose transgender conditions.

"Many of the presentations in the public media concerning childhood GID give the impression that a child with cross-gender behavior needs to change to the new gender or at least should be evaluated for such a change," he wrote. "Very little information in the public domain talks about the normality of gender questioning and gender role exploration and the rarity of an actual change. The burden of that education is going to fall on the pediatrician."

Once the pediatrician verifies GID, other specialists need to weigh in.

"Pediatric endocrinologists should work with a mental health professional who will support this diagnosis or who can vet the patient for this diagnosis," Meyer said in an interview with Endocrine News.

Transgender is not a mindset, it is a condition that is most likely hardwired into a person from the onset.

"A transgender patient says 'change my body, not my mind,'" explained Milton Diamond, a sexologist with a research focus on transitional and intersex conditions. "A therapist tries to get them to think they're delusional and they don't think they are." Diamond says transgenderism is in a person's genes. In his research on transexuality in twins, he has found that among identical twins, if one transitions, the other does also in about 40 percent of the cases. With fraternal twins, this usually does not happen—only 4 percent of these twins do.

His studies have also shown that transgenders' brains are more similar to the gender they want to be than to their biological gender.

"Experiments show that just the way people are right or left-handed, individuals that are transgender are shown to hear and smell like their preferred gender," added Diamond. (Except for taste and touch, men generally underperform in the sensory department compared with women.)

Spack, who co-directs the Gender Management Service, or GeMS, at Boston Children's Hospital, one of the United States' first gender identity pediatric clinics, champions early treatment before patients reach adulthood.

During his 40-year career, he says he has treated some 200 adult transgender patients who would have benefited from biological clock-stopping drugs. Male-to-female adult patients often suffer physically and psychologically—battling male pattern hair loss, undergoing voice training, having their thyroid cartilage shaved to remove their Adam's apples, and feeling stuck in a body that's too big for a typical female. The late transformation can also be expensive. Patients spend thousands of dollars on hair removal, breast augmentation surgery, and facial feminization surgery.

When American women transition to men at an adult age, their height is typically 5 feet 4 inches, considerably below the mean of 5 feet 10 inches for men. Such patients would have menstruated monthly for years and would face complicated breast reduction to attain a flat chest with an appropriately located areola and nipple.

The lack of availability of medical services for transgenders 20 years ago was "a wasteland," Spack told a packed audience at ENDO 2012 in Houston. In 2009 he co-authored The Endocrine Society Guideline that recommended the use of GnRH analogues in prepubertal,

Tanner Stage 2 children and lifetime use of sex-changing hormones with monitoring for potential health risks.

"There was an attitudinal shift to be able to say that The Endocrine Society supports this," said Spack. Today a dozen pediatric endocrinology transgender programs exist in the United States compared with two or three a few years ago.

Although attitudes about treatment are changing, Spack said transgender kids are not being treated soon enough. In his own practice, he advocates starting puberty blockers earlier than in the Society guidelines of under the age of 16. The best age for boys, he says, is 12–14 years, while they are at Tanner Stage 2, and have a testicular volume of 4–6 cc; girls should come in younger, at age 10–12 years, with Tanner Stage 2 breast development.

"If a biological female comes in at 15, she's physically a woman and may have been menstruating for three years," he said. She would have already reached her peak height, which might have been augmented with earlier GnRH analogues. If she starts blockers at ages 10–13, she would not need a mastectomy because Tanner 2/3 breasts recede with treatment.

"It's becoming clear that the most desirable physical result with the least physical intervention is to prevent pubertal progression in the first place," Spack said.

Adult transgender genotypic males outnumber genotypic females by a three-to-one ratio while in cohorts under age 21, the sex ratios are equal, he said. The reason for the disparity among transgender adults is mostly cultural; most Westernized countries accept women who are "masculine" in looks and behavior, so a girl may have more difficulty in identifying the depth of her feelings or convincing family and doctors of them.

Spack's GeMS program is modeled after the Dutch program that was created by Peggy Cohen-Kettenis, Ph.D., in Amsterdam. The premise of both programs is to treat the patient's natural puberty like an unintended precocity. Dutch physicians administer GnRH analogues to patients at Tanner Stages 2–3, in an attempt to buy more diagnostic time and ensure that patients really want to transition to the other gender.

If at age 16, patients decide to proceed with the transition, they are put on cross-sex steroids such as testosterone and estradiol. The next step is gonadectomies (e.g., oophorectomy, hysterectomy, feminizing genitoplasty with orchiectomies), surgeries that cannot be lawfully performed in the Netherlands and North America until patients are 18. Mental health counseling is continuous and formal evaluations take place at each major decision point in the process.

Before entering Spack's program, patients must be between Tanner Stages 2 and 5 (10 years or above for boys and 9 years or above for girls) and have been in counseling with a gender therapist for six months. The therapist is required to write a referral letter recommending pharmacologic endocrine intervention and stating that other than depression and anxiety associated with gender nonconformity, the patient has no severe psychopathology. Patients must also have the support of both custodial parents.

Once these requirements are established, Spack and his interdisciplinary staff of endocrinologists, urologists, gynecologists, geneticists, psychologists, medical ethicists, and social workers are called into action. Candidates for medication undergo a rigorous five-hour battery of psychological tests and a physical examination to determine pubertal stage.

In his ENDO 2012 lecture, Spack explained that before Tanner 2, most patients are willing to live in both genders. "It's hard to distinguish whether they will desist or persist in becoming transgender and there is no litmus test before Tanner 2 puberty," said Spack. Very few of his patients or those in the Dutch program decide to stay their biological gender after beginning pubertal blockers. The Dutch have treated more than 100 patients with GnRH who have reached over 18 years of age. Spack has seen 105 new patients ages 10–19 since 2007; more than a third of his patients (40) have been Tanner Stage 2–3 and have received GnRH treatment.

Once the psychiatrist and endocrinologist have given the greenlight, the patient begins with one of several GnRH analogues, either a depo injection of Leuprolide that lasts one to three months or an inch-long implant of Histerlin that lasts two years. The latter shuts down gonadotrophic secretion very quickly—within a couple of weeks. The patient undergoes a state of biologic limbo, in which secondary sexual characteristics such as breast budding, testicular enlargement, and axillary and torso hair growth are halted. Height and bone mass, however, still proceed at a pre-pubertal rate.

Usually between ages 14 and 16, patients still look prepubertal compared with the maturity of their peers. Although the delay can be psychologically challenging for the patients who may desire to look like their preferred genders, the slowdown gives them an opportunity to reconsider the transition. GnRH analogues are reversible. Cessation of them usually results in patients restarting their genetically intended puberty within six months.

Although the treatments are considered safe, they are not risk-free. Most transgenders become infertile as a result of the hormonal switching medications. Estrogens diminish sperm production in males, and testosterone's cessation of menses can cause polycystic ovaries in women; these changes usually lead to infertility. Some late-pubertal male patients have opted for sperm banking, but equivalent options for women are limited. Egg freezing is an arduous and expensive procedure requiring ovarian hyperstimulation with HCG, akin to women undergoing in vitro fertilization, and not as likely to be successful, especially if the ovaries are immature when GnRH-suppressed.

"It's hard to have a conversation about fertility when the patient is 12 or 14 years old," said Spack. "It's important for patients to continue to be in psychotherapy during this long diagnostic phase so they can fully understand the implication of taking cross-steroids, even though they are waiting anxiously to get them."

Another risk is cancer. Girls who have breasts and undergo testosterone treatment need regular mammogram screening as adult men; those who have their uteruses while on testosterone may develop endometrial cancer. Both risks can be mitigated by surgical removal of the organs.

Among the arguments for using pubertal blockers to gain more diagnostic time is that patients will not need as many cross-sex hormones later in the transition process. Fewer estrogens in patients means a decreased risk of blood clotting and pulmonary embolism; fewer androgens reduces the likelihood of hypertension. Another plus, Spack said, is that most male-to-female adult patients who took GnRH analogues end up with appropriate size breasts for their frame and never feel the need to have further reconstructive surgery.

For Jack and Janice, not having options may be a case of life and death. According to Youth Pride Inc., a U.S. advocacy group for lesbian, gay, bisexual, transgender, and questioning youth, about two thirds of transgender youth have reported being verbally, physically, and sexually attacked by either their peers or an adult family member, and one third have attempted suicide.

"A lot of people are concerned that delaying puberty may cause some harm," said Meyer. "On a whole, much less harm is done by giving blockers than by not giving blockers."

JACQUELINE RUTTIMANN is a freelance writer living in Chevy Chase, Maryland.

Michelle Cretella    **NO**

I'm a Pediatrician. Here's What I Did When a Little Boy Patient Said He Was a Girl

"**C**ongratulations, it's a boy!" Or, "Congratulations, it's a girl!"

As a pediatrician for nearly 20 years, that's how many of my patient relationships began. Our bodies declare our sex.

Biological sex is not assigned. Sex is determined at conception by our DNA and is stamped into every cell of our bodies. Human sexuality is binary. You either have a normal Y chromosome, and develop into a male, or you don't, and you will develop into a female. There are at least 6,500 genetic differences between men and women. Hormones and surgery cannot change this.

An identity is not biological, it is psychological. It has to do with thinking and feeling. Thoughts and feelings are not biologically hardwired. Our thinking and feeling may be factually right or factually wrong.

If I walk into my doctor's office today and say, "Hi, I'm Margaret Thatcher," my physician will say I am delusional and give me an anti-psychotic. Yet, if instead, I walked in and said, "I'm a man," he would say, "Congratulations, you're transgender."

If I were to say, "Doc, I am suicidal because I'm an amputee trapped in a normal body, please cut off my leg," I will be diagnosed with body identity integrity disorder. But if I walk into that doctor's office and say, "I am a man, sign me up for a double mastectomy," my physician will. See, if you want to cut off a leg or an arm you're mentally ill, but if you want to cut off healthy breasts or a penis, you're transgender.

No one is born transgender. If gender identity were hardwired in the brain before birth, identical twins would have the same gender identity 100 percent of the time. But they don't.

I had one patient we'll call Andy. Between the ages of 3 and 5, he increasingly played with girls and "girl toys" and said he was a girl. I referred the parents and Andy to a therapist. Sometimes mental illness of a parent or abuse of the child are factors, but more commonly, the child has misperceived family dynamics and internalized a false belief.

In the middle of one session, Andy put down the toy truck, held onto a Barbie, and said, "Mommy and Daddy, you don't love me when I'm a boy." When Andy was 3, his sister with special needs was born, and required significantly more of his parents' attention. Andy misperceived this as "Mommy and Daddy love girls. If I want them to love me, I have to be a girl." With family therapy Andy got better.

Today, Andy's parents would be told, "This is who Andy really is. You must ensure that everyone treats him as a girl, or else he will commit suicide."

As Andy approaches puberty, the experts would put him on puberty blockers so he can continue to impersonate a girl.

It doesn't matter that we've never tested puberty blockers in biologically normal children. It doesn't matter that when blockers are used to treat prostate cancer in men, and gynecological problems in women, they cause problems with memory. We don't need testing. We need to arrest his physical development now, or he will kill himself.

But this is not true. Instead, when supported in their biological sex through natural puberty, the vast majority of gender-confused children get better. Yet, we chemically castrate gender-confused children with puberty blockers. Then we permanently sterilize many of them by adding cross-sex hormones, which also put them at risk for heart disease, strokes, diabetes, cancers, and even the very emotional problems that the gender experts claim to be treating.

P.S. If a girl who insists she is male has been on testosterone daily for one year, she is cleared to get a bilateral mastectomy at age 16. Mind you, the American Academy of Pediatrics recently came out with a report that urges pediatricians to caution teenagers about getting tattoos because they are essentially permanent and can cause scarring. But this same AAP is 110 percent in support of 16-year-old girls getting a double mastectomy, even without parental consent, so long as the girl insists that she is a man, and has been taking testosterone daily for one year.

To indoctrinate all children from preschool forward with the lie that they could be trapped in the wrong body disrupts the very foundation of a child's reality testing. If they can't trust the reality of their physical bodies, who or what can they trust? Transgender ideology in schools is psychological abuse that often leads to chemical castration, sterilization, and surgical mutilation.

Michelle Cretella, M.D., is president of the American College of Pediatricians, a national organization of pediatricians and other health care professionals dedicated to the health and well-being of children.

EXPLORING THE ISSUE

Should Parents Allow Puberty Blocking Hormones for Their Transgender Children?

Critical Thinking and Reflection

1. Can you identify the emotional, moral, intellectual, and social components in Ruttimann's argument?
2. Can you identify the emotional, moral, intellectual, and social components in Cretella's argument?
3. Can you identify your own emotional, moral, intellectual, and social responses to this issue?
4. What are some similarities and differences between your responses and those of the authors?

Is There Common Ground?

In this case, as in others within this book, the common ground here is the care and protection of children. Both sides of the argument want the best for the children involved in these scenarios. Indeed, in each case, both sides believe that their answer to the challenge represents the most humane and caring response to these children and their parents. Where the two sides diverge, however, is in their belief about whether or not people should be encouraged to conform to the gendered norms that exist in the cultures of the United States. As the cultural understanding of gender becomes more complex, it has the potential to expand gender categories and allow people to identify their gender in a myriad of ways that may or may not be consistent with their biological sex. As gender and biological sex become less entangled, it may be possible that medical treatment is less sought after by gender nonconforming children and adults.

Additional Resources

Brill, S. and Pepper, R. (2008). *The Transgender Child: A Handbook for Families and Professionals*. Cleis Press: San Francisco.

Ehrensaft, D. (2011). *Gender Born, Gender Made: Raising Healthy Gender-Nonconforming Children*. The Experiment: New York.

Pessin-Whedbee. (2016). *Who Are You?: The Kid's Guide to Gender Identity*. Jessica Kingsley Publishers: London, UK.

Internet References . . .

Mermaids

https://www.mermaidsuk.org.uk/

Trans Kids Purple Rainbow Foundation

http://www.transkidspurplerainbow.org/

Trans Youth Family Allies

http://www.imatyfa.org/

Unit 4

UNIT

Families and Systems

*F*amilies don't exist in a vacuum. Each family unit is connected in meaningful ways to larger social systems. Education systems interact with most families on a daily basis. Legal systems create rules by which families must abide. Systems of privilege and oppression marginalize some families while offering others protection and privilege. This unit explores some of the important ways that families and systems interact with one another, and the effects that those interactions have on the members of those families.

Selected, Edited, and with Issue Framing Material by:
Don Dyson, *Widener University*

ISSUE

Should Illegal Immigrant Families Be Able to Send Their Children to Public Schools?

YES: William Brennan, from Majority Opinion, *Plyler v. Doe*, U.S. Supreme Court (1982)

NO: Warren Burger, from Dissenting Opinion, *Plyler v. Doe*, U.S. Supreme Court (1982)

Learning Outcomes
After reading this issue, you will be able to: • Identify legal criteria such as the due process clause, the equal protection clause, and fundamental rights. • Compare and contrast whether the U.S. Constitution protects undocumented immigrant children who reside in the United States. • Evaluate the impact of this Supreme Court decision on illegal U.S. border crossings.

ISSUE SUMMARY

YES: William Brennan is regarded as one of the greatest intellectual leaders of the twentieth-century Supreme Court. He was regarded for writing extraordinarily forward-thinking opinions, especially regarding civil rights and civil liberties. This case proves no exception, as he captures an issue that seems even more pertinent today than when the Supreme Court addressed it. Brennan believes that children who are in the country and undocumented have a constitutional right to a public education.

NO: Warren Burger was the Chief Justice of the Supreme Court during a time in which it was slowly moving in a more conservative direction. He was an instrumental voice in many cases before the Supreme Court that had a more conservative outcome. Burger believes that undocumented immigrant children have no constitutional right to an education.

Although the percentage of the U.S. population that is foreign born has not increased significantly, there is a significant change in the country of origin from decades past. According to the Census Bureau, during 1960, 75 percent of those who were foreign born were from Europe. By 2009, over 80 percent of those who are foreign born are from Latin American and Asian countries (53.1 percent from Latin America, 27.7 percent from Asia, 12.7 percent from Europe, 3.9 percent from Africa, and 2.7 percent from other regions).

When looking at the data from specific countries, Mexico was the largest, accounting for almost 30 percent of foreign-born population, totaling approximately

11.5 million. The second-largest country of birth was China, representing just over 5 percent of the foreign-born population.

In 1960, the foreign born settled in traditional gateway states: New York, California, Texas, Florida, and Illinois. Today, foreign-born residents are increasingly likely to settle in states and communities that may not have a history of having large populations of foreign-born residents. Despite this, half of all foreign-born residents today live in California, New York, Texas, and Florida. According to public opinion polling, Gallup regularly asks a random sample of Americans the following question, "In your view, should immigration be kept at its present level, increased, or decreased?" In 2011, 43 percent of respondents, a plurality, argued that it should be decreased, 35 percent felt it should remain at its present level, and 18 percent of respondents felt it should be increased. How do these numbers compare and contrast with the general public's views at other periods in American history? According to their polling, there were periods of time in which larger numbers of Americans wanted to see decreased immigration, such as after 9/11 (58 percent) and during the mid-1990s (65 percent), when California voters supported reporting undocumented immigrant students to the Immigration and Naturalization Service. The poll's 18 percent support for increased immigration is tied for the highest percentage that response has ever received: in 1965, the first year that Gallup asked that question. Most Americans view immigration as a good thing for the country (57 percent) versus a bad thing (37 percent). The face of immigration has changed in the United States over recent decades. While in the previous decades it was largely European, more recently it is largely Hispanic and African. It is also found in more varied places than the traditional states associated with immigration. While in the mid-1990s the backlash to immigration was seen in California, today the backlash often occurs from untraditional places, sometimes rural and fairly distant from the U.S.-Mexican border.

Views about immigration are not necessarily the same as views about illegal immigration. For example, the state of Arizona passed a highly restrictive law targeting undocumented immigrants, and the United States filed suit, saying that the law is unconstitutional. However, 50 percent of Americans oppose the U.S. lawsuit while only 33 percent support it. When divided by political ideology, support for the lawsuit varies significantly: 56 percent of Democrats, 27 percent of Independents, and 11 percent of Republicans support the lawsuit. The concern that many states have is over undocumented immigration. In some cases, undocumented immigrants can comprise a sizable number of students. In challenging economic times when many districts are laying off teachers, a number of U.S.-born citizens voicing dismay and even anger at the public resources that are directed toward undocumented immigrants. There are school districts across the United States that were accustomed to having a small population of students who speak English as a second language. Today, many districts are seeing a steady increase in the number of speakers of English as a second language. Sometimes a backlash ensues, and visitors are looking for ways to adjust their instruction to correspond with this need. A case like this raises critical

questions about the role of education and the role of the Constitution regarding education:

- What is the purpose and function of education in the United States today?
- What is the cost of sending undocumented immigrants to public schools?
- What is the value of sending undocumented immigrants to public schools?
- What is the cost of keeping undocumented immigrants out of public schools?
- What is the value of keeping undocumented immigrants out of public schools?

Immigration has played a critical role throughout American history, as has education. Public education has historically allowed many generations to improve their economic situation compared to that of their parents. Many children who are here illegally, and may have been here since they were infants, want the same opportunities as everyone else. At the same time, there are limited resources directed to public education. Adding more students, and in many cases adding more specialized teachers, creates additional expenses that the public education system would otherwise not need to assume. Also, allowing undocumented immigrants access to public schooling arguably proves to be a compelling incentive to come to the country illegally. The U.S. Constitution provides a wide array of protections. This case raises important questions not just about public education, but also constitutional rights:

- Do those rights and protections in the U.S. Constitution apply to everyone within the U.S. borders?
- Do the rights and protections in the U.S. Constitution apply only to U.S. citizens?
- Do constitutional protections vary depending on whether or not something is a fundamental right?

The U.S. Constitution applies certain rights regardless of popular opinion. In fact, the entire point of having rights enumerated in the Constitution is to keep certain rights from being at the whim of the majority. When the Constitution was written, there was not the sort of formal process for immigration that exists today.

Another perspective to view this from is one of safety and security. For example, proponents of the rights of undocumented immigrants will often say that it is dangerous to leave children on the streets all day. Having them social welfare legislation. Both the importance of education in maintaining our basic institutions and the lasting impact of its deprivation on the life of the child mark the distinction. The "American people have always regarded education and [the] acquisition of knowledge as matters of supreme importance." But neither is it merely some governmental "benefit" indistinguishable from other forms of social welfare legislation. Both the importance of education in maintaining our basic institutions and the lasting impact of its deprivation on the life of the child mark the distinction. The "American people have always regarded education and [the] acquisition of knowledge as matters of supreme importance." We have recognized "the public schools as a most vital civic institution for the preservation of a democratic system of government." We have recognized "the public schools as a most vital civic institution for the preservation of a democratic system of government," and as the primary vehicle for transmitting "the values on which our society rests" (BRENNAN, J., concurring), and as the primary vehicle for transmitting "the values on which our society rests."

[A]s . . . pointed out early in our history, . . . some degree of education is necessary to prepare citizens to participate effectively and intelligently in our open political system if we are to preserve freedom and independence.

And these historic perceptions of the public schools as inculcating fundamental values necessary to the maintenance of a democratic political system have been confirmed by the observations of social scientists.

In addition, education provides the basic tools by which individuals might lead economically productive lives to the benefit of us all. In sum, education has a fundamental role in maintaining the fabric of our society. We cannot ignore the significant social costs borne by our Nation when select groups are denied the means to absorb the values and skills upon which our social order rests.

In addition to the pivotal role of education in sustaining our political and cultural heritage, denial of education to some isolated group of children poses an affront of the goals of the Equal Protection Clause: the on of governmental barriers presenting unreasonstacles to advancement on the basis of individual aradoxically, by depriving the children of any disgroup of an education, we foreclose the means by at group might raise the level of esteem in which by the majority. But more directly, "education individuals to be self-reliant and self-sufficient ts in society." Illiteracy is an enduring disability to read and write will handicap the individ- rived of a basic education each and every day

of his life. The inestimable toll of that deprivation on the social, economic, intellectual, and psychological wellbeing of the individual, and the obstacle it poses to individual achievement, make it most difficult to reconcile the cost or the principle of a status based denial of basic education with the framework of equality embodied in the Equal Protection Clause. What we said 28 years ago in 221. Illiteracy is an enduring disability. The inability to read and write will handicap the individual deprived of a basic education each and every day of his life. The inestimable toll of that deprivation on the social, economic, intellectual, and psychological wellbeing of the individual, and the obstacle it poses to individual achievement, make it most difficult to reconcile the cost or the principle of a status-based denial of basic education with the framework of equality embodied in the Equal Protection Clause. What we said 28 years ago in *Brown v. Board of Education* (1954) still holds true:

Today, education is perhaps the most important function of state and local governments. Compulsory school attendance laws and the great expenditures for education both demonstrate our recognition of the importance of education to our democratic society. It is required in the performance of our most basic public responsibilities, even service in the armed forces. It is the very foundation of good citizenship. Today it is a principal instrument in awakening the child to cultural values, in preparing him for later professional training, and in helping him to adjust normally to his environment. In these days, it is doubtful that any child may reasonably be expected to succeed in life if he is denied the opportunity of an education. Such an opportunity, where the state has undertaken to provide it, is a right which must be made available to all on equal terms.

B

These well-settled principles allow us to determine the proper level of deference to be afforded [the Texas law]. Undocumented aliens cannot be treated as a suspect class, because their presence in this country in violation of federal law is not a "constitutional irrelevancy." Nor is education a fundamental right; a State need not justify by compelling necessity every variation in the manner in which education is provided to its population. But more is involved in these cases than the abstract question whether [the Texas law] discriminates against a suspect class, or whether education is a fundamental right. [The Texas law] imposes a lifetime hardship on a discrete class of children not accountable for their disabling status. The

behaving productively in schools will keep them engaged in ways that are beneficial to the larger society. Opponents of the rights of undocumented immigrants argue that such a system encourages dangerous and violent people to come to the United States, and that they use our laws to take advantage of U.S. citizens. Last, analyze the role of race and how that affects views about immigration:

- What role do you feel that race plays in views about immigration today?
- How are the changing demographics of American society influencing views about immigration and public education?
- How would you compare and contrast social problems and immigration (e.g., violence caused by immigrants) between generations past and today?
- How would you compare and contrast ingenuity and immigration between generations past and today?

Race has often played a significant role in American society, and definitions of whiteness and racial minorities have been reconstructed throughout American history. Immigration today, both documented and undocumented, is having a clear impact on American demographics and American culture. The relationship between race and immigration is a topic that merits close examination. This chapter contains excerpts from a Supreme Court opinion about whether undocumented immigrants have a right to attend public schools. This court case is not a recent one, yet the topic remains a priority and a major concern for a large number of Americans. What do we learn from the fact that such an issue remains divisive within our society for decades? When examining the articles in this chapter, apply them to the Legal Framework overview in the Introduction. Do your beliefs in this case fit more under Originalism or Living Document? Consider the larger implications of these decisions.

YES ⬅

William Brennan

Majority Opinion, *Plyler v. Doe*

Justice Brennan delivered the opinion of the Court.

The question presented by these cases is whether, consistent with the Equal Protection Clause of the Fourteenth Amendment, Texas may deny to undocumented school-age children the free public education that it provides to children who are citizens of the United States or legally admitted aliens. . . .

I

In May, 1975, the Texas Legislature revised its education laws to withhold from local school districts any state funds for the education of children who were not "legally admitted" into the United States. The 1975 revision also authorized local school districts to deny enrollment in their public schools to children not "legally admitted" to the country. These cases involve constitutional challenges to those provisions.

This is a class action, filed in the United States District Court for the Eastern District of Texas in September, 1977, on behalf of certain school-age children of Mexican origin residing in Smith County, Tex., who could not establish that they had been legally admitted into the United States. The action complained of the exclusion of plaintiff children from the public schools of the Tyler Independent School District. . . . The State of Texas intervened as a party-defendant. After certifying a class consisting of all undocumented school-age children of Mexican origin residing within the School District, the District Court preliminarily enjoined defendants from denying a free education to members of the plaintiff class. In December, 1977, the court conducted an extensive hearing on plaintiffs' motion for permanent injunctive relief. . . .

II

The Fourteenth Amendment provides that

[n]o State shall . . . deprive any person of life, liberty, or property, without due process of law; nor deny to

any person within its jurisdiction the equal protection of the laws.

(emphasis added.) Appellants argue at the outset that undocumented aliens, because of their immigration status, are not "persons within the jurisdiction" of the State of Texas, and that they therefore have no right to the equal protection of Texas law. We reject this argument. Whatever his status under the immigration laws, an alien is surely a "person" in any ordinary sense of that term. Aliens, even aliens whose presence in this country is unlawful, have long been recognized as "persons" guaranteed due process of law by the Fifth and Fourteenth Amendments. Indeed, we have clearly held that the Fifth Amendment protects aliens whose presence in this country is unlawful from invidious discrimination by the Federal Government. . . .

The Fourteenth Amendment to the Constitution is not confined to the protection of citizens. It says:

Nor shall any state deprive any person of life, liberty, or property without due process of law; nor deny to any person within its jurisdiction the equal protection of the laws.

These provisions are universal in their application, to all persons within the territorial jurisdiction, without regard to any differences of race, of color, or of nationality, and the protection of the laws is a pledge of the protection of equal laws.

In concluding that "all persons within the territory of the United States," including aliens unlawfully present, may invoke the Fifth and Sixth Amendments to challenge actions of the Federal Government, we reasoned from the understanding that the Fourteenth Amendment was designed to afford its protection to all within the boundaries of a State. Our cases applying the Equal Protection Clause reflect the same territorial theme:

Manifestly, the obligation of the State to give the protection of equal laws can be performed only where its laws operate, that is, within its own jurisdiction. It is there that the equality of legal right must be maintained. That obligation is imposed by the Constitution upon the States severally as governmental entities, each responsible for its own laws establishing the rights and duties of persons within its borders. . . .

Is it not essential to the unity of the people that the citizens of each State shall be entitled to all the privileges and immunities of citizens in the several States? Is it not essential to the unity of the Government and the unity of the people that all persons, *whether citizens or strangers, within this land,* shall have equal protection in every State in this Union in the rights of life and liberty and property?

Senator Howard, also a member of the Joint Committee of Fifteen, and the floor manager of the Amendment in the Senate, was no less explicit about the broad objectives of the Amendment, and the intention to make its provisions applicable to all who "may happen to be" within the jurisdiction of a State:

The last two clauses of the first section of the amendment disable a State from depriving not merely a citizen of the United States, but *any person, whoever he may be,* of life, liberty, or property without due process of law, or from denying to him the equal protection of the laws of the State. This abolishes all class legislation in the States and does away with the injustice of subjecting one caste of persons to a code not applicable to another. . . . It will, if adopted by the States, forever disable every one of them from passing laws trenching upon those fundamental rights and privileges which pertain to citizens of the United States, *and to all persons who may happen to be within their jurisdiction.* . . .

Our conclusion that the illegal aliens who are plaintiffs in these cases may claim the benefit of the Fourteenth Amendment's guarantee of equal protection only begins the inquiry. The more difficult question is whether the Equal Protection Clause has been violated by the refusal of the State of Texas to reimburse local school boards for the education of children who cannot demonstrate that their presence within the United States is lawful, or by the imposition by those school boards of the burden of tuition on those children. It is to this question that we now turn. . . .

III

A

Sheer incapability or lax enforcement of the laws barring entry into this country, coupled with the failure to establish an effective bar to the employment of undocumented aliens, has resulted in the creation of a substantial "shadow population" of illegal migrants—numbering in the millions—within our borders. This situation raises the specter of a permanent caste of undocumented resident aliens, encouraged by some to remain here as a sou[rce of] cheap labor, but nevertheless denied the benefits tha[t] society makes available to citizens and lawful resid[ents.] The existence of such an underclass presents most diff[icult] problems for a Nation that prides itself on adherence [to] principles of equality under law.

The children who are plaintiffs in these cases a[re] special members of this underclass. Persuasive argumen[ts] support the view that a State may withhold its beneficen[ce] from those whose very presence within the United State[s] is the product of their own unlawful conduct. These argu[ments] do not apply with the same force to classifications imposing disabilities on the minor children of such illegal entrants. At the least, those who elect to enter our territory by stealth and in violation of our law should be prepared to bear the consequences, including, but not limited to, deportation. But the children of those illegal entrants are not comparably situated. Their "parents have the ability to conform their conduct to societal norms," and presumably the ability to remove themselves from the State's jurisdiction; but the children who are plaintiffs in these cases "can affect neither their parents' conduct nor their own status." Even if the State found it expedient to control the conduct of adults by acting against their children, legislation directing the onus of a parent's misconduct against his children does not comport with fundamental conceptions of justice.

[V]isiting . . . condemnation on the head of a[n] infant is illogical and unjust. Moreover, imposing disabi[lities] on the . . . child is contrary to the basic concept of o[ur] system that legal burdens should bear some relation[ship] to individual responsibility or wrongdoing. Obvious[ly,] child is responsible for his birth, and penalizing th[e] child is an ineffectual—as well as unjust—way of d[eterring] the parent.

Of course, undocumented status is no[t] to any proper legislative goal. Nor is undoc[umented sta]tus an absolutely immutable characteristic, product of conscious, indeed unlawful, a[ction. If Texas law] is directed against children, discriminatory burden on the basis of [a charac]tic over which children can have littl[e] difficult to conceive of a rational ju[stification for penal]izing these children for their prese[nce in the United] States. Yet that appears to be pr[ecisely the effect of the] Texas law].

Public education is not a [right granted to individu]als by the Constitution. But [neither is it merely some gov]ernmental "benefit" indistin[guishable from]

stigma of illiteracy will mark them for the rest of their lives. By denying these children a basic education, we deny them the ability to live within the structure of our civic institutions, and foreclose any realistic possibility that they will contribute in even the smallest way to the progress of our Nation. In determining the rationality of [the Texas law], we may appropriately take into account its costs to the Nation and to the innocent children who are its victims. In light of these countervailing costs, the discrimination contained in [the Texas law] can hardly be considered rational unless it furthers some substantial goal of the State. . . .

IV

As we recognized in *De Canas v. Bica* (1976), the States do have some authority to act with respect to illegal aliens, at least where such action mirrors federal objectives and furthers a legitimate state goal. In *De Canas,* the State's program reflected Congress' intention to bar from employment all aliens except those possessing a grant of permission to work in this country. *Id.* at 361. In contrast, there is no indication that the disability imposed by [the Texas law] corresponds to any identifiable congressional policy. The State does not claim that the conservation of state educational resources was ever a congressional concern in restricting immigration. More importantly, the classification reflected in [the Texas law] does not operate harmoniously within the federal program.

To be sure, like all persons who have entered the United States unlawfully, these children are subject to deportation. But there is no assurance that a child subject to deportation will ever be deported. An illegal entrant might be granted federal permission to continue to reside in this country, or even to become a citizen. In light of the discretionary federal power to grant relief from deportation, a State cannot realistically determine that any particular undocumented child will in fact be deported until after deportation proceedings have been completed. It would, of course, be most difficult for the State to justify a denial of education to a child enjoying an inchoate federal permission to remain. . . .

V

First, appellants appear to suggest that the State may seek to protect itself from an influx of illegal immigrants. While a State might have an interest in mitigating the potentially harsh economic effects of sudden shifts in population, [the Texas law] hardly offers an effective method of dealing with an urgent demographic or economic problem. There is no evidence in the record suggesting that illegal entrants impose any significant burden on the State's economy. To the contrary, the available evidence suggests that illegal aliens underutilize public services, while contributing their labor to the local economy and tax money to the state. The dominant incentive for illegal entry into the State of Texas is the availability of employment; few if any illegal immigrants come to this country, or presumably to the State of Texas, in order to avail themselves of a free education. Thus, even making the doubtful assumption that the net impact of illegal aliens on the economy of the State is negative, we think it clear that "[c]harging tuition to undocumented children constitutes a ludicrously ineffectual attempt to stem the tide of illegal immigration," at least when compared with the alternative of prohibiting the employment of illegal aliens.

Second, while it is apparent that a State may "not . . . reduce expenditures for education by barring [some arbitrarily chosen class of] children from its schools," appellants suggest that undocumented children are appropriately singled out for exclusion because of the special burdens they impose on the State's ability to provide high-quality public education. But the record in no way supports the claim that exclusion of undocumented children is likely to improve the overall quality of education in the State. . . .

Finally, appellants suggest that undocumented children are appropriately singled out because their unlawful presence within the United States renders them less likely than other children to remain within the boundaries of the State, and to put their education to productive social or political use within the State. Even assuming that such an interest is legitimate, it is an interest that is most difficult to quantify. The State has no assurance that any child, citizen or not, will employ the education provided by the State within the confines of the State's borders. In any event, the record is clear that many of the undocumented children disabled by this classification will remain in this country indefinitely, and that some will become lawful residents or citizens of the United States. It is difficult to understand precisely what the State hopes to achieve by promoting the creation and perpetuation of a subclass of illiterates within our boundaries, surely adding to the problems and costs of unemployment, welfare, and crime. It is thus clear that whatever savings might be achieved by denying these children an education, they are wholly insubstantial in light of the costs involved to these children, the State, and the Nation.

VI

If the State is to deny a discrete group of innocent children the free public education that it offers to other children residing within its borders, that denial must be justified by a showing that it furthers some substantial state interest. No such showing was made here. Accordingly, the judgment of the Court of Appeals in each of these cases is

Affirmed.

> * Together with No. 80-1934, Texas et al. v. Certain Named and Unnamed Undocumented Alien Children et al., also on appeal from the same court.

WILLIAM BRENNAN is regarded as one of the greatest intellectual leaders of the twentieth-century Supreme Court. He was regarded for writing extraordinarily forward-thinking opinions, especially regarding civil rights and civil liberties. This case proves no exception as he captures an issue that seems even more pertinent today than when the Supreme Court addressed this issue. Brennan believes that children who are in the country and undocumented have a constitutional right to public education.

Warren Burger

 **NO**

Dissenting Opinion, *Plyler v. Doe*

Chief Justice Burger, with whom Justice White, Justice Rehnquist, and Justice O'Connor join, dissenting.

Were it our business to set the Nation's social policy, I would agree without hesitation that it is senseless for an enlightened society to deprive any children—including illegal aliens—of an elementary education. I fully agree that it would be folly—and wrong—to tolerate creation of a segment of society made up of illiterate persons, many having a limited or no command of our language. However, the Constitution does not constitute us as "Platonic Guardians," nor does it vest in this Court the authority to strike down laws because they do not meet our standards of desirable social policy, "wisdom," or "common sense." We trespass on the assigned function of the political branches under our structure of limited and separated powers when we assume policymaking role as the Court does today.

The Court makes no attempt to disguise that it is acting to make up for Congress' lack of "effective leadership" in dealing with the serious national problems caused by the influx of uncountable millions of illegal aliens across our borders. The failure of enforcement of the immigration laws over more than a decade and the inherent difficulty and expense of sealing our vast borders have combined to create a grave socioeconomic dilemma. It is a dilemma that has not yet even been fully assessed, let alone addressed. However, it is not the function of the Judiciary to provide "effective leadership" simply because the political branches of government fail to do so.

The Court's holding today manifests the justly criticized judicial tendency to attempt speedy and wholesale formulation of "remedies" for the failures—or simply the laggard pace—of the political processes of our system of government. The Court employs, and, in my view, abuses, the Fourteenth Amendment in an effort to become an omnipotent and omniscient problem solver. That the motives for doing so are noble and compassionate does not alter the fact that the Court distorts our constitutional function to make amends for the defaults of others.

I

In a sense, the Court's opinion rests on such a unique confluence of theories and rationales that it will likely stand for little beyond the results in these particular cases. Yet the extent to which the Court departs from principled constitutional adjudication is nonetheless disturbing. I have no quarrel with the conclusion that the Equal Protection Clause of the Fourteenth Amendment *applies* to aliens who, after their illegal entry into this country, are indeed physically "within the jurisdiction" of a state. However, as the Court concedes, this "only begins the inquiry." The Equal Protection Clause does not mandate identical treatment of different categories of persons.

The dispositive issue in these cases, simply put, is whether, for purposes of allocating its finite resources, a state has a legitimate reason to differentiate between persons who are lawfully within the state and those who are unlawfully there. The distinction the State of Texas has drawn—based not only upon its own legitimate interests but on classifications established by the Federal Government in its immigration laws and policies—is not unconstitutional.

A

The Court acknowledges that, except in those cases when state classifications disadvantage a "suspect class" or impinge upon a "fundamental right," the Equal Protection Clause permits a state "substantial latitude" in distinguishing between different groups of persons. Moreover, the Court expressly—and correctly—rejects any suggestion that illegal aliens are a suspect class or that education is a fundamental right. Yet by patching together bits and pieces of what might be termed quasi-suspect-class and quasi-fundamental-rights analysis, the Court spins out a theory custom-tailored to the facts of these cases.

In the end, we are told little more than that the level of scrutiny employed to strike down the Texas law applies only when illegal alien children are deprived of a public

Supreme Court of the United States, 1982.

education. If ever a court was guilty of an unabashedly result-oriented approach, this case is a prime example.

(1)

The Court first suggests that these illegal alien children, although not a suspect class, are entitled to special solicitude under the Equal Protection Clause because they lack "control" over or "responsibility" for their unlawful entry into this country. Similarly, the Court appears to take the position that [the Texas law] is presumptively "irrational" because it has the effect of imposing "penalties" on "innocent" children. However, the Equal Protection Clause does not preclude legislators from classifying among persons on the basis of factors and characteristics over which individuals may be said to lack "control." Indeed, in some circumstances, persons generally, and children in particular, may have little control over or responsibility for such things as their ill health, need for public assistance, or place of residence. Yet a state legislature is not barred from considering, for example, relevant differences between the mentally healthy and the mentally ill, or between the residents of different counties simply because these may be factors unrelated to individual choice or to any "wrongdoing." The Equal Protection Clause protects against arbitrary and irrational classifications, and against invidious discrimination stemming from prejudice and hostility; it is not an all-encompassing "equalizer" designed to eradicate every distinction for which persons are not "responsible."

The Court does not presume to suggest that appellees' purported lack of culpability for their illegal status prevents them from being deported or otherwise "penalized" under federal law. Yet would deportation be any less a "penalty" than denial of privileges provided to legal residents? Illegality of presence in the United States does not—and need not—depend on some amorphous concept of "guilt" or "innocence" concerning an alien's entry. Similarly, a state's use of federal immigration status as a basis for legislative classification is not necessarily rendered suspect for its failure to take such factors into account.

The Court's analogy to cases involving discrimination against illegitimate children is grossly misleading. The State has not thrust any disabilities upon appellees due to their "status of birth." Rather, appellees' status is predicated upon the circumstances of their concededly illegal presence in this country, and is a direct result of Congress' obviously valid exercise of its "broad constitutional powers" in the field of immigration and naturalization. This Court has recognized that, in allocating governmental benefits to a given class of aliens, one "may take into account the character of the relationship between the alien and this country." When that "relationship" is a federally prohibited one, there can, of course, be no presumption that a state has a constitutional duty to include illegal aliens among the recipients of its governmental benefits.

(2)

The second strand of the Court's analysis rests on the premise that, although public education is not a constitutionally guaranteed right, "neither is it merely some governmental 'benefit' indistinguishable from other forms of social welfare legislation." Whatever meaning or relevance this opaque observation might have in some other context it simply has no bearing on the issues at hand. Indeed, it is never made clear what the Court's opinion means on this score.

The importance of education is beyond dispute. Yet we have held repeatedly that the importance of a governmental service does not elevate it to the status of a "fundamental right" for purposes of equal protection analysis. In *San Antonio Independent School Dist.*, JUSTICE POWELL, speaking for the Court, expressly rejected the proposition that state laws dealing with public education are subject to special scrutiny under the Equal Protection Clause. Moreover, the Court points to no meaningful way to distinguish between education and other governmental benefits in this context. Is the Court suggesting that education is more "fundamental" than food, shelter, or medical care?

The Equal Protection Clause guarantees similar treatment of similarly situated persons, but it does not mandate a constitutional hierarchy of governmental services. JUSTICE POWELL, speaking for the Court in *San Antonio Independent School Dist.* put it well in stating that, to the extent this Court raises or lowers the degree of "judicial scrutiny" in equal protection cases according to a transient Court majority's view of the societal importance of the interest affected, we "assum[e] a legislative role, and one for which the Court lacks both authority and competence." Yet that is precisely what the Court does today.

The central question in these cases, as in every equal protection case not involving truly fundamental rights "explicitly or implicitly guaranteed by the Constitution," *San Antonio Independent School Dist.* is whether there is some legitimate basis for a legislative distinction between different classes of persons. The fact that the distinction is drawn in legislation affecting access to public education—as opposed to legislation allocating other important governmental benefits, such as public assistance, health care, or housing—cannot make a difference in the level of scrutiny applied.

B

Once it is conceded—as the Court does—that illegal aliens are not a suspect class, and that education is not a fundamental right, our inquiry should focus on and be limited to whether the legislative classification at issue bears a rational relationship to a legitimate state purpose.

The State contends primarily that [the Texas law] serves to prevent undue depletion of its limited revenues available for education, and to preserve the fiscal integrity of the State's school-financing system against an ever-increasing flood of illegal aliens—aliens over whose entry or continued presence it has no control. Of course such fiscal concerns alone could not justify discrimination against a suspect class or an arbitrary and irrational denial of benefits to a particular group of persons. Yet I assume no Member of this Court would argue that prudent conservation of finite state revenues is, *per se*, an illegitimate goal. Indeed, the numerous classifications this Court has sustained in social welfare legislation were invariably related to the limited amount of revenues available to spend on any given program or set of programs. The significant question here is whether the requirement of tuition from illegal aliens who attend the public schools—as well as from residents of other states, for example—is a rational and reasonable means of furthering the State's legitimate fiscal ends.

Without laboring what will undoubtedly seem obvious to many, it simply is not "irrational" for a state to conclude that it does not have the same responsibility to provide benefits for persons whose very presence in the state and this country is illegal as it does to provide for persons lawfully present. By definition, illegal aliens have no right whatever to be here, and the state may reasonably, and constitutionally, elect not to provide them with governmental services at the expense of those who are lawfully in the state. In *De Canas v. Bica* (1976), we held that a State may protect its fiscal interests and lawfully resident labor force from the deleterious effects on its economy resulting from the employment of illegal aliens.

And, only recently, this Court made clear that a State has a legitimate interest in protecting and preserving the quality of its schools and "the right of its own *bona fide residents* to attend such institutions on a preferential tuition basis." The Court has failed to offer even a plausible explanation why illegality of residence in this country is not a factor that may legitimately bear upon the bona fides of state residence and entitlement to the benefits of lawful residence.

It is significant that the Federal Government has seen fit to exclude illegal aliens from numerous social welfare programs, such as the food stamp program, the old-age assistance, aid to families with dependent children, aid to the blind, aid to the permanently and totally disabled, and supplemental security income programs, the Medicare hospital insurance benefits program, and the Medicaid hospital insurance benefits for the aged and disabled program. Although these exclusions do not conclusively demonstrate the constitutionality of the State's use of the same classification for comparable purposes, at the very least they tend to support the rationality of excluding illegal alien residents of a state from such programs so as to preserve the state's finite revenues for the benefit of lawful residents.

The Court maintains—as if this were the issue—that "barring undocumented children from local schools would not necessarily improve the quality of education provided in those schools." However, the legitimacy of barring illegal aliens from programs such as Medicare or Medicaid does not depend on a showing that the barrier would "improve the quality" of medical care given to persons lawfully entitled to participate in such programs. Modern education, like medical care, is enormously expensive, and there can be no doubt that very large added costs will fall on the State or its local school districts as a result of the inclusion of illegal aliens in the tuition-free public schools. The State may, in its discretion, use any savings resulting from its tuition requirement to "improve the quality of education" in the public school system, or to enhance the funds available for other social programs, or to reduce the tax burden placed on its residents; each of these ends is 'legitimate.'" The State need not show, as the Court implies, that the incremental cost of educating illegal aliens will send it into bankruptcy, or have a "'grave impact on the quality of education;'" that is not dispositive under a "rational basis" scrutiny. In the absence of a constitutional imperative to provide for the education of illegal aliens, the State may "rationally" choose to take advantage of whatever savings will accrue from limiting access to the tuition-free public schools to its own lawful residents, excluding even citizens of neighboring States.

Denying a free education to illegal alien children is not a choice I would make were I a legislator. Apart from compassionate considerations, the long-range costs of excluding any children from the public schools may well outweigh the costs of educating them. But that is not the issue; the fact that there are sound policy arguments against the Texas Legislature's choice does not render that choice an unconstitutional one.

II

The Constitution does not provide a cure for every social ill, nor does it vest judges with a mandate to try to remedy every social problem. Moreover, when this Court rushes in to remedy what it perceives to be the failings of the political processes, it deprives those processes of an opportunity to function. When the political institutions are not forced to exercise constitutionally allocated powers and responsibilities, those powers, like muscles not used, tend to atrophy. Today's cases, I regret to say, present yet another example of unwarranted judicial action which, in the long run, tends to contribute to the weakening of our political processes.

Congress, "vested by the Constitution with the responsibility of protecting our borders and legislating with respect to aliens" bears primary responsibility for addressing the problems occasioned by the millions of illegal aliens flooding across our southern border. Similarly, it is for Congress, and not this Court, to assess the "social costs borne by our Nation when select groups are denied the means to absorb the values and skills upon which our social order rests." While the "specter of a permanent caste" of illegal Mexican residents of the United States is indeed a disturbing one, it is but one segment of a larger problem, which is for the political branches to solve. I find it difficult to believe that Congress would long tolerate such a self-destructive result—that it would fail to deport these illegal alien families or to provide for the education of their children. Yet instead of allowing the political processes to run their course—albeit with some delay—the Court seeks to do Congress' job for it, compensating for congressional inaction. It is not unreasonable to think that this encourages the political branches to pass their problems to the Judiciary.

The solution to this seemingly intractable problem is to defer to the political processes, unpalatable as that may be to some.

1. It does not follow, however, that a state should bear the costs of educating children whose illegal presence in this country results from the default of the political branches of the Federal Government. A state has no power to prevent unlawful immigration, and no power to deport illegal aliens; those powers are reserved exclusively to Congress and the Executive. If the Federal Government, properly chargeable with deporting illegal aliens, fails to do so, it should bear the burdens of their presence here. Surely if illegal alien children can be identified for purposes of this litigation, their parents can be identified for purposes of prompt deportation.

2. The Department of Justice recently estimated the number of illegal aliens within the United States at between 3 and 6 million.

3. The Court implies, for example, that the Fourteenth Amendment would not require a state to provide welfare benefits to illegal aliens.

4. Both the opinion of the Court and JUSTICE POWELL's concurrence imply that appellees are being "penalized" because their parents are illegal entrants. However, Texas has classified appellees on the basis of their own illegal status, not that of their parents. Children born in this country to illegal alien parents, including some of appellees' siblings, are not excluded from the Texas schools. Nor does Texas discriminate against appellees because of their Mexican origin or citizenship. Texas provides a free public education to countless thousands of Mexican immigrants who are lawfully in this country.

5. Appellees "lack control" over their illegal residence in this country in the same sense as lawfully resident children lack control over the school district in which their parents reside. Yet in *San Antonio Independent School Dist. v. Rodriguez* we declined to review under "heightened scrutiny" a claim that a State discriminated against residents of less wealthy school districts in its provision of educational benefits. There was no suggestion in that case that a child's "lack of responsibility" for his residence in a particular school district had any relevance to the proper standard of review of his claims. The result was that children lawfully here but residing in different counties received different treatment.

6. Indeed, even children of illegal alien parents born in the United States can be said to be "penalized" when their parents are deported.

7. It is true that the Constitution imposes lesser constraints on the Federal Government than on the states with regard to discrimination against lawfully admitted aliens. This is because "Congress and the President have broad power over immigration and naturalization which the States do not possess," Hampton, supra, at 95, and because state discrimination against legally resident aliens conflicts with and alters the conditions lawfully imposed by Congress upon admission, naturalization, and residence of aliens in the United States or the several states. However, the same cannot be said when Congress has decreed that certain aliens should not be admitted to the United States at all.

8. In support of this conclusion, the Court's opinion strings together quotations drawn from cases addressing such diverse matters as the right of individuals under the Due Process Clause to learn a foreign language; the First Amendment

prohibition against state-mandated religious exercises in the public schools; the First Amendment prohibition against state-mandated religious exercises in the public schools; and state impingements upon the free exercise of religion; and state impingements upon the free exercise of religion. However, not every isolated utterance of this Court retains force when wrested from the context in which it was made. . . .

10. The Texas law might also be justified as a means of deterring unlawful immigration. While regulation of immigration is an exclusively federal function, a state may take steps, consistent with federal immigration policy, to protect its economy and ability to provide governmental services from the "deleterious effects" of a massive influx of illegal immigrants. The Court maintains that denying illegal aliens a free public education is an "ineffectual" means of deterring unlawful immigration, at least when compared to a prohibition against the employment of illegal aliens. Perhaps that is correct, but it is not dispositive; the Equal Protection Clause does not mandate that a state choose either the most effective and all-encompassing means of addressing a problem or none at all. Texas might rationally conclude that more significant "demographic or economic problem[s]" are engendered by the illegal entry into the State of entire families of aliens for indefinite periods than by the periodic sojourns of single adults who intend to leave the State after short-term or seasonal employment. It blinks reality to maintain that the availability of governmental services such as education plays no role in an alien family's decision to enter, or remain in, this country; certainly, the availability of a free bilingual public education might well influence an alien to bring his children, rather than travel alone for better job opportunities.

11. The Court suggests that the State's classification is improper because "[a]n illegal entrant might be granted federal permission to continue to reside in this country, or even to become a citizen." However, once an illegal alien is given federal permission to remain, he is no longer subject to exclusion from the tuition-free public schools under [the Texas law]. The Court acknowledges that the Tyler Independent School District provides a free public education to any alien who has obtained, or is in the process of obtaining, documentation from the United States Immigration and Naturalization Service. Thus, Texas has not taken it upon itself to determine which aliens are or are not entitled to United States residence. JUSTICE BLACKMUN's assertion that the Texas [law] will be applied to aliens "who may well be entitled to . . . remain in the United States," is wholly without foundation.

12. The Court's opinion is disingenuous when it suggests that the State has merely picked a "disfavored group" and arbitrarily defined its members as nonresidents. Appellees' "disfavored status" stems from the very fact that federal law explicitly prohibits them from being in this country. Moreover, the analogies to Virginians or legally admitted Mexican citizens entering Texas are spurious. A Virginian's right to migrate to Texas, without penalty, is protected by the Constitution; and a lawfully admitted alien's right to enter the State is likewise protected by federal law.

13. The District Court so concluded primarily because the State would decrease its funding to local school districts in proportion to the exclusion of illegal alien children. 458 F.Supp. at 577.

14. I assume no Member of the Court would challenge Texas' right to charge tuition to students residing across the border in Louisiana who seek to attend the nearest school in Texas.

15. Professor Bickel noted that judicial review can have a "tendency over time seriously to weaken the democratic process." He reiterated James Bradley Thayer's observation that

"the exercise of [the power of judicial review], even when unavoidable, is always attended with a serious evil, namely, that the correction of legislative mistakes comes from the outside, and the people thus lose the political experience, and the moral education and stimulus that comes from fighting the question out in the ordinary way, and correcting their own errors. The tendency of a common and easy resort to this great function, now lamentably too common, is to dwarf the political capacity of the people, and to deaden its sense of moral responsibility."

WARREN BURGER was the Chief Justice of the Supreme Court during a time in which it was slowly moving into a more conservative direction. He was an instrumental voice in many cases before the Supreme Court that had a more conservative outcome. Burger believes that undocumented immigrant children have no constitutional right to education.

EXPLORING THE ISSUE

Should Illegal Immigrant Families Be Able to Send Their Children to Public Schools?

Critical Thinking and Reflection

1. Can you identify the emotional, moral, intellectual, and social components in Brennan's argument?
2. Can you identify the emotional, moral, intellectual, and social components in Burger's argument?
3. Can you identify your own emotional, moral, intellectual, and social responses to this issue?
4. What are some similarities and differences between your responses and the authors'?

Is There Common Ground?

There are clear and distinct differences in this case regarding what should occur related to undocumented immigrant rights and public schooling. However, there is little disagreement that there are a substantial number of undocumented immigrants in the United States today. Some estimates say that the number of undocumented immigrants meets or exceeds 11 million. Many of these undocumented immigrants are children in public schools. The result is that some children are not U.S. citizens but will spend their entire childhood in this country, therefore feeling little different about their place in the United States than that of those who are citizens. Most would agree that immigration has historically had a positive impact on American society. Whether one agrees with the current system that is in place, everyone has a vested interest in fostering a system of immigration that is in the best interest of America's future. How should this affect acceptance, financial aid, and state tuition rates for colleges and universities? What are the implications on this ruling for future citizenship of undocumented immigrants?

Additional Resources

The American Civil Liberties Union on immigrant rights:

www.aclu.org/immigrants-rights

Taking action on immigration reform through Change.org:

http://immigration.change.org/

The National Network for Immigration and Refugee Rights:

www.nnirr.org/

End Illegal Immigration works to stop undocumented immigration:

www.endillegalimmigration.com/

Conservative USA calls to stop illegal immigration immediately:

www.conservativeusa.org/immigration.htm

Internet References . . .

Immigrant Solidarity Network

www.immigrantsolidarity.org/

National Council of La Raza

www.nclr.org/

US Immigration Support

www.usimmigrationsupport.org/

Selected, Edited, and with Issue Framing Material by:
Don Dyson, *Widener University*

ISSUE

Should Teachers in Schools Have Firearms?

YES: Michael W. Goldberg, from "I'm a School Psychologist—And I Think Teachers Should Be Armed," *Forward* (2018)

NO: Eugene Scott, from "A Big Question in the Debate About Arming Teachers: What About Racial Bias?" *Washington Post* (2018)

Learning Outcomes
After reading this issue, you will be able to: <ul><li>Identify two challenges in preventing school shootings.</li><li>Evaluate the effectiveness of arming teachers as a strategy to prevent school shootings.</li><li>Compare and contrast viewpoints on arming teachers.</li></ul>

ISSUE SUMMARY

YES: Michael W. Goldberg is a School Psychologist. He earned his Masters in Psychology at SUNY New Paltz, and was born in Brooklyn in 1963, where he was raised by his Orthodox Jewish grandparents. He argues that arming specially trained teachers will decrease the likelihood of school shootings as well as decrease subsequent trauma for students.

NO: Eugene Scott writes about identity politics for The Fix. He was previously a breaking news reporter at CNN Politics. Scott argues that in schools, where racial bias among teachers has been well documented, arming teachers will likely result in the unwarranted deaths of students of color.

The first school shooting on record in the United States happened in the mid 1700s. Since that time, there have been consistent experiences of schools being a location where gun violence occurs.

Flash forward to 1999 in Littleton, Colorado. On April 20th of that year, two students entered Columbine High School armed with multiple firearms. They had been planning the attack for over a year. By the end of the rampage, they had killed 12 students and one teacher, wounded 27 other students, and turned the guns on themselves. It was the deadliest school shooting in U.S. history. There was strong media reaction to the murders. The President called for stricter gun laws. But in the end, the only response was a Colorado law that prevented the purchase of firearms for a juvenile and the re-authorization of a background check program.

According to The Washington Post, in the time between the Columbine shooting and the end of October 2018, approximately 219,000 students have experienced gun violence in school. In that report, they state that 143 students, teachers, and staff have been killed and 288 people have been injured. Those number are the topic of some debate because the U.S. government does not track school shootings, and as a result, researchers have had to piece together statistics on gun violence in schools from news accounts, government records, and other sources. Perhaps what is most alarming about that controversy is the focus on the reporting of numbers rather than on the reality that students and teachers are wounded and killed with some degree of regularity in our nation's schools.

Since Columbine, there have been a number of high-profile school shootings. The massacre at Sandy Hook Elementary School in Newtown, CT, shocked the world not only with the number of fatalities (20 students and six adults), but with the age of the student victims, all of whom were six or seven years old. In the year 2018, three high-profile incidents occurred. At Marshall County High School in Benton, KY, two people were killed and 18 wounded. At Marjory Stoneman Douglas High School in Parkland, FL, 17 people were killed and 14 injured. At Santa Fe High School in Santa Fe, TX, 10 people were killed and three injured. And these are just the incidents that gathered the most media attention. The reality of racism in our nation results in the underreporting of violent school incidents in areas where the majority of the students are people of color.

While these are just a few of the incidents that have occurred, it is important to remember that there are thousands more students who were not killed or wounded who are affected by gun violence in schools. Survivors mourn their friends and try to put their lives back together; parents and caregivers worry about their children's well-being; students across the country worry about whether or not it could happen at their school.

In a poll (conducted in March and April of 2018 by the Pew Research Center) of 13–17 year olds across the United States, the majority of teens (57%) fear that a shooting could happen in their school, with 25% of teens very worried about the possibility. Only 13% of those surveyed were not worried at all about a shooting in their school. Add to that the concern of parents, 63% of whom were at least somewhat worried that a shooting could occur at their child's school.

That same poll asked students what actions they thought would be most effective in preventing a school shooting from occurring. Overwhelmingly, teens identified programs that supported mental health screening and evaluation and preventing people with mental illness from purchasing guns as the most likely to be at least somewhat effective (86% each). They followed that with metal detectors in schools at 79% and banning assault-style weapons at 66%.

When parents of teens were polled during the same time period, 89% agreed that increased mental health screening would be very or somewhat effective in preventing school shootings. They also agreed on other effective strategies: preventing people with mental illness from purchasing guns (85%), metal detectors in schools (80%), and banning assault-style weapons (61%); although this last strategy was sharply divided along partisan political lines (34% of republicans and 81% of democrats.)

One strategy that has been offered by some is the arming of schoolteachers and staff. In March of 2018, the Trump administration proposed a program that would provide rigorous firearms training for specially qualified personnel. This included a program to encourage military and police veterans to start second careers in schools across the country. While the proposal met with immediate criticism from many, others supported and even championed the idea.

Important to note in this debate is that teens in the Pew study mentioned above, who spend the most time with public school teachers out of all polled, did not strongly support the idea of arming teachers. Only 12% believed that arming teachers would be very effective, while 35% believed it would be not at all effective. Of parents polled, only 47% overall believed that strategy would be at least somewhat effective. Those results were again divided sharply across partisan lines with only 24% of democrats but 78% of republicans believing that the strategy might be at least somewhat effective. Of note in these results in that when the data are broken down by race, Black teens were the least likely to support arming teacher as an effective strategy.

Research has consistently shown that teachers and other school staff hold implicit anti-black biases. An implicit bias occurs when someone holds unconscious positive or negative perceptions and/or stereotypes about a group of people. These biases inform the ways in which teachers respond differently to similar behaviors depending upon the racial perception they hold about the student. Some would argue that arming teachers who are known to hold anti-black biases might result in teachers responding with deadly force to black students more than to white students. This same argument is currently occurring in the field of law enforcement.

It is into that debate that the authors in this issue write. As you read the articles provided, consider a few important questions: What might be the benefits of arming teachers? What might some of the challenges be? Do you think that a teacher is in a good position to prevent gun violence in school? What prevention strategy do you believe would work best?

YES ⬎

Michael W. Goldberg

I'm A School Psychologist — And I Think Teachers Should Be Armed

Scribe, the Forward's curated contributor network, features a wide array of Jewish thought leaders brought together to give our readers a 360 degree view of the world around us. Here you will find a wide array of writers discussing news, religion, politics, culture, tech, and more.

The views and opinions expressed in this article are the author's own and do not necessarily reflect those of the Forward.

I've been a School Psychologist for the past 20 years. In the wake of the school shootings in Florida, I am brought right back to December 7, 2017, the day of the deadly mass shooting at the high school I currently serve. In the aftermath, I helped to counsel students through the trauma caused by direct exposure to a murderous terrorist act — including nightmares, uncontrollable and unpredictable floods of tears, senseless "what if" questions, anxious obsessing and survivors' guilt.

I also have a unique perspective on the school shooting problem, having been both a mental health professional and a licensed concealed firearm carrier for the past 24 years.

In addition to zero bullying tolerance, empathy building, and lockdown drills in our schools, we must bolster our self-defense. Specifically, law-abiding, psychologically stable, specially trained staff should carry concealed weapons.

This would reduce our students' trauma and has the potential to stop terror immediately — or deter it from occurring in the first place.

A Centers for Disease Control study commissioned by President Obama, "Priorities for Research to Reduce the Threat of Firearm-Related Violence," supports this idea. The report concludes that "self-defense can be an important crime deterrent":

"Studies that directly assessed the effect of actual defensive uses of guns (i.e., incidents in which a gun was 'used' by the crime victim in the sense of attacking or threatening an offender) have found consistently lower injury rates among gun-using crime victims compared with victims who used other self-protective strategies."

A 1985 survey by the Justice department, "Armed Criminal in America — A Survey of Incarcerated Felons," found that 54 percent of respondents agreed or strongly agreed with the statement, "A criminal is not going to mess around with a victim he knows is armed with a gun, and 74 percent also agreed that "One reason burglars avoid houses when people are at home is that they fear being shot." The study also reported that a third of the felons said they personally had been "scared off, shot at, wounded or captured by an armed victim" and two-thirds said that they knew at least one other criminal who had been as well.

It follows that the majority of would-be school shooters would be deterred from attacking a school if they knew that they would likely be confronted by armed staff prior to accomplishing their evil deed.

Arming teachers is also likely to reduce trauma for our students.

In my experience counseling sessions after our school shooting, I found that feeling totally defenseless increased the severity of the trauma for children and staff. On the other hand, if both children and staff knew the school had means to thwart the killer, this knowledge would serve to reduce their fear of a potential traumatic assault. Many at my school needlessly experienced severe emotional trauma because they were helpless to stop the violence. Helplessness in the face of violence is an emotion that amplifies the effects of trauma, and likely contributes to Post Traumatic Stress Disorder. I'm convinced that if highly-trained school staff were armed, and the children were aware of it, the emotional stress during any school shooting would be reduced significantly. More importantly, school shootings may not even occur, and lost lives might still be with us today.

Perhaps the greatest argument against highly-trained armed school staff is that this would result in more deaths to students through the accidental discharge of a firearm. This appears a reasonable concern, but in reality is greatly exaggerated. For example, In 2007, there were 220 unintentional firearm deaths of children under age 13. Over 12 times as many children died from drowning during the same period. Because these accidental gun death statistics include deaths caused by drunks, drug users, children, criminals and novice gun users, in all likelihood, accidents from guns occur a lot less frequently in the hands of highly trained and responsible personnel. And we can never fully count the bodies saved from deterrence and successful use of a gun for self-defense.

The topic of having guns on school grounds provokes strong visceral reactions, but relying on reason and logic is the better way to save children's lives. Guns, which have no intrinsic motivation of their own, stir phobic responses and are assigned evil attributes. However, we need to stop our children from being slaughtered in a place they should feel safe and welcomed. The next school shooting is imminent if we continue as is. I propose that schools continue to fine-tune proactive measures like anti-bullying and empathy skill development, and defensive procedures that are proven effective (like lockdown drills, but also consider a more active defense measure — carefully screened and highly trained school staff willing to take on the enormous responsibility of being competent and armed in a safe fashion on school grounds. My own experience as a School Psychologist and my understanding of the research indicates that this would reduce emotional trauma as well as reduce the amount of school shootings, saving and improving the lives of our most valuable resource — our children.

The views and opinions expressed in this article are the author's own and do not necessarily reflect those of the Forward.

Michael W. Goldberg is a School Psychologist. He earned his Masters in Psychology at SUNY New Paltz, and was born in Brooklyn in 1963, where he was raised by his Orthodox Jewish grandparents.

Eugene Scott  **NO**

A Big Question in the Debate About Arming Teachers: What About Racial Bias?

In the wake of the school shooting that killed 17, President Trump and the National Rifle Association's main proposal to prevent another tragedy like the one in Parkland, Fla., has been to arm teachers.

NRA chief Wayne La Pierre told a crowd at a conservative gathering that "our banks, our airports, our NBA games ... are all more protected than our children at school."

"Highly trained, gun-adept, teachers/coaches would solve the problem instantly, before police arrive," the president tweeted Thursday.

But that desire has led some Americans, especially those who discuss race and politics, to raise questions: Will we be arming all teachers, including black teachers or education professionals who teach in mostly minority districts? It's a worthwhile question, given the police killings of unarmed black men in recent years.

It's another layer to the conversation about how racialized the debate around gun violence can be. There has not been a mass shooting in a predominantly minority high school that compares to the shooting at Marjory Stoneman Douglas High School, a school of mostly white students in a fairly affluent suburb. But some activists have pointed out that there are some students who face gun violence in their community on an almost daily basis.

"Another tragic moment. But there are folks in communities that I know who have been burying their kids for a long time because guns have been in their communities. Parents have been grieving because they've been putting their babies in [the] ground," Eddie S. Glaude, a Princeton University religion and African American studies professor, told MSNBC host Stephanie Ruhle on Thursday.

Glaude added that it took "certain kinds of people to die for us to get this question on the table."

When it comes to arming teachers and the factor race might play, two issues are being raised: (1) Arming teachers of black students who may have a racial bias, and (2) arming black teachers and education workers, who face their own risks carrying a weapon.

The Internet was quick to remind us that Philando Castile, a cafeteria supervisor at a public school in St. Paul, Minn., was shot dead by a police officer after he told him he was carrying a licensed firearm.

Efforts to tackle school violence have disproportionately impacted black students through arrests and restraint, according to the U.S. Department of Education. Although black students were only 16 percent of the total student enrollment during the 2011-12 school year, they made up 27 percent of the students referred to law enforcement and nearly double — 31 percent — of the students involved in a school-related arrest, according to data from the U.S. Department of Education office for civil rights.

Ashley Nicole Black, a writer for late-night show "Full Frontal with Samantha Bee," mentioned how carrying a gun could have added to her already-tense relationship with a racist teacher.

"All I can picture is every racist teacher who lashed out at me verbally or physically over the years and what would have happened if that person had a gun? Yeah, there are more good, kind, teachers ... but they're not gonna be the ones signing up for guns," Black tweeted.

Kelly Wickham Hurst, CEO of Being Black at School, a nonprofit that addresses issues impacting black students, asked: "How long before a teacher feels the need to make use of Stand Your Ground while on a school campus?"

Multiple studies, including one from the Yale University Child Study Center, have shown that implicit bias against black students shapes how teachers respond to them. That's not to imply explicitly that white teachers will be using guns against black students, but it does factor into how students of color are disciplined.

"Implicit biases do not begin with black men and police. They begin with black preschoolers and their teachers, if not earlier. Implicit bias is like the wind: You can't see it, but you can sure see its effects," Yale child psychology professor Walter S. Gilliam previously told The Post.

Bree Newsome, an activist who attracted national attention after a mass shooting in a Charleston, S.C., church, argued that the idea that arming teachers with guns will protect youths doesn't seem to take black youths into account.

Michael Harriot, host of the podcast "The Black One," wrote that the idea of black educators carrying guns isn't likely to attract lasting support because history has shown that conservatives do not support gun ownership among black Americans as much as they claim.

"If black people arm themselves, America always figures out a way to disarm them through legislation," he wrote for the Root. "While no one doubts the strength of the American brand of racism, the theoretical use of America's anti-black sentiment as a legislative, race-based Jedi mind trick ignores an important reality: It won't work."

Nearly 6 in 10 — 59 percent — think America would be less safe if more people had guns, according to a recent Quinnipiac poll. And only 20 percent say armed teachers are the answer to making schools safer.

More than half of Americans do not think the Parkland shooting could have been prevented had teachers been armed, according to a Washington Post-ABC poll. The school did have an armed school resource officer assigned to protect students, but he reportedly took a defensive position outside the school and did not enter the building during the shooting.

The sample size for how black people feel on this issue was too small to break out. But the current conversation about school safety appears to have more black Americans drawing attention to the consequences arming teachers could have in schools where implicit biases exist, particularly against black students who are deemed threatening.

EUGENE SCOTT writes about identity politics for The Fix. He was previously a breaking news reporter at CNN Politics.

EXPLORING THE ISSUE

Should Teachers in Schools Have Firearms?

Critical Thinking and Reflection

1. Can you identify the emotional, moral, intellectual, and social components in Goldberg's argument?
2. Can you identify the emotional, moral, intellectual, and social components in Scott's argument?
3. Can you identify your own emotional, moral, intellectual, and social reactions to this issue?
4. What are some similarities and differences between your reactions and the authors'?

Is There Common Ground?

There are few parents, teachers, or lawmakers who do not think that keeping children safe in their school settings is of vital importance. Therein lies the common ground of the issue. The challenge to agreement is the ways in which people think it is best to accomplish that goal. Specifically around this issue, it seems clear that those who support gun ownership and use believe that having well trained, armed professionals in schools will help to prevent school shootings. On the other side, those who oppose the idea argue that there are no instances on record where an armed school professional *prevented* a school shooting. On an issue that is so divided along partisan political lines, it is difficult to see where resolution and agreement might occur.

Additional Resources

Benbenishty, R. & Ashty, R.A. (2005). *School Violence in Context: Culture, Neighborhood, Family, School, and Gender.* Oxford University Press: New York.

Druck, K. (2003). *How to Talk to Your Kids about School Violence.* Onomotopoeia, Inc.: New York.

Jimerson, S., Nickerson, A., Mayer, M. & Furlong, M. (2012). *Handbook of School Violence and School Safety: International Research and Practice* 2nd Edition. Routledge: New York.

Internet References . . .

The National Center for Healthy, Safe Children

https://healthysafechildren.org/

The National Child Traumatic Stress Network

www.nctsn.org/

The National Resource Center for Mental Health Promotion and Youth Violence Prevention's Trauma, Violence and School Shooting

www.youth.gov

Selected, Edited, and with Issue Framing Material by:
Don Dyson, *Widener University*

ISSUE

Should Cyber-Bullies Be Prosecuted?

YES: Brianna Flavin, from "Is Cyberbullying Illegal? When Comments Turn Criminal," Rasmussen College Blog (2017)

NO: J. Graffeo, from "People v Marquan M." *New York State Law Reporting Bureau* (2014)

Learning Outcomes

After reading this issue, you will be able to:

- Identify three of the key challenges of cyberbullying.
- Identify the rates of cyberbullying in schools.
- Identify challenges to prosecuting cyberbullies.

ISSUE SUMMARY

YES: Brianna Flavin is a freelance writer, content marketer, adjunct professor, and poet. She argues that cyberbullying is culturally pervasive and should be criminalized to prevent tragedies such as teen suicide and school shootings.

NO: The opposing view is presented by the verdict of the New York Court of Appeals in a case that argued that the cyberbullying law enacted was considered a violation of the defendant's First Amendment free speech.

" **A**bout two years ago, I was cyber bullied. Former friends of mine posted hate blogs, and most recently I found a YouTube video of them burning my picture with the theme song of I hope you die. The funny thing is the video was posted nearly two years ago. The scary thing is, even though I survived it. I pray that my college professors will not look up my name. If they do they will find it. To me this is a serious concept. I flirted with the idea of taking my own life during the time. That's the thing. Information spreads fast. With me it was no different. I was being attacked in my own living room." *16 year-old boy*

"Cyber Bullying is a serious topic! I was bullied and began to cut myself . . . You may want to know why . . . time to tell I was bullied, stalked, and harassed. Never to my face but online the people who bullied me would make fake pages and put me on

them saying I'm how and everything I'm willing 'to do' with a guy, but nothing on them were true . . . They told people to walk up to me and ask me if I was a hoe, lesbian, dyke, slut, pregnant. etc. I couldn't take it anymore I was on the verge of suicide and when you're going through this you want to handle it alone, but truthfully you can't. So I began to cut. For everything I was going through. I got help. I came clean to a trusted adult and they told my mom everything my mom got very upset and began to take pills to solve her problems. I got madder and cut even more then I finally said no! STOP I haven't cut in a month and 5 days . . . i use to cut every day. So to wrap this up I'm done cutting my mom's still on pills and I told the police (about the bullying) and guess what. The sites and texts are gone!!! :)" *14 year-old girl*

Bullying has existed among people for as long as anyone can remember. For years, people have engaged in

---

behavior that was meant to intimidate, harass, embarrass, and humiliate. In today's electronic world, however, bullies have far more access to resources and audiences for their bullying than ever before. The access afforded by technology has changed the nature of bullying in significant ways.

In the past, bullies largely had to rely on face-to-face opportunities to intimidate their victims, and their tactics could be observed in real time and easily attributed to them. Now, bullying can happen 24 hours a day. Bullies can use the anonymity that technology allows to prevent people from identifying them as the perpetrators, and their bullying has an audience much wider than those who are in the immediate vicinity when it occurs.

Cyberbullying is bullying that takes place through the use of computers, cell phones, tablets, game consoles, and other electronic devices. Cyberbullying can occur through email, Instant Messaging Services (IMS), Short Messaging Services (SMS/Text), and social media platforms like Twitter, Tumblr, Instagram, Snapchat, and Facebook. Basically anywhere that people create, view, or comment on content posted by another person.

There are a few things that set cyberbullying apart from other forms of bullying. First, is the ease with which the bullying can be completely anonymous. Screen names that have no relationship to a person's identity and email accounts that require no personal information to establish contribute to a feeling of anonymity that can allow for increased cruelty and decreased fear of being caught. Second, electronic platforms have the capacity to reach a much larger audience for bullying than in-person options. This is especially true when you consider that a single twitter account may have hundreds to hundreds of thousands of followers. Third, electronic bullying is relatively permanent. Unless a post or comment is specifically removed, pictures, comments, and other hurtful or humiliating content remains accessible indefinitely. This can result in both the accumulation of bullying content as well as easy accessibility in ways that prolong the exposure of the victim to the harassment. As seen in the quote above, content can remain accessible for many years after it is first posted. Finally, because cyberbullying happens in spaces

that are not always known by or accessible to parents and teachers, it often goes unnoticed. As a result, people suffer in silence.

The frequency of cyberbullying is difficult to assess. According to the most recent Youth Risk Behavior Survey (YRBS) done by the United States Centers for Disease Control and Prevention (CDC), 14.5% of high school students were electronically bullied in 2017. That compares to 24% of middle school students identified in 2015. While it appears from the statistics that cyberbullying decreases with age, it highlights that children who are younger and more vulnerable to the experience are also more likely to be the targets.

It is also important to identify some of the outcomes of the experience of being cyberbullied. Lower of self-esteem, poor school performance, depression, and anxiety have all been linked to cyberbullying. In some cases, cyberbullying has been found to be a factor in youth suicide. As a result, something that is easy, insidious, and difficult to identify can lead to catastrophic outcomes.

Brandy Vela, Meghan Meier, Amanda Todd, Ryan Halligan, Jessica Logan, Jessica Laney, Hannah Smith, Audrie Pott, Erin and Shannon Gallagher, Alexis Pilkington, and Rehtaeh Parsons. Each of these young people was the victim of cyberbullying so severe, and in some cases so prolonged, that they ended up taking their own lives. And this list is far from exhaustive.

Because of the nature of cyberbullying, prosecuting it as a crime can be difficult. Many states have bullying laws on their books, but they are often inconsistent and the penalties vary widely. There is also a good deal of disagreement among lawmakers about whether attention should be paid to cyberbullying when there are limited resources in the criminal justice system and, some argue, far more physically dangerous crimes that the time and attention available.

It is into this argument that the authors in this issue offer their work. As you read each piece, and yourself some important questions: Is bullying enough of a problem that legislation should be written? Are people becoming too dependent on others to save them from hurt feelings? If cyberbullying was a crime, what would a just penalty be?

YES

Brianna Flavin

Is Cyberbullying Illegal? When Comments Turn Criminal

It's no surprise that cyberbullying has been a hot topic lately. With the rapid progression of technological abilities, the age-old issue of bullying has moved to the more anonymous—but no less harmful—digital world.

Recent research reports that 58 percent of kids admit to receiving hurtful comments online. About 75 percent of students have visited a website bashing another student while about 70 percent of students report seeing frequent bullying online.

And with the denouncement of cyberbullying by national figures, the problem is well on its way to attracting unprecedented attention. But in the midst of it all, it's difficult to parse what cyberbullying really means at a legal level.

Is cyberbullying illegal? Could it result in jail time? Keep reading for expert insights and clarity on the legal ramifications of cyberbullying.

What is cyberbullying, anyway?

"Cyberbullying is the platform the twenty-first century bully uses to inflict pain and humiliation upon another," says author and speaker Dr. John DeGarmo of The Foster Care Institute. "The use of technology to embarrass, threaten, tease, harass or even target another person." DeGarmo emphasizes the danger of cyberbullying in how inescapable it can be.

"Today's bully can follow the targeted victim wherever that child may go," he explains. "Whether the child is in school, at home … whenever that bullied child has access to online technology, he or she can be bullied." He adds that this form of bullying can be non-stop; twenty-four hours a day, seven days a week.

"Today's bully can follow the targeted victim wherever that child may go."DeGarmo stresses that bullying is on the upswing. Online platforms create easy, accessible opportunities for harassment—to the point that witnessing cruelty online is the norm for many. "Younger people

see that on Twitter all the time," he says. "It's become part of their daily lives, and it's a breakdown of compassion."

Because cyberbullies can't witness the effect of their words, they use less restraint than they would in face-to-face situations. This emotional and physical detachment allows them to harass others, in some cases without truly realizing they've become a bully. But if you are thinking cyberbullying can never harm someone as much as a punch or getting shoved into a locker, think again.

"We see a significant number of young people who have experienced cyberbullying," says Dr. Jeff Nalin of Paradigm Malibu. "We have seen young people traumatized from a variety of events ranging from character assassination to revenge porn and taunts to engage in destructive behaviors, including suicide."

With the possibility of such severe ramifications, it begs the question: Is this a criminal offense?

Is cyberbullying a crime?

"Yes, there can be legal consequences," says attorney and founder of Carter Law Firm, Ruth Carter. "Depending on the rules of your state and the circumstances involved, discipline can include expulsion from school, criminal charges for harassment and/or civil lawsuits for defamation and other harms."

> "The last thing anyone wants is a suicide or school shooting because of cyberbullying."

DeGarmo adds that due to the prevalence of the issue, most schools have created specific policies for cyberbullying. "Ten years ago, no one gave much thought to this issue," he says. "But now, schools are paying more attention. The last thing anyone wants is a suicide or school shooting because of cyberbullying."

The consequences for cyberbullies depend on the specific circumstance. Many cyberbullying cases wind up getting prosecuted as harassment. Some cases result in civil court, while others might warrant criminal charges and prosecution for hate crimes, impersonation, harassment, cyberbullying and violations under the Computer Fraud and Abuse Act (CFAA).

In addition to the larger laws, individual states have their own rules for cyberbullying. Stop bullying.gov offers a state-by-state map to highlight the specific policies.

But where do we draw the line between what cyberbullying is and what it isn't? What are some of the specific crimes cyberbullying can fall under? See this quick list below for reference.

Here is a list of potentially criminal forms of cyberbullying, as listed by Stomp Out Bullying:

- Harassing someone, especially if the harassment is based on gender, race or other protected classes
- Making violent threats
- Making death threats
- Making obscene and harassing phone calls and texts
- Sexting
- Sextortion, which is sexual exploitation
- Child pornography
- Stalking someone
- Committing hate crimes
- Taking a photo of someone in a place where they expect privacy
- Extortion

If you are unsure about whether or not a specific behavior counts as cyberbullying, Carter says the best course of action is to ask for help. "Review the rules and go to the proper authority, depending on what avenue you're pursuing and ask if a particular behavior or situation is a violation," she suggests.

Carter advises anyone feeling harassed by a possible cyberbully to keep copies of harassing messages, screenshots of social media posts and video of the date, profile information of who posted it and the URL.

What are the long-term consequences of cyberbullying?

Cyberbullying could land you in court, get you fired, expelled or even arrested. But in addition to the trouble cyberbullies might face with authorities for a specific instance, both Carter and DeGarmo mention more long-term consequences.

"What goes online stays online," DeGarmo says. "People can find it. Those posts and comments won't just go away."

"The courts have already ruled that there's no such thing as privacy online." DeGarmo recalls seeing applicants lose job opportunities because their potential employers went online to research the candidates and their social media platforms. "It's becoming a more common practice for employers," he says. "What you thought was justified or funny in the moment may be tomorrow's regret," Carter points out. "Once you put something out there, you can never fully take it back. My rule is don't put anything online that you wouldn't put on the front page of a newspaper."

Carter has worked on several cases where social media posts became evidence or significant research factors in court. "The courts have already ruled that there's no such thing as privacy online," she adds.

Where is the issue of cyberbullying headed?

"Our culture has made a major shift for the better in identifying and addressing face-to-face bullying," Nalin says. "Because the media is currently putting energy and focus on cyberbullying, it seems likely that we will be able to do the same in the online arena."

Indeed, many anti-bullying campaigns are calling for increased uniformity and policy in how our society deals with cyberbullying. Sameer Hinduja recently wrote on the topic on behalf of the Cyberbullying Research Center. "We go into schools all the time and administrators simply don't know what they should do (and not do) to *really* make a difference," he wrote. He calls for clear, practical guidance from the federal government for schools to understand how to reduce online (and offline) harassment and promote peer respect, tolerance and kindness.

"I hope the lesson of 'think before you post' is being instilled and frequently repeated to young people when they get their first device or social media accounts," Carter says. "If you're angry, upset or in another heightened emotional state, don't post about it." If you feel you need to vent about it, she suggests writing it down or creating a video for personal use. But she urges you never to put it on the internet, regardless of the privacy settings.

Crime and technology

So is cyberbullying illegal? The answer to that is that it can be, and it is increasingly likely to have consequences for perpetrators. As cyberbullying has attracted greater attention, parents, educators, lawmakers and tech companies are hustling to create solutions. But the speed at which our technological capabilities develop is hard to match in legal infrastructure and the justice system.

Cyberbullying isn't the only issue where technology and the legal system crosses wires.

BRIANNA FLAVIN is a freelance writer, content marketer, adjunct professor, and poet.

J. Graffeo

 **NO**

People v Marquan M.

Corey Stoughton, for appellant.
Thomas Marcelle, for intervenor-respondent
County of Albany.
Advocates for Children of New York et al.,
amici curiae.

Defendant, a 15-year-old high school student, anonymously posted sexual information about fellow classmates on a publicly-accessible internet website. He was criminally prosecuted for "cyberbullying" under a local law enacted by the Albany County Legislature. We [*2] are asked to decide whether this cyberbullying statute comports with the Free Speech Clause of the First Amendment.

Bullying by children in schools has long been a prevalent problem but its psychological effects were not studied in earnest until the 1970s (see Hyojin Koo, A Time Line of the Evolution of School Bullying in Differing Social Contexts, 8 Asia Pacific Educ Rev 107 [2007]). Since then, "[b]ullying among school-aged youth" has "increasingly be[en] recognized as an important problem affecting well-being and social functioning," as well as "a potentially more serious threat to healthy youth development" (Tonja R. Nansel et al., Bullying Behaviors Among U.S. Youth, 285 Journal of the Am Med Assn 2094 [2001]). At its core, bullying represents an imbalance of power between the aggressor and victim that often manifests in behaviors that are "verbal (e.g., name-calling, threats), physical (e.g., hitting), or psychological (e.g., rumors, shunning/exclusion)" (id. at 2094; see Koo, supra at 112). Based on the recognized harmful effects of bullying, many schools and communities now sponsor anti-bullying campaigns in order to reduce incidents of such damaging behaviors.

Educators and legislators across the nation have endeavored to craft policies designed to counter the adverse impact of bullying on children. New York, for example, enacted the "Dignity for All Students Act" in 2010 (see L 2010, ch 482, § 2; Education Law §§ 10 et seq.), declaring that our State must "afford all students in public schools an environment free of discrimination and harassment" caused by "bullying, taunting or intimidation" (Education Law § 10). In furtherance of this objective, the State prohibited discrimination and bullying on public school property or at school functions (see Education Law § 12 [1]). The Act relied on the creation and implementation of school board policies to reduce bullying in schools through the appropriate training of personnel, mandatory instruction for students on civility and tolerance, and reporting requirements (see Education Law § 13). The Act did not criminalize bullying behaviors; instead, it incorporated educational penalties such as suspension from school.

Despite these efforts, the problem of bullying continues, and has been exacerbated by technological innovations and the widespread dissemination of electronic information using social media sites. The advent of the internet with "twenty-four hour connectivity and social networking" means that "[b]ullying that begins in school follows students home every day" and "bullying through the use of technology can begin away from school property" (L 2012, ch 102, § 1). Regardless of how or where bullying occurs, it "affects the school environment and disrupts the educational process, impeding the ability of students to learn and too often causing devastating effects on students' health and well-being" (id.; see e.g. American Psychiatric Assn, Resolution on Bullying Among Children & Youth [2004]). The use of computers and electronic devices to engage in this pernicious behavior is commonly referred to as "cyberbullying" (see e.g. Education Law § 11 [8]; L 2012, ch 102, § 1; Simone Robers et al., Indicators of School Crime & [*3]Safety: 2012, at 44, Natl Ctr for Educ Statistics, U.S. Depts of Educ & Justice [2013]). Unlike traditional bullying, victims of cyberbullying can be "relentlessly and anonymously attack[ed] twenty-four hours a day for the whole world to witness. There is simply no escape"[FN1].

The Dignity for All Students Act did not originally appear to encompass cyberbullying, particularly acts of bullying that occur off school premises. As the ramifications of cyberbullying on social networking sites spilled into the educational environment, in 2012, the State Legislature amended the Act to expand the types of prohibited bullying conduct covered by its provisions. It added a proscription on bullying that applied to "any form of electronic communication" (Education Law § 11 [8]), including any off-campus activities that "foreseeably create a risk of substantial disruption within the school environment, where it is foreseeable that the conduct, threats, intimidation or abuse might reach school property" (Education Law § 11 [7]).

Before the addition of the 2012 amendments to the Dignity for All Students Act, elected officials in Albany County decided to tackle the problem of cyberbullying. They determined there was a need to criminalize such conduct because the "State Legislature ha[d] failed to address th[e] problem" of "non-physical bullying behaviors transmitted by electronic means" (Albany County Local Law No. 11 of 2010, § 1). In 2010, the Albany County Legislature adopted a new crime the offense of cyberbullying which was defined as "any act of communicating or causing a communication to be sent by mechanical or electronic means, including posting statements on the internet or through a computer or email network, disseminating embarrassing or sexually explicit photographs; disseminating private, personal, false or sexual information, or sending hate mail, with no legitimate private, personal, or public purpose, with the intent to harass, annoy, threaten, abuse, taunt, intimidate, torment, humiliate, or otherwise inflict significant emotional harm on another person" (id. § 2)

The provision outlawed cyberbullying against "any minor or person" situated in the county (id. § 3)[FN2]. Knowingly engaging in this activity was deemed to be a misdemeanor offense punishable by [*4]up to one year in jail and a $1,000 fine (see id. § 4). The statute, which included a severability clause (see id. § 7), became effective in November 2010.

A month later, defendant Marquan M., a student attending Cohoes High School in Albany County, used the social networking website "Facebook" to create a page bearing the pseudonym "Cohoes Flame." He anonymously posted photographs of high-school classmates and other adolescents, with detailed descriptions of their alleged sexual practices and predilections, sexual partners and other types of personal information. The descriptive captions, which were vulgar and offensive, prompted responsive electronic messages that threatened the creator of the website with physical harm.

A police investigation revealed that defendant was the author of the Cohoes Flame postings. He admitted his involvement and was charged with cyberbullying under Albany County's local law. Defendant moved to dismiss, arguing that the statute violated his right to free speech under the First Amendment. After City Court denied defendant's motion, he pleaded guilty to one count of cyberbullying but reserved his right to raise his constitutional arguments on appeal. County Court affirmed, concluding that the local law was constitutional to the extent it outlawed such activities directed at minors, and held that the application of the provision to defendant's Facebook posts did not contravene his First Amendment rights. A Judge of this Court granted defendant leave to appeal (21 NY3d 1043 [2013]).

Defendant contends that Albany County's cyberbullying law violates the Free Speech Clause of the First Amendment because it is overbroad in that it includes a wide array of protected expression, and is unlawfully vague since it does not give fair notice to the public of the proscribed conduct. The County concedes that certain aspects of the cyberbullying law are invalid but maintains that those portions are severable, rendering the remainder of the act constitutional if construed in accordance with the legislative purpose of the enactment. Interpreted in this restrictive manner, the County asserts that the cyberbullying law covers only particular types of electronic communications containing information of a sexual nature pertaining to minors and only if the sender intends to inflict emotional harm on a child or children.

Under the Free Speech Clause of the First Amendment, the government generally "has no power to restrict expression because of its message, its ideas, its subject matter, or its [*5]content" (United States v Stevens, 559 US 460, 468 [2010] [internal quotation marks omitted]). Consequently, it is well established that prohibitions of pure speech must be limited to communications that qualify as fighting words, true threats, incitement, obscenity, child pornography, fraud, defamation or statements integral to criminal conduct (see United States v Alvarez, __ US __, 132 S Ct 2537, 2544 [2012]; Brown v Entertainment Merchants Assn., __ US __, 131 S Ct 2729, 2733 [2011]; People v Dietze, 75 NY2d 47, 52 [1989]). Outside of such recognized categories, speech is presumptively protected and generally cannot be curtailed by the government (see United States v Alvarez, 132 S Ct at 2543-2544; Brown v Entertainment Merchants Assn., 131 S Ct at 2734; United States v Stevens, 559 US at 468-469).

Yet, the government unquestionably has a compelling interest in protecting children from harmful publications or materials (see Reno v American Civil Liberties Union, 521 US 844, 875 [1997]; see also Brown v Entertainment Merchants Assn., 131 S Ct at 2736; see generally

Bethel School Dist. No. 403 v Fraser, 478 US 675, 682 [1986]). Cyberbullying is not conceptually immune from government regulation, so we may assume, for the purposes of this case, that the First Amendment permits the prohibition of cyberbullying directed at children, depending on how that activity is defined (see generally Brown v Entertainment Merchants Assn., 131 S Ct at 2735-2736, 2741; cf. United States v Elonis, 730 F3d 321 [3d Cir 2013] [affirming conviction premised on threatening Facebook posts], cert granted __ US __ [June 16, 2014]). Our task therefore is to determine whether the specific statutory language of the Albany County legislative enactment can comfortably coexist with the right to free speech.[FN3]

Challenges to statutes under the Free Speech Clause are usually premised on the overbreadth and vagueness doctrines. A regulation of speech is overbroad if constitutionally-protected expression may be "chilled" by the provision because it facially "prohibits a real and substantial amount of" expression guarded by the First Amendment (People v Barton, 8 NY3d 70, 75 [2006]). This type of facial challenge, which is restricted to cases implicating the First Amendment, requires a court to assess the wording of the statute "without reference to the defendant's conduct" (People v Stuart, 100 NY2d 412, 421 [2003]) to decide whether "a substantial number of its applications are unconstitutional, judged in relation to the statute's plainly legitimate sweep" (United States v Stevens, 559 US at 473 [internal quotation marks omitted]). A law that is overbroad cannot be validly applied against any individual (see People v Stuart, 100 NY2d at 421, citing Tribe, American Constitutional Law § 12-32, at 1036 [2d ed 1988]). In contrast, a statute is seen by the courts as vague if "it fails to give a citizen adequate [*6]notice of the nature of proscribed conduct, and permits arbitrary and discriminatory enforcement" (People v Shack, 86 NY2d 529, 538 [1995]). Hence, the government has the burden of demonstrating that a regulation of speech is constitutionally permissible (see United States v Playboy Entertainment Group, 529 US 803, 816-817 [2000]; cf. People v Davis, 13 NY3d 17, 23 [2009]).

A First Amendment analysis begins with an examination of the text of the challenged legislation since "it is impossible to determine whether a statute reaches too far without first knowing what the statute covers" (United States v Williams, 553 US 285, 293 [2008]). In this regard, fundamental principles of statutory interpretation are controlling. Chief among them is the precept that "clear and unequivocal statutory language is presumptively entitled to authoritative effect" (People v Suber, 19 NY3d 247, 252 [2012]; see e.g. People v Williams, 19 NY3d 100, 103 [2012]).

Based on the text of the statute at issue, it is evident that Albany County "create[d] a criminal prohibition of alarming breadth" (United States v Stevens, 559 US at 474). The language of the local law embraces a wide array of applications that prohibit types of protected speech far beyond the cyberbullying of children (see id. at 473-474; People v Barton, 8 NY3d at 75). As written, the Albany County law in its broadest sense criminalizes "any act of communicating . . . by mechanical or electronic means . . . with no legitimate . . . personal . . . purpose, with the intent to harass [or] annoy. . . another person." On its face, the law covers communications aimed at adults, and fictitious or corporate entities, even though the county legislature justified passage of the provision based on the detrimental effects that cyberbullying has on school-aged children. The county law also lists particular examples of covered communications, such as "posting statements on the internet or through a computer or email network, disseminating embarrassing or sexually explicit photographs; disseminating private, personal, false or sexual information, or sending hate mail." But such methods of expression are not limited to instances of cyberbullying the law includes every conceivable form of electronic communication, such as telephone conversations, a ham radio transmission or even a telegram. In addition, the provision pertains to electronic communications that are meant to "harass, annoy . . . taunt . . . [or] humiliate" any person or entity, not just those that are intended to "threaten, abuse . . . intimidate, torment . . . or otherwise inflict significant emotional harm on" a child. In considering the facial implications, it appears that the provision would criminalize a broad spectrum of speech outside the popular understanding of cyberbullying, including, for example: an email disclosing private information about a corporation or a telephone conversation meant to annoy an adult.

The County admits that the text of the statute is too broad and that certain aspects of its contents encroach on recognized areas of protected free speech. Because the law "imposes a restriction on the content of protected speech, it is invalid unless" the County "can demonstrate [*7]that it passes strict scrutiny that is, unless it is justified by a compelling government interest and is narrowly drawn to serve that interest" (Brown v Entertainment Merchants Assn., 131 S Ct at 2738). For this reason, the County asks us to sever the offending portions and declare that the remainder of the law survives strict scrutiny. What remains, in the County's view, is a tightly circumscribed cyberbullying law that includes only three types of electronic communications sent with the intent to inflict emotional harm on a child: (1) sexually explicit photographs; (2) private or personal sexual information; and (3) false sexual information with no legitimate public, personal or private purpose.

It is true, as the County urges, that a court should strive to save a statute when confronted with a Free Speech challenge (see e.g. People ex rel. Alpha Portland Cement Co. v Knapp, 230 NY 48, 62-63 [1920], cert denied 256 US 702 [1921]). But departure from a textual analysis is appropriate only if the statutory language is "fairly susceptible" to an interpretation that satisfies applicable First Amendment requirements (People v Dietze, 75 NY2d at 52; see e.g. United States v Stevens, 559 US at 481). The doctrine of separation of governmental powers prevents a court from rewriting a legislative enactment through the creative use of a severability clause when the result is incompatible with the language of the statute (see e.g. People v Dietze, 75 NY2d at 52-53; Reno v American Civil Liberties Union, 521 US at 884-885). And special concerns arise in the First Amendment context excessive judicial revision of an overbroad statute may lead to vagueness problems because "the statutory language would signify one thing but, as a matter of judicial decision, would stand for something entirely different. Under those circumstances, persons of ordinary intelligence reading [the law] could not know what it actually meant" (People v Dietze, 75 NY2d at 53; see e.g. City of Houston, Texas v Hill, 482 US 451, 468-469 [1987]).

We conclude that it is not a permissible use of judicial authority for us to employ the severance doctrine to the extent suggested by the County or the dissent. It is possible to sever the portion of the cyberbullying law that applies to adults and other entities because this would require a simple deletion of the phrase "or person" from the definition of the offense. But doing so would not cure all of the law's constitutional ills. As we have recently made clear, the First Amendment protects annoying and embarrassing speech (see e.g. People v Golb, __ NY3d __, 2014 NY Slip Op 03426 [May 13, 2014]; People v Dietze, 75 NY2d at 52-53), even if a child may be exposed to it (see Brown v Entertainment Merchants Assn., 131 S Ct at 2736), so those references would also need to be excised from the definitional section. And, the First Amendment forbids the government from deciding whether protected speech qualifies as "legitimate," as Albany County has attempted to do (see Snyder v Phelps, __ US __, 131 S Ct 1207, 1220 [2011], quoting Erznoznik v Jacksonville, 422 US 205, 210-211 [1975]; cf. People v [*8]Shack,

86 NY2d at 536-537)[FN4]. It is undisputed that the Albany County statute was motivated by the laudable public purpose of shielding children from cyberbullying. The text of the cyberbullying law, however, does not adequately reflect an intent to restrict its reach to the three discrete types of electronic bullying of a sexual nature designed to cause emotional harm to children. Hence, to accept the County's proposed interpretation, we would need to significantly modify the applications of the county law, resulting in the amended scope bearing little resemblance to the actual language of the law. Such a judicial rewrite encroaches on the authority of the legislative body that crafted the provision and enters the realm of vagueness because any person who reads it would lack fair notice of what is legal and what constitutes a crime. Even if the First Amendment allows a cyberbullying statute of the limited nature proposed by Albany County, the local law here was not drafted in that manner. Albany County therefore has not met its burden of proving that the restrictions on speech contained in its cyberbullying law survive strict scrutiny.

There is undoubtedly general consensus that defendant's Facebook communications were repulsive and harmful to the subjects of his rants, and potentially created a risk of physical or emotional injury based on the private nature of the comments. He identified specific adolescents with photographs, described their purported sexual practices and posted the information on a website accessible world-wide. Unlike traditional bullying, which usually takes place by a face-to-face encounter, defendant used the advantages of the internet to attack his victims from a safe distance, twenty-four hours a day, while cloaked in anonymity. Although the First Amendment may not give defendant the right to engage in these activities, the text of Albany County's law envelops far more than acts of cyberbullying against children by criminalizing a variety of constitutionally-protected modes of expression. We therefore hold that Albany County's Local Law No. 11 of 2010 as drafted is overbroad and facially invalid under the Free Speech Clause of the First Amendment.

Accordingly, the order of County Court should be reversed and the accusatory instrument dismissed.

Verdict of the New York Court of Appeals.

EXPLORING THE ISSUE

Should Cyber-Bullies Be Prosecuted?

Critical Thinking and Reflection

1. Can you identify the emotional, moral, intellectual, and social components in Brianna's argument?
2. Can you identify the emotional, moral, intellectual, and social components in the New York Court of Appeals' argument?
3. Can you identify your own emotional, moral, intellectual, and social responses to this issue?
4. What are some similarities and differences between your responses and the authors'?

Is There Common Ground?

There is definitely common ground here. On both sides of this argument there is agreement that cyberbullying has negative and sometimes catastrophic results. And, in both cases, the authors argue that there need to be programs in place that work to end cyberbullying. The difference arises when considering the role of law enforcement in the issue. Some argue that prevention programs and sanctions for offenses should be enough. Others insist that without legal action, some people will continue in behavior that can result in the loss of life.

Additional Resources

Goldman, C. (2012). *Bullied: What Every Parent, Teacher, and Kid Needs to Know About Ending the Cycle of Fear.* Harper Collins: New York.

Heitner, D. (2016). *Screenwise: Helping Kids Thrive (and Survive) in Their Digital World.* BiblioMotion, Inc.: New York.

Lohmann, R.C. & Taylor, J.V. (2013). *The Bullying Workbook for Teens: Activities to Help You Deal with Social Aggression and Cyberbullying.* New Harbinger Publications, Inc.: Oakland, CA.

Internet References . . .

Cyberbullying Research Center

https://cyberbullying.org/

Pacer's National Bullying Prevention Center

https://www.pacer.org/bullying/

StopBullying.gov

https://www.stopbullying.gov/

Selected, Edited, and with Issue Framing Material by:
Don Dyson, *Widener University*

ISSUE

Should Parents of School Shooters Be Held Responsible for Their Children's Actions?

YES: **Alia E. Dastagir**, from "After a School Shooting, are Parents to Blame?" *USA Today* (2018)

NO: **John Cassidy,** from "America's Failure to Protect Its Children from School Shootings is a National Disgrace," *The New Yorker* (2018)

Learning Outcomes

After reading this issue, you will be able to:

- Identify two factors common to school shootings.
- Identify two ways that parents may be criminally responsible for their child's actions.
- Differentiate between emotion and reason in the arguments presented.

ISSUE SUMMARY

YES: Alia E. Dastagir is a reporter covering cultural issues, including gender, race, and sexuality. She argues studies consistently show that teen violence is mitigated by consistent, nurturing adult influence and that those adults need to take their responsibility seriously.

NO: John Cassidy has been a staff writer at *The New Yorker* since 1995. In 2012, he began writing a daily column about politics and economics on newyorker.com. Cassidy argues that the federal government, in its unwillingness to stand up to gun lobbyists, is responsible for the ongoing epidemic of school shootings.

In the issue, "Should Teachers in Schools Have Firearms?" of this book, we took a look at the issue of school shootings and considered the discussion of whether or not arming teachers was a good way to prevent such tragedies. In this issue, we look at some of the aftermath of a school shooting. Specifically, this issue focuses on the question of parental responsibility for the actions of a child who has already committed a school shooting.

The question of whether or not a child's bad behavior is entirely their own responsibility or the responsibility of their parents has been one asked for many years about many different issues. When someone's child is behaving in a way that an adult does not like in a grocery store or a restaurant, frequently the response is frustration and anger with the parent. When some folks hear of a group of adolescents vandalizing a random building, often the thought is, "Where are their parents?!"

Attempts to connect children's criminal behaviors to their parents are not new. In fact, in 2009, a group of researchers (Hoeve, Dubas, Eichelsheim, van der Lan, Smeenk & Gerris) did a meta-analysis of 161 studies that examined the connection between parenting and delinquency. In their findings, they identified that up to 11% of the difference between in delinquency rates were connected with the amount of parental monitoring that occurs, the psychological control of the parents over their children, and negative parental attributes such as hostility and rejection. These data seem to run counter to the idea that more controlling parents will decrease rates of childhood delinquency.

When it comes to the issue of school violence, and specifically gun violence in school, the facts point to access to guns at home being a significant part of school shooting narratives. The Wall Street Journal reported in April of 2018 that of the mass school shootings that had occurred since 1990 only 20 reports had information about where students procured the weapons for their attack. Of those 20, 17 shooters got their guns at home, with a few of those getting guns from other relatives. In these cases, it is difficult not to speculate that if the parents had secured their weapons in ways that were not accessible to their children, disaster may have been averted.

There are a few ways that the legal system has attempted to hold parents responsible for the criminal behavior of their children. One of those is statues that address "contributing to the delinquency of a minor." In most cases, this requires some direct action on the part of the parent, which is not usually the case in school shooting situations. The other is child firearm access prevention laws. These laws, in general, say that a parent can be held criminally liable for leaving firearms in places where children can easily access them. This is meant to be a deterrent for careless gun ownership by parents, and is sometimes discussed as a preventive measure in school shootings. While many states have such laws on their books, they are rarely enforced. Consider what it would take to enforce such laws. Investigators would have to obtain a search warrant in order to check on whether or not the parent was properly storing their weapon, and that would have to occur before a shooting in order for it to be preventive in any way. Considering the invasiveness of those necessities, there are few people who would argue that they should be regularly enforced and even fewer who would agree to random searches of their homes.

In addition, these laws only apply to minor children. In some of the deadliest school shootings on record, the young people involved were just at or above the state's age of majority. As a result, the laws could not be applied.

It is also important to consider that legally holding parents responsible for the actions of their children will likely disproportionally affect people of lower socioeconomic status. Those who have less access to money and resources are often forced to work longer hours in order to make ends meet, which means that they have less available time to monitor their children's behaviors. Consider as well the challenge faced by single parents who do not have another parent to help share that burden. Combine poverty with single parenthood and the odds continue to stack up against those who are already disadvantaged.

Finally, it is important to consider that the "troubled youth" with absent or uninvolved parents does not hold universally true in the cases of school shooters. Consider the case of Columbine High School shooter Dylan Klebold. Dylan's father, Tom, was a work-from-home dad who regularly spent time with his son. They shared interest in sports, worked together to fix cars, and played chess regularly. His mother, Sue Klebold, was active in his life as well; taxiing him and his brother to their various appointments, organizing events for Dylan and his friends all while working with disabled students at a community college. Both his mother and his father were actively involved in Dylan's life in significant ways. And that did not stop him from planning a massacre at his school for close to a year and carrying out that plan.

From where, then, does the argument arise that parents should be held responsible for the criminal acts of their children? Many arguments come from a person's personal experience with their own parents. They remember the rules in their household, the ways in which their parents would keep track of them, the punishments that would occur if the rules were broken, and the fear they had of being caught engaging in any kind of wrongdoing. This argument is based largely in the fuzzy nostalgia of a time gone by when children didn't talk back to their parents, sipped rootbeer floats at the local pop shop and stayed out of trouble. The challenge with this argument is that for as long as there have been children, some of them have committed crimes.

As you read these articles, remember that it is in large part human nature to want to find someone to blame when faced with unspeakable tragedy. Some blame themselves, wondering whether or not if they might have done something differently, the tragedy would have been averted. Sue Klebold has spoken of that often. Others want to blame society and the corrosion of values they believe once kept people safer and happier. When we have no explanation for tragedy, we create an explanation to help us cope.

As you read these articles, consider some important questions: What are the ways that the authors are seeking to find solutions to unspeakable tragedy? From where does each argument arise? How realistic is it to hold your parents responsible for your behaviors? Would you want that to happen?

YES ⬅

Alia E. Dastagir

After a School Shooting, are Parents to Blame?

19-year-old Nikolas Cruz is described by his classmates and investigators as a troubled teen with a history of "disturbing" posts on social media. Cruz is charged with 17 counts of premeditated murder in Wednesday's Florida high school shooting.

Family matters. But not in the way some may think.

Last week, a 19-year-old with an AR-15-style assault weapon was accused of walking into a Florida high school and killing 17 people. This week, the nation is embroiled in a debate about who's to blame.

It's the guns. It's the kids. It's gang violence and broken health care and corrupt politicians and violent video games. It's the drugs. It's Russia. It's President Trump. On Thursday, a Florida middle school teacher weighed in with a Facebook post that has since gone viral, declaring it's the parents.

Kelly Guthrie Raley's post, which was picked up by Fox News, had more than 600,000 shares as of Sunday afternoon:

"I grew up with guns. Everyone knows that. But you know what? My parents NEVER supported any bad behavior from me. I was terrified of doing something bad at school, as I would have not had a life until I corrected the problem and straightened my ass out. My parents invaded my life. They knew where I was ALL the time. They made me have a curfew. They made me wake them up when I got home. They made me respect their rules. They had full control of their house, and at any time could and would go through every inch of my bedroom, backpack, pockets, anything! Parents: it's time to STEP UP!"

Comments read, "Parents have got to do better" and "These horrible acts of violence will continue to happen if their REAL cause is not addressed." The sentiments Raley expressed were pervasive on social media: Tweets and Facebook posts blamed a lack of parental discipline for shootings like the one at Marjory Stoneman Douglas High School.

Guns have always been around and you never heard about school shootings. Now school shootings are becoming the norm. This isn't a gun issue; it's a parental and society issue. God taken out of schools, parents failing to discipline their children, and creating entitled kids.

Liberals want to blame the school-shootings on gun control. The problem is how our society has allowed people to grow up without consequences, discipline and a sense of ownership. They want to take guns from responsible citizens because their group can't cope with stress.

But how much are parents to blame? Is lenient parenting part of the problem? After the 2012 Sandy Hook Elementary School shooting in Newtown, Conn., when 20-year-old Adam Lanza fatally shot 20 children and six adults, the National Science Foundation asked researchers to look at what is known and unknown about youth violence. Published in 2016, the report found families do play roles that can either increase or decrease violence. It did not, however, find support for "harsh" parenting, which is viewed as a risk factor.

Researchers said children who had a lower risk of youth violence had "close attachment bonds with consistently supportive caregivers" and experienced "effective and developmentally sensitive parenting."

Raley's argument does not fit neatly in the case of the accused Florida shooter. Nikolas Cruz was adopted. His adoptive mother, Lynda Cruz, died of pneumonia in November and his adoptive father died in 2004. Ethan Trieu, 17 — who was friends on and off with Cruz since the sixth grade — said Cruz changed significantly after the death of his father.

What little we know of Cruz's life does not suggest he lacked discipline or that his family was unaware he was struggling. Neighbors told *The New York Times* that Lynda Cruz "called sheriff's deputies to the house numerous times in an effort to keep Mr. Cruz in line."

Broward County Mayor Beam Furr said during an interview with CNN that Cruz had received treatment at a mental health clinic. The family friends Cruz moved in with after his mother's death took him to a therapist for his depression.

"Mental illness cannot be fixed by parents or caretakers alone either because they are often not financially equipped to do so nor trained to deal with it," said Susanne Babbel, PhD, a trauma therapist. "Children and teenagers with mental illness often need a team of providers but many times do not receive adequate support, nor does the parent or caretaker who tries to meet their child's needs."

When Raley shared her post the morning after the shooting, she might not have been aware of those circumstances of Cruz's life. However, those details were reported by the time many others, including Fox News, picked it up.

One reason her post may have resonated is because she tapped into the frustration other teachers share. Raley notes there were times when she would try to work with families whose children had discipline problems at school and was met with a "horrendous lack of parental support." She isn't alone.

Research suggests one of the major causes of teacher burnout, a long-documented social problem, is the emotional exhaustion they experience while dealing with students' behavioral problems.

In just 45 days, there have been at least six school shootings that have wounded or killed students in the United States. The student survivors of Wednesday's massacre declared "we will be the last." For that to become a reality, people on both sides of the debate — those who share Raley's view and those who do not — will need to at least consider her final thought.

"Those 17 lives mattered," she wrote. "When are we going to take our own responsibility seriously?"

Anne Godlasky contributed.

ALIA E. DASTAGIR is a reporter covering cultural issues, including gender, race and sexuality.

John Cassidy    **NO**

America's Failure To Protect Its Children From School Shootings Is A National Disgrace

Early on Wednesday afternoon, Marjory Stoneman Douglas High School, in Parkland, Florida, had a fire drill, an eleventh-grader named Gabriella Figueroa told MSNBC's Brian Williams. "Then we heard gunshots," Figueroa said. "Then it went to code red. And then it was crazy."

An individual with deadly intent was in the school building, holding an assault weapon that was designed for fighting wars. As Figueroa's use of the term "code red" indicated, such an event is no longer considered an aberration. All across the country, school boards drill their teachers and students in how to respond to such an emergency. Code yellow: turn cell phones to silent, return to the classroom, and follow the teacher's instructions. Code red: find a secure area immediately, lock the door, close the blinds, turn off the lights, do not move.

This lockdown wasn't a drill, of course. By the time it was over, seventeen people had been shot dead, and more than a dozen had been wounded. "Bodies were lying in the hallway," another eyewitness told Fox News. "People were killed in the hallway." Police later identified the suspected killer as Nikolas Cruz, a nineteen-year-old former student who had been expelled for discipline problems.

After Cruz fled the scene—he was arrested shortly after the shooting, in neighboring Coral Springs—news helicopters captured footage of students walking and running from the school, some of them carrying flowers and cards. It was Valentine's Day, after all. By that point, the authorities had secured the area around the school. There were heavily armed cops, police cars, bomb-squad trucks, and F.B.I. vehicles. The mayor of Parkland, a former teacher named Beam Furr, told CNN, "It's all being fairly well coördinated, and everyone is doing everything they can."

But were they? On Twitter, President Donald Trump offered his "prayers and condolences to the families of the victims," adding that "no child, teacher, or anyone else should ever feel unsafe in an American school." Fox News interviewed Marco Rubio, Florida's junior senator, who has an A-plus rating from the National Rifle Association. "I hope people reserve judgment.... The facts of this are important," Rubio said. As soon as the facts are clear, Rubio went on, "we can have a deeper conversation about why these things happen." The forty-six-year-old Republican added, "It's a terrible situation. It's amazing the amount of carnage that one individual can carry out in such a short period of time."

Yet some pertinent facts are already known. According to local police, Cruz was armed with an AR-15 assault-style rifle—the same type of gun that Adam Lanza used to kill twenty-six pupils and staff at Sandy Hook Elementary School, in December, 2012. Evidently, Rubio still isn't aware of the power of such weapons, which fire bullets that can penetrate a steel helmet from a distance of five hundred yards. When fired from close range at civilians who aren't wearing body armor, the bullets from an AR-15 don't merely penetrate the human body—they tear it apart. It "looks like a grenade went off in there," Peter Rhee, a trauma surgeon at the University of Arizona, told *Wired*.

To spare the families of the victims—and the public at large—additional anguish, these sorts of details are often glossed over in the aftermath of mass shootings. But it's surely long past time that we acknowledged these facts, and that we begin to more fully discuss the complicity of N.R.A.-backed politicians like Rubio, and Florida's governor, Rick Scott, in maintaining the environment that allows these tragedies to happen again and again and again.

One of the first duties of any government is to protect its citizens, through collective action, from violent threats they'd otherwise have to fend off themselves. Even most libertarians accept this principle. But when it comes to mass shootings, the Republican Party falls back on constitutional arguments that have no proper basis in history, and it refuses to budge from this stance. Nothing can shift it—not Sandy Hook, not the Orlando night-club shooting, not the Las Vegas massacre, not weekly shootings in schools. (According to the *Guardian*, Wednesday's attack in Parkland was the eighth school shooting this year that has resulted in death or injury.) Nothing.

The Democrats aren't entirely blameless, either. In 2009 and 2010, when they controlled the White House and both houses of Congress, they failed to take some steps that were obviously necessary, such as closing the gun-show loophole for background checks and reinstating the Clinton Administration's ban on assault weapons, which the Bush Administration allowed to expire.

The Republicans bear the primary responsibility, though. Ever since Sandy Hook, it is their craven subservience to the gun lobby that has prevented meaningful action, even as the carnage that Rubio referred to has continued. "Turn on your televisions right now and you are going to see scenes of children running for their lives,"

Chris Murphy, the junior Democratic senator for Connecticut, said on the Senate floor on Wednesday afternoon. "Let me just note once again for my colleagues: this happens nowhere else other than the United States of America. This epidemic of mass slaughter, this scourge of school shooting after school shooting, it only happens here. Not because of coincidence, not because of bad luck, but as a consequence of our inaction. We are responsible for a level of mass atrocity that happens in this country with zero parallel anywhere else."

The key concept in that excellent peroration was responsibility. Even with the blood of defenseless children flowing along the corridors of schoolhouses, the U.S. government has abdicated its duty to protect. And that, it bears repeating ad nauseam, is a national disgrace.

John Cassidy has been a staff writer at *The New Yorker* since 1995. In 2012, he began writing a daily column about politics and economics on newyorker.com.

EXPLORING THE ISSUE

Should Parents of School Shooters Be Held Responsible for Their Children's Actions?

Critical Thinking and Reflection

1. Can you identify the emotional, moral, intellectual, and social components in Alia's argument?
2. Can you identify the emotional, moral, intellectual, and social components in Cassidy's argument?
3. Can you identify your own emotional, moral, intellectual, and social responses to this issue?
4. What are some similarities and differences between your responses and the authors'?

Is There Common Ground?

The common ground here is found in both authors' desire to place accountability and blame somewhere. While this is a natural human reaction, it does beg the question whether there is any place to find blame other than in the actions of the individual school shooters. This is especially difficult to do when the shooters turn their guns on themselves. In those instances there is no one left to hold responsible for the tragedy at hand. Some would argue that these acts, and the reasons behind them, are far too complex to boil down to one responsible party. Perhaps the common ground is there. If more people took more responsibility in many of these areas, we might see the frequency of these violent and tragic incidents decrease.

Additional Resources

Duffy, P.M. (2014). *Parenting Your Delinquent, Defiant, or Out-of-Control Teen: How to Help Your Teen Stay in School and Out of Trouble Using an Innovative Multisystemic Approach*. New Harbinger Publications: Oakland, CA.

Faber, A. (2012). *How to Talk so Kids Will Listen and Listen so Kids Will Talk*. Simon & Schuster: New York.

Faber, A. (2005). *How to Talk so Teens Will Listen and Listen so Teens Will Talk*. Harper Collins: New York.

Internet References . . .

FindLaw: Parent liability basics

https://family.findlaw.com/parental-rights-and-liability/parental-liability-basics.html

The Relationship Between Parenting and Delinquency: A meta analysis

https://link.springer.com/article/10.1007/s10802-009-9310-8

Selected, Edited, and with Issue Framing Material by:
Don Dyson, *Widener University*

ISSUE

Is the Criminal Justice System Unfair to Black Families?

YES: Samantha Daley, from "The Criminal Justice System is Failing Black Families," *Rewire.News* (2014)

NO: Kay S. Hymowitz, from "Did Mass Incarceration Destroy the Black Family? No, and Here's Why," *City Journal* (2015)

Learning Outcomes

After reading this issue, you will be able to:

- Define the Rule of Law.
- Identify three negative effects that unequal treatment by law enforcement have on Black people.
- Compare and contrast the treatment of African American and white people by law enforcement.

ISSUE SUMMARY

YES: Samantha Daley is a reproductive justice activist and a supervisor at a homeless shelter for youth and a writer in Echoing Ida, a project of Forward Together. She argues that the criminal justice system's biased treatment toward black families creates a system that passes down racial disadvantage from generation to generation.

NO: Kay S. Hymowitz is the William E. Simon Fellow at the Manhattan Institute and a contributing editor of *City Journal*. She writes extensively on childhood, family issues, poverty, and cultural change in America. She argues that issues within Black families are an under-considered part of the mass incarceration problem.

The last issue of this edition of Taking Sides: Family and Personal Relationships attempts to address, at least in part, the debate about the criminal justice system and the way that it interacts with African American families. Entire volumes have been written on this subject, so I do not present this summary as comprehensive in any way. What I do hope to present is some context for the conversation and a brief look into some of the issues that frame the discussion.

On one side of this argument, there sits the rule of law. In essence, the rule of law is the belief that constraints are needed to keep individuals and institutions from exercising power against others. It includes the idea that all people are equally subject to those laws. Many of us have heard the saying "everyone is equal under the law," and many people believe it.

Most statues of Lady Justice depict her wearing a blindfold. The blindfold is used to symbol objectivity; to communicate the idea that the law is applied objectively to everyone regardless of power, wealth, or identity. It is a symbol that sits in thousands of courtrooms across the United States and purports to mete out justice without partiality.

For many people in the United States, their lives have supported this reality. Their experiences with law enforcement have taught them that when they disobey the law, they face the consequences. When they exceed the speed limit, they get a ticket. When they commit tax fraud, they face trial and jail time. If they steal, they are arrested, stand trial, and go to prison.

This extends into their interactions with the police. The concept of "fair policing" involves a number of important factors: being neutral, even handed, and equitable in the way that people are treated; giving voice to citizens to tell their side of the story; interacting with dignity and politeness; and being accountable by offering reasonable explanations for reasonable behavior. For many folks, this has consistently been their experience when dealing with law enforcement. As a result, they make the choice to trust the police and to convey them authority to enforce the law.

As a result of this experience, when people see others who are being stopped or accosted by the police their first thought is to imagine what that person did wrong. They unconsciously attribute respect and authority to the police and assume guilt and wrongdoing of the person with whom an officer is interacting. They believe, implicitly, that the law, and by extension its enforcers, are just and fair. What many people who have this experience do not understand is that this is not many African American people's experience with the criminal justice system.

To understand this different perspective, it is helpful to consider the history of law enforcement and people of color. From the time of slavery, law enforcement was used to enforce the subjugation of black men and women. Officers of the law enforced slave owners' rights and often participated in hunting down escaped slaves and returning them to their shackles. In the antebellum South, police officers were regularly involved in lynch mobs and other forms of violence against black and brown bodies. In the North, police were actively involved in supporting illegal activities that enforced black exclusion from living or even walking in certain communities. Some argue, in fact, that one of the main purposes of police forces has always been to police black bodies in ways that protect white sensitivities. And while this is an historical reality, they argue that it has unjustly continued to present day. The result, they argue, is a system of state-sponsored violence used disproportionately against Black people.

In recent years, the media has given much more attention to the shooting of unarmed black men by police. For many white Americans this has been shocking, despite the reality that people of color have been trying to call attention to that reality for decades. Young Black men are 21 times more likely to be shot by police than their white peers. White men who engage in mass shootings are apprehended by the police with little fanfare and are escorted to jail to await trial. Black men who sell loose cigarettes are brutalized and killed before they even get taken into custody. When communities of color see this behavior over and over again, they lose their faith in the idea of "fair policing."

This historical reality and countless present-day examples of unequal treatment of Black people by law enforcement have resulted in increased depression, stress, and other mental health issues in Black families. Studies have shown that it results in an increased perception of vulnerability, a constantly heightened sense of threat, an intense reaction to the lack of fairness, decreased social status and self-worth, and consistent triggering of past trauma. In addition, researchers have identified the concept of "spill" that occurs for Black people after reports of police violence against Black bodies. Each time an incident of police violence is reported, Black women, men, and children experience a series of days in which their well-being is challenged and they experience more difficulty navigating their everyday lives. Black people do not have to be present with the violence; a news report can cause them to experience symptoms of depression and anxiety.

When most white people think about getting sat down by their parents to have "the talk," their minds go immediately to that awkward moment when their dad tried to explain the birds and the bees. They are unaware that in many Black families, "the talk" is often about the specific ways that they need to behave in any interactions that they have with police officers in order to keep themselves alive. Think about that. Parents regularly have to coach their children in specific tactics in order to avoid giving police officers any reason to escalate a situation into violence. That conversation usually involves acting in submissive and docile ways, regardless of the treatment that they receive from the officer.

It is important to remember that most Black people would like to have a good relationship with law enforcement. They would like their families and property to be protected from those who mean them harm. The challenge is that the system, as it exists, threatens them more than it supports them.

Some questions to consider as you read: What has been your experience with law enforcement throughout your life? Do you think that the criminal justice system practices fair policing? What effect do you think that a constant state of fear and concern might have on someone's reaction to getting stopped by a police officer?

YES

Samantha Daley

The Criminal Justice System Is Failing Black Families

Dr. Dorothy Roberts is right: Incarceration of women "inflicts incalculable damage to communities .... [transferring] racial disadvantage to the next generation."

Marissa Alexander's story resonates with me, not because I am a mother, or even a past victim of domestic violence, but because my life has been greatly affected by the systematic expansion of the prison system and excessive criminalization of my community.

CNN/YouTube

This piece is published in collaboration with Echoing Ida, a Forward Together project.

Marissa Alexander, a Florida mother of three, is currently undergoing a retrial and facing 60 years in prison for firing a warning shot into the air to ward off her abusive and estranged husband. Though the bullet didn't hurt anyone, Alexander would be serving a 20-year sentence if the ruling had not been overturned following her first trial. She is Black and a woman, and that's all those who prosecuted her cared to know.

Her imprisonment and the historical injustices suffered by so many Black and brown people have led to a major uproar and deeper conversation about the criminalization of Black women and how it has significant effects on the Black family structure. The criminalization of the Black community is breaking up the Black family and by doing so is perpetuating the cycles of poverty and oppression in our society, especially when Black children are being put in foster care at a greater rate than other children.

Now that I've shared some of Alexander's story, here is a snapshot of mine.

It's 3:00 a.m. I am awakened by bright lights and men with big attitudes. Police officers have entered my mother's home without warrants, guns at the ready, pointed at my 18-year-old brother. I have never felt more in danger than I did at that point, surrounded by individuals whom I'm supposed to trust to protect me. Instantly I realize that my little brother, whom they assume is my big brother—the person they are really after, for missing a court date—is a threat simply because of his Black maleness.

My big brother is not home that night, but the police find him at a friends' house a few weeks later. I recall seeing my brother's scars on his arms and shoulders from that day. The wounds never healed properly from the dogs that the police unleashed on him; the dogs bit into him to the muscle, and the scars, visible and invisible, never fully healed. He was handcuffed and hauled away, and I was left behind—writing to him while he was in jail, then prison.

He was a criminal and he was Black; that's all the police cared to know when they treated him in that violent manner.

Marissa Alexander's story resonates with me, not because I am a mother, or even a past victim of domestic violence, but because even before the moment police stormed my home, my life has been greatly affected by the systematic expansion of the prison system and excessive criminalization of my community. At a time when lines are drawn on the value of Black lives, we must unearth and fight how the unjust system harms most those who are already suffering.

While the specifics of Alexander's trial and defense are unique, she is not alone. Thirty percent of African-American women have experienced domestic abuse, putting their lives in constant danger. This has been seen time and time again, and is currently a mainstream issue because of video that surfaced of Ray Rice abusing his now wife in an elevator. Although the Ray Rice/NFL scandal has received international attention and criticism, so many more women experience this violence every day and will be forgotten when the next big story hits. There is a clear link between intimate partner violence and a person's ability to maintain bodily autonomy and care for their children—two crucial tenets of reproductive justice. She may have successfully shooed away her abuser, but instead of supporting her in finding safety and protecting her children, the state has relinquished Alexander's freedom and her ability to bond with her youngest child.

Another way the justice system affects the Black family can be seen in how incarceration disproportionately affects people of color. Keeping a family structure intact is nearly impossible with the incarceration of a parent. Separated children are often put into foster care, even though studies show that children raised in the foster care system are more likely to end up in the criminal justice system in the future.

Dr. Dorothy Roberts is right: Incarceration of women "inflicts incalculable damage to communities .... [transferring] racial disadvantage to the next generation."

Roberts has also clearly laid out the intersections of the foster care and prison systems and their disproportionate impact on Black women. She writes that the fact that one-third of foster care children are Black and landed there after being removed from Black women's care "is evidence of a form of punitive governance that perpetuates social inequality."

Nearly 80 percent of women behind bars are mothers serving time for offenses largely related to domestic violence, sexual abuse, drug addiction, other health problems, and homelessness. In fact, over three-quarters of the women sitting in prisons have histories of severe violence by an intimate partner as adults, and 82 percent suffered physical or sexual abuse as children. This is another example of how the justice system fails women who are actually in need of counseling programs, support groups, and treatment programs so that they can live and raise their families in a productive and healthy way.

Instead, from 1986 to 1991 the incarceration rate of Black women drug offenders increased 828 percent. In 2010, Black women were put in jail at nearly three times the rate of white women. And, the majority of jailed women lived with their minor children before their arrest. These trends do not seem to be slowing.

The criminalization of Black women makes it nearly impossible for Black women to care for our families. When we do try and protect our families we're punished, as in the case of Marissa Alexander, and even when we're not punished our children are being harassed and harmed. This injustice toward Black mothers cannot continue!

Far from rehabilitating in the ways our communities need, this system is attempting to break us.

There was never a mention of drug rehab programs or rehabilitation programs to help my brother rejoin and be productive in society.

The disproportionate and constant surveillance, harassment, threats, arrests, and family separation experienced by my older brother, and many Black men and women in my community, illustrates how our justice system fails people of color, and hurts the communities that need justice most.

Amidst this dire situation, if there's one thing I know about my folks, it is that we are resilient: We will find a way to survive, fight back, and keep on. Organizations and individuals are seeing this attack on families of color and are taking a stand to protect our family and communities. SisterSong and the Free Marissa Now campaign joined together over the summer to host "Standing Our Ground"—an event to discuss the intersections of the (in)justice system and reproductive justice in the case of Marissa Alexander and others, and to shed light on attacks of this on communities of color throughout the nation. Having attended the conference, I was struck by all the organizations and beautiful women of color who showed up–bringing their expertise and experiences to the table. I knew I was not alone. My story, our suffering is connected. That power and the determination to win the battle for our rights and the rights of our families are carrying me through the events in Ferguson, Missouri, where a senseless killing and the outrage that followed show us that our basic rights to live are being challenged.

Conversations like these are lifting the veil that has obscured the connections between domestic violence, reproductive justice, and the criminalization our communities experience for simply being. Things will only improve when Black women and mothers are seen as human–when our lives are treated as they matter as much as anyone else's; when our bodies and privacy cannot be violated, and if they are the incidents are met with public outrage; and when communities join together to fight laws that turn those suffering from violence into criminals.

It's become clear that in order for our people to survive and thrive we must call out this unjust criminal system, and take a stand for ourselves. The "American dream" sold to us never included communities of color, and doesn't enable us to raise our families in safe environments. We as women of color–often the foundation and heads of our households–need to start trusting ourselves and making our own seats at the table. No longer should officers be able to push us around in our own homes and take away our right to protect our families.

We are the experts on our communities while those in power are just outsiders looking in with no real connections to our day-to-day lives and lived experiences. We're told that prisons are supposed to protect our families from danger, but in reality the policing of our communities and families presents a danger so grave, I question whether we can survive it. We must stop living in fear and call out those in positions of power and the policies they create that are out to harm and hinder our communities. We must join together and stop being our toughest critics, because now more than ever our communities are under attack. We have come to a time in history, again, where simply being able to walk outside and live our lives is being threatened. We are resilient as a community and our resilience is being challenged. It's no longer time to be on the defensive; it's time we stand because it's clear that our justice system isn't looking out for us.

SAMANTHA DALEY is a reproductive justice activist and a supervisor at a homeless shelter for youth and a writer in Echoing Ida, a project of Forward Together.

Kay S. Hymowitz

 **NO**

Did Mass Incarceration Destroy the Black Family?

No, and Here's Why.

As riots in Ferguson and Baltimore heated up this past winter and spring, so did denunciations of a criminal-justice system that has placed a disproportionate number of black men behind bars. One widely aired theory holds that not only are racial disparities and mass incarceration patently unjust on their own terms, but they also lead to chaos in poor urban families. Black men's absence "disrupts family formation, leading both to lower marriage rates and higher rates of childbirth outside marriage," pronounced a widely discussed *New York Times* article, "1.5 Million Missing Black Men." Hillary Clinton auditioned the theory in the first policy speech of her presidential campaign. "When we talk about one and a half million missing African-American men," she said at Columbia University in April, "we're talking about missing husbands, missing fathers, missing brothers."

The missing-men theory of family breakdown has the virtue of being easy to grasp: men who are locked up are obviously not going to be either desirable husbands or engaged fathers. It also bypasses thorny and deadlocked debates about economics and culture. Still, it has a big problem: it's at odds with the facts.

Consider the first graph (below), which traces the percentage of births to black unmarried women between 1960 and 2013. As the sixties began, 20 percent of all black births were to single mothers. By 1965, black "illegitimacy," in the parlance of the time, had reached 24 percent and become the subject of Daniel Patrick Moynihan's prophetic but ill-fated report "The Negro Family: The Case for National Action." That number, startling at the time, turned out to be only the ground floor of a steep 30-year climb. By 1980, more than half of black children were born to unmarried mothers. The number peaked at 72.5 percent in 2010.

Now look at the second graph, tracing the number of black men admitted to state and federal prisons over this same period. In the 1960s and early 1970s, as nonmarital births raced upward, mass incarceration was not yet a glimmer in policymakers' eyes. The black prison population hovered at a relatively low level, showing no serious trend up or down. In 1975 came the first signs of a clear increase, but it wasn't until 1980 that the numbers of black men admitted to state and federal prisons really mushroomed. (Though the graph doesn't show it, the same trends were true for white men, though their prison-admission rate per 1,000 is far lower.) Throughout the 1990s and most of the first decade of the 2000s, the prison population grew to historical highs. In 2008, the black (and white) prison population peaked; since then, it has declined, though only slightly.

The two graphs together show that the black family was in deep disarray well before America's experiment in mass incarceration. If anything, the timing of the two problems points to the *opposite* causation from the one assumed by "missing-men" theorists: as the family unraveled, crime increased—the homicide rate doubled between the early 1960s and late 1970s, with more than half of the offenders being black—leading to calls for tougher sentencing and more bad guys behind bars. In other words, family breakdown led to more crime and more crowded prisons. That theory also jibes with abundant research showing that boys who grow up without a father in the home are at greater risk of criminal behavior.

We shouldn't take this alternative theory too far. Crime and prison rates are unlikely to have a single cause: demographics, policing and sentencing policies, environmental toxins, and who knows what else may all play some role. Perhaps the most controversial of those policies was what came to be known as the War on Drugs,

Family Breakdown and Black Incarceration

Percentage of Births to Unmarried Black Women, 1960–2013

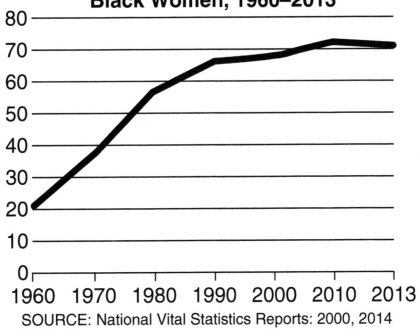

SOURCE: National Vital Statistics Reports: 2000, 2014

Prision Admissions for Black Males, 1960–2011

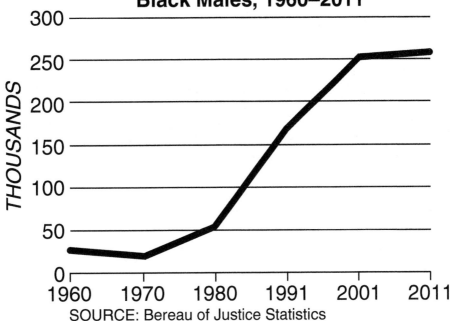

SOURCE: Bereau of Justice Statistics

first declared by President Richard Nixon in 1971. There's little question that the government's hard line on drugs eventually put large numbers of black (and, again, white) men behind bars.

However, if the War on Drugs played any role in shaping the contemporary black family, it's almost impossible to decipher from the data. Despite Nixon's early 1970s call to arms, the War on Drugs didn't lead to many casualties until well into the next decade. As of 1979, only 5.7 percent of U.S. prisoners were incarcerated for drug offenses. Yet as we've just seen, by that time, nearly half of black births were already to single mothers. The number of men imprisoned for drug crimes rose only modestly until 1990, four years after Congress passed the Anti-Drug Abuse Act, legislating harsher sentences for crack cocaine, a move often cited as a cause of the disproportionately black prison population. Far from leading to more fatherless children, the growing number of black men imprisoned for drugs coincided with a flattening out of the percentage of black single mothers, after a 30-plus-year upward climb.

In fact, whatever its evils, the War on Drugs doesn't take us far in explaining prison racial disparities. That's not the impression you'll get from the punditry class. "More than half of federal prisoners are incarcerated for drug crimes in 2010," goes a typical formulation, from the *Huffington Post*. It's true, as far as it goes—but "federal prisoners" make up only about 14 percent of all incarcerated men. In the far larger state system, the majority of black men are doing time for violent crimes. Between the federal and state system, almost two and a half times the number of black men are serving sentences for murder, assault, and the like than they are for using and selling drugs. Today, violent criminals continue to make up by far the largest cohort of the freshman class of prisoners—black, white, and Hispanic.

The preponderance of violent prisoners muddies another plank of the missing-men theory: that mass incarceration of black adults has harmed black children. Researchers have made a compelling case that when fathers go to prison, their absence takes a toll on their kids. Boys, especially, have more behavioral problems, including aggressive acting out and lower educational achievement. But the lessons of those findings are far from clear. You can construct a reasonable argument that the children of men sentenced for drug offenses—and the communities they live in—would be better off if fewer fathers were behind bars. When it comes to men prone to violence, though, that supposition is ambiguous, at best.

The difficult truth avoided by most missing-men adherents is that men doing prison time are part of a larger population that doesn't provide much in the way of paternal care, even if they never were locked up. According to research from the Fragile Families project, the vast majority of poor black fathers are unmarried, though it's also the case that those in jail are the *least* likely to be married. That same population is less likely to be living with their children and their children's mother than unmarried white or Hispanic fathers, a fact that lessens their sons' and daughters' chances in life. It's true that black nonresidential fathers have been found to be more involved with their kids in the early years than comparable white and Hispanic dads. But that only lasts until the kids are nine or so; after that, poor black fathers are actually more likely to have exited their children's lives than other men—another blow to children's well-being. Part of the reason for this is "multi-partner fertility"—social-science-speak for having children by more than one partner. Multi-partner fertility, with the complex families it creates, is extremely common in poor black neighborhoods. (Again, it's twice as prevalent among incarcerated men.) Serial parental relationships, breakups, disappearances, a line of step-siblings and parents: they're all part of what sociologists Laura Tach and Kathryn Edin call the "family-go-round." These traits are linked to the same behavioral problems experienced by boys whose fathers have been jailed.

None of this means that incarceration policies aren't ready for an overhaul. The country needs a vigorous examination of mandatory-sentencing laws, the War on Drugs, and racial arrest and sentencing disparities. But that debate should not be used to evade the realities of family life in neighborhoods like Ferguson and Baltimore's Sandtown. Evasion has been the preferred modus vivendi over the past 50 years, ever since Moynihan's warning of rising fatherlessness in the ghetto drew sharp condemnation. Look where it's gotten us.

KAY S. HYMOWITZ is the William E. Simon Fellow at the Manhattan Institute and a contributing editor of City Journal.

EXPLORING THE ISSUE

Is the Criminal Justice System Unfair to Black Families?

Critical Thinking and Reflection

1. Can you identify the emotional, moral, intellectual, and social components in Samantha's argument?
2. Can you identify the emotional, moral, intellectual, and social components in Kay's argument?
3. Can you identify your own emotional, moral, intellectual, and social responses to this issue?
4. What are some similarities and differences between your responses and the authors'?

Is There Common Ground?

In even this very polarized issue, there is common ground to be found. Both sides, I would argue, would support the Rule of Law. The difference that sets them apart from one another is that one side believes that the equitable treatment that is inherent in the definition of the Rule of Law is already firmly in place. The other side would argue that the Rule of Law, as it is currently practiced, is far from equitable. It is not that they do not want a criminal justice system that upholds the law fairly and equitably. It is that they do not believe that the current system does this.

Additional Resources

Hill, M.L. (2016). *Nobody: Casualties of America's War on the Vulnerable, from Ferguson to Flint and Beyond.* Simon & Schuster: New York.

Yancy, G. & del Guadalupe Davidson, M. (2016). *Our Black Sons Matter: Mothers Talk about Fears, Sorrows, and Hopes.* Rowan and Littlefield: Lanham, MD.

Internet References . . .

Black Lives Matter

https://blacklivesmatter.com/

Color of Change

www.colorofchange.org

W.K. Kellogg Foundation: Racial Equity Resource Guide

http://www.racialequityresourceguide.org/